Chinese San Francisco, 1850–1943

ASIAN AMERICA
A series edited by Gordon H. Chang

The increasing size and diversity of the Asian American population, its growing significance in American society and culture, and the expanded appreciation, both popular and scholarly, of the importance of Asian Americans in
the country's present and past—all these developments have converged to
stimulate wide interest in scholarly work on topics related to the Asian
American experience. The general recognition of the pivotal role that race
and ethnicity have played in American life, and in relations between the
United States and other countries, has also fostered this heightened attention. Although Asian Americans were a subject of serious inquiry in the late
nineteenth and early twentieth centuries, they were subsequently ignored by
the mainstream scholarly community for several decades. In recent years,
however, this neglect has ended, with an increasing number of writers examining a good many aspects of Asian American life and culture. Moreover,
many students of American society are recognizing that the study of issues
related to Asian America speak to, and may be essential for, many current
discussions on the part of the informed public and various scholarly communities. The Stanford series on Asian America seeks to address these interests. The series will include work from the humanities and social sciences,
including history, anthropology, political science, American studies, law, literary criticism, sociology, and interdisciplinary and policy studies.

Chinese
San Francisco,
1850–1943

A TRANS-PACIFIC COMMUNITY

Yong Chen

STANFORD UNIVERSITY PRESS

STANFORD, CALIFORNIA

Stanford University Press
Stanford, California
© 2000 by the Board of Trustees of the
Leland Stanford Junior University

Printed in the United States of America
CIP data appear at the end of the book

Published with the assistance of the Edgar M. Kahn Memorial Fund

To my parents

Contents

Acknowledgments

I was able to write this book thanks to the generous support that many people in both the United States and China have offered me since 1989, when I first started working on it as a Ph.D. dissertation at Cornell University. The dissertation benefited from the thoughtful comments of my dissertation committee members Nick Salvatore and Mary Beth Norton, who both read it in its entirety, and of Richard Polenburg and my fellow graduate students at Cornell: Timothy Billings, John Fousek, and Michael Bussel, who read parts of it. I remain deeply indebted to Michael Kammen, my advisor at Cornell. He has been an exemplary and inspiring teacher ever since I first met him in Beijing in 1983. Gary Okihiro, who joined the Cornell faculty and my dissertation committee in 1988, read not only the dissertation but also drafts of the book manuscript. Both the perceptive comments that he has offered me and his own work have been critical for the development of my study.

I could not have completed the book without the support of my colleagues in the History Department and the Asian American Studies Program at the University of California, Irvine (UCI). Many—including Karl Hufbauer, John Liu, Spencer Olin, Ken Pomeranz, and Bin Wong—read parts of the project at its different stages and extended valuable advice.

Another colleague and a dear friend, Anne Walthall, closely read and perceptively critiqued first the dissertation and later the book manuscript, both in their entirety. Teaching and working with my students in Asian American Studies courses at UCI has increased my understanding of critical historical issues that I deal with in my written work.

My thanks also go to people at other institutions, including Hong Cheng, Zhenghua Dong, Mario Garcia, Qitao Guo, Pat Keats, Him Mark Lai, Xiaohe Ma, Dayong Niu, Wei-chi Poon, Shichang Ouyang, Ronald Takaki, Emily Wolff, and Maochun Yu. My heartfelt thanks go to Gordon Chang for his encouragement and detailed suggestions. His intellectual insights have helped me to improve and better contextualize my book. I owe much to my editors at Stanford University Press. Muriel Bell impressed me not only with her kindness and professionalism but also with her intellectual wisdom, and Stacey Lynn was consistently patient and helpful. My copy editor, Ruth Barzel, did an extremely fine job in assisting me to improve the manuscript.

I would like to express my sincere gratitude to Elizabeth Abbott, Sandy Yee Man Leung, Dr. Thomas Quin Kong, and Cynthia Soo for allowing me to use their private collections. For their help with my research, I am grateful to the staff at numerous libraries, including the Olin Library of Cornell University; the library of the San Diego Historical Society; the Library of Congress; the East Asian Library of Columbia University; New York City Public Library; the East Asian Library of the University of California, Los Angeles; the library of the California Historical Society; the National Archives in Laguna Niguel; and the Asiatic Library, the Bancroft Library, and the Asian American Studies Library of the University of California, Berkeley. I also thank the hardworking employees at the interlibrary loan departments of the Olin Library and UCI's main library for their superb service.

I received several fellowships from Cornell University and a predoctoral fellowship from UCI for the writing of the dissertation. Two career-development awards from UCI gave me valuable release time from teaching so that I could focus on this book and other research projects.

I would also like to thank the *Western Historical Quarterly* for allowing me to use parts of an article originally published there. Portions of chapter 1 were first published, in slightly different form, as "The Internal Origins of

Chinese Immigration to California Reconsidered," *Western Historical Quarterly* (winter 1997): 520–46. Copyright by the Western History Association. Used by permission.

My parents' support and love, which they provide from their home across the Pacific Ocean, have been a key source of strength and served to put the notion of "trans-Pacific community" in perspective for me. Their frequent questions about my progress on the book helped drive me to complete it. Most important, I thank my wife, Rosalind, for her careful and critical reading of early drafts of the study and for her immeasurable support and patience.

Y.C.

Note on Translation and Transliteration

In translating sources originally written in Chinese, I have made every effort to retain the authenticity and integrity of the original text. In a study of the world of early Chinese Americans as they understood and lived it, the need for and significance of respecting textual authenticity are self-evident. Chinese was the primary language of Chinese San Francisco during this period and constituted a crucial part of Chinese American culture. The linguistic notions constructed therein reveal, and at the time reinforced, people's mentality, values, customs, and social relations.

Not all the features and subtleties of the original text can be retained in translation, however. For instance, many Chinese documents used in this study appear in classical or semiclassical forms that are condensed, concise, full of references to ancient legends and historical events, and often without punctuation. To retain the original style of these texts would be beyond even Jack Kerouac (who wrote his 1957 novel *On the Road* without punctuation). I have made no attempt to match the original text with Chaucerian or Shakespearean English. Citations from Chinese texts are rendered in simple, straightforward language. Several rules for translations and transliterations that I have followed are explained below.

The issue I have had to deal with most frequently involves converting the names of people, places, and organizations from Chinese into English. Many of these names are Chinese versions, including translations or transliterations, of identical names in English. When the Chinese version of an English term contains new meaning or sentiment, such as "the barbarian language" (meaning English) or "the 'Flowery-Flag' Country" (the United States), it is translated into English exactly as it is phrased in Chinese. Other Chinese translations without cultural alterations and additions in the Chinese text, such as "Theodore Roosevelt," and "the Workingmens' Party," have been restored back to their proper English forms.

Most Chinese names of people and places are transliterated in pinyin, a modern system of romanization, which has been used in post-1949 China and is gaining increasing acceptance in the West. For academic reasons, these names are romanized according to their pronunciation in present-day Chinese (Mandarin) rather than in any Cantonese dialect. The names of people are transliterated according to their original order in Chinese, that is, the last name comes first and is separated from the rest of the name with a space. The given name (which often contains two characters) is transliterated as one word. There are a few exceptions, however. Certain old forms of transliteration or romanization of certain Chinese names, such as "Sun Yat-sen," "Taipei" and "Canton," remain unchanged, because they have been widely used and accepted for a long time. Romanization of the names of some relatively anonymous people, such as Ah Quin and Ng Poon Chew, also reflect the form of the name adopted by these people themselves. The titles of most Chinese-language sources are transliterated with their meaning explained in English. The names of a few sources are translated in order to capture their important meaning in Chinese. For example, the most important Chinese American newspaper during the first half of the twentieth century is cited as "The Chinese-Western Daily," (translation) rather than "Chung Sai Yat Po" (Cantonese transliteration). Those sources that already have English titles, such as several Chinese-language newspapers, are not given new translations.

Finally, the Chinese used a different calendar, a lunar calendar, before the 1911 revolution. In most cases Chinese dates, which appeared in the order of year-month-day, are converted to their corresponding Western-style dates. In doing this I have consulted various reference books, especially Zheng Hesheng's *Jinshi Zhongxishiri Duizhaobiao* (Modern Chinese and Western historical dates in contrast).

Chinese San Francisco, 1850–1943

Introduction

In the summer of 1995 I spent a great deal of time in the microfilm reading room of the National Archives in Laguna Niguel, California, collecting data for this book. One day a white woman in her sixties sitting next to me asked me what I was working on. I told her that I was reading nineteenth-century census schedules regarding the Chinese in San Francisco. "Are you also trying to find information about your ancestors?" she asked, thinking I was doing the same kind of genealogical research on my family as she was on hers. I hesitated, not knowing how to respond. I would have to say no, I thought, because I am not Cantonese (most of the early Chinese immigrants to the United States came from the Pearl River Delta Region near Canton) and no one in my family had come to the United States prior to my arrival at Cornell University in 1985 to attend graduate school. Yet the history of those early immigrants has so profoundly shaped my own American experience that they have become more than ancestors to me. At that moment, I realized more consciously than ever how much what I was writing was also about myself. In the words of Stuart Hall, "the 'I' who writes here must also be thought of as, itself, 'enunciated'. We all write and speak from a particular place and time, from a history and a culture which is specific. What we say is always 'in context', *positioned.*"[1]

Conceived during the early part of my graduate career, this work had a humble and simple genesis. It was not driven by any theoretical ambition or preoccupation (I had just arrived from a society where such a preoccupation reduced many allegedly historical writings to temporal, petty ideological, jargon-infested exercises). Nor did it start with much historiographical knowledge of Chinese American history. The initial intellectual stimulus came from Alexander Saxton's *The Indispensable Enemy*, which I read for a graduate seminar taught by the historian Nick Salvatore. The failure of this otherwise excellent study of anti-Chinese racism in California's white labor movement to allow for any Chinese voice inspired my desire to know more about the feelings of the Chinese. At a more personal level, my choice of topic represented a longing to make sense of my existence in Chinatown-less rural upstate New York by connecting with immigrant pioneers from China.

I finally decided to focus my work on Chinese San Francisco from 1850 to 1943. After the first major wave of Chinese immigration to the United States during the Gold Rush, San Francisco's Chinese population emerged quickly as the most significant and largest Chinese American community, and it remained so for the rest of the period. Almost all Chinese Americans had left their footprints there. Many used it as a gateway between the Old World and the New. Others went there to work, recreate, and socialize. Its important social institutions, like the Zhonghua [Chinese] Huiguan (which eventually adopted a formal English name, the Chinese Consolidated Benevolent Association, and was commonly known as the "Six Companies"), once organized a majority of the Chinese American population. Chinese immigrants (especially those in the West) called Chinese San Francisco *dabu* (meaning "the big city," or "the first city"), a term that captured its significance in Chinese American life.

In this volume the reader will hear competing voices that tried to define Chinese San Francisco and, ultimately, Chinese America. As the most visible Chinese community in America, Chinese San Francisco also occupied a prominent place in white American consciousness. Its conspicuousness did not come about just as a result of its demographic size. Enhancing its visibility was its rich cultural distinctiveness. The old-timer San Franciscan Charles Dobie observed in 1939, "There are Chinatowns in other American cities still. But it must be conceded that San Francisco's Chinatown always has been the most significant expression of this alien people dwelling in our midst. It ranks first in numbers and in wealth of transplanted traditions. To know the Chinatown in San Francisco is to know every other Chinatown in the United States."[2] Dobie's statement undoubtedly fails to acknowledge the richness and complexity of the experiences of Chinese Americans living in different communities across the nation. It nevertheless helps to reveal the extent to which public attention focused on Chinese San Francisco.

Just as important as Chinese San Francisco's cultural distinctiveness is its physical location in the heart of San Francisco. Chinatown's location augmented the perception that it was a direct threat to the city's social and racial order. In 1906 the *New York Times* expressed a widely held view that San Francisco's Chinatown took up public space where it did not belong:

> The old Franciscan Chinatown was a much greater blemish and absurdity than that of New York. For it occupied the slope of the hill at the base of which is the chief commercial quarter, and the top of which is the chief residential quarter. No Franciscan of those parts could pass from his business to his home or back again without passing through it. What is more, his womankind could not "go shopping" without traversing it.

"Our little Chinatown on the other hand," the report went on, "modestly withdraws itself where nobody need ever enter it who does not betake himself to it for that express purpose."[3] The history of Chinese San Francisco tells us a great deal about white America's efforts to designate the proper space for the Chinese in society—not only geographically but also in its emerging racial hierarchy.

My primary goal in this study is to revisit the world of Chinese immigrants as they knew and experienced it themselves, instead of viewing their history from non-Chinese perspectives and contexts. A notion that vividly captures the essence of early Chinese life is "China in America." Although originally coined by the nineteenth-century anthropologist Stewart Culin, "China in America" was not an exclusively white term. Chinatown's residents themselves recognized the community's multilayered ties to China. An editorial in *The Chinese-Western Daily*, Chinese Americans' major newspaper, called Chinatown "the epitome of China." In reference to the popular phrase "China in America," the editorial continued: "Although the Chinese and outsiders used the same expression, they each see different things." "For Westerners," it noted, "the notion refers to the outward appearance of China."[4] The editorial clearly expressed an awareness of the differences between Chinese and white observers' perspective and comprehension with regards to recording and interpreting Chinese life. I must point out that my emphasis on such differences should not be construed as a rejection of the objectivity of history. It is simply a recognition that historical objectivity exists in multiple dimensions.

Therefore this study is not focused on how Chinese Americans were victimized or exploited by non-Chinese outsiders. Much has been written on those topics, as we will see. More important, Chinese Americans did not live just to serve as footnotes to socioeconomic and political developments and forces in the New World. This study seeks to understand things that motivated them to live, work, and persevere. It attempts to demonstrate how they comprehended and articulated the meanings of their American experiences based on their own backgrounds and historical memories. It is a story of how they built a community in the largest metropolis of the American West between 1850 and 1943.

To achieve this goal, I have made a conscious attempt to uncover and make use of Chinese-language sources.[5] During the entire period of my study, Chinese remained the primary language for a majority of Chinese Americans. Although such sources are not as comprehensive as are those in English in their accounts of certain aspects of Chinese American history, they give access to the meaning of Chinese Americans' existence as parents and children, as theatergoers and gamblers, and as clan and *huiguan* members. Huiguan, or home-district associations, were known as "companies" among white Americans. Those sources also enable us to appreciate Chinese Americans' efforts to control their own lives, and they reveal how they viewed the world and people around them.

There were common cultural systems (in both ideology and practice) constructed and communicated in linguistic codes, which the entire community, instead of just a few privileged members, could understand. Recognizing the existence of such systems is central to comprehending the importance of Chinese-language sources, especially those in the public domain such as editorials, advertisements, and announcements. After all, we must recognize that the different dialects spoken by various immigrant groups all originated from and shared the same written form—a written language that had taken shape in China many centuries before. The issue of written language invites questions about literacy. As we will see later, in the 1880s Stewart Culin asserted that a majority of the Chinese American population could read. While we do not have statistics to prove that assertion, it is perfectly clear that the written language was of enormous significance for

Chinese San Francisco, which demonstrated a strong, long-standing demand for written materials. Early in the twentieth century, for example, the relatively small community sustained four major dailies, all of which enjoyed longevity.

That assumption about common cultural systems is not made to deny the fact that social gaps were created by people's differing genders, literacy levels, and class interests. Such gaps remind us of the limitations of Chinese-language sources as representations that register not only past events but also traces of their authors' subjectivity. The unrespectable and the illiterate are unlikely to be adequately represented in surviving historical texts. In addition, we should take into consideration the autonomy of contemporary audiences, who might consciously or unconsciously misread messages in various written documents. Undeniably, such misreading sometimes took place.

It is equally undeniable, however, that sufficient cultural coherence held Chinese San Francisco together as a community to allow its members to use Chinese, directly or indirectly, as a medium of communication. In this study, nevertheless, I am more interested in representing the meaning of words and texts as they were understood by contemporary readers than in deciphering the puzzles they might otherwise contain. I am more interested in how written documents can open windows into historical reality and mentality concerning the community than in their authors' subjectivity or aesthetics. Indeed, a critical and contextual reading of such sources demonstrates that they were not totally divorced from social reality. In fact, many ideas discussed and promoted at various public forums were transformed into social practice.

To reconstruct Chinese San Franciscans' world from their own point of view also requires us to respect and try to use their own terminology, instead of employing the concepts and words invented for our times, especially those intended for only a few specialists. Such a reconstruction, in other words, demands that we preserve the integrity of these historical texts. However inherently subjective they may be, and in whatever way, that subjectivity is less of a hazard than the temptation to read our own anachronistic biases into such texts.

Readers will encounter a wide range of sources—private and public, fictional and statistical, and in both Chinese and English. Analyzing them calls for an interdisciplinary approach. But principally and ultimately my approach is historical. My intent is to write a history built on solid historical evidence. It is based on a conviction regarded by some as increasingly old-fashioned that it is a historian's obligation to seek historical truth, which includes social realities that existed independent of people's consciousness. While the creation of all historical sources involves the subjectivity of their authors, some contain less truth about such realities than others. In fact, the tremendous amount of anti-Chinese propaganda that in the nineteenth century distorted facts about Chinese America has in several cases succeeded in contaminating historical sources and knowledge. We will consider two myths that were first created and popularized by the anti-Chinese movement: first, that Chinese emigration to America was a desperate flight from impoverishment and other problems at home, and, second, that nearly all Chinese women in America were prostitutes.

Emerging from historical sources, *Chinese San Francisco* is a story about a community that maintained its cultural distinctiveness. It serves to demonstrate the failure and invalidity of wholesale assimilation as a social practice and as a political ideology and rhetoric. In the introduction to the 1970 edition of their 1963 landmark study, Nathan Glazer and Daniel Patrick Moynihan declared: "The ethnic pattern was American, more American than the assimilationist."[6] Adding an important chapter to the epic of America's cultural diversity, Chinatown in many ways resembled the white ethnic communities, such as Kleindeutschland, Irishtown, and Little Italy. As they did in non-Chinese ethnic communities, in Chinese San Francisco social institutions rose to aid the immigrants and offer protection against discrimination. Like their white ethnic counterparts, the Chinese understood the cultural importance of language, and the numerous schools that thrived in Chinese San Francisco remind us of the parochial or Hebrew schools in non-Chinese communities.[7] The non-English press that once prospered in so many other contexts also played an important role in Chinese life.[8] Finally, like many other ethnic groups that maintained lasting connections to their ancestral lands, the Chinese in the United States remained strongly attached to China.

Chinese San Francisco, however, was more than just another Anglo ethnic community. The Chinese American experience was significantly different from that of European groups. Coming to the New World across a different ocean, Chinese Americans encountered far greater hostility when they arrived. This racial hostility, which was deeply rooted in American history, limited their political rights and stunted the growth of their community. In the American West many European immigrants themselves joined the anti-Chinese crusade, in part to demonstrate their white-ness and thereby their American-ness. The effort to end Chinese immigration, which was formalized as a law forbidding the entry of Chinese immigrants into the country in 1882, succeeded in reducing the Chinese presence. In addition, the 1882 law reiterated the rule stating that Chinese immigrants could not become naturalized citizens.[9] In California and elsewhere in the American West anti-miscegenation laws made it illegal for Chinese to marry whites, and alien land acts passed early in the twentieth century denied Chinese the right to own land. Anti-Chinese discrimination also prevented Chinese America from making the transition from a predominantly "bachelor society" to a family-based community. All the hostility undoubtedly contributed to making Chinatown an especially attractive haven for Chinese Americans.

Nevertheless, Chinese San Francisco was far from a mere creation of anti-Chinese racism. In fact, it constantly defied the wishes of anti-Chinese forces. Moreover, during the post–Civil Rights Movement period the Chinese and other minority groups have demonstrated a desire similar to that of the African American population to maintain their own community and culture. The impetus toward community building arose out of the needs of the immigrants themselves.

Most important of all, *Chinese San Francisco* is a story about the emergence and development of a Pacific Rim community. Many Chinese Americans comprehended their experiences in the context of the trans-Pacific world, rather than solely in that of American society. While working and living in America they maintained strong memories of both the emigrant communities in South Guangdong and of their historical heritage. Such memories were not merely nostalgic sentiments but embodied very real, not imagined, personal, economic, and political ties.

Such ties became precious resources that helped to reinforce the immigrants' cultural identity, gave meaning to their American existence, and served as a source of hope and strength for enduring life's daily harshness. "Happy Chinaman!" exclaimed an African American woman early in the twentieth century, "[y]ou can go back to your village and enjoy your money.

This is my village, my home, yet am I an outcast."[10] For Chinese immigrants, their homeland (although not as easily returned to as the aforementioned woman believed) not only offered them a possible escape from racial oppression but also gave them energy and support in their struggle against it. In other words, trans-Pacific ties empowered the immigrants in their pursuit of both the American dream and rights.

In Chinatown, Chinese Americans found a fertile environment in which to nourish collective memories of their shared past and to maintain their trans-Pacific ties. At the same time Chinese San Francisco's American roots grew deeper and deeper, making it a true Pacific Rim community. After the 1906 earthquake Chinatown thwarted the last serious attempt made to relocate it and quickly rose from the ruins to reclaim its position as a permanent and highly visible part of the city. An internal acculturation had been under way, resulting from individual immigrants' varied efforts to adapt to the new social conditions. The community increasingly participated in American politics and celebrated American holidays such as the Fourth of July. It changed its outward look by discarding the old way of dressing, and the queue. More important, Chinese San Franciscans adopted prevailing Social Darwinistic ideas as a way to comprehend their plight in America, and that of China in international relations. Acculturation (namely, change in behavior and knowledge), nevertheless, constituted no "assimilation" or becoming part of Anglo America. For most Chinese Americans it did not signify the diminishing of their trans-Pacific ties or the loss of their cultural identity. Even in cases where individual Chinese might have desired to embrace completely the Anglo-American way of life, such a desire did not alter white America's prejudicial perceptions of them as alien, exotic creatures.

While Chinese Americans directly and openly challenged discrimination on many different occasions, internally they developed yet another approach that emphasized self-improvement and atonement. The origin of discrimination, they argued, lay in the weakness of China and in the problems within Chinese America. They believed that in order to successfully fight racism they must help strengthen China and improve their community. Recognizing the existence of such an ideology helps to explain the rise of nationalistic sentiments among Chinese Americans.

Several issues regarding terminology need a brief explanation. The term "Chinese Americans" is sometimes used interchangeably with "Chinese immigrants" in this book. The foreign birth of the immigrant Chinese did not render them less "American" than other groups around them. In 1880, for example, over 44 percent of San Francisco's population was foreign born. Overall, the term "Chinese Americans" in my text is more comprehensive and includes those with legal citizenship. We must remember, however, that few early immigrants adopted the term to identify themselves. My use of such a concept that only began to gain prevalence after World War II is not intended to slight the differences in sensibility and consciousness between early Chinese Americans and their counterparts in the late twentieth century. I also use the word "Chinese" to describe immigrants of Cantonese origins. This was a national identity that they had developed long before coming to the United States, instead of being a post-immigrant invention. Within Chinese American communities most people identified themselves by their home country, county, or village. In their home communities in China, where they were called "Gold Mountaineers," their American connections became markers of their collective identity. "Chinese San Francisco" refers to the Chinese community throughout the city. It was centered in Chinatown, but at different times a varying number of its members were scattered among other parts of the city. Finally, the term "white men" is a historical notion introduced and publicized by white men themselves. Many nineteenth-century male Californians of European descent adopted it to highlight their white-ness and de-emphasize their ethnicity. Although the term included groups that were significantly different from one another, it became a vital legal concept and an indicator of status that entailed exclusive political, social, and economic privileges.

The book covers two time periods. The opening chapter describes travels back to the pre-emigration emigrant communities in an effort to explore the socioeconomic, cultural, and mental conditions that led to California-bound migration. Students of American immigration have traditionally focused on the immigrants' American encounters. The analysis in chapter 1 serves as a reminder that their lives, however, began long before their arrival in America. Chapters 2 and 3, the first two chapters of part I, attempt to reconstruct Chinese San Francisco's changing demographic, social, and economic landscape. Chapter 4 discusses the life and mentality of a temporary Chinese San Franciscan. Chapter 5 analyzes Chinese San Franciscans' sense of identity, and the community's public expression. The next five chapters, which constitute part II, deal with a new era in Chinese San Francisco history that began with the 1905 protest against Chinese exclusion and the 1906

San Francisco earthquake. Chapters 6 and 7 seek to uncover the nature and the political and ideological roots of the reform efforts and mentality that posed a serious challenge to old traditions. The fruit of those efforts, namely acculturation, is the topic of chapter 8. Chapter 9 examines the ties that the transformed communities maintained with China. The story ends with the repeal of the Chinese exclusion acts in 1943 that came about as a result of China's long war of resistance against Japanese aggression, which is analyzed in the last chapter. During that war, Chinese Americans combined their efforts to aid China and to fight against racism directed toward themselves in America. The repeal provides conclusive evidence that the Chinese American experience must be understood in the trans-Pacific context.

This study has benefited from and adds to the increasingly rich scholarship on Chinese America. The numerous studies of issues concerning anti-Chinese discrimination have made it easier for me to explore and focus on other, sometimes ignored, aspects of Chinese life.[11] Although previous studies have investigated some of these aspects, mine attempts to represent a synthetic view of a Chinese American community and culture, a view seen through both collective and individualized lenses.[12] Recently several historians have made fruitful efforts to advance our understanding of those individuals who were quite acculturated.[13] In my book I have tried to uncover the mentality and life of others, including a significant number of second-generation Chinese Americans, who remained more "Chinese" and made up a majority of the community throughout our period.

It is the complex experiences of early Chinese Americans themselves that have propelled me to take an interdisciplinary, transnational approach. In recent years more and more scholars have recognized the significance of this approach in understanding not only Chinese America but also other Asian American groups, as we can tell from the growing popularity of words such as "trans-Pacific" and "global."[14] I do not seek to offer new theories about why we should problematize the "solid" and "isolated" constructs and boundaries of "Asia," "America," and individual nations. My contribution lies in my extensive use of both Chinese- and English-language sources in a systematic effort to demonstrate the formation and development of an early trans-Pacific community.

ONE

Revisiting the Pre-Emigration Old World

On August 4, 1850, while white Californians (many of them newcomers who had arrived in California during the Gold Rush) were still waiting for the federal government to approve their petition to join the union, the *Mary Ann Folliott* sailed into the harbor of San Francisco after a 63-day voyage from Hong Kong. Aboard were nearly fifty "unidentified" Chinese.[1] They were among the thousands of gold seekers who had begun to voyage across the Pacific Ocean from South China shortly after the discovery of gold at Sutter's Mill in January 1848.[2]

The arrival of these 49'ers opened a new chapter in California history and in the nation's history of race relations. It marked the beginning of a large-scale Chinese presence in America, which would soon become a focal point in the national discourse of race. In California especially, where the pioneering 49'ers and their followers soon became a leading minority group and a major labor force, they helped transform the economic and social landscape.

The book begins, however, with an inquiry into the Pearl River Delta Region in South China during the pre-emigration years, a region that not only sent the Gold Rushers but also remained the main source of China's America-bound emigration for over a century. We know much about the world that they entered and its reaction to them. But we need to pay more attention to the world they had left. From their own perspective, after all, their venturesome journey to the New World was but an extension of their experiences in a different historical context. Revisiting the Old World can help to reveal the natural and social ecology that nurtured the body and mind of the immigrants and gave them the temples, theaters, social relations, and many other traditions that were later transplanted in the New World. Going back can also shed light on the collective backgrounds and mentality of these pioneers who, like the "unidentified" passengers on the *Mary Ann Folliott*, left few traces of themselves as individuals and have remained anonymous.

My intention in this chapter is not to offer a comprehensive history of the region but to provide some insights into a couple of fundamental but unanswered questions. The first and foremost question is a rather straightforward one: why did the mid-nineteenth-century Chinese exodus to California originate from the Pearl River Region? In attempting to answer this question, it is extremely important to consider the pioneers' journey, because it played a pivotal role in generating a continuous flow of migrants from the delta region in what immigration scholars call "chain migration," making the region the main source of China's U.S.-bound emigration until after World War II.

To understand the genesis of Chinese emigration we need to fully appreciate the socioeconomic realities of the region, especially its economic vitality. It was home to one of China's oldest and most developed market-oriented economies. This economy bred not only a relatively high degree of prosperity but also gave rise to individuals willing to venture away from home to pursue money-making opportunities. This helps explain why news about the discovery of gold quickly triggered the first wave of emigration to California.

Moreover, the region was also culturally vital as a result of its geographical location at the forefront of China's maritime frontier. For decades before the Opium War the provincial capital of Canton (now spelled Guangzhou) served not only as the regional economic center but also as the nation's sole official port for trade with the West. Therefore, the delta was China's oldest focal point of contact with America and other Western countries.[3] Coming to China to pursue their varied interests in Chinese markets and Chinese souls, American merchants and missionaries congregated there and disseminated information about the New World. Of particular importance were the region's evolving California ties, through which the news of the discovery of gold reached local residents. In short, increasing Sino-American contact in South China before 1850 set the stage for the establishment of another condition necessary for mid-nineteenth-century Chinese emigration.

This argument marks a departure from the prevailing interpretation, which views Chinese emigration as a panic-stricken, hunger-driven flight from poverty and other socioeconomic difficulties. As I have stated elsewhere, whatever problems China may have been experiencing at the time, they do not fully explain the origins of mid-nineteenth-century emigration from the delta to California.[4] Nor do they completely represent the socioeconomic realities there. I must admit that I am not the first to come to this "new" interpretation. Nineteenth-century contemporaries, including non-Chinese observers, held the same view. In 1855 the Rev. William Speer, then a missionary among Chinese immigrants in California who had served in the delta for several years, pointed out that residents in coastal Guangdong "are better acquainted with other countries than any other portion of the Chinese." He went on: "They are . . . the richest people in the Empire. When the news of the discovery of gold . . . reached them, it was natural that they, above all other Chinese, should rush to California."[5] My research supports Speer's view. While we do not know how individual early emigrants made the decision to leave for California, it is clear that their departure constituted no rushed, massive exodus. In fact, fewer than seventy thousand people chose to go to California between 1849 and 1859.[6] The 1860 federal census reports a Chinese American population (primarily on the West Coast, especially in California) of about thirty-five thousand, which is less than one-fourth the size of the Chinese community in Java during the same time.[7]

The second question that this chapter deals with concerns mentality: early Chinese perceptions of America. I will concentrate on three of the earliest Chinese written works about the United States, taking a close look at each text itself. I will not attempt an exclusively textual reading that centers on the authors' aesthetics. Rather, my intention is to unearth key words and phrases that offer glimpses into larger societal trends. Although not written by emigrants, these texts came from and help to shed light on the historical environment that also generated Chinese emigration. They suggest that the knowledge about the United States available in the emigrant region was quite limited, reminding us that the New World remained an unfamiliar place for the emigrants, just as China was for most Americans at the time.

Socioeconomic Conditions Reconstructed

Guangdong, designated a province during the Qing Dynasty, is at the southeast end of mainland China. To the south is the vast South Sea, embracing the province along a coastline of several thousand kilometers. The mild, warm climate, along with plentiful precipitation, gives farmers in most areas multiple harvesting seasons (three for grains and seven for natural silk). The Pearl River Delta is the "pearl" of the province. "Every locality in Shunde is full of water and can be reached by boat. Rivers flow in different directions," reported the gazetteer for Shunde, one of the delta counties. There were, it went on, "profitable mulberry-tree fields and fish ponds. Natural silk is produced annually. Men and women live by their own exertion. The poor lease their land from the rich, who collect the rent. . . . Others specialize in different kinds of crafts and occupations that are found throughout the townships," ranging from weaving to making various utensils.[8]

This portrait of prosperity and brisk commodity production stands in stark contrast with the image of impoverishment and a traditional agrarian economy that current scholarship has of the delta area. Only an in-depth examination of the rich local documents, especially county gazetteers, reveals the real conditions there.[9] What follows is historical archeology or empirical social history.

The world the California-bound immigrants left was not a one-dimensional, stagnant and closed society. Instead, the Pearl River Delta was (and still is) one of the most dynamic areas in China. For local residents, migration was not a new concept. A long-standing Chinese frontier, Guangdong Province had been populated through continuous migration from the north beginning in the Qing Dynasty (221–206 B.C.). Such internal migration began to step up during the Tang Dynasty (618–907). In the Pearl River Delta the migrants from the north and their descendants helped to transform thousands of acres of marshland into agricultural fields. Generations of human labor accelerated the work of the Northern, Eastern, and Western Rivers that for centuries had been pushing the delta farther and farther into the sea by filling it with silt. The physical metamorphosis of the region was well remembered and recorded. The following is a passage from the gazetteer for one of the delta counties, Nanhai, about a mountain in the west of the county: "It used to stand in the middle of ocean waves. In several thousand years, the sand and mud brought down by two rivers accumulated around the mountain, gradually making it far away from the water."[10] Starting largely from the Song Dynasty (960–1279) onward, people built dams to create and protect agricultural lands across the delta area.

Settlers from the north also profoundly transformed the region's social landscape by introducing the culture of China's ethnic majority, the Han people. This helps to explain why, despite its cultural uniqueness and its physical distance from the country's social and political center, the region had strong and inherent ties with "mainstream" Chinese culture. Local residents' distinctive dialects were based on and preserved significant elements of classic Chinese.[11] In many of the temples that constituted a conspicuous mark in the regional landscape, people worshipped deities that had national, rather than only regional, followings. As we will see later, some of them were figures central to China's national history that had been deified. Equally conspicuous were the "citang" or clan buildings. The clan existed as a significant social and economic entity. Each clan often lived in its own structure. The rich clans owned land, fruit trees, and fish ponds and could afford to build massive, fortress-like compounds. The many genealogies that traced the clans' ancestral roots to central China were but one indication of Cantonese people's lasting historical memories of their geographical and cultural origins. Therefore, I must add, it is not culturally erroneous to use the word "Chinese" in reference to America's Cantonese immigrants.

Waves of southbound overland migration also created some of the most important social discord in the delta society, including the animosity between the Hakka and Bendi groups. The word *bendi* (meaning "natives" in Chinese) refers to those who established their presence earlier than the Hakka (meaning "guest people") in the province. The latter spoke a different dialect and lived in the mountainous areas and, in many cases, worked as tenant peasants. Occupying an even lower social status were those known as *dan*, who lived by the water on their boats and made a living mostly by fishing. The fifty thousand dan households on rivers south of Canton were descendants of a non-han ethnic group named *yue*.[12] The "natives" did not allow intermarriages with these people, indicating not only a significant social gap between them but also the prejudice of the former.[13]

The presence of non-Asians had further complicated the social structure and consciousness of the region. As an eighteenth-century writer named Fan

Duanang reported, for example, during the Ming Dynasty (1368–1644) many rich families in Canton bought black slaves to serve as house guards, a phenomenon that had started in the Tang Dynasty.[14] Later on the black slaves in Macao who served and lived among Europeans maintained some contact with Chinese residents—there were laws regarding crimes committed by Chinese and blacks together. More important, they remained a prominent presence in Chinese minds, if the numerous writings about them are any indication. Chinese writers from the Tang years earlier had called such blacks *guinu* (meaning ghost slaves) and considered them scarcely human. Fan believed that "they came from mountains beyond the oceans and lived on raw food. After being captured, they were fed cooked food . . . if they survive they can learn to understand but not speak the human language."[15] It is interesting to note how Fan used the categories of raw and cooked food to differentiate between the blacks and their civilized masters.

As markers of the delta's transformative process, many inland waterways existed to link different counties, and offered access to the sea. Several counties were located right along the long, curved coastline that was inlaid with fine harbors. Thanks to such favorable natural conditions, the region was a busy place for domestic and international trade. The Qing government blessed the region in another way by designating Canton as China's sole port for international trade between 1757 and the end of the Opium War. Even for decades after other ports had opened as a result of the Opium War, it maintained its significance in international trade.

Therefore a dynamic economy emerged in the delta long before the mid-nineteenth century, an economy that was characterized by the production of agricultural and nonagricultural commodities for domestic and international markets.[16] Such a market-oriented economy constituted the foundation of the region's prosperity, a fact that became common knowledge after the Ming Dynasty. In a valuable book about Guangdong written in the seventeenth century, Qu Dajun, a native of Nanhai (another delta county) and a perceptive writer, noted that many people there were engaged in commerce-related activities, and some became wealthy.[17] It also made possible a population growth that exceeded that which a subsistence economy could have sustained.[18]

By the eighteenth century the province no longer had an agricultural system that could produce enough food for its population. In fact, it had a long history of reliance on neighboring Guangxi Province for the supply of rice, the staple of local residents' diet. Guangdong's dependence on Guangxi for rice supplies remained so important in the 1830s that foreigners in China noticed it. In 1833 the *Chinese Repository* reported that "large quantities of rice" were imported from Guangxi.[19]

The province was unable to be self-sufficient in grain production in part because many people were involved, one way or another, in the more profitable market economy.[20] Even among those who continued to work in the fields, many chose to grow various cash crops such as oranges, sugar cane, and tobacco, instead of food crops to consume themselves. Commenting disapprovingly on the Cantonese people's lack of interest in traditional agriculture, the governor of Guangxi stated early in the eighteenth century that they failed to grow enough rice because they "are very greedy and are always going after profit."[21] The governor's attitude and language reflected the dominant way of thinking among the Chinese elite that regarded agriculture as the essential and proper way to make a living. China's rulers in Beijing were also aware of and worried about Cantonese people's active participation in commodity production and exchange. As early as the eighteenth century the Emperor Yongzheng more than once exhorted his subjects in Guangdong not to abandon traditional agriculture in favor of profit.[22]

Guangdong used the profit from trade to import food supplies from elsewhere to feed its growing population. *The Nanhai Xianzhi* reported that "Guangdong is limited in its territory and dense in population. Few are engaged in agriculture. Six to seven out of every ten people are engaged in commerce. Trade is the most profitable of all."[23] The authors of the county gazetteer did not mean to suggest that a majority of the people were merchants per se. The words "commerce" and "trade" used here were loosely defined and referred to varied market-driven economic activities, including the production of different agricultural and nonagricultural commodities. And engagement in such activities did not prevent many people from participating in grain cultivation on a part-time basis.

Economic conditions in different regions of Guangdong varied significantly. The market-oriented economy was most advanced in the Pearl River Delta in the eastern part of the province, thanks mainly to its geographic advantages. As early as 1730 the Emperor Yongzheng noted: "East Guangdong is surrounded by the ocean on three sides, where merchants arrive from various provinces and foreign barbarians come with money to purchase goods. Trade is very heavy."[24]

An extensive network of local markets served to connect the communities in the region into one economic zone, which extended to nearby Macao and, later on, Hong Kong. During the eighteenth and the early nineteenth centuries the number of markets significantly increased in many areas across Guangdong, especially in the Pearl River Delta.[25] Many in the delta specialized in certain kinds of products, such as longan (a popular local fruit), medicine, spices, and pearls.[26]

As the center of the regional economy, Canton had become a busy metropolitan city of regional and international trade by the early nineteenth century, when Americans arrived in increasing numbers. A young American named W. C. Hunter recalled later what he had seen upon entering this busy port city in February 1825 aboard the *Citizen*: "It was then crowded with native vessels . . . these brought cargoes from Teenpak and places on the coast south-westward of Macao. . . . The number of cargo boats from the interior, of passenger boats, floating residences and up-country craft . . . was prodigious."[27]

Of the boats sighted by Hunter, many would have come from the emigrant counties, especially the *sanyi* (meaning "three-district") counties of Nanhai, Panyu, and Shunde, located south of Canton. The sanyi area had the most developed economy. Panyu County, where "commercial vessels come from all over," had been a focal point of trade since the Song Dynasty (690–1279).[28]

Like Panyu, Nanhai also had a strong tradition of commerce starting long before the mid-nineteenth century. The provincial gazetteer of Guangdong, one of the most important sources of the history of the province, reports that since the Song Dynasty "Nanhai has been a metropolis in Guangdong," where foreign merchants came with goods, like pearls, to trade with local people. By that time it already had a reputation for affluence.[29]

During the early Qing Dynasty a commercialized economy in Nanhai continued to thrive because of its proximity to the major ports of trade in East Guangdong. The regional network of inland waterways afforded the county easy access to the market in nearby Canton. Over time regular boat service was also established between Nanhai and Macao as well as Hong Kong. The goods that arrived at the local marketplaces in the county often came directly from the so-called Thirteen Hang (*hang* was then commonly spelled *hong*) in Canton, which are among the most important trading firms in modern Chinese history. In fact, some of the wealthiest and most influential hang merchants, including a very powerful merchant named Houqua, who had local as well as international business ties, were natives of this county, as we will see later.[30]

The local merchants and others involved in transporting the goods worked together and hard. One of the major export products of this county was silk. The silk merchants collected their goods from the producing villages and shipped them to the urban markets on "small but solidly built" boats. Often traveling together, the boats took off at sunset and arrived at their destination at dawn. The boatmen oared their way hard and loud, announcing their collective presence to assure the safety of the cargo in the darkness of the night.[31] Besides silk, Nanhai also produced other marketable commodities, such as fish. In a village named Jiujiang fish ponds were most residents' primary source of livelihood.[32]

In like fashion, Shunde County developed an economy that produced items such as silk and fish for the market, rather than mere subsistence crops. The county gazetteer estimated that less than half of the population was engaged solely in producing grain.[33] Fish ponds and mulberry-tree fields yielded two of the county's major commodities with high market values. The county was also known for its profitable hemp products, which were sold as far away as Jiangsu and Zhejiang Provinces hundreds of miles away.[34] The provincial gazetteer of Guangdong reported that during the Qing Dynasty Shunde's farming and fishing industries were "better than any other district [in the province]." This authoritative source attributed the county's economic strength to its geographical location and natural resources: "Shunde is located by the ocean and has vast and fertile land."[35]

What is more, the delta region had such an advanced market-driven economy that some villages became specialized in certain products. In a "watery" district known as Chen Village, for example, most people made their living by growing longan. The tens of thousands of longan trees formed a distinctive scene. The numerous longan markets within the county offered a convenient channel of sales for the longan farmers. The residents also produced other fruits, including lichees and oranges, which were sold "nearby and afar." They developed such a good reputation as fruit-tree specialists that people elsewhere who wanted to enter the same business came to buy saplings from them.[36]

Shunde's commodities reached both domestic and international markets. Besides the fruit trees, the county was known for its silk products. Two Frenchmen visited the silk territory of Shunde late in 1844, when they were traveling on boat from Canton to Macao. One of them, I. Hedde, noted in a lengthy report that "The foreign trade consumes a great deal of these [silk products]."[37] Such continued silk production shows that despite the damage to the textile industry brought about by the Opium War and its aftermath, at least in the 1840s the local economy was far from being totally destroyed. Some sectors in the regional economy that were connected to foreign trade, such as the silk industry and sugar-cane production, remained strong and even grew after the war.

In any event, the county gazetteer estimated that, overall, 60 percent of the people in Shunde worked in the fields (not necessarily solely in food-crop production), 20 percent were artisans, and the remaining 20 percent were in commerce. Because of its commercial development, by the mid-nineteenth century this county's economy was thriving, in relative terms, and its unemployment rate was low. The authors of the county gazetteer reported several times that "few people are idle and lazy."[38]

Within the delta not all the emigrant counties reached the same level of economic development. Nor were they all integrated into the regional market network to the same extent or in the same manner. For example, in Xinning County, which is situated on the southwest periphery of the delta area, the economy was less developed, and more people were engaged in agriculture, as compared with the sanyi counties. With less extensive and direct connections to the outside markets than their counterparts elsewhere, the Xinning merchants did business mostly locally and seldom traveled far.[39] Also situated on the periphery, to the west of Xinning, Enping County had a similar economic structure; most people were in agriculture, and local merchants handled their business needs locally. Few outside merchants were to be found in the county.[40]

Nevertheless, what we find in those counties was not a pure traditional agrarian economy. In Xinning County, for instance, there were over seventy local marketplaces in the mid-nineteenth century. What is more, people in the less-prosperous *siyi* (meaning "four counties" and referring to Xinning, Xinhui, Enping, and Kaiping) area, traveled to work in more developed market economies. During the fall and winter seasons and during times of poor harvest, people from these two counties, especially Xinning County, went to other counties, such as Nanhai County, to seek employment as artisans and other types of workers.[41] These less-developed counties entered the region's commercial network as suppliers of labor.

Such differences between the sanyi counties and those like Xinning reflected the regional economic structure. It is necessary to note that such structural differences were transplanted to the New World. It was common knowledge among immigrants that while those from Xinning and other less-developed counties were likely to be laborers, merchants tended to be from the sanyi counties. As a major supplier of labor in the economy of the Pearl River Delta, Xinning had a ready pool of laborers with the necessary experience and willingness to travel and work elsewhere. The position that it occupied in the regional market economy helps to explain why it eventually became the single most important sending county during the first century of Chinese labor immigration. By comparison, the rich tradition in commerce in the sanyi counties offered sanyi people various vital resources, making it relatively more likely that they would become merchants in the United States.

Much evidence supports the argument that the early emigrants were not from impoverished families or communities. The gazetteer of Xinning, probably the least prosperous of all the emigrant counties, contains valuable information about the plight of some of the families, especially wives, of men who had gone overseas. Although limited and perhaps not even always representative, such information sheds light on the vanished men's family background and the conditions in their native community.

One woman named Li was engaged to an emigrant before his departure. Disappointed by the young man's failure to come back, her anxious father started making arrangements for her to marry someone else. She sent a family servant to get the sister of her fiancé to help persuade her father to change his mind. Realizing that he was unpersuadable, she eventually went to live with her fiancé's family and supported herself by weaving while waiting for the man, who never returned.[42] Most such women profiled in the local document were wives, or rather widows, of husbands who died or simply disappeared on their journey overseas. No evidence suggests that they were from the poorest families, though they were not very rich. They struggled but were nonetheless able to raise their offspring and, in some cases, take care of their parents-in-law on their own, without any help from their vanished spouses. Their ability to do so clearly shows that the communities, which their men had left and where these women continued to live, were not totally impoverished.

In short, the most important socioeconomic characteristic of the emigrant communities was not impoverishment that resulted from the disintegration of a traditional agrarian economy. Rather, it was economic vitality. Generated by the region's long-standing market economy, that vitality helps to explain its relative prosperity.

My analysis deals primarily with the mid-nineteenth century, but it is necessary to note that the relatively highly commercialized economy in the delta continued to exist for decades thereafter. For example, the mulberry cultivation and fish breeding in Shunde County discussed earlier remained a distinct feature of its economy as late as the 1920s. As the historian David Faure has shown in his study of Jiangsu and Guangdong, between 1870 and 1930 the delta region, along with other areas in these two provinces that also produced cash crops for export, experienced "considerable prosperity."[43]

Moreover, it is worth noting that the scholarship on nineteenth-century and early twentieth-century European labor immigration once supported the view that European emigration was a flight from poverty and hunger. That view has been increasingly challenged in recent years. As John Bodnar states, for example, "the image of poor peasants fleeing to America has also dominated much of the scholarship on Italian emigrants but closer analysis reveals that the very poor seldom left." It becomes increasingly clear that immigrants from European countries such as Italy and Germany were likely to have occupied positions somewhere in the middle and lower-middle levels of their home societies.[44]

Students of Chinese emigration do not have documents like the British Register of Emigration that Bernard Bailyn used in his study of English emigrants, *Voyagers to the West*.[45] We cannot pinpoint statistically the pre-emigration social and economic status of the early emigrants from China. But it is fairly clear that while most of them were not rich, it is unlikely that they were among the poorest members of society and that their departure signified primarily an escape from impoverishment. This fact was known to contemporary Americans who were well acquainted with the Chinese, such as the missionary the Rev. William Speer. Later on, anti-Chinese propaganda succeeded in obscuring that fact by claiming that the Chinese immigrants were the lowest social class and were driven by starvation to the United States. In the 1870s S. Wells Williams, once a missionary to China and later a Chinese historian, tried to refute the increasingly popular claim. Referring to those immigrants, Williams noted: "They are not held at home as serfs by feudal barons or great landholders . . . nor compelled to work in mines, factories, or penitentiaries; they are in no particular danger of starving, from which and other evils they hope to escape by running away to America."[46] My examination of some of the major emigrant communities helps to restore a historical fact that has long been buried.

America in Guangdong

The China trade, the locomotive of American expansion across the Pacific Ocean, has an important place in American history. In the late eighteenth and early nineteenth centuries it decorated the households of New England merchants with silks, porcelain, and lacquer. Americans' thirst for Chinese tea, unquenched by the splashes of the Boston Tea Party, remained strong for a long time.[47] What is more, the China trade is of great significance in the early history of the American West. As Arthur M. Johnson and Barry E. Supple wrote, "The China trade proved an important source of men and capital for America's western development."[48] American merchants, especially the influential and close-knit Bostonian China traders such as John M. Forbes, used their profits from the China trade, including the opium trade, to build Western railways.[49]

Most important, the arrival of American traders and missionaries helped to introduce America to Chinese consciousness and established an important condition for Chinese emigration.[50] Beginning with the arrival of the *Empress of China* in 1784, the American commercial presence in China grew quickly.[51] The *Chinese Repository* reported that the number of American ships coming to Canton increased from 5 in the 1786–87 season to 59 by 1832–33.[52] In the late 1830s and early 1840s Americans had the second-largest fleet of foreign vessels, after Britain.[53]

Chinese consciousness of Americans increased during the Daoguang period. When Samuel Shaw and his *Empress of China* crew sailed to China, the Cantonese mistook them for British. By the early nineteenth century, however, they had come to realize that those who shipped under the Stars and Stripes came from a different country. Struck by its colorful flag, local Chinese called that country the "Flowery-Flag Country."[54]

Venturing to Canton with "no other objective than that of commerce," American China traders did not have extensive contact with ordinary residents in noncommercial contexts.[55] But they had ample opportunity to interact with their Chinese counterparts. On the river in the vicinity of the port of Canton, "[t]he crowds of boats," Chinese and foreign, constituted a very memorable scene.[56] The *Chinese Repository* reported in 1833: "The situation of Canton and the policy of the Chinese government . . . have made this city the scene of a very extensive *domestic and foreign commerce*."[57] Some Chinese merchants evidently obtained a certain amount of knowledge about America from such interactions. As early as 1814 one merchant named Pan Shuiguan wrote to "Number One Master [the president] of the Flowery-Flag Country" to file a complaint against some American merchants for dishonest behavior, because he had heard that in America the law was just.[58]

By the 1830s Western merchants in Canton had established their own agencies, located a few yards away from the banks of the Pearl River. Known as "factories," those agencies were housed in buildings nominally under the supervision of the co-hong, a Chinese security-merchant group with the exclusive authorization to deal with foreign trade.[59] The Americans had their own factory, the Kwang-yuen hang, on Old China Street.[60]

The factory setting allowed Americans to interact with their Chinese employees, including the compradores and interpreters, on a daily basis.[61] The Americans also worked and sometimes even forged close relations with Chinese hang merchants, many of whom were natives of the emigrant counties. As we will see later, the Chinese merchants had strong local ties, and they must have passed on what they heard about America to residents in their native communities.

The area where the factories were located became a busy place. Here native Cantonese set up shops, selling liquor, coffee, food, and other goods to foreigners. The busiest place was a three-story building right next to the "factories." It housed a hospital that thousands of people visited over the years after it first came into existence in 1835. The hospital was operated by Dr. Peter Parker, one of the American Protestant missionaries in China.[62]

Traveling along the way paved by Yankee China traders, the missionaries commenced their work in China in 1830.[63] The missionaries arrived for a different purpose, that is, to heed God's command: "Go ye into all the world and preach the gospel to every creature" (Mark xvi. 15). As the Rev. William J. Boone declared in the 1830s, with the largest pagan population on earth, China represented "the most desirable field in the world for the Church to enter in her missionary capacity."[64] The missionaries had a strong sense of mission to "enlighten" the Chinese about America—not only about their country's religion but also about its medicine, technology, history, and geography. They learned the Chinese language and made conscious efforts to communicate with local people. As a result they contacted a wider range of people and played a far more direct role than did merchants in spreading information about America.[65]

The American Board of Commissioners for Foreign Missions dispatched the first American missionaries to China and remained the most active in missionary work in China for years.[66] By 1847 it had sent more workers to China than any other organization. Because of China's anti-Christianity policy adopted under the Emperor Kangxi (1662–1722),[67] the Americans followed a tradition started by the Englishman Robert Morrison: they engaged in a variety of activities rather than focusing on overtly evangelical work.[68] This development is highlighted by the career of Dr. Peter Parker, a medical missionary. Known among the Chinese as a "celebrated" physician, he reached thousands of people by practicing medicine.[69]

It is interesting to note that Parker first learned about China from New England China traders while studying medicine and theology in New Haven. The image of China he acquired was apparently not a rosy one, because he regarded missionary work in China as a sacrifice that would entail enormous danger and uncertainty.[70] Shortly before his departure he confessed his inner anxiety in his diary: "Oh, my God, to thee I may say it, there is something that appears like the feeling of a martyr that possesses my

bosom."[71] In June 1834, when he was publicly dedicated as a China missionary in New York, he told the audience in a farewell speech that it might be
"my last address to you with the living voice."[72]

In late 1835, upon completing his one-year language training course in
Singapore, Parker set up the Ophthalmic Hospital in Canton. By the end of
1847 the hospital had treated over twenty-six thousand patients for a wide
range of diseases.[73] Equally diverse were the social backgrounds of the patients. The Englishman C. Toogood Downing, a frequent visitor to the hospital, noted late in the 1830s that "[a] great number of the Chinese of all
ranks visit the Hospital."[74] According to the hospital's own reports, its patients came from "all conditions and ranks, from the beggar to the highest
functionary under the imperial government."[75] Parker developed a personal
relationship with some of his patients, such as Qiying (Kiying), governor
general of Liangguang at Canton (1844–48). Qiying became an "old friend"
of Parker's and continued to consult him after returning to Beijing.[76]
Another Chinese who would consider Parker an "old friend" was Imperial
Commissioner Lin Zexu. Besides offering medical advice, Parker helped him
translate a book on international law into Chinese.[77] As we will see, Lin was
responsible for the compilation of the influential *Gazetteer of the Four
Continents*, which has a section on the United States.

Parker must have also known many ordinary patients well, especially
those who stayed at the hospital for extended periods or who went there
more than once. Patients showed respect and appreciation for Parker. In 1849
a grateful man named Chushu wrote a poem, calling him "America's noble
and disinterested man." The poem declared: "His country is different from
ours, yet his feelings are the same [as ours]."[78]

The patients clearly heard something about that "different" country at the
hospital. It is very important to note that a great number of Parker's patients
came from major emigrant counties such as Nanhai and Panyu. It is reasonable to believe, therefore, that before they left China some emigrants had
heard something about America from Parker, directly or indirectly.

Inspired by Parker's success, in 1838 Protestant missionaries founded the
Medical Missionary Society in China "in order to give a wider extension,
and a permanency, to the efforts that have already been made to spread the
benefits of rational medicine and surgery among the Chinese."[79] Medical
work constituted just one of the missionaries' many efforts to spread "ra-

tional" knowledge among the Chinese. The missionaries also established schools, including the Morrison School. Founded late in the 1830s in memory of the late Rev. Morrison, the school melded religious teaching with secular subjects. Among its students was Yung Wing. Before arriving in America, as he later revealed in his autobiography, Yung had acquired some knowledge about America from the two American teachers.

Indeed, American missionaries placed great emphasis on introducing nonreligious knowledge to the Chinese. Together with their British coworkers, they formed the Society for the Diffusion of Useful Knowledge in China and published numerous books about the West. One such book, Bridgman's *Meilige hesheng zhilue* (A brief introduction to the United Provinces [States] of America) of 1832, was quite popular among Chinese readers and was later included in Wei Yuan's influential *Haiguo tuzhi* (Illustrated treatise on the sea kingdoms) (to be discussed later). Wei called it an authoritative source on the subject because it was written by a native of that country.[80]

While American missionaries were clearly instrumental in spreading knowledge about America, we must nevertheless not overestimate their impact. First of all, their number remained small. From 1830 to 1847 a total of about forty ordained American missionaries came to China.[81] In 1848 the influential American Board of Commissioners for Foreign Missions had only seven people in Canton.[82] Secondly, the missionaries' proficiency in Chinese was still quite limited, as both contemporary Chinese and Americans noted.[83] Thirdly, profound differences existed between the missionaries and local Chinese. John King Fairbank writes that the American missionary "had the chance to preach and innovate in China only because he was part of the western invasion. Gunfire and the unequal treaties initially gave him his privileged status and opportunity."[84] In fact, some missionaries even acted as representatives of the American government. Naturally, the missionaries' perspective was different from that of the Chinese. An informational pamphlet about China, published at a later time for missionaries, asked the readers to identify and remember the "*good* results" (italics added) of the Opium War, a war that harmed and humiliated China.[85]

Finally, we must recognize Chinese contributions to the development of Sino-American contact. Numerous Cantonese merchants had extensive trans-Pacific connections and investments. Others went to America as sailors, interpreters, students, or servants working for Yankee merchants.[86] News about some of these individuals occasionally reached China. In 1845, for example, the *Chinese Repository* reported that a native of Canton became a naturalized U.S. citizen in Boston after living there for eight years.[87] A few of these individuals wrote about what they saw and experienced in America. One of them was Lin Zhen, who went to the United States as an interpreter in 1847 aboard an American commercial ship and spent over one year in New York and the South. In his *Xihai youji cao* (Accounts of a Journey to the West Sea), he offered terse but interesting observations on a wide range of subjects, showing the depth of his knowledge of American society.[88] He discussed the legal and political institutions, the freedom of the press, and technological innovations. He also noticed the intolerance for other cultures, which were considered "stupid."[89] Such intolerance would be further demonstrated after the arrival of Chinese immigrants.

Emerging Perceptions of Americans

Residents around Canton coined the earliest Chinese terms for both the United States and California. In an effort to gauge the impact of growing Sino-American contact during the Daoguang years, this section considers what went on in Chinese minds rather than the socioeconomic conditions that have been discussed up to this point. I will focus on accounts of the United States given in three books: Xie Qinggao's *Haiwai fanyi lu* or simply *Hailu* (Record of the Seas) of 1820, *Sizhou zhi* (Gazetteer of the four continents) compiled in 1839 under the leadership of Lin Zexu, and Xu Jiyu's *Yinghuan zhilue* (Brief record of the ocean circuit) of 1848.[90] These texts, especially the last two, were widely circulated in the Pearl River Delta and beyond.[91] Therefore, while we cannot assume that they accurately mirror the mind of the average emigrant, a historically grounded contextual reading of such texts can certainly help us understand emerging images and perceptions of the United States in the emigrant region.[92]

Containing the earliest writings about the West in modern Chinese history, these documents embody the increase in knowledge about the United States in the delta region. As a result of that growth, people in South China began to find ways to identify America and European countries individually instead of lumping them all together. What is more, this also tells us that the Chinese did not view and think of Westerners in terms of race, a way of thinking that immigrants carried in the New World. The three texts clearly chronicle the emergence of a body of knowledge about America available in the region. They also remind us that such knowledge available to local people remained quite limited.

In his *Hailu*, a Guangdong native named Xie Qinggao gave us the first written Chinese account of the United States. Finished in 1820, the book is about countries that he had seen or heard about during his fourteen-year career as a seaman on a Western vessel.[93] Its section on America includes the following description: "The country of 'Meiligan' is west of 'Yingjili' [transliteration of "English" in reference to "England"] . . . and is also an isolated island in the ocean. Its territory is a bit narrow. Originally a colony of 'Yingjili,' it is now an independent nation, and its customs are similar to tho'e of 'Yingjili.' This is what is known in Guangdong as the 'Flowery Flag [Country].' "[94]

Evidently Xie had some knowledge of U.S. history. The former sailor was also aware of the relatively new American invention of the steamboat, or "fireboat," that could operate "without manpower."[95] But the characterization of America as an "isolated island" reveals his inability to pinpoint the geographical location of the country, which had not yet appeared on China's world map. Indeed, the short section of about five hundred characters illustrates how little he actually knew about the country that he probably never set foot on. For instance, it said nothing about political practices and social customs except for one sentence on monogamy: "from the king to the commoner, no one has two wives."[96] Overall, the text is marked by vagueness, as is best conveyed in a sentence about America's natural geography: "in the mountains are exotic birds and animals, and their names are unknown."[97]

Yet we must not overlook the historical significance and impact of this piece. It received attention from not only Chinese readers but also from Westerners in Guangdong. The *Chinese Repository* called it "the best" of all Chinese overseas travel books. It would be reasonable to believe that this book aroused people's curiosity and made them "desire, more earnestly than ever before," to see the outside world.[98]

More important, Xie's work serves as a barometer of its times. Its vagueness and inaccuracy, first of all, are indicative of how uninformed China remained as a nation about the West in general and America in particular. By the 1820s and 1830s there were still no consistent ways of translating the names of Western countries. The name of a single country often had several different transliterations, which usually consisted of uncommon characters used solely as phonetic symbols. This caused much confusion.[99] Trying to clarify such confusion regarding the sundry Chinese translations of "America," an official wrote in 1825: " 'Yamolige' was also named 'Yameilige' or 'Milijian.' "[100]

As further evidence of China's unfamiliarity with the West, many Chinese continued to use the old terms *fan* and *yi* (originally meaning "barbarians") in reference to all Westerners.[101] Such terminology not only failed to distinguish Westerners from one another but also contained a strong dose of Chinese cultural superiority. In an attempt to argue that racial bias has not been just a white phenomenon, Frank Dikötter asserts that nonwhite peoples like the Chinese developed prejudiced views about outsiders, including Westerners.[102] It is problematic, however, to see China's sense of cultural superiority as racial prejudice. The Chinese may have been extremely biased, but the words "fan" and "yi" were used in reference to all non-Chinese peoples, Westerners and non-Westerners alike, Therefore, they do not constitute racial categories.[103]

Despite its limitations, Xie's account not only represents the effort to establish a distinctive Chinese term for the United States but also marked the earliest attempt to give it a historically and geographically meaningful definition. The increasing tendency to try to recognize the individuality of America as well as of other Western nations is evident in other documents of the time. Diverging from the old tradition and mentality characterized by a reluctance to acknowledge differences among foreigners, the new tendency was a result of increased contact between the West and China.

In distinguishing individual Western nations the Chinese occasionally used physical features as markers—the English became "red-haired" foreigners, for instance. Nevertheless, it is clear that physical features were not used to group nations into racial categories. Most strikingly absent from the efforts to identify Western nations was any emphasis on skin color. For the most part, the Chinese focused their attention on something that had nothing to do with Westerners' physicality: their national flag.

Numerous national flags of Western countries were prominently displayed in the Canton area. Their "glaring colours," commented an Englishman, "attract the eye from the first moment."[104] For local people, Westerners' eye-catching flags served as more important identity markers than did people's physical characteristics. They called Norway, for example, the "Yellow-Flag Country."[105] And the United States became the "Flowery-Flag Country." Developed by ordinary Cantonese, this term found its way into Xie's book and various other documents that appeared later.

Lin Zexu's *Sizhou zhi* of 1839 allows us to measure the development of China's knowledge of the United States after 1820. To a large degree the book was a product of the socioeconomic and political crisis caused by the opium trade, especially the imminent conflict with Britain. Appointed as imperial commissioner in 1838 to deal with that crisis, Lin was aware of the urgent need to gather information about the outside world, especially the West. The book is based on a variety of sources and reflects the collective efforts of a group of young intellectuals put together by Lin.[106] In 1852 Sir John Francis Davis recalled Lin Zexu's zest for the project:

> When that very active and energetic functionary Lin resided at Canton in his high official capacity . . . he availed himself of the aid of interpreters, and of every work he could procure, either native or foreign, to obtain a knowledge of the Terra incognita, that is, of every country of the world beyond China. For this purpose he availed himself of the Missionary Tracts, the Chinese Month Magazine, a Treatise on Commerce, a Description of the United States, and of England, a work on Geography. . . . Translations were also made of all such articles in the newspapers as contained any thing concerning China.[107]

It is worth noting that Lin's work resulted from the collective effort of a group of researchers and was based on different sources. Clearly, this is a text that tells us more about a society's collective knowledge than about one individual's subjectivity. Let us consider the section on America. In comparison with Xie's text, *Sizhou zhi* covers a wider range of subjects, such as history, government, economy, geography. and population. Its data were also far more substantial and systematic and even included statistics. Topics of interest to the Chinese, such as the fact that there was no king in America, received particular attention.

One of the book's remarkable features is the absence of the kind of bias toward Westerners that characterized contemporary official documents. Instead, it presented positive images of Americans and their social and political institutions. The authors wrote that America's success in quickly becoming a prosperous nation was attributable to its achievement in education that enabled "talents to emerge generation after generation."[108]

While contemporary Westerners regarded the book as containing "nothing interesting,"[109] it was of great value to the Chinese because of the systematic information it assembled. Such information helped establish a meaningful and concrete concept of the United States. A landmark in the development of China's knowledge of the West, *Sizhou zhi* influenced many Chinese and became a basis for Wei Yuan's multivolume *Haiguo tuzhi* (Illustrated treatise on the sea kingdoms), which one historian calls "the single most important geographical work written about the maritime world during the Ching [Qing] period."[110]

A great deal of caution must be exercised in assessing *Sizhou zhi*'s significance, however, because the book was primarily a translation. Most illustrative of its problems is the authors' use of phonetic symbols to transliterate many key concepts, such as "president," "Congress," and "Supreme Court." Such transliterations did not clearly communicate the meaning of those terms. In fact, sometimes the authors themselves failed to understand what important phrases meant. A statement about American colonial history reads: "The English King 'Zanshi' [James] appointed two officials to govern [the colonies], one named 'Landen Ganbani,' and the other 'Boliemao Ganbani.' " Here, the London Company and the Plymouth Company were mistaken for two officials.[111] Such mistakes remind us of what John King Fairbank has called China's "intellectual unpreparedness for Western contact"—unpreparedness that was "evident in the folklore and thought of China in 1840."[112]

After the Opium War (1840–42), while Americans and other Westerners gained many privileges in China through the unequal treaties, more books about the West appeared. One of them was the *Yinghuan zhilue* by Xu Jiyu, a scholar-statesman, who had held various positions in Guangdong and Fujian Provinces and was knowledgeable about developments in coastal areas, and their consequences. In an 1842 essay he proposed a ban of opium smoking and the opium trade. His 1848 book represents another important work about the West in modern China. It is based on his own research and written in his own words.

Xu used vocabulary familiar to Chinese readers, rendering key American concepts in easily understood terms. For example, "Congress" was translated as *gonghui* (public meeting), and "president" as *zongtongling* (commander in chief).[113]

In lively and colorful language Xu recounted events in American history. The following is from a long passage about the War of Independence, in which he praised Washington and gave him a common Chinese family name, "Den": "Afterwards, however, the English army redeployed massively and pushed forward. Den's army was then defeated. The soldiers were so afraid that they wanted to disband and leave, but Den's righteous spirit remained unshaken. He regrouped the remaining army and fought again."[114]

Xu tried to offer the most up-to-date information. Of the number of states, he noted: "Milijian previously had twenty-six parts. Later the number increased to twenty-eight."[115] Xu missed only one of the three states that had been admitted into the union after the publication of Lin Zexu's book. Besides using written sources, he also gathered data from various people for the book. He frequently consulted the American missionary Rev. David Abeel, whose assistance he acknowledged when the book first came out. He also received help from a Chinese, a native of Xiangshan County who had reportedly lived in the United States for four years and had learned to write and speak English "tolerably well."[116]

The appearance of this book signified China's growing awareness of the United States. And after its publication the popular book served to augment that awareness. It was widely circulated and had a significant impact in the delta area and beyond.[117]

Obvious factual mistakes in Xu's text nevertheless reveal the limitations of his knowledge. In his account of Rhode Island, for example, he stated that in Ferdinand Verbiest's record of the seven wonders of the world, "there was a colossal copper man on 'Lode Island.'" That island, Xu thought, was Rhode Island.[118] Again, such mistakes show how limited China's collective knowledge of America still remained. In post–Opium War China, in fact, there were still at least eight different translations for the term "United States of America."[119]

The above discussion illustrates the development of the earliest knowledge about the United States in China, especially in the delta region. It also reveals the limited nature of that knowledge. Its limits suggest the wide physical and cultural gap that existed between the Old World and the New, and help to explain why the first wave of Chinese emigration to the New World did not take place until the news of California gold reached China. The limited nature of China's knowledge of the United States also explains why the first group of Chinese immigrants in America would find their new environment quite unfamiliar.

The California Connection and the Making of Chinese 49'ers

In the final section of this chapter, let us look at the delta's emerging California connections during the Daoguang period. These connections signify the dawn of what we call today the Pacific Rim, and they offer clues about the origins of the mid-nineteenth-century Chinese exodus. For years the American Pacific Coast supplied America's China traders with some of their most marketable goods, including sea-otter skins. California became more important to that trade during the 1830s, when the Pacific Northwest lost its attraction for China traders. That ships visited from China is well documented. *The Emigrants' Guide to Oregon and California* reported that many vessels reached California every year, not only from "the States, England, France, and Russia, but also from the Sandwich Island, the Russian settlements, and China."[120]

Numerous Yankee settlers in California joined the China trade. One of them was Alpheus Basil Thompson, a New England native, who settled in Santa Barbara. We can get a glimpse of California's extensive involvement in that trade from a letter that a Honolulu-based American company, Pierce and Brewer, sent to Thompson on August 9, 1837:

> The Griffon on her arrival back here, will proceed immediately to China, and return here with a cargo.—Should you feel disposed to give Capt. Little orders for China goods we shall be willing to import them . . . either to be delivered on California or at this place. We intend to run her as a regular trader between this place, China & California. . . . The otter Skins are still on hand and are in good order—from Capt. Little you will learn the State of [the] China Market as it regards that article.[121]

San Francisco was America's West Coast center of the China trade. A wide variety of goods from Canton landed there. When the *Mary Ann Folliott* arrived in 1850, besides passengers, it carried various types of merchandise, including "1100 blocks of granite, 155 pkgs furniture, 46 chairs, 1059 wood planks, 1 box curiosities, 136 bags rice, 72 packages Chinese articles."[122] At about the same time the E. and Mickle and Company was conducting an "extensive sale" of "China goods" in its warehouse on the wharf on Clay Street.[123]

There were plenty of customers for such goods. Around 1850 two visitors to San Francisco noticed that Chinese goods were used extensively in numerous places. Inside the building of J. L. Riddle and Company they found that "nearly all the furniture then was of China importation; and very commodious, stylish and comfortable it was, too."[124] In their description of the city in 1852 the authors of *The Annals of San Francisco* mentioned a "large and imposing edifice of granite," occupied by "Adams & Co., express agents, and Page, Bacon & Co., bankers." "The stone for this building," they reported, "was prepared in China and put up in San Francisco by Chinese workmen."[125]

The old-timers in the China trade knew firsthand the best routes across the Pacific. By 1850 a well-traveled route existed from San Francisco to Macao and Canton by way of the Sandwich Islands, Guam, and Manila. This 7,263-mile route was ideal, because it allowed mariners to avoid unfavorable winds and gave them easy access to coal supplies in Sydney and Taiwan.[126]

Traveling on this route, China-bound vessels not only carried goods to the Chinese market but also brought news about events on the other side of the Pacific Ocean. The English-language newspapers published in South China frequently covered such news. Some reports were taken directly from San Francisco–based periodicals, such as the *San Francisco Daily Herald*, the *Daily Alta California*, and the *Daily Journal of Commerce*, which apparently had a trans-Pacific readership. It was via this route that news of California gold would travel to Canton.

The discovery of gold in California did not result in the world "rushing in" immediately, as folklore has it. The news moved rather slowly. It did not get to San Francisco or Los Angeles for a few months. It took even longer to reach China. In January 1849 the Hong Kong–based *China Mail* showed its ignorance of the discovery of gold in California by reporting that "North America produces little [gold], and only in South Carolina."[127] But the knowledge that gold had been discovered in California would soon be widespread. By mid-spring 1849 Americans and other Westerners in Canton had learned of the discovery. On March 26, 1849, in a letter to his brother back in the United States, the American S. Wells Williams wrote: "The discovery of gold in California to such an unlimited extent has thrown our community into the same ferment as elsewhere."[128]

Visiting South China in June and July, Ludvig Verner Helms, a native of Denmark, noted the continued "ferment" in the area: "people at Hong Kong were at this time becoming excited about California." During the trip he met some "gentlemen of the legal profession, who, though doing extremely well, yet wanted to do better, and induced by the exciting news, which every incoming ship brought from California, determined to seek their fortune there."[129]

By early fall articles had appeared in the area's English-language periodicals advising people not to believe the inflated stories. A "letter of Digger in California," published in *The China Mail*, offered a rather realistic account, warning readers not to "imagine some romantic nonsense about finding the gold lying on the surface of the ground and that they have nothing to do but pick it up." "No one but those accustomed to hard work can stand it."[130] Evidently the discovery of gold had already become old news.

Local residents in the emigrant communities were among the first Chinese in China to learn about California gold. While it remains unclear exactly how the news first reached them, individual emigrants could have heard about it from a multitude of different sources. Some would have gotten the news when working as seasonal laborers away from home, and others would have received it directly from Americans like Dr. Peter Parker.

One group that must have played an important role in spreading the word were successful merchants from emigrant counties such as Panyu, Shunde, Nanhai, and Xinhui, who developed close connections with Americans and retained their long-standing local ties. One such merchant was the aforementioned Wu Bingjian (also known as Wu Yihe) (1765?–1843) of Nanhai County, whom Westerners called Houqua (also spelled Howqua). His story illustrates how global some of the local merchants' economic activities had become.

Houqua forged close relations with and generously helped Americans in Canton. The historian Samuel E. Morison writes that the success of Russel & Company "was due to the friendship of Houqua."[131] Houqua also donated a building so that the American missionary Dr. Peter Parker could establish a hospital. The American missionary S. Wells Williams called Houqua "the most remarkable native known to foreigners," praising him for his business "shrewdness and ability."[132] It was widely known among the Chinese that the shrewd merchant himself benefited from dealing with Americans. In reference to such profitable dealings, a San Francisco–based Chinese newspaper noted in 1855 that Houqua's wealth "could not have been acquired from domestic trade alone."[133] According to the local gazetteer Houqua knew very well "how to manage his fortunes and how to do business." The gazetteer reported that "for several decades as a master of international trade, his hands controlled the flow of money and goods."[134]

Houqua is actually the transliteration of the business name that was also used by other male heads of the Wu family at different times. The scope of the family's business activities went beyond national borders. Through its American connections the family invested heavily in "America's western expansion," as Arthur M. Johnson and Barry E. Supple have noted.[135] Descendants of the Wu family and local people in Guangdong knew that the Wus had once been major stock owners of American railroad companies. Evidently the Chinese contributed not only labor but also capital to the development of the American West.

The Wus had deep roots in their native Nanhai County, where everyone knew about their economic success. Locally the Wus had been major contributors to charity and public projects in Nanhai. They were also deeply involved in local affairs and often acted as gentry leaders. During the Red-Turban Rebellion, for instance, the family organized local militia to defend the county.

Finally, numerous Cantonese individuals had been in America before the Gold Rush. Some of them undoubtedly helped to disseminate the news. Legend has it that a man named Chun Ming, who came to California as a merchant and later became a successful gold miner during the Gold Rush, was among the first to break the news to people in the Canton area.[136]

Based on the news that they acquired one way or another, local Chinese formed their image of California, namely, "Jinshan" (meaning "Gold Mountain" or "Country of Gold"). The image was concrete and powerful for those who had experiences with the market economy and understood the significance of commodities. Indeed, gold was what most early emigrants associated with California, and acquiring it was their motivation for going there. The San Francisco–based *Oriental* stated that "Most of the Chinese arriving [from China] in this city are gold-miners," and few came for other reasons.[137]

Chinese emigration to California did not start with large numbers of people rushing to leave their home communities. Rather, it began as a trickle—only a few hundred Chinese arrived in San Francisco in 1849. More emigrants took off as the news of California gold gradually spread. Unlike the Chinese emigration to southeast Asia and the abduction of coolies, the departure of a much smaller number of the first California-bound emigrants received little attention in China. In 1850 the *Chinese Repository* briefly reported that "nearly a thousand Chinese have . . . found their way to California."[138] In late December 1851 S. Wells Williams wrote in Canton that the total number of Chinese emigrants "is estimated at already about 10,000," with each paying $60.00 for the passage.[139] Five hundred and nineteen people left Shunde for California after the news that gold had been discovered arrived. A significant number of them came from Chen Village, which had long specialized in commercialized fruit production.[140]

Clearly, the delta region's connections—unparalleled in China—with America in general and California in particular constitute another important explanation for the timing and geographical origin of Chinese emigration. Among the local Chinese population, few were better acquainted with the United States than people who had close contact with American missionaries. Such contact took place in various contexts, and we do not know precisely how many such locals left for California. But it is clear that one relatively small group among them, namely the Christian-school students and Christian converts, were well represented in Chinese California. When the Rev. William Speer came to San Francisco to start doing missionary work among the Chinese at the end of 1852, he was welcomed by a number of Chinese who "had been instructed in Christian schools in China," as was reported by Ira M. Condit, one of Speer's successors in San Francisco. And the first Chinese Christian missionary church that Speer founded in the city in 1853 included a number of Chinese Christians who had been converted in China.[141]

One of the earliest and most important Christian schools in the East Guangdong area was the Morrison School. Of the six pupils in its first class, three went to the United States in 1847 with their American teacher, the Rev. Samuel R. Browne.[142] At least two of the other three, Lee Kan and Tong K. Achick, joined the early wave of emigration to California in the 1850s.[143]

Based on scattered information in U.S. federal census materials, Chinese-language newspapers, and personal memoirs, we can piece together a sketch of Lee Kan's life. It is unclear whether he had known Speer in China. But the two met shortly after Lee came to the United States in 1852 at the age of 26. Lee became the Chinese-language editor of a bilingual newspaper, *The Oriental*, that Speer started in San Francisco during the 1850s.

Surviving documents do not tell us much about Lee's life and his family in China. It is safe to assume that just like the rest of his classmates at the Morrison School, Lee was not from a rich family.[144] But Lee did not leave for America as an impoverished man fleeing blindly from hunger. He possessed valuable resources, including the knowledge about Americans, and especially about their language, that he had gained at the Morrison School. Such resources proved important for him. Besides becoming a newspaper editor, this Chinese San Franciscan also ran a business at 139 Sacramento Street, advertising his oral and document translation services in newspapers. Beginning in 1869 he worked for the Bank of California, where he remained an employee for a long time. The city directory of 1878 lists Lee Kan as "interpreter [for] Bank of California."[145]

Unlike Lee, most emigrants had not attended missionary schools, and they heard about "Gold Mountain" elsewhere. Like Lee, however, they departed from China at a young age. For these young emigrants the voyage to the New World must have been another means by which to achieve personal upward social mobility. It must have also been part of their family's collective strategy for responding to the economic challenges and opportunities facing them at the time. Most emigrants were men and had various familial responsibilities in China. A great number of them were married. Marriages, sometimes formed shortly before their departure, served as an assurance that they would send money back to their families, as Sucheng Chan has pointed out.[146] These men who left their families were simply doing what many Chinese had done before them. As G. William Skinner has commented, "whereas an ambitious man was likely to leave his local community to work or study elsewhere, his family's residence normally remained unchanged."[147] Carrying their own hopes and those of their loved ones, the emigrants left their families for another continent but promised to come back to them soon. Within the first decade after leaving, about a third of these emigrants kept their promise (the Chinese were but one of numerous immigrant groups that had a high return rate).

A significant number of the Chinese immigrant population, I must add, were in their early twenties or even younger. In many cases the journey across the Pacific must have been as much a way of assuming family responsibility as a step toward greater individual independence. Surviving folk songs contain stories about overseas emigrants. Collected in a later period, one long folk song, entitled "Guofan" ("Going to the land of the Fan"), tells such a story from the point of view of a man who was under 20 years of age:

He had ambitions "as big as the ocean and as high as the sky," and he also had a rather carefree lifestyle involving "prostitution, gambling, and fine dining," for which he was scolded by his parents and relatives. Therefore, he decided to borrow money from friends and relatives to venture overseas. The journey to independence, however, did not end his attachment to his native land or to his parents. The song went, "while in China, I heard about things [and longed to go] overseas; once overseas, I missed China." He also remembered his responsibility to help his family.[148]

I have ventured beyond the Pacific Ocean to the Pearl River Delta in order to comprehend, first of all, the genesis of the first major wave of Asian immigration to America. A dynamic market economy that had existed there for decades produced individuals who were able to appreciate the significance of the news about California gold and who were willing to act on their understanding of the importance of this news.[149] As we have also seen, the Pearl River Delta area's connections with the United States, including California, afforded local people vital awareness of the New World, especially of opportunities in California.

Rather than overemphasizing the emigrant region's socioeconomic hardships, as previous studies have tended to do, in this chapter I have focused on its economic and cultural vitality. This perspective allows us to view the Chinese exodus as a rational decision made by emigrants based on their experience and knowledge, rather than as a flight forced by desperation. It also allows us to appreciate the emigrants' aspirations toward upward social mobility for themselves and for their families.

This chapter also seeks to shed light on another equally important aspect of the world that the emigrants left behind, namely, local people's knowledge of and perceptions about America. Understanding the Old World enables us to better comprehend immigrants' experience in the New. Evidence shows that while information about America was more readily available in the delta area than it was elsewhere in China, it remained indirect and scattered. With little in-depth knowledge about America, emigrants did not leave China to become acculturated. Instead, they remained in their own cultural paradigm. Much like Yankee merchants who were enticed by fabled Chinese wealth to sail westward, Chinese immigrants ventured to California for its gold, which is why they called it the "Gold Mountain."

In conclusion, my analysis underscores the importance of non-American histories and sources, especially the experiences of nonwhite immigrants, for uncovering the history of the American West. For a long time many viewed that history as one of the westward movement of European immigrants and Euro-Americans—a view that was "fixed in American history by Frederick Jackson Turner, but popularized by a host of writers," in George Sanchez's words.[150] The arrival of Chinese and, later, other Asian immigrants who came to the West Coast from the East, as well as the arrival of Mexicans who hailed from south of the national border, enriched and redefined the meaning of the American West. More important, the world of those people remained transnational—shaped not only by what they encountered in America but also by memories of their home communities and by the personal, socioeconomic, and political ties that they maintained therein over time. For these immigrants, especially those who traveled back and forth between two countries, national borders—natural and artificial—symbolized both disruptions and points of conjunction in their lives. A better understanding of their native communities, in short, will aid us in our effort to appreciate not only the reasons for their initial departure from the native countries but also their experiences as immigrants who helped build America's multicultural West.

PART ONE

The Rise of Chinese San Francisco

Introduction

Unlike Americans in China, who enjoyed a great deal of privilege, the Chinese immigrant pioneers became a target of growing xenophobia in California,[1] where they were considered "by some as only a little superior to the negro, and by others as somewhat inferior."[2] The xenophobia reflected an evolving struggle to determine the future of California society at a time of rapid demographic changes.[3] At the heart of the struggle was the issue of race. The state constitution, adopted at the 1849 convention, made clear white Californians' desire to keep political power to themselves by declaring that only "white male" citizens "shall be entitled to vote at all elections."[4] This desire had deep roots in American history—the 1849 clause echoed a principle established by the 1790 Immigration and Naturalization Act, which stated that only white men could become naturalized citizens—a principle that was later reaffirmed in various court cases and legislation.

The emergence of California's xenophobia precedes Chinese immigration.[5] As their visibility increased, however, the Chinese soon found themselves at center stage in California's racialized politics. Shortly after the constitutional convention they became the state's leading minority. In 1860 and 1870 they accounted for about 9 percent of its total population and a higher percentage of its labor force. The immigrants' physical appearance and lifestyle rendered them "easily distinguished" by white Californians.[6] While America denied them fundamental political rights, the Qing Court was unable and, for a long time, unwilling to offer any protection. In a word, the Chinese represented a culturally distinguishable and politically vulnerable minority group.

Beginning in the 1870s the anti-Chinese movement became a dominant force in California politics, enjoying widespread support. Hostility toward the Chinese was certainly based on racism. But it is also important to recognize that the anti-Chinese choir consisted of groups with different agendas and interests. Capitalists, who needed and profited from Chinese labor, knew that a hostile environment would make such labor socially controllable and economically exploitable. For the white labor movement anti-Chinese antagonism became a unifying factor and a powerful organizational tool.[7] It enabled white ethnic workers (many of them immigrants), in particular, to reinvent themselves as members of the white race by highlighting their white-ness and de-emphasizing their ethnicity.[8]

Marking the climax of the anti-Chinese political climate, the passage of the 1882 Chinese Exclusion Act sent a chilling message to the Chinese across the nation. For Chinese San Franciscans, in particular, 1882 was memorably cold—in December a record three inches of snow fell in the city. As the first and most important piece of such legislation, the 1882 act illustrates the salience of class and race in what was called the "Chinese question." The law suspended Chinese labor immigration for ten years and prohibited any federal or state court from granting citizenship to Chinese immigrants. It also illustrated the significance of the "Chinese question" at a national level. Repudiating the pro-Chinese senator George Hoar, the *New York Times* pointed out the helplessness of the Chinese: "We might almost suppose the Massachusetts Senator to be in joke when he lauded the Chinese as inventors of gunpowder, the compass, and the printing-press. Even if we concede these very doubtful claims in behalf of China, they can have no appreciable influence in determining the present question."[9]

Undoubtedly, discrimination had an important impact on Chinese life. Anti-Chinese federal legislation, for example, significantly obstructed the growth of Chinese America. During the eleven years after 1882 Congress passed over ten pieces of legislation to tighten exclusion measures. The Scott Act of 1888, for example, prohibited the return of all Chinese laborers who had departed the United States, including over twenty thousand people who had reentry certificates. In 1904 Congress extended the ban on Chinese labor immigration indefinitely. As a result of such hostile legislation, the Chinese American population decreased after 1890.

Federal legislation also contributed to the long-standing dearth of Chinese women in America. As early as 1875 Congress passed the Page Law, forbidding the immigration of Chinese prostitutes. Because Chinese women traveling to the United States were usually believed to be prostitutes, the law acted to reduce the presence of Chinese females in America.[10] The restrictive acts passed thereafter not only put an end to all Chinese labor immigration but also shattered Chinese immigrant men's hopes of bringing their wives to America.

This study is not about the exploitation and victimization of the Chinese as laborers and as a perceived inferior race in America. Other scholars have already written about these topics, as we have seen. More important, although discrimination created hardships for the immigrants, it never exerted absolute control over their lives. Insofar as immigrants are concerned, the meaning of life was not derived, after all, from the way they were perceived or treated by outsiders. The study tries to comprehend, from the point of view of Chinese Americans themselves, what gave meaning to their experience and from where they drew strength to endure hardships and rebuild their communities.

The following four chapters discuss the formation and development of Chinese San Francisco, throughout the second half of the nineteenth century. The history of this community bears witness to discrimination, but we cannot view Chinatown simply as a segregated urban ethnic enclave created by a hostile environment. Such a view prevents us from appreciating the conscious choices and efforts the pioneers and their followers made in building and maintaining their own community. It hinders our ability to see the internal vitality of Chinatown. Racial prejudice affected but never totally dictated the lives of the immigrants. Chinatown's longevity most clearly underscores its defiance of anti-Chinese forces that persistently tried but failed to eradicate or dislocate this large and visible Chinese community from the heart of the city.

The four chapters in this part take snapshots of the community and of the lives of Chinese San Franciscans from different angles. Chapter 2 uses both quantitative and qualitative sources to locate the position of Chinese San Francisco in Chinese America as well as in the city, demographically, geographically, and economically. Chapter 3 illustrates the importance of Chinatown as a social and cultural center, where various social organizations and recreational institutions were located. Chapter 4 explores the mental world of one individual who, like many of his compatriots, was an impermanent San Franciscan. Chapter 5 examines the collective mentality of Chinese San Franciscans, especially their sense of identity.

Although the chapters touch upon non-Chinese perceptions of Chinatown, my main aim is to illustrate its multilayered meaning to the Chinese. Chinese San Francisco stood as the most important entrepôt through which passed hundreds of thousands of arriving and departing immigrants. For people who lived within Chinatown and for those who lived outside it, it was always a desirable place to work, to meet friends, to recreate, and to shop. All of these things help explain the inner strength and the attraction of Chinatown, which had become the largest Chinese American community by 1870 and remained so for a long time thereafter.[11]

The "First City": Locating Chinese San Francisco

On December 12, 1878, a mostly Chinese crowd gathered at a building on Clay Street to celebrate the opening of the Chinese Consulate (later renamed the consulate general) in San Francisco. It was the right time and place for establishing the first diplomatic office outside Washington, D.C. By then the rising tide of anti-Chinese sentiments had become a formidable political force in the city and throughout the state, and Chinese San Francisco had become the largest and most visible Chinese American community and thereby a focus of attack. On the same day in the state capital delegates at the second constitutional convention (one third of them representatives of the Workingmen's Party of California) were denouncing Chinese immigration during deliberations of the "Chinese question." Announcing his hope of driving the Chinese out of the city and the country, a San Francisco delegate said: "The trouble is how to get the guest out of the house."[1]

White San Franciscans viewed their Chinese neighbors with fear and anxiety. Many supported efforts to deny the Chinese the rights to naturalize and thereby to vote because they believed that, given such rights, the Chinese would become a great political threat "with most dangerous results to the State."[2] Others saw Chinatown as the worst source of filth and diseases. A week prior to the opening of the consulate, Denis Kearney, head of the Workingmen's Party, raided Chinatown in search of lepers and other "nauseating things." Accompanying him were people representing the whole

49

spectrum of the power structure: a judge, a prosecutor, a reporter, and a police officer.[3]

Also on December 12 a young man named Ah Quin arrived from Santa Barbara in San Francisco, where he had landed a few years earlier after leaving China.[4] Chinese San Francisco meant something totally different to Ah Quin and his fellow immigrants than it did to whites. For the immigrants it was a place to work, live, and renew. While working as a cook for white Americans, Ah Quin frequently visited Chinatown, sometimes by streetcar and sometimes on foot, and it remained an important part of his life during his stay in San Francisco. He undoubtedly spent a big chunk of his monthly wage of $25 there, thereby supporting Chinatown economic enterprises. In his diary, which he wrote mostly and imperfectly in English (in an effort to improve his English skills, as we will see), he simply referred to it as "the town" or "town."[5] In the address notes that he kept in Chinese he called San Francisco "Dabu."

"Dabu," meaning "Big City" or "First City," was a Chinese name that Ah Quin and his compatriots gave to San Francisco. They also invented names for other cities. Sacramento was "Second City," and Stockton "Third City." Such names reflect the way early immigrants mapped Chinese America and redefined different cities based on their importance in Chinese American life. The word "Dabu" vividly conveys the immigrants' appreciation of Chinese San Francisco's central importance in their lives.

From the beginning of Chinese immigration, Chinese San Francisco was the major hub of cross-Pacific traffic. Hundreds of thousands of immigrants, along with goods and letters, traveled through it on their way from South China to America, and back. According to the customs records, from 1848 to 1876, 233,136 Chinese arrived in the city, while 93,273 left through the same port.[6] Chen Lanbin, the first Chinese minister to America, noted in 1879 that almost all Chinese in America used "Gold Mountain" as a gateway on their trans-Pacific travels.[7]

Regular announcements in Chinese newspapers about ships sailing between South China and San Francisco are evidence of Chinese San Francisco's continued connection to the Old World. In the early years sail vessels owned by China traders were a chief means of transportation between California and the Canton area. Later they were replaced by steamships owned by ocean-liner companies, especially the Pacific Mail S. S. Company, which started its long-lasting trans-Pacific service in 1867. In comparison with vessels under sail, steamships were both safer and faster, cutting the voyage time by more than half. At the beginning of the twentieth century Pacific Mail faced competition from two other companies: the Toyo Kisen Kaisha Company (a Japanese company), and the Canadian Pacific S. S. Company. All ran extensive advertisements for their regular services in Chinese newspapers, and all had Chinese representatives in San Francisco. The two Chinese representatives of Pacific Mail promised that all of the company's six ships provided passengers with good food, clean and large beds, and rooms for opium smoking.[8]

For immigrants, the existence of Chinese San Francisco meant many things. This chapter seeks to reconstruct its changing demographic, physical, and economic landscape in an effort to establish a collective profile of the community's pioneers, and the physical environment of their existence. Doing so will improve our understanding of Chinese San Francisco's internal vitality and help locate its historical place in Chinese America and in the city of San Francisco.

The Demography of Chinese America

In order to appreciate the demographic significance of Chinese San Francisco it is necessary to take a look at the Chinese American population during this period. The figures used in my discussion stand not as pure statistical evidence but as estimates that also represent the perceptions and the interest of different groups and individuals. On the one hand, it was common knowledge that many deliberately inflated the Chinese presence in an effort to depict it as a threat. In 1876, explaining his earlier interest in the subject, Alfred Wheeler acknowledged that: "It had been alleged then that there was a very large number of Chinese in the State."[9] Although more objective and reliable than popular perceptions and allegations, on the other hand, figures furnished by various government agencies are often inconsistent and tend to underestimate the Chinese population. As we will see, the seemingly simple task of determining the size of Chinese America on the basis of varying figures from a multitude of sources has always been a difficult challenge.

In her pioneering work, *Chinese Immigration*, Mary Coolidge made one of the earliest scholarly attempts to arrive at a reasonable projection of the Chinese American population.[10] Her figures suggest that by 1851 the West Coast Chinese population stood at 7,370 (that population remained predominantly Western for a long time).[11] In the next three decades it grew steadily, increasing in number from 25,116 in 1852 to 46,897 in 1860, to 71,083 in 1870, to 104,991 in 1880. It reached 132,300 in 1882.[12] It must be noted that Coolidge's estimates are higher than the census figures for the entire Chinese American population in America for 1860 and 1870, which were 34,933 and 63,199, respectively.[13] The 1880 census figure for the Chinese American population was 105,465, higher than Coolidge's estimate of the West Coast Chinese population for the same year but lower than her number for 1882.

Coolidge's numbers are based on official and nonofficial documents that were all prepared by white, English-speaking Americans. Figures from Chinese sources, however, suggest that even Coolidge's assessment understates the size of Chinese America. In 1854 *The Golden Hills' News*, a San Francisco–based bilingual paper, estimated that the total number of Chinese "who have arrived in the Gold Mountain [from China] is no less than 40,000 to 50,000."[14] In 1855 the most important Chinese American organizations—the five "companies," as they were referred to by whites, or huiguan, as the Chinese called them—in Chinese San Francisco declared a collective membership of 38,687 (about a thousand Chinese remained nonmembers).[15] Coolidge's figures for the same two years are lower—37,447 and 36,557, respectively.[16] During a trip to the United States in 1876 a Chinese intellectual named Li Gui stated that the Chinese American population numbered about 160,000.[17] This figure is again much higher than Coolidge's assessment of 111,971.[18] Toward the end of this period another Chinese visitor, Liang Qichao, wrote that there were 120,000 Chinese in America, a figure larger than the census figure of 89,693 for 1900. Coolidge did not have an estimate for the year.[19]

Despite the unsystematic nature of surviving Chinese figures, we have reason to believe that they are credible.[20] They depict a demographic trend that can also be detected in other sources. The number offered by Chen Lanbin in 1879 was lower than the one provided by Li Gui in 1876.[21] Likewise, Coolidge's figures also suggest a decline in the Chinese American population during the same period. In addition, figures from different Chinese sources are usually similar for identical periods. In 1878 the six huiguan had a total membership of 148,600, which is very close to Chen Lanbin's figure for 1879.[22] Such figures are based not on subjective guesswork but on firsthand data that the huiguan and the individual writers went to great effort to collect. No Chinese individual made more effort than Liang, who gathered information from Chinese communities in more than twenty cities and interviewed many immigrants for his study of Chinese America, *My Journey to the New Continent.*

While it is fairly clear that American official records underestimated the Chinese American population, its precise size remains an enigma. In 1876 Frank M. Pixley admitted before a congressional committee on Chinese immigration that statistics about the subject matter "cannot be definitely ascertained."[23] An important explanation for this uncertainty is that for a good part of the nineteenth century Chinese immigration was illegal under both Chinese and American laws.

It is not a surprise that Chinese America was underreported in the rather extensive and systematic federal census materials and customs-house records. We must remember that, like other kinds of historical data, statistics are also social representations.[24] Simply put, they are the product of particular historical environments. The problems with such sources did not simply stem from customary bureaucratic incompetence but also had to do with the cultural ignorance of white officials. They often demonstrated an inability or even an unwillingness to identify Chinese immigrants individually. Early records of passengers coming through San Francisco's customs house, for example, usually listed those from China as "unidentified Chinese." Similarly, the federal census recorded many Chinese simply as nameless "China men" in 1850.[25] Later on, they gave a majority of Chinese immigrants the same official first name of "Ah," which, as has been previously mentioned, was in fact an informal prefix. Undoubtedly, cultural barriers hindered the ability of the census takers to gather and keep accurate data. We do not know exactly how many people they failed to count. But we do know from the census manuscripts that some individuals were apparently counted twice.

The various official committees that investigated Chinese immigration were driven more by their overt anti-Chinese agenda than by a desire to gather facts. In its official report, the 1876 congressional committee concluded that "there is not sufficient brain capacity in the Chinese race to fur-nish motive power for self-government."[26] Similarly, the city's Special Committee asserted in 1885 that the alleged filth and immorality of China-town was "inseparable from the very nature of the race."[27]

Anti-Chinese discrimination contributed significantly to the limitations of official American records. After the passage of the Chinese Exclusion Act in 1882, many Chinese "leaked" in from the northern and southern borders, and others came in with forged papers.[28] Those already in the United States tried their best not to offer information about themselves to the authorities. While attempting to gather data in Chinatown in 1876, San Francisco's as-sessor realized that "the Chinese were loath to impart information."[29] After all, they had good reasons not to trust the authorities, whose discriminatory policies and practices frequently breached legal principles and abrogated treaty agreements with China.

On the other side of the Pacific, the Chinese government had long been hostile toward overseas emigration and trade activities, which could result in capital punishment under Article 225 of the Qing penal code in the early part of Qing Dynasty. In treaties with Britain and the United States during the 1860s, the Qing Court acknowledged and demonstrated a desire to regulate overseas migration. In 1875, when it appointed the first mission to America, it began to show some concern over the plight of Chinese immigrants in America.[30] But the government did not officially abandon the policy of pro-hibiting immigrants from returning home until 1894.[31] As a result of such hostility and apathy toward overseas migration in general, early official Chinese records of emigration to the United States are extremely scattered.[32]

Chinese San Francisco: Demographic and Physical Landscape

During the period under discussion a majority of Chinese immigrants spent some time in San Francisco. A significant number of them stayed and worked there. This section chronicles that community's changing demogra-phy and the shifting physical boundaries of Chinatown. My purpose is to illustrate the central importance of Chinese San Francisco in Chinese American life and to locate the space that Chinese San Francisco occupied physically in the city and culturally in the minds of its white residents.

In the early years of Chinese immigration most Chinese went to work in the mines right after their arrival. As early as 1850 those who had found their way into the gold country left their traces in the federal census schedules. No statistical records have survived to tell us how many stayed in San Francisco. The compilers of the *Annals of San Francisco* reported that they were "very numerous," estimating that there were between three and four thousand of them in 1852.[33] During the 1850s an emerging Chinese quarter, known at the time as "Little China," occupied two blocks between Kearny and Stockton Streets, and Sacramento and Jackson Streets.[34] In 1860 there were 2,719 Chinese in the city, according to the federal census. In the next decade the city's Chinese population grew significantly; it reached 12,022 in 1870, making Chinese San Francisco the largest Chinese community in America.[35]

Before we move on, let us first take a close look at the population census manuscripts of 1860 and 1870. They allow us to construct a collective profile of Chinese San Francisco's pioneers during its formative years.[36] Such a profile reveals the community's internal vitality before the anti-Chinese movement became a dominant political force in California. It is that vitality, rather than hostile outside forces, that created Chinatown.

First of all, Chinese San Francisco's vitality came from its youthfulness.[37] In 1860 over 75 percent of its adult population was between 20 and 39 years old. Only a fraction (less than 3 percent) was over 50 years of age. Proportionally, more women (almost 15 percent) than men (less than 9 percent) were in their teens.[38] In 1870 more than 68 percent of the adult population was between 20 and 39; about 2 percent of it was over 50 years of age. For both men and women, those over 50 years old accounted for less than 3 percent of the total population. In terms of percentage, again, more women (about 28 percent) than men (over 15 percent) were in their teens.[39]

It is worth noting that Chinese San Francisco's adult population was considerably younger than the similar age segment of the nation's white population at the time. Of the whites aged 10 and above, less than 44 percent in 1860 and slightly over 41 percent in 1870 were between 20 and 39 years of age. And more than 13 percent of the population in 1860 and more than 15 percent in 1870 were over the age of 50.[40]

It is significant that the Chinese American population at this time included very few women. Women represented a larger proportion in Chinese San Francisco than they did in other Chinese American communities. My

1860 sampling includes 587 women. The occupation of most of them was not identified, but it is likely that many were housewives, servants, or prostitutes. Some made a living in other ways, and a number of those women found their way into the census records, including 1 pharmacist, 4 "store keepers" (managers or owners), 3 cooks, 13 laundry operators, 4 gardeners, and 2 laborers.

Most of the 1,410 women in the 1870 sampling reportedly found employment in prostitution—1,132 were prostitutes and 18 were brothel keepers. The second-largest group were the 68 domestic servants. Again, women continued to work in other occupations. Besides those mentioned in the 1860 case, the 1870 sampling yielded 6 actresses, 3 lodging-house operators, 17 shoe binders, and 18 "tailoresses." There were also 137 housewives. Not all of them were wives of merchants. A few, for example, were married to men identified as laborers.

The census materials also show a significant increase in the number of children during the 1860s. I have collected two samplings of 42 and 390 children from the 1860 and 1870 census manuscripts, respectively.[41] While these numbers do not tell us precisely how many children were in the city, an analysis of the census data reveals much about the community where they lived, and especially about the mentality of their parents' generation.

We must remember that the word "child" is a subjective concept. In my analysis it includes only those who lived with adults as dependents and did not have a listed occupation. A ten-year-old boy who worked as a domestic servant, for example, is not considered a child here. Nor is a thirteen-year-old girl living in a brothel but listed as a house servant.

About half of the 42 children in the 1860 sampling were born in China, and another half in California. The 1870 sampling shows an increase in the number of children in general and in the proportion of California-born children in particular. Of the 198 girls and 192 boys in the 1870 sampling, 283 were born in California, outnumbering the 106 Chinese-born children.[42] Those who were 9 years old or under (that is, who were born after the previous census) accounted for over 94 percent of all California-born children. By comparison, the Chinese-born group was older, with 64 percent being 9 years old and over. And, of this group, all but one child was beyond 3 years of age. The age gap between the two groups reflects the fact that few parents brought babies to the United States.

The census information about these children also offers insights into the long-standing debate over the immigrants' "sojourner mentality." For a long time their relatively high return rate has been seen as evidence of that mentality. But the increase in the number of children in Chinese San Francisco strongly suggests that in the early years more and more immigrants already regarded Chinese San Francisco as their new home community, a place to raise children.[43] Overall, the percentage of children therein doubled between 1860 and 1870, increasing from less than 2 percent to over 4 percent during this period.[44] The presence of Chinese-born children underscores the conscious efforts of parents to pass on to their offspring what they had achieved in America. The increasing number of California-born children suggests that more and more people started a family in the United States. Some of these children were born right after Chinese emigration began, announcing the early arrival of the second generation of Chinese America: the oldest native-born children listed in the 1860 and 1870 samplings were 7 and 13 years of age, respectively.

We must adopt a different approach in our effort to understand the mentality of the immigrants. They did not have to make a choice between being settlers and sojourners or between China and America. Living in a trans-Pacific world, many traveled back and forth between Canton and San Francisco. Similarly, while some parents brought their Chinese-born children to the United States, others sent their offspring back to China for an education. For those Chinese immigrants who had the freedom to make a choice, many chose to be both settlers and sojourners at the same time. They built a community in San Francisco that reflected their trans-Pacific existence: while maintaining close ties to the Old World they rooted themselves deeply in the New.

As the Chinese community grew in number, so did its relative numerical importance in the city. It accounted for less than 5 percent of the city's total population in 1860, according to the federal census figures. A decade later over 8 percent of that population was Chinese. During the 1870s, when Chinese immigration became a heated political subject nationwide, the increasingly visible Chinatown inevitably became the focus of extensive public attention. The intense public discussions devoted to the physical space that Chinatown occupied in the city documented its changing boundaries. More important, they reveal where it was located in white consciousness.

In the summer of 1876 Congress formed a Joint Special Committee to Investigate Chinese Immigration. At the hearings held inside San Francisco's Palace Hotel, Chinatown stood as a pivotal issue. Examining a witness named Donald McLennan, Senator Aaron A. Sargent of the investigation committee framed his question in this way: "Are you not aware that during the last six years it [the Chinese quarter] has extended over additional blocks?" The unequivocally anti-Chinese senator's question represented an attempt to reinforce a threatening image of the expanding Chinatown. McLennan did not respond to the question. Nor did this employer of Chinese labor desire to eradicate the Chinese presence totally. Nevertheless, he acknowledged that Chinatown should be removed to a segregated area away from "the very heart of the city."[45]

Like McLennan, many white residents were keenly aware of and objected to the spatial position of Chinatown in their midst. The politically disfranchised and increasingly socially marginalized Chinese, they believed, did not belong at the center of San Francisco. Therefore, the proposal to remove the Chinese community to a place more commensurate with the Chinese social status kept surfacing until it was finally defeated after the 1906 earthquake.

White American authorities and individuals also sought to determine the physical size of Chinatown. The lack of consensus regarding its precise boundaries underscores their fluidity in reality and in white American consciousness. The estimates that individuals offered during the 1876 congressional hearings and on other occasions varied, ranging from six to eight blocks.[46] In an effort to come up with a rather detailed description of its borders, B. E. Lloyd stated that Chinatown occupied nine blocks: "Chinatown proper . . . consists of sections of two blocks, each of Sacramento, Clay, Washington, Jackson and Pacific Streets, between Kearny and Stockton Streets; and Dupont Street from Sacramento to Pacific Streets, the whole comprising about nine blocks."[47]

In 1885 the city of San Francisco formed its own special committee to probe the Chinese community. According to its report, Chinatown consisted of twelve blocks. The committee defined it as an area "within the boundaries of California street on the south, Kearny Street on the east, Broadway on the north, and Stockton on the west."[48] This is a rather narrow definition of Chinatown that failed to include numerous Chinese businesses on its outskirts. To pinpoint the locality of Chinatown, the committee added an "official map of Chinatown" to its report. Its main objective was apparently to identity the vices of Chinatown, such as Chinese brothels, gambling houses, and opium dens, as well as white brothels and joss houses. These were marked with different colors: green, pink, yellow, blue, and red.

The difficulty of identifying the boundaries of Chinatown had much to do with the fact that it existed not in isolation but right in the middle of a metropolis. What was even more difficult to determine was the size of the city's Chinese population. This difficulty is attributable not only to deliberate attempts to inflate the Chinese presence but also to the physical mobility of the immigrants. Equally important, a significant number of Chinese San Franciscans worked and lived in other parts of the city.

Different numbers for San Francisco's Chinese population given in the 1876 congressional report range from thirty thousand to seventy-five thousand.[49] Most English-language sources indicate that by the late 1870s there were about thirty thousand Chinese throughout the city. The Chinese visitor Li Gui's estimate of forty thousand in 1876 was slightly higher.[50] Chen Lanbin put the number at thirty thousand in 1879.[51] During the rest of the period considered in this chapter, the city's Chinese population remained at about thirty thousand.

The federal census numbers are once again lower than numbers offered by other sources. The census figure of 21,745 for 1880 was lower than Chinese as well as non-Chinese estimates.[52] A tour guide in 1883, for example, reported that there were between thirty thousand and thirty-five thousand Chinese in the city.[53] That report was consistent with the results produced by the city's 1885 committee. Translating its manifest hostility toward the Chinese into a thoroughness in the investigation, it claimed to have visited "every floor and every room" in Chinatown. Recognizing that "no known method of census-taking has ever yet sufficed to furnish an approximate idea even of the number of our Chinese population," the committee devised a new approach. Finding 15,180 bunks in Chinatown, the investigators concluded that there were 30,360 Chinese in Chinatown, based on the assumption that every bunk was occupied by two persons.[54]

The federal census office reported 25,833 Chinese in San Francisco in 1890 and 13,954 in 1900, figures that are again considerably lower than those provided by other sources.[55] In his inquiry into Chinese and Japanese labor in the Pacific states for the U. S. Industrial Commission in 1900, Thomas F.

Turner found a Chinese population of twenty-five thousand in the city.[56] Turner's number is still lower than Liang Qichao's estimate of thirty thousand in 1903.[57] While Chinese San Francisco remained fairly stable after the late 1870s, its size relative to the city's total population shrank.[58] Spatially, however, Chinatown continued to expand, growing to an area of fifteen blocks by the early twentieth century.[59] This is probably because many people moved from other parts of the city to live within Chinatown.

Despite their imprecise nature, the preceding estimates serve to portray the numerical importance of Chinese San Francisco in Chinese America. On the assumption that from the 1870s to the 1900s Chinese San Francisco's population was about thirty thousand, it represented no less than 17 percent in the 1870s and 25 percent in the 1900s of the total Chinese American population. Moreover, we must remember that many Chinese also lived in nearby cities, such as Oakland, where there was also a fairly large Chinese community. In the request he made to the Qing Court to establish a consulate in San Francisco in 1878, Minister Chen Lanbin reported that there were about sixty thousand Chinese in the "Gold Mountain" area.[60]

Many factors contributed to Chinese San Francisco's ability to develop and maintain its relatively high population level. Over the years, especially after 1870, when anti-Chinese violence prevailed throughout the American West, racial discrimination forced many Chinese to give up their residences and jobs elsewhere and move to San Francisco.[61] Hostility within the city drove some Chinese to live within Chinatown. In addition to violence, there existed other forms of discrimination that continued after the organized anti-Chinese movement died out. Outside Chinatown, Coolidge noted, "no other lodging would take in Chinese."[62] In 1900 a cook named Li Rong, who had come back to San Francisco after failing to find lodging in Stockton, was again forced out of his new residence by a white San Franciscan. The experience was so depressing that he contemplated suicide.[63] Naturally, Chinatown became a safe haven for many Chinese. "Here," the Rev. Otis Gibson wrote metaphorically, "they breathe easier." He continued: "The hoodlum's voice has died away in the distance. Here Chinese faces delight the vision, and Chinese voices greet the ear."[64] For immigrants, however, Chinatown was more than a physical shield against hostility. Many were attracted to the economic opportunities offered by Chinese San Francisco, opportunities that became increasingly important when fewer jobs were available in mining and railroad construction beginning in the 1860s.[65]

Chinese San Francisco: The Economy

The Chinese community that started to take shape in the 1850s was no impoverished ghetto; rather it demonstrated significant economic strength. Its dynamic economy was another source of its vitality and helps explain its longevity. As a commercial and later a manufacturing center, Chinese San Francisco attracted many Chinese with its wide variety of Chinese-style goods and services and job opportunities. The varied economic activities and the geographical distribution of the businesses attest to the breadth and depth of its economy and illustrate how intertwined it was with rest of the city.

Chinese San Francisco emerged first as a commercial and service center during the 1850s. At that time the immigrants could obtain various services and goods at both Chinese and non-Chinese firms in the city. They could, for example, deposit their fortunes in non-Chinese financial institutions and spend their extra money on Chinese-style clothes, food, and other supplies in Chinese stores. Of special significance was rice, a major component of the Chinese diet. A large amount of rice was imported from China. In 1853, 404,374 bags of rice were reported to have been imported to the United States. "This rice," reported *The Oriental*, "was chiefly from China, and is consumed by the Chinese."[66] American-produced rice was also available to Chinese customers and was called the "Flowery-Flag rice."[67]

In the 1850s numerous white businesses actively attempted to capitalize on the evolving Chinese customer market. In an advertisement published in the Chinese section of *The Golden Hills' News*, the Miner's Exchange Bank informed Chinese miners that they could deposit their gold dust, exchange it for currency, or open a savings account that would earn them interest at a monthly rate of 1.5 percent.[68] The Wells Fargo and Company advertised similar financial services in Chinese in another newspaper. Other white merchants sold various Chinese goods to the Chinese. One store named O. M. Eder sold Chinese goods ranging from rice to *muer* (an edible fungus; a traditional Chinese food).[69] At a time of increasing hostility toward the Chinese, these merchants carefully worded their Chinese-language advertisements in an effort to distance themselves from the anti-Chinese forces. In addition to reasonable prices, a drugstore named Samuel Adams promised that "all Chinese patrons at the store will surely be treated politely."[70]

Competition from Chinese stores that provided similar goods and scr-vices helps explain white store owners' politeness to their Chinese customers. In fact, by the mid-1850s a sizeable economy had already taken shape in Chinese San Francisco, if the 88 Chinese businesses listed in an 1856 business directory are any indication. By 1856 there were 33 Chinese-owned grocery shops in San Francisco, mostly located along Sacramento Street, with a few on Dupont and Jackson Streets. Second to grocery stores in number were the 15 pharmacies, and 5 doctors. There were also 3 boarding houses, 3 tailors, and 5 restaurants.[71] All these businesses catered to the basic needs of immigrants.

The directory offers additional insights into the geographical location of Chinese San Francisco both as a community and as an economy. Almost all the businesses mentioned above clustered in an area defined by Sacramento, Dupont, Jackson, and Washington Streets, as we are informed by the detailed descriptions of their locations in the directory. Sacramento Street, where 46 businesses were found, appears to have been the economic center of Chinese San Francisco. Thirty-four businesses were on Dupont Street. The businesses on Sacramento Street included 22 of the 33 general stores and groceries, the 3 wood yards, 9 of the 16 drugstores, and 3 of the 5 meat stores. Dupont was a place for shops catering to more diverse needs; it housed the 2 silversmiths, the wood engraver, 4 of the 5 barbers, 9 general stores, 4 of the 5 restaurants, and 3 of the 5 doctors. In the early years the immigrants called Sacramento Street "Tangren Jie" in Chinese, meaning "the street of Chinese people." "Tangren Jie" has since become a synonym for "Chinatown"; the evolution of this term underlines the central importance of Sacramento Street to the Chinese community at the time.

By the late 1870s Dupont (later renamed Grant) had replaced Sacramento Street as the economic center of San Francisco's expanding Chinese community. In 1878 a directory issued by the Wells Fargo and Company's Express, which for years handled letter- and parcel-delivery service for many immigrants, internationally and domestically, listed 423 Chinese firms. Of those businesses, 121 were located on Dupont Street. Sixty firms could be found on Sacramento Street. Another 60 were located on Jackson Street, where only 4 of the 88 businesses listed in the 1856 directory had been located. The increase in the number of Chinese businesses in 1878 on Commercial, Clay, Washington, Jackson, and Pacific Streets and along Dupont and Stockton Streets showed the westward and northward expansion of

Chinatown after the 1850s.[72] Another directory issued by the Wells Fargo and Company's Express in 1882 listed 673 Chinese businesses, of which 143 were located on Dupont Street, 60 on Jackson Street, 55 on Commercial Street, 52 on Sacramento Street, 44 on Washington Street, 42 on Clay Street, 29 on Pacific Street, 21 on Stockton Street, and 16 on Washington Alley.

Needless to say, evidence from those two directories offers only a sketch, rather than a precise indication, of the scope of the Chinese community's economy after the 1850s. It is evident that they did not list all Chinese businesses. The city directories for 1878 and 1882, for example, registered more Chinese businesses. The city directories nonetheless showed a similar pattern of geographical distribution of Chinese businesses as that shown in the Wells Fargo directories. Of the 942 Chinese businesses mentioned in the 1882 city directory, over one hundred and ninety were located on Dupont Street. Other streets that housed more than twenty businesses were Jackson (over one hundred), Washington Street and Washington Alley (over one hundred and twenty on the two combined); Commercial Street (67), Sacramento Street (56), Clay (54), Pacific Street (42), Waverly Place (29), Spofford Street (27), and Stockton Street (20).[73]

Over the years Dupont Street remained the center of economic activities in Chinese San Francisco. In 1902 a directory published by a Chinese newspaper, *The Chinese-Western Daily*, listed 531 businesses and nonbusiness organizations. One hundred and sixty-six of them were located on Dupont Street, 69 on Jackson Street, 48 on Sacramento Street, 45 on Washington and Clay Streets combined, 37 on Stockton Street, 32 on Commercial Street, 26 on Waverly Place, 23 on Washington Alley, and 12 on Pacific Street.[74]

Let us now take an in-depth look at the economy of Chinese San Francisco between the early 1860s and the early 1880s, a period that witnessed the development of the community's commercial and service sector and the emergence of a new manufacturing one. Again, the two Wells Fargo and Company's Express directories offer insights into the kinds of goods and services available in Chinese San Francisco. Before examining them, however, their incompleteness must first be acknowledged. Not only did they fail to report some individual firms, but they also missed a few kinds of businesses, such as the numerous gardeners, altogether. According to census materials, a gardener often operated as a small business, employing a few workers.[75]

As we will see later, however, these two directories were consistent, to a certain degree, in their respective listings. More important, they reported both the Chinese- and English-language names of the businesses listed, making it relatively easy to identify the nature of the businesses. Of particular importance are the descriptive, pre-translation Chinese-language names, which offer clear characterizations of individual firms.[76]

By the late 1870s Chinatown's ability to serve immigrants had expanded enormously. The 131 grocery stores constituted the most important type of business listed in the 1878 directory. Numerous shops that featured certain specialty goods, such as medicine and fruit, also carried groceries, which were apparently money-making products.

In 1878 a greater variety of goods and services were available in comparison to what could be had in the 1850s. For lovers of tofu products, for example, the two "bean cake" shops must have been a special blessing. Those who wanted to take a picture to send to their loved ones in China could go to Lai Yung, the town photographer, at 743 Washington Street. Main Fook Undertaker identified its merchandise in Chinese as "extending-happiness, long-longevity boards," a euphemism for coffins. For customers who could afford luxury goods, there were 10 jewelry shops and 30 "dry goods" stores, where people could shop for goods ranging from new clothes to porcelain products, all especially imported from "Suhang" (Suzhou and Hangzhou, two cities in Jiangsu Province with a long-standing reputation for their silk and other luxury products). There were also seven Japanese and Chinese lacquerware stores, one of which was fittingly called "Wing Fat Fancy Goods."

The number of shops continued to increase after 1878. The 1882 Wells Fargo and Company's directory listed 350 more businesses than the earlier one did. The difference between the number of businesses listed in the two directories does not necessarily serve as a precise index to the actual net growth of the economy. Rather, the difference stemmed in part from the failure of the 1878 directory to register comprehensively the businesses that actually existed at the time.[77] But the increase in the number of businesses that took place between 1878 and 1882 is confirmed by other sources. The city directories for the same years, for example, indicated that the number of businesses increased by 469.

An analysis of these two Chinese directories will offer some insights into the life span of Chinese businesses. As has been mentioned, the two were somewhat consistent with one another. Of the 227 businesses listed in the 1878 Wells Fargo and Company's directory that did not make their way to the 1882 directory, only 17 were picked up by the more comprehensive 1882 city directory. While comparing the Wells Fargo and Company's directories merely provides an inexact barometer of attrition (closure is only one possibility for the "vanishing" of the other 227 stores),[78] it gives us a clear idea about the duration of some businesses. Nearly half of all the businesses in the 1878 directory remained in place in 1882.[79] What is more important, at least more than half of those that catered to the most basic needs of the immigrants survived—including 76 of the 131 grocery and general stores and 12 of the 19 drugstores.

Most of the businesses discussed above were located in Chinatown. But as an economy Chinese San Francisco stretched far beyond Chinatown's boundaries. The 176 laundries in the 1882 Wells Fargo and Company's directory (the 1882 city directory lists the same number), which outnumbered all other types of businesses, for instance, were scattered among 73 different streets across the city, offering services primarily to white clients. Their Chinese names emphatically indicated that these businesses "wash barbarians clothes." Businesses such as laundries found their way into both non-Chinese neighborhoods and into the city's economy. By 1870 the Chinese represented a majority of the city's over two thousand launderers.

At the same time, the Chinese in the laundry business in other parts of the city remained closely connected to Chinese San Francisco's economy. Along with many others who lived and worked in white neighborhoods, including the many servants (a significant number of whom were female) and cooks, they visited Chinatown whenever possible, supporting that economy as consumers. These people participated in and served to bridge the gap between the white and Chinese segments of the city's economy.

I must note that the Chinese American service industry became so important for the entire city that it was used by opponents of the Chinese. Frank M. Pixley, the aforementioned ardent anti-Chinese representative of San Francisco who was present at the 1876 congressional hearing, for example, employed Chinese servants in his household.[80] Many of those who attended mass anti-Chinese rallies and loudly accused the Chinese of "polluting our land" at the height of the anti-Chinese movement during the 1870s would have worn clothes cleaned at Chinese laundries.

Chinese San Franciscans not only washed but also manufactured clothes for their white neighbors. During the 1870s the Chinese became the city's garment industry's main source of labor. Overall, more than a third of the city's Chinese population at the time worked in various manufacturing industries.[81] Some Chinese owned and operated their own factories, making garments, shoes, slippers, cigars, and so on. The emergence of these factories during the 1860s and 1870s turned Chinese San Francisco into a manufacturing center.

Less scattered than the laundries, most Chinese-owned factories were found in Chinatown and its vicinity. But just as the laundries had a white clientele, these factories also produced mostly for the non-Chinese market. While laundry firms and other service and commercial businesses could be found elsewhere across Chinese America, the manufacturing factories were primarily a Chinese San Francisco phenomenon, setting it apart from other Chinese American communities.

Throughout the rest of this period San Francisco's Chinatown remained a manufacturing center. In 1885 the investigating committee of San Francisco identified more than two hundred and fifty manufacturing units in Chinatown that employed a total of over two thousand people.[82] These factories varied in size—the smallest had only one employee, while the largest had three hundred—and engaged in a wide range of industries.[83] The textile industry, the largest of all, employed more than twelve hundred workers in about one hundred factories. According to Thomas F. Turner's report, in 1900 there were 2,579 Chinese workers in San Francisco's Chinatown manufacturing a wide range of goods such as boots and shoes, shirts, overalls, men's clothing, womens' underclothing, and cigars.[84] But the relative significance of Chinese San Francisco in the city's economy had declined. By 1890 even anti-Chinese forces no longer regarded the Chinese as an economic threat in the manufacturing sector.

For the Chinese, the service and especially the manufacturing industries that they entered were battlefields where they combated not only economic odds but also the immense hostility of white San Francisco. In so doing they demonstrated their mental perseverance as well as their resourcefulness. *The Oriental* discussed the opportunities and the frequent changes in the shoe-making industry: "Five years ago there were ten large shoe factories in the 'Big City' [San Francisco], employing over seven hundred barbarian people. . . . Now there are only six such factories, which merely employ two hundred barbarian people. The rest of the employees are Chinese, numbering about a thousand. Other shoe-making shops are small ones all owned by Chinese themselves without one barbarian employee."[85]

The shoe-making industry and industries in general were very volatile because of competition that came from both within the city and from East Coast producers. The Chinese had more difficulty staying in business than their white counterparts. As evidence from various directories suggests, there was a high turnover rate among Chinese manufacturers. Only 8 of the 34 Chinese cigar makers in the 1871 city directory made the 1876 directory, for example. Only 10 of the 39 cigar factories and 14 of the 46 shoe/slipper factories in the 1878 Wells Fargo and Company's directory reappeared in the 1882 directory. Comparing the city directories for the same two years, only 12 of the 60 tobacco-related businesses and only 10 of the 36 shoe/slipper businesses successfully made the transition.

If the turnover rate was indeed so high, this should not be surprising. In industries like these, where Chinese capitalists and laborers came into direct contact and competed directly with their white counterparts, anti-Chinese sentiments were at their height. Here the racial conflict that was often centered on cultural issues such as assimilability and unassimilability in other contexts became a naked economic battle, and racial antagonism became a method of self-promotion on the part of white San Franciscans. White workers in the cigar and other industries launched boycotts against Chinese-made goods. White merchants too boycotted their Chinese competitors. In a politically charged leaflet distributed in the 1880s a retailer in womens' underwear named S. Klarenmeyer urged white San Franciscan consumers to "protect the city from further destruction" and to avoid the "sin" of "assisting the heathens."[86] Therefore, he asked them to stay away from the Chinese and buy his goods, which he claimed were all produced by "white labor." His choice of the word "white" (instead of "American") is worth noting. Used widely in the popular anti-Chinese literature, the word effectively identified the Chinese as the "other" at a time when a substantial portion of the city's population (over 44 percent in 1880 and over 42 percent in 1890) was foreign born.[87]

Another challenge that Chinese businesses faced was that of raising capital. To start and run a manufacturing establishment, in particular, required a substantial amount of money. In 1880 the average sum it took to set up a tobacco factory was about $14,480, an enormous amount of money at the time.[88] While Chinese businesspeople did not have the same financial resources that their white counterparts did, they managed to raise sufficient funds to launch their ventures, thereby demonstrating their resourcefulness and the collective economic strength of the community.[89]

The industrialists were undeniably one of the richest groups and the biggest employers in the community. Many factories employed more than twenty people, and a few had a workforce of more than one hundred. By comparison, businesses in the service sector were much more modest. Laundries, for example, were small operations with little capital, usually amounting to between two hundred and six hundred dollars. Seldom did a laundryman's personal property exceed a thousand dollars, and few shops employed more than ten people. It is worth noting, however, that a few women in the business became property owners, including a fifteen-year-old named Low Ing who reported one hundred dollars' worth of personal property in the 1869 census returns.

Besides manufacturers and laundry owners, many other individuals reported personal property in the 1860 and 1870 population census manuscripts. These individuals included owners or managers of various stores, lodging houses, and other businesses, as well as butchers, clerks, tailors, carpenters, fishermen, doctors, druggists, and those who identified themselves as merchants. Many of them, such as tailors and clothing-store keepers, possessed personal property similar to the amount owned by laundry owners. A number of white-collar professionals, such as interpreters and photographers, also reported personal property worth from four hundred to eight hundred dollars. Running a brothel could be profitable as well. By 1870 numerous brothel operators, both men and women, had accumulated some wealth.

The richest individuals were found among the grocery/general-store owners and those recorded as merchants in the census returns. In the 1870 census returns I have identified 44 store (primarily general and grocery stores) owners who reportedly owned five thousand dollars or more worth of personal property. A few had personal wealth valued at over twenty-five thousand dollars. The wealth of the two richest, Ah Chinn and Ah Kim, was valued at thirty thousand dollars. This propertied class was relatively young: a majority of them were between 20 and 39 years old.

At a time when little support could be expected from white financial institutions, Chinese San Francisco's internal resources were extremely important for its economic development. Many immigrants relied on traditions and social relations formed in the Old World to pool capital in order to open small businesses. A frequently used method of raising money was to form an informal *hui* (revolving credit association), a centuries-old practice in China.[90] The hui must have served a lot of people well. The Chinese were known for their propensity to open their own businesses after they had amassed enough skills and capital. Sometimes businessmen with extra capital would form partnerships especially for the purpose of lending money to others. One such partnership had to file a lawsuit when it could not collect on time the money it had loaned to a woman.[91] To launch more ambitious projects later on, merchants used Chinese-language newspapers to reach potential investors. Finally, another source of Chinese San Francisco's economic strength came from the propertyless ordinary men and women (sometimes boys or girls), who supported the ethnic economy with both labor and avenues of consumption (tourist spending did not become a major source of revenue until later).

The bustling economy in commerce and manufacturing constituted another important reason for Chinese San Francisco's vitality. This economy helped maintain a sizeable population and contributed to the perpetuation of Chinese San Francisco as a community. The importance of the businesses, however, should not be understood only in economic terms. In providing the immigrants with Chinese-style goods and services, the various economic institutions also played a culturally important role in helping them maintain their way of life.

The demographic and economic landscape of Chinese San Francisco sketched in this chapter helps illustrate its central significance in Chinese American life. It also enables us to appreciate the internal vigor that provided the energy to sustain the community in its formative years and beyond. Clearly, the creation of Chinatown cannot be attributed to discrimination. As we have seen, it stood, located in the "heart of the city," as testimony to Chinese America's defiance of the will of anti-Chinese crusaders.

THREE

The Social Landscape of Chinese San Francisco

For a long time Chinatown remained a social and cultural center of Chinese America. It was the first major permanent physical space that the mobile Chinese American population carved out for itself. Besides economic opportunities, it offered the immigrants a sense of belonging in an unfamiliar and unfriendly society. Here they established social organizations in an attempt to organize a coherent community, transplanting Old World traditions that served to unite as well as divide them. Here they communicated with one another in their native tongue. Here they enjoyed the smell of familiar foods, the Cantonese music emanating from the theaters, and everything that made Chinatown an appealing place to recreate and to socialize. Here they reinforced memories of their collective past.

This chapter examines several major social and recreational Chinese San Franciscan institutions that helped establish the trans-Pacific foundation of the evolving Chinese American community. Learning about these institutions, which touched the lives of thousands of immigrants in various ways, enables us to see that social and cultural traditions constituted vital resources for the community. More important, it allows us to appreciate the meaning and significance of Chinese San Francisco in Chinese American life.

After we discuss two social institutions in the first section of this chapter, we will turn to different recreational establishments that represented another attraction of Chinese San Francisco. Some of them provided entertainment suitable for all, and others catered solely to bachelor men. Understanding them helps reveal the nature of life in the community. Often, places of recreation existed as cultural institutions, serving to reconnect immigrants to their cultural heritage. The recreational institutions were economic entities as well; a few profited from them, and others were exploited.

More than anything else, these recreational institutions were symbols of the community and of the Chinese way of life in the eyes of outsiders. While anti-Chinese agitators attacked them vigorously, others exoticized them. I will analyze public perceptions of some of these institutions in an effort to locate Chinese San Francisco in white consciousness. Through this analysis we will see that the immigrants' effort to build a community and culture of their own was a constant battle.

Social Organizations: The Huiguan and Newspapers

Various social organizations mushroomed in Chinatown, providing the social fabric that connected Chinese immigrants to one another. Referring to the large number of such organizations, Mary Coolidge wrote that "every Chinaman is enmeshed in a thousand other relations with his fellows."[1] Liang Qichao found it unthinkable that there were more than 80 various associations in San Francisco.[2]

The plethora of organizations clearly reflects the predominantly bachelor population's dire need of community life. It also established the continued significance of complicated Old World social relations defined by traditional geographical, clan, and linguistic bonds and boundaries that constituted the most important foundation of these organizations. The influence of such organizations often extended beyond San Francisco.

Of central importance were the huiguan. For decades they existed as the most significant Chinese American social institution, and they included an overwhelming majority of Chinese America. The first huiguan is believed to have been the Kong Chow Huiguan,[3] formed probably as early as 1849. In 1853 there were four huiguan.[4] In 1855 the number grew to five.[5] The huiguan buildings loomed large in Chinatown. *The Oriental* gives us a detailed description of the building that housed the Yanghe Huiguan: "As the reader has walked . . . his attention has been attracted by a large frame structure, evidently of Chinese architecture. . . . A pair of lions, carved in wood, guard the wide doorway. . . . The two perpendicular inscriptions on either side are poetical lines. They read, Tseung Kwong Ham Man Li, Sui Hi Po Tung Yan. May the prosperous light fill a thousand leagues; May the auspicious air pervade mankind."[6]

The prominent Chinese motif of the building was not intended to draw the attention of non-Chinese spectators—Chinatown was not a tourist attraction yet. It embodied the cultural traditions that all the huiguan were founded upon. In fact, the huiguan themselves were a long-standing Chinese tradition—people who ventured out of their hometowns had often formed huiguan.[7]

By the mid-1850s the huiguan had established themselves as member-supported organizations with paid staffers, elected officers or "agents," and clearly defined responsibilities. Let us take a look at the Shiyi (four-district) Huiguan, founded by people from the four counties of Xinning, Xinhui, Kaiping, and Enping. It had a servant and three officers, all of whom had been elected to serve a six-month term. At the elections no one expected all members to cast their votes, but the representation of the collective interest of each county group was required. Like others, the Shiyi Huiguan was in part supported by membership dues. The huiguan itemized the things that the money was spent on: "1. The purchase of ground and erection of the building used by us; 2. the salaries of agents and servants; 3. fuel, water, candles and oil; 4. assisting the sick to return; 5. the bestowment of medicines; 6. coffins and funeral expenses; 7. the repairs of tombs; 8. expenses of lawsuits; 9. taxes upon our frame house at Sacramento; 10. drayage, and other outlay, for passengers landing or departing, by ships."[8]

The wide range of services and assistance that the huiguan offered demonstrated its important role in the lives of immigrants. Early in the 1860s the Hehe Huiguan was established, bringing the number of huiguan to six. These huiguan together formed a general body of government, the Zhonghua [Chinese] Huiguan, which—as has been previously mentioned—eventually adopted a formal English name, the Chinese Consolidated Benevolent Association, and was commonly known as the "Six Companies." But the number of the huiguan did not stay at six—in 1903 there were actually eight of them. Nor did all the "companies" remain in business. Over the years some disappeared as their members joined other huiguan or formed new ones.

Individual huiguans' influence fluctuated, corresponding to demographic changes in Chinese America. In the 1850s the Yanghe Huiguan was the biggest, with a membership of fourteen thousand.[9] But both its membership and its clout had declined by the 1870s, when the Ningyang Huiguan became the most powerful huiguan with the largest membership. It had seventy-five thousand members, all from Xinning County.[10] Early in the twentieth century the commanding presence of the Ningyang Huiguan's building in Waverly Place announced the huiguan's eminence. Below the huge characters spelling "Ningyang Huiguan" in front of the building, two couplets acrostically explicated the meaning of the two characters "ning" and "yang": "Ningjing fada" (peacefully prosper) and "Yangde fangheng" (masculine virtues flourish at present).

Together, the huiguan maintained their collective leadership, handling internal affairs in Chinese America. In fighting the mounting anti-Chinese discrimination the Zhonghua Huiguan became Chinese America's most important voice. From 1878 onward the Chinese Embassy in Washington and the consulate general in San Francisco began to share the huiguan's leadership role. New organizations, including political parties established by exiles from China around the turn of the century, came into existence in Chinatown, sometimes competing with the huiguan for influence. But no one could replace the Zhonghua Huiguan as Chinese America's spokesman.

As further evidence of its significance, Chinese San Francisco published not only the first Chinese newspapers in the United States but also more newspapers than any other Chinese American community. Although they were a cultural institution that the immigrants adopted in America, these newspapers offered extensive coverage of events in their native land, thereby bridging the distance between the Old World and the New. They also connected the lives of Chinese immigrants in and outside San Francisco. People not only read the newspapers to get news but also used the advertisement sections to promote their products and services and sometimes to communicate their opinions.

Chinese-language newspapers were evidently in high demand during the period of this study. We have no statistical evidence to support Stewart Culin, who argued in the 1880s: "Nearly all the Chinese in America have passed some of their early years at school, where they learned to write a few of the many characters of their language, and to read it with more or less facility."[11] But it is safe to assume that through the help of their literate fellow countrymen even the illiterate had access, albeit indirect access, to the information in the newspapers.

On April 22, 1854, *The Golden Hills' News* joined *Daily Alta California* and a few others to become one of the first newspapers to appear in California. It was the first newspaper in America with a Chinese section.[12] In January 1855 another bilingual newspaper followed: *The Oriental.* Both newspapers were intended primarily for the Chinese community. Started as a weekly, *The Golden Hills' News* promised to become a semiweekly when "the Chinese generally adopt it."[13] When *The Oriental* started out it was published three times a week, and only one issue had an English section.

Published by white Americans, the two newspapers were nonetheless connected to a part of modern Chinese history that we have seen earlier, namely, the attempts to proselyte the Cantonese. An assistant for *The Golden Hills' News* had lived in China for ten years, probably as a missionary.[14] The Chinese editor of *The Oriental,* Lee Kan, had attended a missionary school in China. The paper's publisher and the editor of its English-language section, the Rev. William Speer, had been a China missionary for four years. The publishers of the two newspapers made clear their intention, that is, to "enlighten" and Christianize the Chinese in the United States. The publisher Speer explicitly stated that his "chief personal motive" was to fulfill "our religious obligation" to the "heathen" Chinese.[15]

This evangelical purpose, however, was notably absent from the mission statement in the Chinese-language section of both newspapers. The newspapers told Chinese readers that their goal was to offer information about the state of commerce and society in America so that readers would not be as easily cheated and mistreated as they had been before.[16] The Chinese editors clearly understood their readers' needs. They must have also understood how hard it was for the immigrants to accept the religion of a society so hostile to them. Despite his close ties to the missionaries, Lee Kan himself remained a professed non-Christian through the late 1870s, and was never baptized.[17] Beginning in 1869 he worked for the Bank of California, enjoying American materialism rather than Christian spirituality.

Indeed, dominating the Chinese sections of these newspapers are mundane matters: events in China and in America, price lists and other business information. Both papers carried lengthy articles explaining the most basic facts about America, revealing and redressing Chinese readers' unfamiliarity with the new social environment. "The 'Flowery-Flag Country,' " *The Golden Hills' News* explained, "is named the United States. Originally there were thirteen states. Later they were united into one country."[18] *The Oriental* informed its Chinese readers that there were 26 letters in the English alphabet and specified how to pronounce them.[19] It acknowledged at another time: "Many Chinese do not know the rules of the 'Flowery-Flag' country. Therefore, they do not do things in accordance with its laws."[20]

The two newspapers mentioned above did not last long—the last trace that we have today of these pioneering enterprises is an August 1856 issue of *The Golden Hills' News*. In the 1860s *The California China Mail and Flying Dragon*, a monthly with occasional Chinese-language pages, appeared.[21] The 1870s and 1880s witnessed a surge of a series of Chinese newspapers, including a daily and at least four weeklies, that coincided with the growth of Chinese San Francisco.[22] One of these papers was *Tangfan Gongbao* (meaning "China and barbarian newspaper"), which started in the 1870s. While its Chinese title varied during its long period of existence, it maintained its English title, *The Oriental*. It was one of the first Chinese-American newspapers published solely in Chinese. Aware of its significance, the publishers Chock Wong and J. Hoffman proclaimed that it "is read by all Chinese in this city and elsewhere. . . . This is the only Chinese newspaper in this country."[23] It was believed to have had seven hundred regular subscribers, mostly in San Francisco.[24] But we should not regard it as a strictly local paper. Given the migratory lifestyle of the immigrants and the multilayered connections among them, the impact of the paper must have extended elsewhere as well. During the first decade of the twentieth century Chinese San Francisco entered its golden age of newspaper publication with the emergence of four major Chinese dailies. All Chinese owned, printed solely in Chinese, and produced by stereotype (earlier newspapers were produced by lithograph), they served to mark Chinatown as the information and communication capital of Chinese America.

Sex in an Imbalanced World

Houses of prostitution emerged as a significant fixture in the social landscape of Chinatown from its beginning, providing an important form of recreation for Chinese men. The issue of prostitution offers us an opportunity to come into contact not only with the male patrons of brothels but also with Chinese women who were often seen as prostitutes and who seldom commanded much attention otherwise.[25] Moreover, in vehemently condemning prostitution as one of the virulent Chinese vices, white San Franciscans made plain their attitude toward their Chinese neighbors, and especially toward Chinese women.[26] Complicating the situation is the fact that white men frequented Chinese brothels and Chinese men called on white prostitutes. All these issues rendered houses of prostitution a revealing intersection of gender, class, and race.

Prostitution was not a solely Chinese phenomenon in the city, which allowed brothels to operate openly until 1917, when the state's 1913 Redlight Abatement Law took effect. Yet Chinese prostitution received an extraordinary amount of public attention. And Chinese prostitutes were often the ones singled out by the police. In reference to such prejudicial treatment by the police, the *California Police Gazette* admitted in 1859 that "[t]he officers do not pitch into WHITE females who pursue the same course."[27]

The voluminous records left by non-Chinese authors about the subject do not represent the Chinese point of view. Within the predominantly male Chinese community,[28] while prostitution was sometimes criticized for the violence it created, it was regarded as an indispensable institution because of the population imbalance.

Nowhere in Chinese America was the service of prostitutes more available than it was in Chinatown. About half of the Chinese women that had migrated to America after 1848 stayed in San Francisco. While a large number of them undoubtedly became prostitutes, we do not know exactly how many did so. For reasons to be discussed later, the enormous amount of attention focused on the issue of prostitution generated much misinformation from the early 1850s on.

Federal census materials suggest that between 1860 and 1880 hundreds of Chinese prostitutes worked in San Francisco.[29] In 1885 an investigating committee for the city of San Francisco stated that among the city's female Chinese population were 567 professional prostitutes, and 761 others whose status was questionable.[30] In 1900 *The Chinese-Western Daily* reported "a large number" of Chinese brothels in San Francisco.[31]

Ah Quin's diary gives us a glimpse of the experience of a Chinese patron of prostitutes. While living in San Francisco he spent much of his leisure time in Chinatown, busying himself with numerous activities, such as socializing with friends and going to the theater. And the brothel was often a part of his itinerary there. Occasionally he went to a brothel just to have sex. On February 6, 1880, for example, after spending a busy afternoon in Chinatown, he went "to fuck a whore at Sac. [Sacramento] St."[32]

Overall, however, his brothel visits were not simply about having sex but also represented a way of "taking a rest." In fact, in his diary Ah Quin sometimes used the word "rest" in reference to visiting a prostitute. Here is his schedule in the Chinatown area for Sunday, January 25, 1880. During the day he attended a Sunday service and later a Bible study session at the Presbyterian church run by the pastor, the Rev. A. W. Loomis. He then went to hear the sermon delivered by a Chinese pastor at Fook Yam Tang [also spelled Foke Yam Tong in other documents, meaning the "good-news house"], a mission school in Chinatown proper that offered services in Chinese, before walking to the Rev. Gibson's mission school for another Bible study session. Between these events he went to some friends' places to socialize and rest. He ended the long day by going "to rest in [a] Chinese whore house till 11 [pm]."[33]

We must avoid reading too much into the text written by one whose English was apparently not fluent enough to allow him to express his subtle feelings through a nuanced choice of words. Nevertheless, "rest" clearly appears to be a critical word here, which Ah Quin chose consistently to characterize such activities as going to bed at night and relaxing briefly at a friend's place. Later in his life when he had a family and a house in San Diego he frequently used expressions such as "in house rest" and "rest in bed" in his diary to describe his moments of relaxation away from work. Evidently, therefore, for this young bachelor, brothel-going during his San Francisco years represented a form of rest in the company of a prostitute.

Brothels did not guarantee good sex. Ah Quin noted in his diary on the same Sunday night in 1880: "A bad Chinese woman room, only fuck once. So mad her."[34] Clearly, he was not only physically unsatisfied but he also disliked the environment. Nevertheless, he still spent hours there to "rest" until late at night.

It is interesting that on that Sunday Ah Quin's brothel visit was preceded by his attendance at church services and Bible studies. That he did both does not mean that Ah Quin was not a sincere believer; ample evidence suggests that he was throughout much of his life in America. His engagement in these two kinds of activities helps to underscore his two different needs—spiritual and worldly.

Not all houses of prostitution were equally accessible. Like its white counterpart, Chinese prostitution had its own hierarchy. In the early years, according to Herbert Asbury, the upscale houses of prostitution were called parlor houses and were often "sumptuously furnished with a great clutter of teakwood and bamboo, embroidered hangings, soft couches and clouds of fragrant incense."[35] Those who attempted to taste what they could ill afford had to pay a high price. *The Oriental* published the story of one Chinese man's visit to a parlor house, where he ordered a fancy banquet and had a wonderful time with the prostitute. The next morning, facing the bill, the penniless and hopeless man cut his throat "to pay for one night's pleasure with his life!"[36]

The blood that this man shed in the parlor house reminds us that violence was a part of the world of prostitution. And the prostitutes themselves were sometimes the victims. In a report of the murder of a prostitute in December 1875, *The Oriental* put it in a larger context: "Within the eleventh month, several of our fellow Chinese were brutally murdered. Their deaths are connected to prostitution and gambling houses. These are the two places where people waste their money and lose their lives. . . . On the eighth day of this month, a prostitute named Xijiao on "Old Lusun Street" [Ross Alley] was killed by her lover with a knife."[37]

The death of Xijiao became big news in Chinese San Francisco in part because she was one of the best-known prostitutes in town. The report in *The Oriental* portrayed her this way: she was not an extremely beautiful woman, but her face "was pretty enough to be pleasing to the eye." Although the report was evidently written from a traditional male point of view, it contained a rather detailed biography of this woman. She was acquired by her "adopted mother," a brothel owner, at a very young age. When she grew up her adopted mother turned her into a prostitute instead of finding her a husband. After receiving countless customers over the years, she became tired of her profession. Eventually she fell in love with one of her customers, who was willing to pay several hundred dollars for her freedom. The prospect of losing such a valuable laborer angered the brothel owner, who conspired to stir up jealousy by revealing her marriage plan to her patrons. In the brawl that ensued Xijiao saved her lover but was killed herself.[38]

Xijiao was clearly a victim of oppression and eventually of violence. Her story also suggests that some prostitutes formed stable relationships with a special patron, called a "lover."[39] In another report in *The Oriental*, the lover of one prostitute had the courage to display his affection in public: After the prostitute fainted in a theater her well-dressed lover carried her back to her house. Realizing that she had lost her shoes in the theater, he went back to fetch them for her. "What a devoted lover," the newspaper exclaimed.[40]

There is no need to verify all the vivid but anecdotal details in those stories. Together, such newspaper stories constitute a collective narrative about the world of prostitution. The descriptive narrative communicated the community's degree of unspoken tolerance toward prostitution; it viewed prostitution not as glorious or even desirable, but as a fact of life for young men who—desperate and hungry for companionship and love—were in constant search of a place to rest. Carrying a moral message for men, the first two of the three preceding articles warned against the self-indulgence and violence associated with prostitution. But none of them condemned the prostitutes.

Few historical documents represent the issue of prostitution from the perspective of the prostitutes themselves. If the brothel was a place to relax for men such as Ah Quin, for most prostitutes it was a place where they were exploited and oppressed by both white Americans and Chinese men. Peggy Pascoe has written: "Compared to white American prostitutes of the same period, Chinese prostitutes were particularly powerless; in fact, many were kept in conditions that render some truth to the sensational stereotype of the 'Chinese slave girl.' "[41] Another scholar concurs: "It was extremely difficult for Chinese prostitutes to better their situation."[42]

Nevertheless a few women, such as the "famous or infamous" woman Ah Toy, dug some gold by working as prostitutes from the Gold Rush years on.[43] Some of these women eventually became brothel owners. The 1870 manuscript census, for example, records a number of female brothel keepers (operators or owners). Most of them owned some property, ranging in value from one hundred to seven hundred dollars, and some were only in their twenties.[44] Some of these brothel keepers must have been entrepreneurial-minded prostitutes before becoming madams themselves.

Female brothel owners appeared to enjoy a fairly high standing in the community. One such businesswoman was Ah Joan, who had business dealings with men on various occasions. Sometimes she was able to borrow money from male lenders rather easily. In 1882 she obtained a loan of five hundred dollars, without security, from a businessman named Chin Kem You who knew her only by sight. He later sued her when she failed to pay the debt on time.[45]

For most prostitutes and other women in bondage, marriage to a Chinese man was a more practical way out. Needless to say, such marriages also salvaged the man from the restless, lonely life of the bachelor and offered both parties the possibility of family life that was so hard to achieve in the immigrant community. Some of these women were rescued by white missionaries before their marriage. Ah Quin's wife, Sue Leong, appears to have been one such woman.[46]

The rescue mission homes run by missionaries offered these women still another way out of their trap. Praising such rescue efforts, M. G. C. Edholm wrote in 1892 that they produced "many a pleasing romance of love and courtship, happy marriage and a loving home, echoing with the laughter of little children."[47] Recently, scholars have pointed out that in dealing with the rescued, the rescuers demonstrated "an unyielding belief in the superiority of Victorian cultural values, to the point of self-righteousness."[48] But self-righteousness was not their cardinal flaw. Instead of judging them by our standards, we must recognize that in doing what they saw as aiding helpless prostitutes the sympathetic missionary rescuers set themselves apart from anti-Chinese crusaders. Contemporary Chinese openly acknowledged the good intention of the missionaries. Late in 1875 *The Oriental* carried an article protesting against the accusation spreading in the community that Rev. Otis Gibson's mission was actually a hiding place for prostitutes. It praised Gibson as "a man of honesty and virtue" and pointed out that "despite the disputes between him and the [six] companies," he fought the attempts to drive away the Chinese "on numerous occasions." The article concluded that for prostitutes, "escaping to the mission house is like coming to heaven from hell."[49]

While the missionaries undoubtedly saved some women from the exploitation of Chinese men, they did not save any from the racial oppression of white America. The rescue stories even provided ammunition for the anti-Chinese movement by directing public attention toward Chinese prostitution. Sometimes the rescue efforts themselves amounted to direct assaults on the Chinese community. One of the most famous missionary rescuers was Donaldina Cameron, who devoted over forty years (1895–1938) to the Chinese Presbyterian Mission Home.[50] When she forced her way into the community to raid what she believed to be brothels and rescued the (allegedly) slave girls, she was usually accompanied by the notoriously anti-Chinese city police, thereby unveiling the source of her authority and support. It is probably not purely accidental, therefore, that the emergence of the first institutionalized rescue efforts during the 1870s coincided with the escalation in scale and intensity of organized anti-Chinese activities.[51]

The anti-Chinese forces devoted much energy to and focused much attention on the issue of prostitution, making it a centerpiece in the heated debate over "the Chinese question" during the 1870s and 1880s.[52] Reminiscent of the public's mood in those years, the popular writer Herbert Asbury wrote in the 1930s: "Prostitution was the principal, and by far the most remunerative, activity of Chinatown's criminal element."[53] As the historian Elmer Clarence Sandmeyer put it, "[n]o phase of the Chinese question attracted more attention than that of prostitution."[54]

Anti-Chinese hostility significantly contaminated the voluminous English-language historical documents concerning Chinese prostitution. They tell us more about public perceptions and attitudes regarding Chinese women than about Chinese prostitutes' actual world. In 1876 a congressional committee conducted a month-long investigation of Chinese immigration in San Francisco, marking the growing intensity of the nation's anti-Chinese sentiments.[55] Reflecting the mood of the dominant society, the investigation devoted a great deal of attention to Chinese prostitution. It was mentioned in over forty-five different places in the lengthy official report—much more often than Chinese "vices" such as opium smoking and gambling. The investigation created an unusual public forum in which individuals could express and register their personal opinions on Chinese prostitution. The following is from the testimony of a San Francisco policeman named James R. Rogers:

> As far as the Chinese women are concerned in San Francisco, with very few exceptions, I look upon them as prostitutes. The exceptions are very rare where they are not prostitutes.
> Q. How as to their being free women?—A. I do not look upon them as such.

Q. What are they?—A. I look upon them as slaves, sold for such and such an amount of money to be worked out at prostitution.[56]

Rogers' opinions were well publicized, and he offered them before two other important committees on Chinese immigration: a senate committee of California that came to San Francisco to conduct its investigation earlier in 1876 and a special committee of the city government in 1885. His testimony exemplifies white America's efforts to obliterate the existence of Chinese women other than prostitutes. On a different occasion, J. W. Buel commented that of the two thousand Chinese women in San Francisco, "there are not a half-dozen who possess any virtue."[57]

Such a view was echoed even by those sympathetic toward the Chinese. In 1877 the Rev. Otis Gibson suggested, in a less venomous tone but in like fashion, that "nearly all the [six thousand] Chinese women in America" were brought in as prostitutes. He created the impression that except for the several "small-footed" wives of merchants, all others arrived as prostitutes in bondage: "I have seen, perhaps, a half-dozen small-footed women in this country, but their number is very small indeed. The feet of little girls doomed to a life of prostitution are never bound."[58] A few years earlier another missionary among the Chinese, the Rev. A. W. Loomis, stated more explicitly: "Nearly all the Chinese women in California are a disgrace to their nation."[59]

In reality, however, there were Chinese women who worked as shoe binders, servants, tailors, launderers, and gardeners, as well as some who were married and some who worked in brothels. Some achieved certain financial success at a young age. The fifteen-year-old laundrywoman named Low Ing to whom I have referred before, for example, owned one hundred dollars worth of personal property in 1860.[60] Although the census takers did not record any information about the foot size of such nonprostitute working women, it is likely that many of them were not "small footed." Back in their native communities in South China such working women never bound their feet. Foot binding took place primarily among "the upper and upper-middle class" women, as a local gazetteer from the emigrant region reported.[61]

It is not surprising that some of these immigrant women who worked in such a wide variety of industries found their way into the census records. Women in emigrant communities had worked to support themselves for a long time. In Shunde County, for example, "both men and women worked to earn a living" in its market-oriented economy.[62] It is highly likely that there were more such working women than the census takers actually identified. Some would have been mistaken for prostitutes. It is evident that the census takers had a very strong inclination to register females, including even very young little girls, as prostitutes. In the 1870 federal census, for instance, a five-year-old girl was entered as a prostitute.

According to Lucie Cheng's computation, the census takers reported 101 Chinese brothels in 1880.[63] But even the thorough investigation conducted by the hostile special committee of San Francisco, which set out to identify the vices in Chinatown, was able to report only 68 Chinese houses of prostitution there in 1885.[64] The *San Francisco Call* was enraged that the map failed to mark "three places occupied by Chinese females" as brothels.[65] The newspaper had no evidence that the women there were prostitutes. Its logic was based on a widely held assumption: all places where only females resided must be houses of prostitution.

In 1870 and 1880, when prostitution was recognized as an occupation in federal census schedules, the census takers, and many others, evidently shared the same assumption, which has also been accepted by some scholars of Chinese America today.[66] But the assumption is clearly problematic. As Janice E. Stockard has shown, for a long time in the Pearl River Delta area unmarried young women sometimes lived together in "girls' houses" and formed close relationships with one another.[67] In Shunde County, again, many young women established such strong bonds that they would refuse to marry men.[68] During a recent research trip to Shunde, I learned that the "girls' houses" and the strong bond young women established there had deep historical roots. These women were called *zishu nu* (self-combed women), because they combed their hair in a special way during a ceremony in which they declared their determination to live on their own. Several such women would find their own houses, where they lived together as "sworn sisters," and adopted children. They became financially independent, supporting themselves in the textile industry. Such a spirit of independence is also found among some married women, who declined to move into their husbands' households after the wedding.[69]

Chinese immigrants transplanted so much of their cultural heritage and way of life in America that it is only logical that women too carried on their unorthodox traditions. For one thing, they maintained close connections among themselves, helping and passing information to one another. In an 1884 civil case a Chinese woman testified in the Superior Court of the City and County of San Francisco: "The husbands know that the women have good many acquaintances, and they ask them to get the money through their acquaintances."[70] Furthermore, some of the alleged houses of prostitution could have been "girls' houses" or simply places where only women, including those who lived away from their husbands or lovers for whatever reasons, resided. This helps explain the presence of little children in numerous so-called houses of prostitution. It also helps explain why sometimes when women were arrested as prostitutes their husbands suddenly emerged. In one such case, about fourteen or fifteen women were arrested by police on charges of prostitution based on the information provided by the Rev. Gibson, but it turned out that all of them had husbands.[71] Clearly, Chinese American women, who have often been perceived as exclusively childless and familyless prostitutes, actually had more diverse and complex experiences.

Some contemporary Chinese themselves believed that the number of prostitutes in Chinatown was overstated. But their opinions were either ignored or suppressed. In April 1876 a 28-year-old Chinese San Franciscan identified as Ah You told the California senate committee that of all the women in San Francisco, only "two or three hundred" were prostitutes and a few hundred were married.[72] A police officer immediately gave a rebuttal. Furthermore, it is interesting to note that Ah You's testimony, translated by a white man, was partially misrepresented. In the senate committee report, Ah You was cited as saying that he had never heard of any women being sold. According to a Chinese newspaper report, his actual statement was "he has never heard of any woman being forcefully sold into prostitution against her will."[73] Ah You's estimate that there were only a couple of hundred Chinese prostitutes was not taken seriously. And the misrepresentation certainly did not add credibility to his estimate.

Those who deliberately inflated the number of Chinese prostitutes did not do so to create what James Moy calls the stereotype of "the sexually available Asian woman."[74] We must remember that representations of the Chinese should be understood historically. From the 1860s to the 1880s, by depicting them as a menace in a number of ways, the growing anti-Chinese forces sought to exclude Chinese women as well as men, not to establish their availability.

Portraying all Chinese women as "slave girls" reinforced the perception that Chinese immigration introduced slavery to the Republic. Of various kinds of slaves in China, Russell H. Conwell wrote in 1871: "The worst features of Chinese bondage is [*sic*] seen in the dealings with females."[75] A pamphlet published by the Workingmen's Party of California around the late 1870s offers a more elaborate account of the Chinese woman: "She has reached the lowest step in vice and worthlessness. At home, she is a slave, bought and sold. . . . It has been her fortune to be picked up by some agent for California. She comes here a slave."[76]

The Chinese were undesirable also because they were accused of being a source of pollution. They "polluted" the racial purity of California.[77] They also supposedly polluted the city physically, where "they have in the alleys and around their houses . . . old rags slop-holes, excrement and vile refuse animal matter."[78] The brothel was often represented as one of the filthiest places in Chinatown. The report of the city's 1885 investigation committee includes this description of a Chinese brothel: "The slops and filth generated in this underground slum are flung into the street as an extra generous contribution to the rotting garbage that daily accumulates there."[79]

This alleged pollution enabled health officials and experts to play an important role in establishing the image of Chinatown, and especially Chinese prostitution, as an alarming threat to public health.[80] Reorganized with much political power in 1870, the city's Board of Health made regular house-to-house inspections in Chinatown.[81] Headed by Mayor I. S. Kalloch, a member of the Workingmen's Party, early in the 1880s the board had four other members, all medical doctors. In 1880 a committee appointed by the board concluded that because of its filth and venereal diseases, Chinatown threatened to "imperil the health of our citizens."[82]

Anti-Chinese crusaders made every effort to associate the Chinese with contagious diseases, calling the Chinese immigrant "the moon-eyed leper."[83] In fact, leprosy was regarded as a Chinese disease that resulted from, as a city health official named Dr. John L. Meares contended, "generations of syphilis."[84] Such effort had an apparent effect. Because of "rumors that the smallpox the Chinese have is extremely contagious," *The Oriental* reported in 1876, white Americans "refuse all Chinese fruit sellers, launders and visitors to enter their house."[85]

Chinese prostitutes were accused of spreading another, supposedly related, contagious disease: syphilis. After attacking the Chinese in the first part of his 1862 *Chinese Immigration and the Physiological Causes of the Decay of the Nation*, Dr. Arthur B. Stout turned to the subject of syphilis and its "deeply engrafted poison."[86] Suggested implicitly in Stout's pamphlet, the connection between the Chinese and the disease was made completely clear later on. In 1876 Dr. Hugh H. Toland declared that Chinese prostitutes were responsible for nine-tenths of the syphilis cases in San Francisco. He asserted that his white patients "think diseases contracted from Chinawomen are harder to cure than those contracted elsewhere," adding "nearly all the boys in town, who have venereal disease, contracted it in Chinatown."[87] While the doctor tactfully led his audience to imagine the hazard of the diseases Chinese women carried, he left no doubt that they were the main source of syphilis and that they endangered innocent white boys. Because Toland was a member of the health board and the founder of the Toland Medical College (which he transferred as a gift to the University of California), his testimony appeared in numerous places.

Most important of all, Chinese immigration was perceived as a racial peril, as Dr. Arthur B. Stout articulated in 1862: "If the world mourns the presence of a Negro race in the Eastern and Southern States, what tear may be shed when . . . the great West is overwhelmed."[88] He envisioned an American West populated by a pure, superior white race. "[B]y commingling with the Eastern Asiatics," he warned, "we are creating degenerate hybrids."[89] Praised as "the first tocsin of alarm,"[90] Stout's pamphlet was recycled and republicized by the anti-Chinese crusaders in the 1870s.[91]

For these crusaders the racial threat came not only from Chinese prostitutes seducing innocent white males. The momentary mingling of Chinese men and white women in brothels represented another serious problem. Ah Quin was one such man. He did not show any preference for white prostitutes over Chinese ones, as some contemporaries believed Chinese men did. We do not know whether he attached any racial meaning to the transactions that took place in the white brothel. It is clear, however, that white San Franciscans were worried about the racial implications of such intimacy between Chinese men and white women. The city's investigation committee communicated its worry in its 1885 report. Referring to these women, it lamented: "their mode of life seems to be modeled after that of the Mongolian, to a larger extent than the manners and customs of the race to which they belong."[92] On its "official map of Chinatown," the committee used blue ink to mark the 36 white houses of prostitution in the Chinese community. The hysteria over the issue of prostitution epitomized the intensity of anti-Chinese hostility during the 1870s and 1880s. It also contributed to shaping long-lasting public perceptions of the Chinese community, and especially of Chinese women.

Opium

From the first years of Chinese immigration, opium provided another avenue of relaxation and recreation for the mostly nondrinking Chinese population.[93] The immigrant community was more critical of opium than it was of prostitution. Alarmed by its prevalence among the Chinese, in 1856 *The Oriental* strongly exhorted people to stay away from opium use because it was unlawful and unfilial.[94]

Despite internal criticism and the city's attempt to ban opium smoking, the habit remained a prevalent fixture of life in Chinatown. Besides the numerous retailers who specialized solely in opium, many other stores also carried opium products. Shun Fook, for instance, was identified by its English name as a grocery store, but in an 1882 directory its Chinese name emphatically stated that it also sold opium.[95] The opium merchants ran elaborate newspaper advertisements, trying to reach customers both in and outside San Francisco. Different kinds of opium were available depending on how much customers could afford to pay.

In the mid-1870s the wholesale price for the two best grades of opium, the Li Yun and the Fuk Lung, was about $1.36 an ounce, making it quite an expensive commodity. To provide some perspective, at this time white sugar sold at about $0.01 a pound and rice at about $0.06 a pound.[96] Customers had to pay more at retail stores or in opium dens. For a regular user, who consumed about six pounds of opium a year, the total price could exceed $150, equal to several months' income for the average immigrant laborer. Even the regular consumption of cheaper products could still be quite costly and could affect the smoker's ability to help his family. H. H. Kane, a contemporary drug expert, called the opium pipe "a pauperizing agent."[97] This is why the habit was criticized among the Chinese as being unfilial.

For white Americans opium use represented another immoral Chinese vice. It was perceived as less threatening than prostitution, however. At the time many medical experts believed that alcohol, a social problem never associated with the Chinese, was more dangerous to society. Comparing the two in 1881, Dr. Fred Heman Hubbard stated that "the effect of opium is peculiarly soothing and tranquilizing. . . . The effects of liquor or wine, as compared with those of opium, are coarse and brutalizing."[98] The missionary Frederick J. Masters noted at the end of the century: "The Chinaman may yell over his drinking game, and curse and swear at the gaming table, but he quiets down in the opium den."[99] The Rev. Ira Condit wrote in like fashion later: "Opium does not lead a person to crime and deeds of violence as the drinking of liquor does."[100]

Even those who were hostile to the Chinese admitted that opium consumption did not make them a social threat. Dr. John L. Meares declared publicly in 1876: "It is rather better for us that they should smoke opium, for if they drank liquor to some excess, I do not know what would become of us. . . . When they smoke opium they are inoffensive so far as we are concerned, because when they get under its influence they drop off and go to sleep."

Over time, opium smoking was put on display for the increasing number of white tourists as a sign of Chinese inferiority and degradation. In 1876 Meares commented: "The higher civilizations prefer liquor—alcohol. Take it as a rule, the use of other stimulants than alcohol is looked upon as more degrading."[101] "In all manner of pose, and in all stages of stupor or idiocy," B. E. Lloyd wrote of a scene of degradation in an opium den in the 1870s, "the opium smokers, [are] each clinging to his pipe endeavoring to get one more full 'whiff,' with the tenacity of a drowning man hanging to a floating wreck."[102]

Opponents of Chinese immigration were quick to claim that the Chinese opium users' habit was physically and mentally self-destructive, contributing to their racial degeneration. A few sympathetic contemporaries repudiated the tendency to exaggerate the ruinous effects of opium use. In a detailed report about opium smoking in Chinatown, the missionary Frederick J. Masters wrote: "A great deal of exaggeration is found in half we read of the effects of opium smoking on the system. It is a mistake to suppose that when a man begins to smoke the drug, he begins to lose strength and waste away."[103] B. S. Brooks, longtime resident of San Francisco, said in 1876 that the Chinese "have not stupefied themselves with opium."[104] He concluded that "as for one to be addicted to the use of opium so as to affect him physically, there is not one per cent."[105] "Upon the subject of the pathological effects of opium-smoking upon the individual and the nation," H. H. Kane contended, "there has been a great deal of unintentional misunderstanding and exaggeration."[106]

According to what appears to be one overestimate made by the American Opium Commission at an international conference in Shanghai, at the turn of the century about 45 percent of the Chinese in America smoked opium. About a third of them were habitual or heavy users (regular smokers who consumed six pounds a year each).[107] At the same time, the Rev. Ira Condit estimated that between 30 and 40 percent of Chinese men smoked opium in San Francisco.[108]

The American Opium Commission called 22 percent of the users "social smokers" (one ounce per year), who took the drug only on very special occasions as a matter of courtesy. The word "social" serves to reveal that many smoked opium because it offered an opportunity for companionship. A "very decided factor," H. H. Kane commented, "is the fact of the companionship, two usually smoking together."[109]

The smoky, crowded opium dens not only offered companionship but also re-created an aspect of social life that had permeated South China by the mid-nineteenth century. Anti-Chinese forces considered opium smoking a vice "transplanted by the Chinese to American soil."[110] Although it did not turn the Chinese smokers themselves into a physical threat to white society, it could spread to white Americans—a concern that Frederick J. Masters expressed explicitly: "The most serious phase of the opium evil is that the vice is spreading amongst depraved white people of both sexes."[111]

Such concerns prompted efforts to address white America's emerging drug problem. It is interesting to note that those efforts converged with the attempts to exclude Chinese immigration. The supplement to the 1880 Sino-American treaty that allowed the United States to enact exclusion laws banned the importation of opium to the United States from China.[112] That ban was written into federal legislation in 1887.

White America evidently enjoyed early success in its endeavor to link a nonwhite race and drug use. Chinese immigrants, however, were not responsible for introducing the drug to the United States—it had arrived long before them.[113] On the contrary, it was Americans who, along with the British, were responsible for creating a large-scale drug problem in China during the Daoguang years (1821–50).[114] Before the Opium War American players in the China trade, such as Perkins & Company and Russel & Company, became important suppliers for China's increasing inhaling population.[115] In negotiating the 1858 Sino-American treaty with China, American officials managed to lift the ban on opium importation to China. Because of its geographical location the Pearl River Delta became one of the most heavily infected areas. In the United States the insignificant-looking, small opium dens were located primarily in the backstreets of Chinatown (in the mid-1880s, for example, there was no single opium place on Dupont, Washington, Clay, and Sacramento Streets). Nevertheless, they represented an extension of an important chapter of nineteenth-century Chinese history. They serve as a reminder of how big a part events in modern China played in shaping the immigrants' lives.

The Immigrant Theater

A much more genuinely Chinese tradition that had been around a great deal longer was the theater. The theater was not only a place for recreation; it also helped sustain the community's collective historical memory and cultural identity. Many of the daily and nightly performances in the drama houses represented "the reproduction of very ancient historical events."[116] During his visit to San Francisco early in the 1880s the Englishman George Augustus Sala noticed that in the Chinese theaters "the play generally represents some historical train of events extending through the entire dominion of dynasty or an interesting national epoch."[117] The integration of historical as well as moral teachings into dramas seems to have been the product of a conscious effort. A placard inside the Royal Chinese Theatre during the 1880s revealed the pedagogical purpose of the theatrical performances, that is, to combine "pleasure, or amusement . . . with instruction."[118] For the immigrants, theatergoing meant reexperiencing a host of cultural traditions. Besides historical events, gods from Chinese folk religion were often featured in the drama, and sometimes statues of them stood in the theater hall to "witness and preside over the performance."[119]

In many cases, the actors and, sometimes, actresses came from Guangdong to perform. They brought the immigrants closer to their native society
not only by re-creating Chinese history and traditions on the stage but also
through their off-stage contact with residents in Chinatown. While he lived
in San Francisco, the brothelgoer Ah Quin was also a theatergoer, and in his
diary he mentioned performers from China.[120] Sometimes he went to talk to
such performers. On June 10, 1879, for example, he went "to see the new
actress[es] come from China, one is name[d] Kwai Fai Yin, the other is
name[d] Luing Chork."

The Chinese theater had accompanied the immigrants to the New World
from the very beginning. As early as 1852 a regular Chinese dramatic company started to perform "pieces in their native language." In 1853 another
theater was opened. The 1870s was a golden period for the immigrant theater. In September 1875 there were eleven Chinese troupes in San Francisco,
each of which had at least 28 players. The names of these players printed in
the Chinese newspaper indicate that a number of them were women.[121] In
the late 1870s and early 1880s the Chinese American community supported
four regular theaters—two on Jackson Street and two on Washington
Street—all of which Ah Quin visited.[122]

Internally, the theater existed as a self-sufficient social unit with its own
hierarchy. At the top were managers and some musicians, for whom the theater could be a profitable business. The performers were mostly propertyless
young men trying to make a living. At the bottom, the laborers provided
food and other basic services. In 1870 the Sun Heen Lok Theater Company,
for example, employed 45 people altogether, including 5 laborers, 2 carpenters, and 3 cooks.[123] The manager, a man named Lun Heen who was in his
forties, had ten thousand dollars' worth of personal property. The company
included 10 musicians and 1 chief actor. Of the other 23 actors, 18 were
young men under the age of 30, and only two were over 40 years old, meaning that the company resembled the general Chinese American population
in terms of age.

The Chinese theater aroused considerable public interest. From the early
1850s non-Chinese visitors came to watch Chinese drama. In their writings
they represented it as a novelty and emphasized its conspicuously alien features, instead of depicting it as a menace or vice. "Of the objects of interest
in the Chinese 'Quarter' of San Francisco which appeal most strongly to
the stranger's curiosity," one wrote in 1882, "the theatres occupy a foremost

place."[124] Such curiosity was accompanied by a deep sense of contempt for the unfamiliar. In 1876 B. E. Lloyd wrote to indicate its unartistic nature: "There are no pretensions to elegance, comfort, or artistic finish in any part of the building. A circle and gallery, furnished with common benches, perhaps two or three private boxes. . . . The stage is simply a raised platform, having no drop-curtain nor scenes."[125] In like fashion, Sala characterized the stage for the Royal Theatre in 1880: "It had no 'flies', no 'wings', no 'flats', 'drops', or 'set-pieces', no curtain, green or otherwise, and, in fact, no shifting or permanent scenery of any kind."[126]

Most white observers were unable to appreciate the artistic quality of the Chinese theater. They were not art connoisseurs on the level of Bertolt Brecht but were simply spectators, driven by curiosity to gaze on the strangeness of a nonwhite race represented by the Chinese in the audience.[127] A traveler named Iza Duffus Hardy wrote of his experience in a Chinatown theater: "We looked around curiously. The audience was . . . quite as interesting as the stage. In all the crowded theatre there was not a white face outside our box. Nothing but Chinese, packed close as sardines; ranks upon ranks of smooth-shaven olive faces, black hats, blouses, and pigtails."[128] Around the turn of the century Joseph Carey, a member of the American Historical Association, stated that "no visit to Chinatown would be complete without an inspection of its theatre and study of the audience." "There were altogether a thousand persons present," continued Carey, "and it was indeed a strange sight to look into their faces, dressed all alike as they were, and all seemingly looking alike."[129] Visitors like these came to the theaters not as regular theatergoers. Their attention was seldom focused on the performance on the stage. For them, observing the Chinese audience became part of their theatrical experience.

Language was another barrier that made it difficult for nineteenth-century white viewers to appreciate Chinese drama. Of non-Chinese visitors to the Chinese theater, Mrs. E. M. Green noted: "The faces of these onlookers bear that stupid expression always noticeable in people listening to a language they do not understand."[130] One such onlooker, William Brewer, confessed in his diary in 1863 that he did not know whether what he saw in the theater "was opera, tragedy, or comedy, or a mixture of the three, I have no idea."[131]

What was music to the Chinese, whites considered offensive noise.

Russell H. Conwell concluded: "Chinese theatres . . . can scarcely be declared either amusing or instructive to the European or American spectator."[132] "If the tone of the gongs which deafen your ears at each dinner hour in your fashionable hotel suit your taste for music, then perhaps you might be able to appreciate a Chinese concert," he continued, "but if that offends your ear, then be careful. . . . Such a noise!"[133] By the early 1880s, to reduce that "noise" the city had passed an ordinance mandating that all the Chinese theaters must close their doors by midnight.

We must not focus our discussion solely on what the Chinese theater signified in white consciousness, because it was never intended for Americans or Europeans. Its audience was predominantly Chinese. What the immigrant theatergoers enjoyed in the early years was actually Cantonese opera. Formed during the late Ming and early Qing Dynasties on the basis of several different branches of the Chinese opera, it had become a popular form of entertainment in the Canton region by the Daoguang period.[134] Traveling troupes performed in small towns and rural areas, making Chinese opera an important part of the popular culture.

For many years theatergoing remained a significant recreational activity for the Chinese in San Francisco. And it was quite affordable. As late as the early twentieth century, according to Mrs. E. M. Green, the price of a ticket to the theater was only 20 cents (50 cents for non-Chinese) and the poor could go for free.[135] Its affordability certainly helped the theater maintain its popularity. In his diary Ah Quin noticed huge crowds in the theater.[136] In 1880 Sala found twelve hundred people in the Royal Theatre.[137] Describing the audience in a Chinese theater, George H. Fitch wrote: "Packed is the proper word, for they are sitting on low benches, and each bench accommodates as many persons as the seats of a horse-car when the rush for home and dinner has set in."[138]

Chinese San Franciscans came to the theaters not simply for the familiar historical plots staged there. They also came to relax and to socialize, as is indicated by the informality that characterized theatergoing. One visitor reported in the late 1860s: "The audience smoked incessantly and chatted together."[139] Before the performance began people were "calling across the theater, exchanging jokes or the compliments of the season."[140] "The actors," Lloyd wrote, "when not engaged with a part, occupy seats at the rear of the stage—still in view of the audience—where they eat and smoke incessantly."[141] Sala described the informality of the theater scene in detail: "One third at least, of the audience are smoking cigars or cigarettes, not impregnated with opium, as some travellers would make you believe. . . . Another third of the audience are eating something—goodness knows what it is; but it is something, no doubt, that the white man would consider nasty. During the performance slim Chinese boys, bearing napkin-covered baskets, elbow and shin their way between the benches."[142]

For the Chinese, theatergoing was a casual recreational activity as well as a group excursion. Individuals often visited the theater houses together with friends, and they entered and left the theaters as they wished. Often accompanied by his Chinese friends, Ah Quin visited the theaters frequently—sometimes he would go twice a day—and at any time of the day he preferred. Moreover, the duration of each of his visits varied—from half an hour to a few hours. The theater, which was open during the daytime and until late at night, was a convenient place for Chinese immigrants to recuperate from their daily toil. In the cozy environment of the theater hall that often recalled a familiar past, they could also forget hostile realities. As Burden McDowell perceptively pointed out long ago, "To a down-trodden and unhappy people, who have long given up the hope of substantial justice in real life, an agreeable improbability will always be preferable to a disagreeable truth on the stage."[143]

As a site of collective memory and a place for socializing and relaxation, the theater was a favorite destination of Chinese San Franciscan men and women. The gallery reserved for women offered them a rare gathering place. The theater epitomizes the significance of Chinese San Francisco as the cultural headquarters of Chinese America. While opium dens and brothels could be found in smaller Chinese communities, the immigrant theater existed only in Chinese San Francisco until other major Chinese communities such as New York's Chinatown were established.

The social and recreational institutions discussed in this chapter further demonstrate the significance of Chinese San Francisco as the "capital" of Chinese America. As the first permanent community that Chinese immigrants established for themselves, it offered more than economic opportunities. It housed institutions that organized and linked the lives of these immigrants. It also existed as a place for them to revive collective memories and to re-create a familiar way of life.

Chinese San Francisco represented a focal point in the heated debate over Chinese immigration. Much of the assault on the community was centered around its recreational institutions, a fact that reveals the cultural dimensions of racial antagonism. The anti-Chinese movement sought to eliminate not only the economic competition of Chinese labor but also what it perceived to be an alien culture.

As we have seen, the attack on the Chinese and their way of life created negative stereotypes and contaminated historical documents regarding Chinese America. This reminds us that the various English-language historical sources were usually written by non-Chinese authors from their point of view, and were intended for non-Chinese audiences. Much work needs to be done to destabilize deeply embedded assumptions based on such documents. In order to do so we must view the history of Chinese Americans from their own perspective and using their own sources.

FOUR

"China in America": The World of Ah Quin

This chapter attempts to gauge the perimeters of the early Chinese Americans' world. The word "world" here refers not simply to their temporal physical environment but to a state of mind and consciousness based on shared experiences and memories and on common world views and social relations. It offered a framework that allowed them to fathom the meaning of their experience. It did not eradicate various internal conflicts but simply provided terms in which to comprehend such conflicts. For people who were perceived as an "inferior" race and who lived in spatially limited settlements, it was a world that transcended class lines. For people who remained physically mobile in the United States and who maintained strong trans-Pacific ties, this world also transcended the physical boundaries of these settlements and national borders.

Our attention in this chapter will focus on Ah Quin, whom we have encountered as a theatergoer and a brothelgoer. His story offers valuable insights into the history of Chinese America. He was one of the thousands of immigrants who ventured to California at a very young age, leaving their families behind. A native of one of the siyi counties named Kaiping, Ah Quin was under the age of fifteen upon his first landing in San Francisco around 1863.[1] His Chinese name was Tan Congkuan (as spelled in pinyin). As happened in many other cases, the new family name "Quin" came about as a result of American authorities' comprehension, or rather incomprehension, of the second part of his given name in Chinese, "kuan." We do not know the exact circumstances under which he came to America, but evidence suggests that he was part of the Chinese "chain migration." His diary and correspondence notes mention relatives (including a brother) and fellow villagers in America. It is possible that some earlier comers among them brought him to California from China. While we do not know if Ah Quin directly helped anyone from his own village to join the trans-Pacific migration, it is clear that many people, mostly with the last name of Tan (namely, Tom or Hom), followed him to San Diego when he became a labor recruiter.[2]

Ah Quin lived in San Francisco for a relatively short time. He came to the city to work in December 1878 and left to settle in San Diego late in October 1880. During the nineteenth century a majority of Chinese immigrants to the United States stayed in San Francisco for varied lengths of time. For Ah Quin and for many other Chinese who moved on to live and work elsewhere, San Francisco retained its significance and magnetism as a cultural and business center and an enjoyable place to visit. Like that of many other immigrants, Ah Quin's world remained trans-Pacific: while demonstrating his willingness and ability to adapt in various ways, he stayed connected with his Chinese friends and relatives in both China and America and with Chinese traditions, such as the Chinese theater, Chinese food, and chess.

Needless to say, our diarist was no prototypical Chinese immigrant. Several things set him apart from most Chinese, including his Christianity and his relative proficiency in English. Many of his descendants believe he encountered both through his contact with American missionaries in China. Most important, he left valuable personal documents, especially a diary that intermittently covers the period between 1877 and 1902. Candid and often unpolished, these private documents afford us a rare opportunity to take a close look at the daily surroundings and the innermost world of an early immigrant.

What follows is not a conventional biography but an anatomy of Ah Quin's mentality.[3] It is an attempt to understand the collective world that he shared so intimately with his compatriots, rather than simply to psychologically analyze a single individual. Ah Quin's records have limitations. Often terse and simple, they rarely go beyond his own daily encounters. His ability to articulate his thoughts and emotions in a diary written mostly in

English was hampered by an imperfect command of his second language. Therefore, in an effort to achieve a more complete understanding of a world that belonged to immigrants collectively, other sources will be used to expand on the documents Ah Quin left. It was a world different from our own and from that of contemporary white Americans.

Between the Old World and the New

Chinese American communities were marked by their undisguised cultural uniqueness. Across the nation, no Chinese community was more evocative of "China" in the minds of white Americans than was San Francisco's Chinatown. Beginning in the 1850s it was "often called 'Little China.' "[4] White observers invented various ways of referring to it that captured its Chineseness, such as the "Pacific Province of China" and "Little China in the City of the Golden Gate."[5]

During the high tide of anti-Chinese sentiments the community's cultural distinctiveness was exploited to promote the image of the Chinese as an inferior and dangerously foreign race. One writer commented in 1878: "It *is* China, unmitigated, debased, idolatrous, unmoved as a rock in the ocean, with the surges of Christian civilization washing the walls of its dwellings."[6] Visitors to Chinatown often requested police escort to protect them "against the possible dangers."[7]

Over time, as Chinese immigration was banned and its perceived threat diminished, Chinatown became an object of curiosity as a tourist attraction, and less emphasis was placed on its danger. A city guide of 1897 noted: "If the average citizen of San Francisco were asked to place his finger on that part of his city which is the most attractive to strangers and at the same time the most objectionable to himself, he should be sure to indicate Chinatown."[8] Its commercial value in bringing tourist dollars prompted efforts to perpetuate Chinatown's peculiarity. Around the turn of the century "China" became the assigned code of Chinese users' telephone lines. The telephone number for Leon Hop & Company was "China. 142," for example.[9] Completed in 1909, the new China telephone office that handled Chinatown phone lines became an instant showplace, with its saliently Chinese motif.

For many white tourists, Chinatown satisfied not only their curiosity about the unfamiliar but also their need to rediscover their superiority. For them Chinatown stood as a site of comparison: one between progress and stagnation, between vices and morality, between dirtiness and hygiene, and between paganism and Christianity. In his lengthy eyewitness description of Chinatown in 1901, the famous lecturer Charles W. Stoddard had this to say: "The air is laden with the fumes of smoking sandalwood and strange odors of the East; and the streets, swarming with coolies, resound with the echoes of an unknown tongue. There is hardly room for us to pass; we pick our way, and are sometimes curiously regarded by slanted-eyed pagans."[10]

Non-Chinese visitors observing the trans-Pacific ties in Chinese life centered their attention on the outward appearance of Chinatown. For the immigrants themselves, however, such ties were of far more profound significance, defining the meaning of their striving in the New World. First and foremost were their strong personal bonds to their families and friends in their native communities, which many regarded as their ultimate home.

Like many others, Ah Quin journeyed to America with family responsibility in mind. On November 30, 1877, he wrote about his concern that his old father needed clothes: "Dream about my father He said to [reach] old age [of] almost 71 and want some cloth."[11] Ah Quin was evidently not from a very affluent family. But it must not have been at the very bottom of society, because it had been able to afford to provide some education for Ah Quin. His handwriting and prose, both quite adequate, indicate that he had gone through a few years of schooling in China.

While working as a cook from 1877 to 1878 in a mining camp on the small island of Coal Harbor off the coast of the Alaska Peninsula, Ah Quin thought and dreamed about his family frequently. In his diary entry for December 1, 1877, his broken English figuratively displays a broken heart: "Fell [feel] very sorry for my Parents [who] is get[ting] old nobody take care them I have one brother [who] is about 12 year old but he cant support them."[12] Clearly, Ah Quin was unhappy about his inability to fulfill his responsibilities as a son. At the time he was actually in debt. This bothered him so much that he had a nightmare: "My friend Lam Bo in Santa Barbara ask my Father about [what] I owe him so my father rebuke me and scare me."[13] This unpunctuated sentence sketches the uninterrupted patriarchal authority of a stern father, who continued to haunt the son across the Pacific Ocean.

Ah Quin's concern for his parents and friends back home remained a constant theme of his diary in the early years. On the "gloomy and cold" day of December 10, 1877, he thought of them again and wrote sadly: "Sorry for relations or my Parent[s] in China and friendship because I may not see them no more."[14] Even the "fine and warm" weather on January 29, 1878, did not comfort him, because the coming Chinese New Year made him even more homesick and heightened his awareness of his unfulfilled family responsibility. He wrote: "Felt very sorry for my Parents in China no body take care [of] them and the time new year come it gives them more terrable [trouble] prepare every things new for they [their] happy new year and feel sad about me left so long and cry when I pray for them."[15] A sincere but poor Christian, he could only pray for his parents, as he did on December 8, 1877: "[It is] my birth day [I] pray to God may bless my parents in China."[16]

Ah Quin frequently wrote to his family and friends in China. Probably starting shortly after he left Alaska, he sent modest sums of money back rather frequently. The regular communication between Ah Quin and his loved ones back home unveils the important position they occupied in his world. Following are a few examples of the things Ah Quin sent his mother in 1879 and early 1880.

In May 1879 Ah Quin sent a letter and $30. On October 4, 1879, he sent another letter along with $20, which were given to "Ah Yaw [who] handed to Hi Kowe [to] bring it to her."[17] On December 6, 1879, he recorded: "a. l. [a letter] to Yan Row and 10 dollar it gave to Tom send it to my Mother in Chi[na]."[18] A few days later he gave a letter and $10 to a fellow Chinese "to take back to my mother in person," along with $1 for his grandmother.[19]

It is also interesting to note how Ah Quin relied on his friends to stay in touch with people in China. In fact, individual immigrants traveling back and forth usually served as regular and trusted messengers. On December 5, 1889, Chinese minister Cui Guoyin noted in his diary that U.S. customs officials in San Francisco found nearly twenty thousand letters placed in Chinese passengers' luggage in three arriving ships, in violation of postal regulations.[20]

Sometimes the Chinese used the U.S. postal services. Describing the San Francisco post office during the Gold Rush, William Taylor noted that one of its two windows was for "the navy and army, the French, Spanish, Chinese, clergy, and the ladies."[21] In the early 1850s the post office, located on the corner of Clay and Dupont Streets, shipped mail dispatches to China twice a month.[22] By the early 1880s the post office offered more services, including money-order services. But it also imposed restrictions. At that time packages weighing more than four pounds "will not be carried in the mails."[23] For Chinese customers, using the postal service not only involved inconvenience but also made them susceptible to abuse.

Various institutions in Chinatown provided more convenient mail service. For decades many stores offered such a service. Later, postal agencies emerged. One such agency advertised its business for letter and money delivery between the "Gold Mountain" and Kaiping, Enping, and Xinning Counties. Even if the delivery had to be made "to villages in the country, far away or nearby," door-to-door delivery was promised.[24] The agency had three representatives in San Francisco alone. Such extensive trans-Pacific communication helped immigrants stay connected with their loved ones in China and expanded the scope of their world.

The immigrants' families in China had a similarly strong desire to stay in touch. That desire surfaced when family members placed advertisements in newspapers asking about the whereabouts of people who had disappeared in America. These advertisements also remind us of the precarious nature of life in the New World for some immigrants. In one case a son looked for his vanished father who had sent letters and money back shortly after his departure in 1852.[25] In another case a couple tried to find their missing son, who would have been 41 years of age in 1903.[26]

There is no evidence that women publicly sought help to find their missing husbands, which would have been deemed socially inappropriate. Local gazetteers in the Pearl River Delta recorded many *jiefu*—women who remained chaste and did not marry again after their husbands died or simply vanished overseas. The gazetteer for Xinning County, the most important source of United States–bound emigration, reported an unusually high number of such women. We have mentioned such women, who were considered models of chastity, in previous discussions of the region's socioeconomic conditions. In addition to giving us insights into the lives of Chinese immigrants who came to the United States, these women's stories shed light on the immigrants' wives, and especially on the difficulties those who became widows encountered.

Nearly all these women assumed the family responsibility that their men had left behind. In many cases a woman would have been waiting for years before news of her husband's death made her widowhood official. Some women who remained "widows" had actually never been married to their men. In one such case, after the man she was engaged to died overseas, a woman named Chen decided, "in great sorrow," to maintain her chastity to honor him. She supported herself by weaving. Sympathetic villagers helped her to adopt a son "in order to continue his family line."[27] According to the dominant ideology of womanhood, when a woman was engaged to a man, she was considered a member of his family. And marrying another man was considered unchaste.

These women's plight was recorded in numerous folk songs that originated in the emigrant region and traveled with the immigrants to the New World. One such song documents a woman's complaint about her immigrant husband: "[After] leaving the hometown, heading overseas, [he] does not think about home for eight to ten years; the willow trees are brilliant and the fields green, the young woman in her chamber is unhappy with her heart broken."[28]

Family ties represented only one layer of the immigrants' multileveled connections to their native land. For many these ties constituted a heritage to be passed on and remembered over generations. Ah Quin's commercial and personal ties to China remained close in the later years of his life, as has been documented by his entries of numerous people and businesses in South China in his address notes. His trans-Pacific connections later became transgenerational. Of the twelve children born to him and his wife, the two oldest sons, George and Thomas, quite closely resembled their father: both had high foreheads and small mouths with full lips.[29] But they had inherited more than a physical resemblance from him. Shortly after September 1910, 25-year-old George and 22-year-old Thomas returned to their father's native land and married two young women from two different counties in Guangdong. Their experience was by no means unusual. At that time many Chinese men went to China to find spouses, in part because of the unbalanced ratio of men to women in Chinese America. As happened in many such cases, Ah Quin apparently arranged his sons' marriages through his connections. In fact, George's wife's name and the address of her father in Canton are in Ah Quin's address notes prior to 1910, suggesting that Ah Quin had some knowledge of her family prior to the marriage. Years later, in 1956, George's son went to Hong Kong (he could no longer enter Guangdong after 1949) and found his bride there.[30] Nothing symbolizes the continuation of heritage more clearly than does a Chinese immigrant's American-born male descendants going to China and returning to the United States with Chinese brides.

Such transgenerational cultural transmission manifested itself in other ways as well. Thomas lived on to assume his father's title as the unofficial mayor of San Diego's Chinatown. During a recent interview one of George's children told me that "Uncle Tom" remained "very Chinese" throughout his life. "Uncle Frank," one of Thomas's younger brothers, also remained "very Chinese." Frank could write and read Chinese and continued to send money to relatives in China. He also urged members of the next generation to follow in his footsteps, saying that doing so was their responsibility.

Three of Ah Quin's daughters took the opposite paths, electing to marry Caucasians. Each must have had her own particular reasons for choosing her spouse. These three marriages nevertheless follow a broader pattern in Asian American history: women tend to marry outside their ethnic communities more often than men. It also seems clear that none of Ah Quin's daughters went back to China to find a husband. This confirms yet another pattern: until very recently most of those Chinese who went to the Pearl River Delta to find a spouse were men.

In the nineteenth century most Chinese immigrants to the United States traveled back to China. This type of "reverse migration" occurred right after Chinese immigration to the country first began. In 1853, one year after a record 20,026 Chinese immigrants had arrived, 4,421 people returned to China, outnumbering those coming to the United States.[31] So-called return migration was not always the end of the American journey for those who sailed back to China. After returning to China, many said farewell to their loved ones and crossed the Pacific once again.

Scholars of Chinese American history often mention two important reasons for reverse migration: discrimination and the unbalanced ratio of men to women in Chinese America. Reverse migration, however, occurred among southern European immigrants to America and in other cases of international immigration where the two factors mentioned above were not always present. To better comprehend Chinese immigrants' strong desire to return to China, therefore, we must also look at the cultural traditions and socioeconomic forces at work within Chinese society. Most important of all, we must understand the significance of the native community in immigrants' minds and lives.

In her 1986 study Carol B. Brettel illustrates the importance of what she calls "migration to return" in the history of Portuguese migration. She concludes that this "can be viewed in the Portuguese context as an ideology that defines or gives meaning to experience."[32] For many Chinese the act of returning signified not only their commitment to family responsibility but also a mentality, if not an ideology, that was deeply rooted in their homeland. In their minds the native community remained the center of their world and the place in which to achieve ultimate self-fulfillment. Only there could their experiences overseas, especially their success, be fully appreciated and meaningfully acknowledged. Indeed, it was common to seek *ronggui* (meaning "a glorious return").[33] In 1907 *The Chinese-Western Daily* critically reflected on the prevalence of the notion of ronggui within the community in earlier years: "Whenever three or five hundred dollars were accumulated in a few years, we felt that if we did not return home it would be like 'wearing silk in darkness.'"[34] Even those with nothing to show off still hoped to return to their native place. As an old Chinese saying went, they were like falling leaves going back to their roots.

So many of the returning immigrants went through San Francisco that the Zhonghua Huiguan seized the opportunity to exercise its social authority. It issued special permits to make sure, as the Rev. Ira M. Condit noted, that "they are not running away from debts or claims against them, and that they have paid the dues" that each huiguan required of each passenger.[35] The departure dues constituted a major source of revenue for the huiguan and other organizations. Late in the nineteenth century dues were nine dollars for each passenger. They went up to eleven dollars early in the twentieth century. Of that amount, three dollars went to the Zhonghua Huiguan, four dollars and fifty cents to charity societies, one dollar to the Chinese Hospital, and one dollar to financing the fight against anti-Chinese legislation.[36] Liang Qichao noted at the time that the American authorities sanctioned and protected the right of the huiguan to collect money from all departing Chinese, except for converted Christians.[37]

Not all Chinese immigrants who wished to go back could do so in their lifetime, as intermittent reports of suicides and sudden deaths in Chinese newspapers remind us. Unable to return alive, many immigrants requested that their bodies or ashes be sent back so that they could be reunited with their loved ones. That wish, wrote the Rev. A. W. Loomis, demonstrated the immigrant's "love for his native land, and the desire that his last resting-place shall be where the ashes of his kindred lie."[38]

The community's collective effort made to ship the dead to China started as early as the mid-1850s.[39] On May 14, 1855, the *Sunny South*, leaving San Francisco for China, carried the remains of 70 Chinese.[40] A few months later, on the night of November 12, 1855, the bones of another 20 people arrived by boat from Sacramento for transportation to China. This practice understandably came under attack at the height of the anti-Chinese movement. In the 1870s the city of San Francisco even tried to prohibit it.

Sending bodies back to China was not only time consuming but also entailed "a considerable expense."[41] It involved raising funds, locating the graves, exhuming the bodies, and purchasing coffins. White America's hostility added a new cost. In 1886 Zhang Yinhuan received a report from the consulate in San Francisco saying that white authorities charged ten dollars for every coffin sent to China. In a letter to the State Department Zhang protested that discrimination "is now applied to dried bones."[42]

The tradition nevertheless persisted because the community invested many resources to sustain it. Numerous charity organizations specialized in the task, which individuals also supported. On April 28, 1856, 336 coffins were shipped back to China. Two hundred and twenty-eight of them were handled by eight charity groups, and the remaining eight by relatives.

In 1862 the Panyu charity house under the Sanyi Huiguan carried out its first operation to ship the remains of deceased Panyu natives back to their land of origin. By the spring of 1863 the charity house had raised more than twenty-five thousand dollars and had shipped the remains of 258 people at an actual cost of $20,500. Transported back to their native community, as one Panyu man noted, the deceased could finally "rest in peace."[43]

In 1903 the number of such charity organizations in San Francisco increased to nine. There was so much support for them in the community that they often stayed in business for a relatively long period of time. One such organization was the Paoan Tang, which had apparently been in existence from the 1850s. Some of these organizations were even able to save a considerable amount of money. The energy and money that the living spent in carrying out the wishes of the dead reveals the importance the Chinese placed on the native land as the ultimate place of rest.

Ah Quin joined the "reverse migration" traffic once in 1867. But he showed no wish to return to his homeland even in his old age, and he remained in San Diego until his sudden death in a motorcycle accident in 1914. He was buried in the city's Mount Hope Cemetery. It remains unclear when or whether he made a decision to stay in America. Possibly he realized that his American journey would not be temporary as early as 1877, when he wrote of his parents: "I may not see them any more."[44] As we will see, the very next year he cut his queue, an important cultural symbol.

What is more, his constant efforts to improve his English suggest that he was preparing himself for a long-term career in America. We do not know when he began making such efforts, but his English handwriting already showed signs of considerable practice by 1877. One important reason for his keeping a diary primarily in English was to learn the language. In fact, Ah Quin's various writings leave no doubt that he had a much better command of Chinese than he did of English. The Chinese passages in the diary, which are more nuanced than the English parts, show that he could accurately describe complicated meanings and occurrences in his native language. They also show that his Chinese vocabulary was more sophisticated than his English one. This becomes even clearer in a glossary that he made late in the nineteenth century, in which he used multiword, sometimes quite elaborate, explanations in Chinese for English words. Many of the English words are rather rudimentary, such as "appearance," "disappearance," and "alcohol."[45]

We will discuss the issue of assimilation later. Suffice it to say that Ah Quin's language exercise did not alter his consciousness of cultural identity. This is not to deny the cultural significance of language acquisition in general. Living in an era of overt anti-Chinese racism, Ah Quin as well as many others learned English more in an attempt to benefit from its practical value than to gain social acceptance. His new language skills did not weaken his ties with Chinese people but rather enabled him to serve them—he worked as a court interpreter in cases involving Chinese and translated a book on assaying into Chinese.

The immigrants' way of life too bore the imprint of Old World traditions. One such tradition was Chinese medicine. Its practitioners used terms, recipes, and techniques derived from ancient classics.[46] They often claimed to have secret recipes that had been handed down by ancestors from generation to generation. Such claims indicate how much tradition was respected in the community.

In the eyes of white Americans the alien-looking Chinese drugstores presented another "interesting feature of the Chinese quarter in our American cities."[47] For them, Chinese medicine was something not only unfamiliar but also "mystified," offering concrete evidence of the "vast superiority of our system."[48] In an article on the subject, the Rev. A. W. Loomis made an elaborate list of medicines taken from the human body: "Hair—cut fine and used in plasters. . . . Teeth filings. Ears. Exuvia. Parings of finger and toe nails of pregnant women. . . . Blood. The placenta. The gall; and other things which cannot be written in the *Overland*."[49] There is no need to examine the subject from a medical point of view—what Loomis presented is not a medical discussion but a cultural message to the general public, a message about Chinese mysteriousness and inferiority.

For the immigrants themselves, however, the numerous Chinese doctors and drugstores in San Francisco and elsewhere provided a trusted and familiar alternative to Western medicine. Several huiguan presidents noted in 1876 that few Chinese would go to a Western hospital.[50] In 1875 only 68 of the 3,975 patients in the San Francisco City and County Hospital were Chinese.[51] This low percentage was the result of two factors. In seeking Western medicine, first, Chinese patients encountered not only unfamiliarity but also hostility. In fact, in the 1870s the city's health board passed a resolution in an attempt to close City and County Hospital to the Chinese population.[52] Second, by comparison, Chinese medicine was not only familiar but also simple, convenient, and inexpensive. As newspaper advertisements show, Chinese doctors and drugstores offered ready-made medicines that could be purchased by mail or in person. Writing about the popularity of non-Western medicine among the Chinese, Culin noted: "[When] ill they take one prescription after another, and drink quantities of unpalatable tea every night."[53] The Rev. A. W. Loomis reported in 1869: "There are in San Francisco a dozen or more establishments where Chinese medicines are prepared and sold, and business is said to be very profitable."[54]

The business was indeed so profitable that Chinese doctors were among San Francisco's rich and famous. One of them was Li Po Tai, reportedly one of the first Chinese medical experts in the United States. By 1870 the 42-year-old physician had already accumulated at least forty thousand dollars in real estate property and twelve hundred dollars in personal property.[55] It was believed that "The returns from his practice for many years before his death [in 1893] was amounted to seventy-five thousand dollars a year."[56] Located on Washington Street in the late 1870s and early 1880s, his office received a total of 150 to 300 Chinese and non-Chinese patients each day.

Ah Quin's diary again allows us to look at the general picture from the personal level. While in San Francisco the young Ah Quin was quite healthy, but his need for medical attention increased when he grew older. He preferred Chinese medicine over Western medicine for himself and for his family, though he used the latter occasionally. On March 24, 1891, when Sue (his wife) was sick, he wrote in the diary: "Tonight . . . her heart very bad. So I get a pill call[ed] in China Shiqiang Ball for her. It is good and fulfill cure her." Relieved by her recovery, he was able to "sleep much." At another time, when he was sick himself on a later date, he went with his friend Yan Row to a Chinese medical expert in the Wing Fung store, who felt his pulse before giving a prescription. Along with the medicine, Ah Quin took some Majiahong tea. He wrote about this experience in a long paragraph written completely in Chinese. Either he wanted to write in his native language because he was sick and it was easier, or else the special medical terms were too Chinese to be recorded in English.[57]

For less serious illnesses the Quins would take a dietary approach, eating special foods. On August 31, 1892, for example, Ah Quin wrote: "To day is [not] well the head and heart bother me. lay in bed all day and night just have some rice oyster soup," which he took again the next day.[58] In mid-July 1892, when Ah Quin was not feeling well, his wife cooked him Chinese ginseng for several days.

To fully appreciate the world of Ah Quin and his fellow immigrants and the significance of tradition therein, we must take a look at the political structure of Chinese America. Because this is a topic that Ah Quin did not cover in his private diary, we have to use other sources. And we have to digress from discussions of issues pertinent to Ah Quin's immediate surroundings.

Simply put, the highest power in "China in America" was held by people coming directly from China rather than by Chinese immigrants. The presidents of the powerful huiguan, first of all, were scholars chosen from their home districts in the Old World, who had passed the civil service examinations at different levels. Obviously a voluntary adoption of China's centuries-old method of selecting officials, this practice tells us that tradition served as the mandate that legitimated power.[59]

This practice started in the 1850s, according to William Hoy.[60] And it gradually became an established custom by the late nineteenth century. In the 1870s the presidents of all huiguan stayed on in San Francisco after their tenure, if their testimony before the 1876 California Senate Committee is to be believed.[61] Some were engaged in other activities at the same time. One of them, for instance, was the owner of a small business in San Francisco.[62] In subsequent years this custom of selecting huiguan presidents from China was institutionalized and written into the constitution of the Zhonghua Huiguan. From 1881 on, for example, all fourteen presidents of the Ningyang Huiguan were such scholars, and thirteen of them had earned high-level scholarly titles.[63] Gradually most of the chosen scholars came solely to serve as president, and returned to China afterwards.

Beginning in the mid-1880s the name of each selected huiguan president had to be reported to the Chinese embassy in Washington, D.C., and to the governor of Guangdong. This does not, however, signal the Chinese government's total control over the immigrant community. Rather it was an expedient measure that gave the presidents diplomat status for travel purposes so that their arrival would not be hampered by the exclusion laws. Each huiguan handled the selection of its president.

In 1903 Liang Qichao, who had been deeply influenced by Western ideas, found this custom highly disturbing and viewed it as an obstacle to reform and progress. "The strangest of all," he stated, "is that every huiguan has to choose a 'jingshi,' or a 'juren,' or a 'xiucai' as the president, which costs from 1,000 to 2,000 dollars every year."[64] What was more upsetting for Liang, was that "the chosen scholars, in their tenure of one, or two, or three years, can neither understand a word nor do anything but sit and eat. Often they would make arbitrary decisions and cruelly oppress the people. But all their countrymen . . . accept this fact without protest."[65]

While Liang may have been correct about the presidents' ignorance of American customs and language, his preoccupation with the Western idea of progress explains his disdain for the immigrant community's need and respect for tradition. Possessing various scholarly titles (as official acknowledgment of their knowledge in the classical Confucian learning), the huiguan presidents embodied Chinese cultural heritage. In Chinese San Francisco association with that heritage carried more weight than did familiarity with American society.

Ah Quin's Christianity and his knowledge of English were certainly great personal assets; they awarded him both access to the white American world and social and economic benefits: at church he met numerous white Americans, and his language skills opened opportunities for him to work as a labor recruiter and court interpreter. These personal resources, however, did not help Ah Quin ascend in the social order within the large Chinese community in San Francisco while he was there. Even if he had stayed there longer, the situation might not have been different. Lee Kant was another Chinese who had good English-language skills and established a close relationship with the white missionaries. Yet although Lee lived in Chinese San Francisco for many years he never became part of the power structure. Knowledge of white America and its language did not lead to a ticket to the core of power. People like Lee Kant wielded some social and economic clout as interpreters and as agents or representatives of American firms, but they were unable to compete with the scholars for political influence. In fact, among their compatriots they were "resented" more than "respected."[66] This helps explain why after moving to and settling down in San Diego Ah Quin was able to put his social resources to better use, and became the most influential man in the much smaller Chinese community there.[67]

As further evidence of the political importance of tradition, Chinese Americans welcomed the leadership role of the Chinese embassy in Washington and especially of the consulate in San Francisco—both established in 1878.[68] The immigrant community for years had longed for the Chinese government's protection. In 1868 the first Chinese mission headed by the American Anson Burlingame was well received by the Chinese upon its arrival in San Francisco.[69] At the Guangzhou Huiguan community leaders held a banquet to welcome the Chinese officials of the envoy. Music played, drums beat, and colorful decorations characterized the event. The festivities vividly reflected the joy and hope the visiting envoy brought to the community that had received little protection from the Qing government against anti-

Chinese discrimination. An antithetical poetic couplet hanging on the wall read: "For years of sojourning, we labored flowing clouds, the moon and stars without the blessing of his Majesty; Now meeting [the officials] in the foreign land, how can we not present celery and wine, together to share the affection for our country."[70]

The "blessing" referred to his Majesty's protection that had yet to come. The immigrants' wish for it grew stronger in the 1870s. In 1876 the huiguan presidents wrote to a Chinese official in Washington for help and advice in dealing with growing hostility.[71] In response, in a letter that was published in *The Oriental* the official suggested that they ask for a consulate in the city so that the Chinese there would not be mistreated as much as they had been before. He stated that the absence of a consulate was one of the "reasons why the Chinese are bullied."[72] The editors who decided to publish the official's letter apparently believed that it addressed concerns that were felt throughout the community.

News of the Qing Court's appointment of Chen Lanbin as minister to America quickly reached and brought hope to Chinese San Francisco even before it became official at the end of 1875. The Chinese expected that the Chinese officials would not only offer legal protection against outside discrimination but would also regulate internal affairs and curb lawlessness within the community. On September 8, 1875, *The Oriental* published a conversation between a Chinese and a white man who tried to find out "whether the Chinese wish to have the [Qing] officials here." "We Chinese people are eagerly waiting for the arrival of the officials day and night," the Chinese man told the white man. He went on to express his hope that they would bring peace and order to the community: "With the officials' presence all Chinese will obey the Imperial laws, and will not commit violence any more."[73]

Time would prove that the diplomats had limited power. Though expected to act as protectors, sometimes they were humiliated themselves. On April 7, 1886, for example, when minister Zhang Yinhuan first reached San Francisco, custom officials refused to allow him to land, giving the high-ranking official firsthand experience with racial discrimination. He was finally permitted to land after threatening to return to China immediately.[74]

Nevertheless, the immigrants' expectations were not totally unrealistic. All seven Chinese ministers between 1878 and 1905 regarded it as one of their main tasks to represent the interests of Chinese immigrants on various occasions.[75] A case in point is that of the aftermath of the 1885 massacre of 51 Chinese laborers working in the largest coal mines along the Union Pacific Railroad in Rock Springs, Wyoming—a massacre that shocked the entire nation.[76] Minister Zheng Zhaoru, a native of Xiangshan (later Zhongshan) County, was actively involved in the investigation of the massacre and in seeking justice. Although the culprits were never punished and the U.S. government agreed only to pay some monetary compensation, Chinese Americans appreciated Zheng's efforts. A book documenting those efforts was published and sold in San Francisco's Chinatown, publicizing them within the community. Zheng's successor, Zhang Yinhuan, received instructions from his superior in China within days of his arrival in Washington to continue what was left unfinished regarding the 1885 massacre.

We must not forget the differences between the officials and immigrants in terms of class background and perspective. Zheng Zhaoru, for example, strongly advocated the idea that China itself should restrict immigration, a policy of self-restraint that did not reflect the interests and wishes of common immigrants and that was unpopular both in Chinese America and in the emigrant communities.[77] But in dealing with outside hostility, Chinese immigrants saw an important ally in the officials and eagerly sought their support. In 1900, for instance, huiguan leaders asked Minister Wu Tingfang to organize a collective protest against discrimination.[78]

The ministers also found themselves playing the role of mediators at times of internal conflict, especially during the violent tong wars. They saw that role as closely related to their mission to protect the immigrants against discrimination. In response to a bloody tong war in Chinatown in 1886, Zhang Yinhuan issued an order to the community, declaring: "It is my responsibility to protect the Chinese. In order for the Chinese not to be mistreated by non-Chinese, however, the Chinese have to live peacefully with one another."[79] He then promised to contact local officials in China to find ways to punish unrepentant culprits. The assistance of local authorities in China was a powerful weapon that the ministers resorted to using quite often.

The consulate general in San Francisco was more closely involved in Chinese San Francisco's affairs than was the embassy. The former was actively engaged in the struggle against anti-Chinese discrimination. For that purpose it hired as vice consul an American lawyer named Frederick A. Bee, who had defended Chinese miners in El Dorado County as early as 1855 and who appeared at the 1876 congressional hearing as the attorney for the Zhonghua Huiguan. In September 1885 Minister Zheng Zhaoru sent him to Rock Springs to collect evidence about the massacre from white Americans, while two Chinese officials gathered information from their compatriots.[80]

Not all consulate officials were dispatched by the Chinese government from China. Sometimes the consulate employed ex-huiguan leaders, which enhanced its effectiveness in dealing with community affairs. In 1888, for instance, two such officials came to work for the consulate. In approving their employment a senior embassy official especially praised one candidate for his discipline and elegant handwriting (a critical criterion for judging a scholar-statesman) and pointed out: "In the Gold Mountain, where Chinese and foreigners live together . . . his knowledge of the people and place [of Chinese San Francisco] can help to resolve disputes."[81]

Consulate officials were also directly involved in matters concerning the welfare of the community. A case in point is the building of a Chinese hospital that would provide free service for all.[82] Before the establishment of the consulate, Chinese San Franciscans had health agencies. In 1870, for example, there was the Chinese Asylum on Pine Street with eleven people on staff, including two doctors and a cook. Most of the patients were laborers.[83] Understanding the difficulties that the Chinese had in obtaining adequate medical care, the consul general, together with the Zhonghua Huiguan, started to collect money to build a Chinese hospital. In 1888 he instructed huiguan officials involved in the project to coordinate closely with one another without dodging responsibilities.[84] A piece of land was purchased outside Chinatown in the name of the consul general. But the city forbade the subsequent building plan because of objections to the sole use of Chinese medicine. In 1899 the consulate general rekindled the aborted project and chose a new site on Sacramento Street. It not only mobilized community resources but also tried to enlist support from white San Franciscans. At a meeting held inside the consulate general a charitable society was formed for fund-raising. Consul General Ho Yow was elected chairman of the Chinese committee, and John Fryer of the University of California was elected president of the society.[85]

From time to time the consulate general attempted to regulate social behavior. By the beginning of the twentieth century organized tours profited from the staged dirtiness and immorality that tarnished Chinatown's image. In June 1905 the consul general forbade Chinese participation in such tours, along with certain kinds of public behavior: "No Chinese tour guides are allowed to show Westerners [Chinese] women with bound feet; no Chinese tour guides are allowed to show Westerners opium dens and whore houses; no Chinese women are allowed to smoke cigarettes in theatres; and all Chinese men and women must wear socks to go out on the street."[86]

With the authority to approve the board members for the Zhonghua Huiguan, the consulate general stood at the top of the political structure of Chinese San Francisco. A photograph of the consulate officials and the huiguan presidents, taken during the Chinese New Year celebration of 1902, vividly illustrates the hierarchy of Chinese San Francisco: sitting right in the middle is the consul general.[87]

New World Existence

Earlier, we took a look at different types of economic interactions that occurred between Chinese and non-Chinese San Franciscans. Chinese and non-Chinese also interacted in noneconomic settings. Ah Quin for one encountered white Americans of various backgrounds and knew some of them fairly well. Occasionally, a "big" name was dropped in his address notes. The name "Geo. Bruce Cortelyou" appears there twice. In one place he noted: "President Roosevelt Point him as the Secretary of the Department of Commerce and Labor." No evidence suggests that Ah Quin personally knew or had met George B. Cortelyou, who served as secretary of commerce and labor between 1903 and 1904. But Ah Quin's notes give us a sense of the extent of his awareness of events in the dominant society late in his life. Having associated with white Americans long enough, he had not only acquired work and language skills but also had learned some of their habits. He occasionally drank coffee. And during his San Diego years he also acquired a drinking problem. Problems with alcohol consumption were seldom associated with the Chinese at the time.

When he lived among white Americans Ah Quin felt and sometimes even bowed to the pressure to alter his Chinese-ness. In his diary he recorded in some detail the moment he had his queue cut by a white man named E. J. Gourley in June 1878. It was a conscious act of acculturation on the part of a young Chinese eager to be accepted by others around him. Of his transformed appearance Ah Quin wrote: "It is just look like the white people not like our china [Chinese people] any more." He carefully watched the reactions of the white men he tried to please: "Gourley and Mr. A. K. Thompson . . . [were] very glad and laugh[ed] at me."[88] He gave a few hairs to them, but he saved the rest instead of throwing it away. He wanted to "remember it in my life." If this act signals a cultural concession, it is only a partial one. Moreover, he left intact for quite some time another cultural marker, his Chinese-style attire, even though he knew it invited public attention. In a report of Ah Quin's return to San Diego with his bride the *San Diego Union* commented that although they were both Christians they still wore Chinese-style garb.[89]

Apparently, while Ah Quin's story contains much evidence of acculturation or behavioral adaptation, overall it is not one of "assimilation" as the concept was defined in nineteenth-century white America. His lifestyle offers plenty of insights into this issue. While he learned to cook non-Chinese food for white Americans to make a living, for example, he always preferred Chinese food himself. Moreover, his relations with white Americans were formed, for the most part, out of necessity and were characterized by striking formality. Whenever Ah Quin mentioned the name of a white person, he would attach a "Mr.," "Mrs.," or "Rev." Such appellations clearly mark the social distance separating them, a distance created by the institutionalized racial hierarchy in a society that demanded that nonwhites defer to members of the white race. In the accepted social lexicon of the time, by comparison, Chinese immigrant men were called "boys" or "Chinamen"—words that clearly indicated their position in that hierarchy. In his memoir, Walter Bellon, an official of San Diego's health department early in the twentieth century, recalled that the police chief described Ah Quin as "the finest Chinaman I have ever known."[90] The seemingly condescending tone of this description reminds us that the police chief's relationship with Ah Quin was anything but one between equals.

Indeed, little evidence points to any personal or intimate relationship that took place on an equal basis between Ah Quin and his non-Chinese acquaintances—if we exclude the brief moments he bought in white brothels. Despite his various encounters with whites, he lived in the Chinese community and shared his social life with his fellow Chinese. In reference to his Chinese friends, instead of a "Mr.," he often wrote an "Ah," a name prefix commonly used in South China. The gazetteer of Panyu explained that local people applied it to family members such as grandparents, parents, siblings, and children.[91] In addition, it was also used among friends. Indeed, the things that Ah Quin did together with his Chinese friends were usually of the most personal and private nature. It is with them, rather than with his white acquaintances, that he went to Chinese theaters, had quick and inexpensive meals in Chinese restaurants, visited houses of prostitution, and played Chinese games.

Nothing is more private than moments of relaxation. While in San Francisco Ah Quin shared many such moments with his Chinese friends, usually in a small room. Their relationship was so close that after one tiring work day Ah Quin slept in the same bed with his friend, Tom Chin.[92] Later, when he was fairly well established as a businessman in San Diego he continued to rest in friends' places when he was out of town. During a business trip to Los Angeles in December 1884, for instance, he went to Chinese theaters and restaurants and spent the night with his Chinese friends.[93] Apparently his way of life did not change much, despite his newfound social and geographical mobility.

Indeed, socializing with his friends revealed his essential Chinese-ness. Earlier in his life Ah Quin displayed an eagerness to rekindle old friendships during the first few days of his return to San Francisco from a non-Chinese environment: between December 12 and 15, 1878, he spent almost all his time visiting friends and Chinese theaters. Every single day Ah Quin kept himself busy until after midnight.

Thereafter, Ah Quin's Christianity, which had once been ardent, gradually waned. He never lost his faith entirely—in San Diego he continued to attend a Presbyterian church between D and Eighth Streets. If his diary is any indication, however, Christianity ceased to occupy the same central position in his life that it had during his lonely Alaska years. In his diary entries of later years, descriptions of his mundane interactions with other Chinese and of business and family matters replace the lengthy biblical citations and records of his church activities that had filled it earlier. To understand such everyday matters that diverted his attention and time away from religion, let us take a look at one day (August 15, 1891) in Ah Quin's life.

After getting up at around 8:00 A.M. and having his breakfast after 9:00 A.M. he spent the rest of the morning building a fence in order to prevent Wong Hai (his servant at the time) from going to see Gui Lon, the woman next door. Then he went to get $30 from the bank for a Chinese with whom Ah Quin was conducting a business transaction. After supper at 4:14 P.M. he played Chinese chess with a friend until 7:10 P.M. There were other things occupying his day as well. At some point he decided to fire Chin Quon, whom he thought was lazy. At noon his wife went to see a Chinese woman, Tam Ung, "and ask her who is [has] told a lie against" her. This incident clearly involved a number of people, including Ah Quin himself. Speaking of another man who was involved, Ah Quin wrote in his diary: "I may [act] against him hard."[94]

The preceding diary entry portrays a Chinese living, working, socializing, and quarreling with others in the community. Ah Quin's world was not confined to one locale even after he settled down in San Diego. Its boundaries were defined socially, rather than geographically, by his connections with his relatives, friends, and other kinds of associates on both sides of the Pacific Ocean. Earlier we saw his connections in the emigrant region. Within the United States Ah Quin maintained regular contact with many compatriots elsewhere. The most frequently mentioned places in his documents are within California—home to a majority of the Chinese American population at the time—including Santa Barbara, San Francisco, San Diego, Los Angeles, and San Bernardino. Occasionally he would receive letters from friends in places outside California, such as Prescott, Arizona. And his address notes include some people in New York City, Seattle, Portland, St. Louis, and so on.

While in most cases we do not know the exact nature of Ah Quin's relations with these people, it is clear that he knew some of them quite well. In his address notes a person named Tanman is recorded as being with the Sam Wing and Thom firm at 211 South Wyoming St., Butte, Montana. Next to this name and address Ah Quin noted in Chinese that Tanman had lost his identification certificate that he had received in San Diego earlier. In the same place Ah Quin also wrote down the certificate number: 101465. Evidently, Ah Quin had helped him.

To understand the expanse of Chinese Americans' world one must recognize their physical mobility. Like many others, Ah Quin was on the move for years. He lived in a number of places, including Seattle, a mining camp in Alaska, Santa Barbara, and San Francisco before he finally settled down in San Diego. Even during his San Diego years he continued to make trips to other cities. Opportunities to work for American businesses, ranging from railroad companies to various factories, constituted a major source of physical mobility for many Chinese laborers. Later, when such opportunities decreased as a result of discrimination, more and more of them traveled to work in major Chinese communities.

Regular listings in Chinese newspapers of ships and, later, trains going between San Francisco and other cities offer additional evidence of the mobility of Chinese immigrants. It is evident that many journeyed between urbanized Chinese communities. In the 1870s ships went from San Francisco to Stockton daily, and three ships left for Sacramento every week.[95] Known among Chinese immigrants as "the second city" and "the third city" respectively, both cities had a sizeable Chinese population. By the beginning of the twentieth century the train had become the major means of transportation for Chinese travelers, as we can tell from the detailed schedules listed in Chinese newspapers.

Time

Immigrants shared cultural traditions that played a more fundamental role than physical mobility in linking their lives and marking the boundaries of their world. As is exemplified by their distinctive conception of time, such traditions afforded them a common framework in which to organize their own lives and understand one another's experiences. We must first note that the word "time" refers to social time, marked and measured by reference points in the calendar system. Calendar systems are historically and culturally constructed to reflect a particular context. The ancient Egyptian calendar, for instance, evolved in a world centered around the flow of the Nile. What is more, a calendar can exist as a mirror and record of culture, as the Jewish and the Islamic calendars show. A nation's calendar helps to maintain memories of its shared heritage. Aware of the significance of calendar systems, the French Revolutionaries designed one of their own, hoping both to "provide a priori frame of reference for all possible memory" and to "open a new book to history."[96]

The old Chinese calendar remained in extensive use in nineteenth-century Chinese America. Although immigrants followed the Western calendar when participating in the American economy, they retained their own calendar to mark the date and punctuate their daily life in their own way.[97] In so doing they exercised some control over their lives.

Day after day, year after year, Ah Quin never forgot to indicate the corresponding Chinese dates (including the day, season, and year) for the Western ones already printed in the notebooks in which he kept his diaries. This demonstrates his awareness of the differences between the two calendar systems, which represented two different ways of life. Community events too were marked according to the Chinese calendar during this period. On June 10, 1854, in announcing the opening of a missionary church, *The Golden Hills' News* informed its Chinese audience that the first sermon would start "at one o'clock on Chinese tenth day of the fifth month." In October 1876 *The Oriental* instructed the community to keep clean and behave properly because a congressional committee on Chinese immigration would arrive in San Francisco "on the eighteenth day of this month, that is," the news report made it clearer to its Chinese audience, "on Chinese third day of the ninth month."[98] Moreover, ship and train schedules posted in the Chinese newspapers were also announced using Chinese dates.

The Chinese calendar served to remind immigrants of their common traditions that had served as markers of seasonal and yearly cycles. Let us take a look at the celebration of the Chinese New Year, the most important traditional holiday. In 1878, in a remote mining camp, Ah Quin celebrated it and remembered his family and friends. This holiday season also brought many immigrants from remote areas to gather in large Chinese communities. The Rev. A. W. Loomis observed: "Our cities and towns which have Chinese streets will have a much larger population at these seasons . . . because all who can be spared, leave the ranch and the lonely mining camp to mingle with the multitudes around the places of amusement."[99]

The Chinese lunar calendar enabled immigrants to stay in touch with activities and changes taking place in China. The lunar year is evenly divided into 24 seasonal periods, marking times to plant and to harvest and times for remembrance and joyful celebrations. It also reminded Chinese Americans of the reigning emperor, for the year in the Chinese calendar was named after him.

As a fundamental part of immigrant culture, the calendar carried Chinese world views. To put this complicated matter in rather simplistic terms, according to the Ganzhi system in the Chinese calendar system, time moved in cycles—in sixty- and twelve-year units. These cycles were supposed to contain an inner order that could explain and even predict the laws governing the motion of the universe and historical changes. They were also believed to predestine the fate of the individual, as a non-Chinese observed: "There is a natural connection in the Chinese mind between the birth of the year and the birth of the man."[100]

Chinese San Franciscans carefully selected certain "lucky days" (*jiri* in Chinese) identified by the lunar calendar on which to open new businesses and to hold other important events like weddings and funerals. Many must have simply respected the practice as a time-honored tradition. After all, few claimed to have a systematic understanding of its complicated structure and deeper significance.

The fortune-tellers did, however. They openly made such claims and were ready to transmit their knowledge to those willing to pay a fair price. Visitors to Chinatown could easily spot a fortune-teller on a street corner. His magic tools often included nothing more than a stool, a little table, and a few cards. In this kind of important business that involved people's futures, tradition appeared again as a source of authority and credibility. After spending seven years in China to perfect his expertise, a fortune-teller named Du Rongbin proclaimed that his skills were now even better than they had been before.[101] A good old family name was also helpful. The Rev. A. W. Loomis wrote that one fortune-teller "proclaimed himself a scion of the family of the renowned Shiu Hong Chit, and divine reckoner by the 'eight diagrams' of man's destiny."[102] Moreover, the fortune-tellers often bragged of being well versed in Confucian Learning—another significant tradition. Loomis noted: "The Book of Changes . . . is held in great veneration for its antiquity and its occult wisdom, which is supposed to be contained in its mystic lines."[103]

Those living outside San Francisco could also benefit from the expertise of these fortune-tellers if they sent their request along with their birth information. A group of people particularly interested in fortune-telling were the gamblers who, as Culin wrote, "are more superstitious than the mass of their countrymen."[104] In a newspaper advertisement for a fortune-teller, a testimonial that allegedly came from a gambler claimed that he had won more than ten thousand dollars by following the fortune-teller's advice.[105]

Furthermore, the Chinese calendar became a basis on which to determine the timing of public events. In 1905 the Zhonghua Huiguan chose an "auspicious day" of the sixth month to issue a public announcement urging all of Chinese America to participate in the global protest against America's anti-Chinese policy.[106] The new Chinese Hospital announced its opening on March 1, 1900, another "lucky day."[107]

A Year in Ah Quin's Life: 1892

We have examined various aspects of Ah Quin's experience in a larger social context. Let us conclude the discussion of his world by taking a focused look at a year in his life. To do so we will use the 1892 diary that has recently resurfaced.[108] At that time, about three decades after his arrival in America, he owned a family store and had investments in a couple of other businesses. In 1892 he did not travel long distances but stayed in touch through correspondence with friends in other Chinese American communities as well as in China.

Indicative of his lifestyle throughout his San Diego years, Ah Quin's attention was centered on his business and on various family and community affairs. Occasionally he found time for church services. He spent much of his leisure time with his Chinese friends. Playing Chinese chess with friends remained a favorite pastime, as we can see from the numerous entries throughout the 1892 diary. April 3 was a typical day for him. It was a Sunday and, as Ah Quin noted, it also was the Qingming holiday (traditionally a time to sweep the graves of loved ones). With no family graves to visit he celebrated the holiday in his own way. He did not go to church but stayed home with his family until 2:00 P.M. He then went to play chess with several different friends until after 6:00 P.M., when he proceeded to see a sick friend named Tam Dip and "talk to him [for] more than one hour."

Ah Quin continued to engage in various business dealings with white Americans. On the Fourth of July he worked the whole day and sold all his firecrackers for $111, turning this American holiday into a profitable day. But in general, as he noted more than once, 1892 was not a good year, economically speaking. On July 14 he wrote: " . . . now so poor time, the money is very poor to make."

He remained a busy man in the Chinese community, participating in funerals and celebrations of births and mediating between parties involved in disputes. He acted as an interpreter when fellow Chinese got into trouble with the authorities. As a community leader he witnessed and recorded incidents of harassment that the Chinese suffered. On June 16, for example, he noted that the police had forced their way into a room to arrest a Chinese man.[109]

In his journal Ah Quin devoted much space to food (Chinese food), revealing its importance in his social life and family life. Besides the regular three daily meals, he loved to have what he called an "extra supper" late at night at home, sometimes with friends. On January 28, for instance, he wrote: "Today is very busy because our end [of] the year of [the Emperor] Quong Shiu 17th year." He invited five people, including a druggist working in his store, to have a New Year's Eve dinner, which was followed by an extra supper. Quite often he cooked for the family.

Family occupied an important place in his life. He was a loving father to his children, accompanying them to school and taking care of them when they were sick. He shared with his wife the responsibility of caring for their "darling" Lily (born in 1891). When his wife was sick Ah Quin stayed home to wash diapers.

After marrying Ah Quin in 1881 at the age of about twenty, Sue Leong appeared in numerous entries in his diary.[110] A devoted spouse, she cooked and did many other things for her husband. Numerous incidents show that she was an independent-minded and strong woman. She played a vital role not only in raising the children but also in managing the family business. On January 20 Ah Quin wrote that because Sue was sick he had to stay "all the afternoon in front store" to "copy bills and watch" and even had supper there. At one time Ah Quin borrowed $50 from Sue, suggesting that she even had some Wnancial independence. Sue had her own friends, sometimes in spite of Ah Quin's objection. One of them was a woman named Chy Doy whom Ah Quin resented greatly because she had married twice. Thousands of miles and nearly three decades away from his native community, Ah Quin apparently still believed in the old cult of female chastity so explicitly expressed in the local gazetteers that we have seen.

Ah Quin's ideas about gender roles constituted a source of disharmony in the family. In the summer a big dispute broke out between the couple concerning a woman named Wong Hi, whom Ah Quin called first a servant and later an adopted daughter—available data, including family photos and descendants' memories, contain no evidence that she was an actual family member. On June 5 Ah Quin wrote in the diary that Sue became very upset when she realized that Ah Quin was unwilling to allow Wong Hi to marry. She even suspected that he desired to have Wong Hi as his second wife, an accusation that Ah Quin denied. For the whole day she was in a bad mood and made him do "much work." Word must have subsequently gone out that Wong Hi was available, because early in July a couple came from Los Angeles as matchmakers. Ah Quin was not at all thrilled about their arrival and did not even want to talk to them. Yet it was inevitable that Wong Hi would marry. On July 17 a man named Wong Sing Yuen from Los Angeles showed up and met briefly with Wong Hi in the afternoon. Everything went so well that an engagement ceremony took place at dinnertime.

But the issue continued to bother Ah Quin and his wife. Ah Quin wrote on August 19: "My wife always quarrel about Wong Hi." The dispute upset him so much that he did not eat anything the entire day. Wong Hi married on August 17. A fairly large crowd attended the wedding, and Sue passed "the wedding cake to all," marking the end of an intriguing, stormy episode in their lives.

In following Ah Quin's footsteps we have sometimes ventured out of San Francisco. He was one of many short-term Chinese San Franciscans who eventually left to pursue opportunities elsewhere. Ah Quin is not to be considered a prototypical Chinese immigrant. In comparison with many others he made more effort to adapt and sometimes even consciously to acculturate. And after making a trip back to China in the early years he stayed in America for the rest of his life. Yet in so many ways he lived in a trans-Pacific world shared by his compatriots, who maintained various ties to their native land while striving to build communities in America. Ah Quin decided to settle in the United States permanently from very early on, yet he remained Chinese in outlook, in his social and personal life, and in his taste for food. He upheld his ties to China and to other Chinese American communities. Most of all, he maintained his cultural identity, as we will see in the next chapter.

FIVE

Collective Identity

In an 1870 article S. Andrews recalled an earlier encounter with a Chinese laundryman in a San Francisco hotel: "John! John! O John!" he called loudly, only to be ignored. Andrews then ran toward him and said: "I want you to do some washing for me, John." " 'Me not John,' " the laundryman replied firmly. Andrews remembered that moment well: "He answered with some dignity, handing me his card, on which I read, 'Hop Long,' "[1] At the time white Americans called all Chinese "indiscriminately by the easy euphonious appellation of 'John.' "[2] Clearly, Hop Long refused the insulting appellation and asserted his own identity.

This chapter deals with the cultural identity of Chinese immigrants. It was not merely oppositional, namely, a reaction to racial oppression, but was based on both memory of the past and experience in the present. Although their political or economic interests were not necessarily similar, that identity embodied a meaningful and tangible element of coherence in their heritage and outlook as well as their daily lives.

Identity is contextual and changes as people's physical, social, and mental circumstances alter. The cultural identity of the Chinese was not static. Yet we must resist the temptation to overstate its fluidity. Insofar as it was a consciousness that dwelled in the minds of the immigrants, it had a significant degree of stability. This is simply because, first of all, the physical arrival of the immigrants in the New World did not suddenly erase rich and powerful memories of experiences and social relations formed in the Old. Erasing such memories was more difficult than changing their class status. For the immigrants, moreover, their Chinese identity was more a social reality than a personal choice. The freedom of individual Chinese to "choose" their cultural identity was significantly constrained by how others saw them. A young Chinese man could decide to abandon everything Chinese in his consciousness and outward appearance, but in either his own communities or in the anti-Chinese white society he still would not become "American" as it was defined by the dominant blocs at the time. Such blocs and others who aspired to join them used the notion of "American" primarily as a political weapon of exclusion. In the public discourse, especially in discussions of Chinese immigration, these groups articulated what the concept did not include, instead of explicating what it did.

Scholars of American immigration have tended to view ethnic (national) consciousness as basically a product of the New World environment that transformed the newcomers "from immigrants to ethnics."[3] In a study based on European immigration, Oscar Handlin points out the immigrants' lack of national identity in that they "defined themselves rather by the place of their birth, the village, or else by the provincial region that shared dialect and custom."[4] Suggesting that in the New World persistent regionalism remained an obstacle to the development of a sense of nationality, Rudolph Vecoli writes of Italians in Chicago: "The experience of emigration did not create a sense of nationality among the Italians strong enough to submerge their parochialism."[5]

But immigrants from Guangdong did not have to come to America to become "Chinese." Instead of being an American invention, the consciousness of their nationality was rooted in strong memories of the national history and in the cultural traditions that Cantonese people had shared with others in China for centuries. Such a culturally defined awareness of nationality laid the basis for the political nationalism that emerged later. Like Vecoli's Contadini in Chicago, Chinese immigrants maintained strong parochial sensibilities. Yet their parochialism coexisted with national identity, which was incarnated in numerous Chinese cultural symbols, such as their manner of dressing and the queue. Similarly, many of the thriving old religious practices, which embodied immigrants' resistance to the efforts of Christian missionaries to acculturate them, were also long-standing national traditions in China.[6]

Undoubtedly the immigrants did not remain unchanged in the New World. Besides acquiring new work and language skills and picking up new habits and hobbies, many also developed an attachment to America over time. For them it existed not only as a job market but also as a home to their communities. This attachment explains why thousands of people wanted to come back to the United States after their return trip to China. Chinese society increasingly recognized the American-ness of the immigrants. Local residents in Guangdong Province called them *Jinshanke*, meaning "Gold Mountaineers" or simply "people who migrated to the Gold Mountain."

In the American context, however, it was their "Chinese-ness" that was emphasized. We must recognize that Chinese immigrants lived in circumstances different from our own and must try to avoid reading today's identity politics into their situations. The cultural identity of these early immigrants was shaped by—and enables us to understand—the dialectical relationship between past memories and present experiences, between historical continuity and change, and between New World conditions and Old World ties. Formed in China, the immigrants' consciousness of their Chinese-ness was, simply put, reinforced by New World conditions, including hostility.

Within Chinese America during this period, it is clear that the varying degrees of cultural adaptation of individual Chinese did not translate into an articulated, collective awareness of being "Chinese American"—a term and a consciousness that began to gain prevalence after World War II. This by no means suggests that the immigrants were not American. Recent scholarship has shown how integral and central the experiences of early Chinese immigrants were to American history, socioeconomically, politically, and legally. What I am trying to suggest is that we need to recognize the vital differences in sensibilities and in the dynamics and perimeter of racial politics between their times and ours.

Collectively, the community maintained its cultural Chinese identity, an identity that served to provide coherence, a sense of direction, and a framework in which to comprehend life in the United States. That identity did not contradict the desire of Chinese Americans to obtain the rights that offered citizenship or membership in society. For them that membership was closely and dialectically related to their country of origin. As many came to realize, they needed support from China, and they had to help build a stronger China in order to attain American constitutional rights. For these reasons the boundaries of Chinese Americans' group identity shifted over the years, but it never collapsed completely during the period under discussion. It was an identity that Chinese Americans not only held dear in their hearts but that they also often asserted openly and proudly.

Social Relations, Memory, and Identity

Instead of a monolithic group consciousness, Chinese Americans had a multitude of identities that existed at different levels in different contexts. Within the immigrant community individuals displayed their strong parochialism by organizing themselves into various associations, resurrecting Old World social relations on the basis of geographical, dialectal, and kinship affiliations.[7] The most significant social organizations, the huiguan, were based primarily on geographical origins, embodying the immigrants' continued attachment to their native communities. The Sanyi (three-county) and Siyi (four-county) Huiguan were both organized by people from neighboring counties, reflecting in part their linguistic unity within the Sanyi and Siyi areas, respectively. Huiguan affiliation became a fundamental part of an individual's identification.

That affiliation was so important that it was carried on to the grave. The inscription on each Chinese tomb specified the home village and county of the dead, as a journalist reported in 1850.[8] Deceased members of the same huiguan were buried together in America before being shipped back to China. The Rev. A. W. Loomis wrote in the 1860s: "The Chinese spirits at Lone Mountain [cemetery] appear to be as clannish as are their surviving relatives in the city; for the dead of the different companies lie in separate enclosures."[9] Years later a visitor to Lone Mountain reported that "the lots used by the different Chinese companies for interment, are each surrounded by a common board or picket fence and at the entrance a sort of canopy is erected, under which is the sign or name of the company."[10] In 1898 the Zhonghua Huiguan bought 40 acres of land outside San Francisco as a cemetery and divided it among individual huiguan. The Sanyi Huiguan issued regulations concerning the use of its allotment, and the first clause stipulated: "Before burying a deceased member, [one] must obtain a certificate from the huiguan, clearly fill it out, and put it in the coffin."[11]

The huiguan reflected complex and often interwoven social relations among the immigrants. The Hehe Huiguan was an association of natives of Xinning County, but only for those with the family name "Yu." Clan affiliation represented another important social relationship. Clan or sur-name associations flourished in Chinese San Francisco. By the early twenti-eth century there were more than thirty of them.[12] Clan associations had their own source of income as well as their own buildings. Common ances-try served as their foundations. When the clan associations rebuilt their headquarters following the 1906 earthquake, their first priority was to restore the shrine for the ancestors. The clans constituted the basic supporting units of the huiguan. Key huiguan positions often rotated among the most power-ful clans.

Names served as important markers of identification. While the last name indicated clan membership, the usually two-character first name contained a character as index to the person's generational status within the clan. Therefore, although census takers and immigration officials often changed the order of the immigrants' names, the latter always kept and used their Chinese names within the community. It is worth noting that as the census and other sources show, in the early years few immigrants used non-Chinese first names. Such names gradually gained currency among American-born Chinese. But all had Chinese names at the same time.[13]

Epitomized by the clan associations and the huiguan, parochialism did not destroy but rather coexisted with the immigrants' national conscious-ness. Nothing more clearly symbolized the harmonious coexistence of local-ism and nationalism than the fluttering of the Chinese national flag, the Yellow Dragon Flag, over the huiguan buildings.[14] I have asserted that their national identity was not an American development. Let us now briefly dis-cuss the complicated issue of nationalism in Chinese history.

Western China scholars have long viewed the formation of the Chinese nation and Chinese nationalism as a relatively recent phenomenon, a view that has been increasingly challenged in recent years.[15] Michael Ng-Quinn convincingly shows that national identity existed in premodern China.[16] Using evidence from Chinese history, Prasenjit Duara offers an insightful criticism of the tendency to emphasize the modernity of nationalism and na-tional consciousness among students of nationalism in general and histori-ans of China in particular.[17]

Much evidence points to the existence of a national culture that had over-come the barriers of dialects and physical distance to encompass the emigrant region. Linguistically, first of all, while there were numerous dialects in Guangdong and other parts of China, their written form was all the same— a written language that has been universally used all over China since the Qing Dynasty (221–207 B.C.).

Moreover, as we will discuss further later, many customs, traditions, and cultural icons that the immigrants brought from their home districts repre- sented the national Chinese culture, rather than local culture. Among them was the dragon. For centuries prior to its appearance on the first Chinese na- tional flag, it had been a divine symbol of the Chinese nation in Chinese mythology and folklore, and of the paramount power of the emperor. It re- mained a powerful cultural symbol among Chinese Americans, who believed it protected the dead.[18] This cultural symbol also constantly featured in holi- day parades.

Most important of all, the Chinese consciousness of immigrants from Guangdong came from enduring memories of the national past. It is im- portant to remember that the ancestors of a majority of Cantonese people began to migrate to Guangdong from the north during the Song Dynasty (960–1279). Memories of their families' pre-migration history had been kept alive in carefully preserved genealogies, a number of which found their way to San Francisco. In one such genealogy dated 1835, the Lu family from Dunhe village of Xiangshan County traced its roots to the fourth century B.C. in Henan Province of central China.[19]

The immigrants remembered the history not only of the family but also of the nation, as is best illustrated by the federation of the Liu, Guan, Zhang, and Zhao clans. These clans came together because they claimed to be the descendants of Liu Bei, Guan Yu (also known as Guan Gong), Zhang Fei, and Zhao Yun, historical figures who lived during the Epoch of the Three Kingdoms (A.D. 220–365). Their legendary bravery and unfaltering loyalty to one another had long been a familiar story in China. Contemporaries like Minister Zhang Yinhuan who visited Chinatown noticed its popularity there. The story also remained a constant motif of historical plays staged in the Chinese theaters. As early as 1852, when the first Chinese troupe per- formed in San Francisco, its opening program included one part about Guan Gong.

Special terms in the Chinese language help us to reconstruct the immi- grants' sense of national identity. From the very beginning of Chinese im- migration they called themselves "*tang* people." One of the oldest terms designating the Chinese and China, "tang" is derived from the term "Tang Dynasty" (618–907), a glorious period in Chinese history. Kept in use for centuries in Guangdong, the word "tang" retained and revealed the Cantonese people's long-standing consciousness of their Chinese-ness. In the language of the immigrants, therefore, "going back to China" was "hui [return to] tang." And they used the term *"tangren"* (the people of China) to designate themselves. Sacramento Street, the center of San Francisco's Chinatown in its early years, was named Tangren Jie, meaning "the street of Chinese People." "Tangren Jie" has since become the synonym for "Chinatown" among Chinese in the United States.

Construction of "the self" is usually connected with that of "the other." On many occasions, tang and fan (barbarian) were used together. A newspaper published in San Francisco in the late nineteenth century, for example, was called the "Tang-Fan" Newspaper. The combined use of those two characters reveals not only early Chinese immigrants' sense of identity but also their understanding of the historical location of their physical being: they were Chinese people in the land of the fan. In light of the previous discussion, it is easy to comprehend why Ah Quin referred to China as "my own country" in his diary.[20]

The New World's new environment, especially the existence of racial antagonism there, undoubtedly enhanced Chinese immigrants' national awareness. The formation of the Zhonghua Huiguan that transcended old ancestral and geographical affiliations was largely a response to the new conditions. The numerous public documents it issued in protest against anti-Chinese racism used terms such as "our Chinese people" or "our countrymen" in reference to Chinese immigrants.[21] In a statement made in 1877 the Zhonghua Huiguan reminded Congress that America and China had the respective obligation to treat fairly "our people resident here" and "your people resident in China."[22] The boundaries between "we" and "you" were clearly marked.

The Christian Church vs. the "Heathen" Temples

The question of assimilation that featured so prominently in the anti-Chinese rhetoric was never a substantive issue for the exclusionists. In 1888, when President Cleveland signed another exclusion act, he declared in a statement to Congress: "The experiment of blending the social habits and mutual race idiosyncrasies of the Chinese laboring classes with these of the great body of the people of the United States has been proved . . . to be in every sense unwise, impolitic, and injurious."[23] Protestant missionaries were among the few in California who attempted to acculturate the Chinese. Such attempts met strong resistance because despite all the missionaries' good intentions the Chinese nonetheless saw them as part of the oppressive society. Resistance also derived from rich Chinese religious traditions. In most cases such traditions had been national rather than local practices in China.

The missionaries started their work early in the 1850s, and for them Chinese San Francisco was of "central" importance.[24] In November 1853 the Presbyterian Rev. William Speer opened the first Chinese mission with only four members.[25] In 1868 the Rev. Otis Gibson established a Methodist Episcopal mission. Around 1870 two other missions appeared: a Congregational mission established by the Rev. W. C. Pond and a Baptist mission established by the Rev. John Francis. During the second half of the nineteenth century numerous missions were also established in other cities throughout California, including Sacramento, Santa Barbara, San Diego, Alameda, Oakland, Los Angeles, and Stockton.

The battle that the missionaries were engaged in was not simply about saving souls. They saw it also as a cultural battle between two divergent ways of life and two different races. In the minds of white Americans Chinese immigration signified the meeting of two civilizations. It marked "the sudden commixture of races" and the "contact of the West and the East," in the words of the Rev. William Speer.[26] Senator John F. Miller said during the 1882 congressional debate over a Chinese exclusion act: "The two great and diverse civilizations have finally met on the American shore of the Pacific Ocean."[27] Christianity and Chinese paganism epitomized the differences between the two civilizations. In the eyes of the missionaries heathenism was a mark of racial and cultural inferiority. Even the Rev. William Speer, a famous defender of the Chinese, noted in 1870 that the Chinese "seem to occupy a superior position compared with other heathen nations, and yet, alas! they are heathen," echoing the sentiments expressed in Bret Harte's infamous "The Heathen Chinee," published in the same year.[28] The missionaries sought not only to proselyte but also to acculturate the Chinese. In fact, in American history Christianization was often a concomitant part of the attempt to Americanize ethnic minorities. In a study of Hawaiian Japanese, Gary Okihiro has written: "Key features of the Americanization movement involved the education and Christianization of the *nisei*."[29]

What differentiated the missionaries from the exclusionists was their greater confidence in the ability of American civilization and, above all, Christianity, to overcome and enlighten inferior and pagan peoples. In an 1856 address to the California legislature, the Rev. William Speer remarked: "The discovery of America, the landing of the pilgrims, the declaration of independence, and the settlement of California, must constitute eras of the new world's advancement, and so of the progress of man, and the triumph of Christianity."[30] Like the pilgrims, the missionaries believed that their generation had a historic mission. In a statement reminiscent of John Winthrop, the Rev. Otis Gibson wrote: "It has been reserved for this nineteenth century and this Republican Government of these United States of America, to witness the first great experiment of aggregated paganism in actual contact with the best form of Christian civilization which the world had ever seen, on Christian soil, in the midst of a Christian people, with Christian institutions, and under the regulations of a powerful Christian Government." In view of such a historic and solemn cause, Gibson warned: "If Christian civilization fails here, it commits deliberate suicide."[31]

Christian missionary work in California was closely connected with that in China. Wesley Woo writes: "Missionary work in China and the conversion of the Chinese in America were viewed as two sides of the same coin."[32] As evidence of such connections, the very first service of the Rev. William Speer's Chinese mission included a sermon by Elija Coleman Bridgman, one of the first two American missionaries to China. Speer himself was a veteran China missionary, and so were many other missionaries in California.[33] Such veteran missionaries constituted a driving force behind the commencement of evangelical work among Chinese immigrants. In 1854, for instance, a former China missionary first urged the Baptist Home Mission Society to establish a mission to the Chinese in California. These veterans' precious experience, especially their ability to speak Chinese (Cantonese in numerous cases), constituted a valuable resource. Praising Speer as "an ideal Christian," a missionary wrote: "I think that he followed the methods to which he had become accustomed in China,—methods which presupposed in the worker quite thorough acquaintance with the Chinese language."[34]

Despite their conviction and experiences, however, the missionaries achieved only limited results. In Chinese San Francisco only a few were converted, according to the missionaries' own accounts.[35] The Presbyterian mission was the first and largest Christian mission in Chinese San Francisco. In 1855 it reported "with regret" its failure to produce any converts.[36] In 1876 it had 69 members, and by then it had received about a hundred people since its establishment.[37] By the close of the century that number had grown to 360.[38] The second largest mission was the Methodist Episcopal mission. For a long time it had been the only mission to secure a chapel, the Foke Yam Tong (the Gospel Temple), in Chinatown proper. In 1876 the mission had about 45 members, and the total number of Chinese converts at the four major missions in San Francisco was 147.[39]

Throughout California there were only three to four hundred Chinese Christians during the 1870s.[40] Around the close of the nineteenth century the number of Chinese Christians on the Pacific Coast rose to a thousand. In all these years the total number of Chinese Christians that different churches had received was two thousand.[41] Despite the potential socio-economic advantages associated with church membership, Christians apparently constituted a very small portion of the Chinese population.[42] If we were to consider other variables, the total number of Chinese converts and their proportion within the Chinese population would be still smaller. Over the years many Chinese Christians had either returned to China or dropped out of the church. Because of the physical mobility of Chinese immigrants, moreover, the number of Chinese recorded as having been received by different churches must have reflected some duplication.

Missionaries also opened numerous Sunday schools. The Rev. William Speer's evening school, where attendance was "irregular," was not very successful.[43] Over time the number of both the schools and of those who attended them increased. In the 1870s there were about fifteen such schools in San Francisco alone. These schools attracted more Chinese than the mission churches did. In the 1870s, while there were less than four hundred Chinese church members, the average total number of people who attended Chinese Sunday schools in California was about one thousand.[44] But this does not mean that Christian missions had a greater influence than is suggested earlier.

Many students at these schools were attracted by secular subjects rather than by religious teachings. In fact, S. Andrews noted in 1870, "the Chinese Sunday schools are not especially schools of religious instruction." Instead they offered lessons in reading, writing, arithmetic, grammar, geography, and so on.[45] Visiting a Sunday school in 1871, Hamilton A. Hill made a similar observation.[46] In reference to the largest Sunday school in San Francisco, Andrews concluded: "It could not be kept up a month if the Bible and catechism were put forward as books for study."[47]

Records left by the missionaries themselves also suggest that secular subjects were much more important than religion in the curriculum of these schools. According to the Rev. Otis Gibson, religious instruction was "interspersed in all the lessons as far as practicable" in his missionary school.[48] In 1870 an average of 71 people attended the evening school of the Presbyterian mission. The mission reported: "Half an hour each evening is devoted to oral lessons, embracing the subjects needful for business education, and designed also to communicate various facts in geography, history, astronomy, and other sciences; together with the important topics of current events."[49] It even had Chinese instructors to teach Chinese classics. As far as evangelical work was concerned, the mission could only report at the end that "at the present time there is an increasing religious interest in our school."[50]

Overall, English lessons remained "the first attraction" to the Chinese.[51] This was especially true among the youth. Many students left after acquiring enough language to conduct their business. Gibson stated regretfully: "Just as fast as these boys and young men acquire a sufficient knowledge of our language to make themselves readily understood in common conversation, they are at once removed from school and placed in business."[52]

The Sunday schools failed not only to guide students to Christianity but also to change these students' customs. In the classroom, as Hamilton A. Hill noted in 1871, all Chinese students "were dressed according to the fashion of their country, each having his pigtail either coiled upon his head or hanging down his back."[53] After many years spent working as a missionary, the Rev. Ira Condit concluded in frustration: "The unique home life, the abounding vices, and the pagan practices which they have carried with them have remained unmodified by the touch of loftier ideals."[54] The modest number of Chinese Christians and the nature of the Sunday schools bespoke the ineffectiveness of Christian missionary work among Chinese. The Rev. Masters conceded that "the work is slow."[55]

Several factors explain the limited influence of Christian missionary work. First, there was not enough support, especially financial support, from white American churches. The Rev. Otis Gibson put it very clearly: "There is reason to believe that the Church at large in America has not clearly appreciated the situation; has not correctly interpreted providential indications; has not carefully measured the responsibility which God has thrust upon her."[56] Fung Chak, a Chinese missionary in Portland, lamented: "Oh, is there no money for the Chinese, however much there may be for others?"[57] Second, America proved not to be a "favorable field for missionary enterprise among Chinese," contrary to the expectations of missionaries like Masters. Its racial prejudice significantly reduced the appeal of its religion. Of an anti-Chinese bill introduced in Congress in 1879, Philip Schaff of the Union Theological Seminary wrote: "A law like this one proposed by Congress would have been a fatal blow to Christian missions among the Chinese now residing in America."[58] Similarly, Masters commented: "The anti-Chinese sentiment of the coast, shared even by some ministers of religion . . . the fresh memories of murdered kinsmen, of riots, boycotts and savage oppression; and the frequent hoodlum assaults made upon defenseless Chinese, even upon their women and children . . . do not make the white man's religion, moral and social life particularly attractive to the average Chinese mind."[59]

Third, as the immigrants fought to preserve their cultural heritage and identity, their own religions served to increase their resistance to the evangelical campaign.[60] In a telling incident that took place in the 1870s, Chinese "heathens" purchased the building of the first Baptist church on Washington Street, replacing "the altar of the living God" with "the incense of idolatry." Gibson understood the symbolic meaning of the event: "The Church of Christ has beaten an ignominious retreat, has surrendered without a struggle one of her strongest fortifications and retreated in disorder before the swarming hosts of idolatry."[61] In a book published at a later time, Mary Bamford offered an explanation of why most Chinese did not accept Christianity: "They've got a good religion already! There isn't much difference between them and us. They've got one good religion and they don't live up to it, and we've got another good religion and we don't live up to it."[62]

Temples constituted an important part of the social landscape in Chinese communities. They were found, as *The Pacific Tourist* stated, "in almost every town containing a few hundred Chinamen."[63] Chinese San Francisco housed the most numerous and elaborate temples—some devoted to one deity, others to several.[64] If the presence of the Christian Church was minimal, that of traditional religion was ubiquitous. Waverly Street was named "Queen-of-Heaven Street" in Chinese, after a temple once located there. In the mid-1880s there were over ten joss houses in Chinatown—used in reference to Chinese idol, "joss" was a corruption of the Portuguese word *deos*, meaning God.[65] Shrines also existed in shops as well as in the Chinese Hospital.[66] Almost all the social organizations, including the huiguan, had their own temples.

It is important to remember that often the "pagan" religions that Christian missionaries combated were not local practices confined to emigrant communities but signified national traditions in China. Many of the deities in the immigrant community, especially the most popular ones, had been widely worshipped in different places in China. One of them was the Queen of Heaven, who originated in South China as a young witch in the tenth and eleventh centuries and had since become a mature female protector of sailors. Several emperors endorsed her as the goddess of navigation. Another popular goddess was Guan Yin, whose temple in Spofford Alley was one of the first Chinese temples in the city. In 1886 numerous Chinese organizations and stores offered money to renovate it. As the Chinese version of the Buddhist deity Avalokitevara, this goddess of mercy had long been popular all over China.

Revered in Chinese San Francisco's pantheon were many historical figures, which once more show the importance of Chinese history in the lives of immigrants. One such figure was Guan Yu, popularly known as Guan Gong, a key figure in the previously mentioned ancient legend about loyal friendship during the Epoch of the Three Kingdoms. He had been canonized in several dynasties since the year 1102 and had been transformed into a god in folk religion. Long before the beginning of Chinese emigration he had become a well-respected deity in the emigrant area. In nineteenth-century Chinese San Francisco this red-faced and black-bearded god was "the *most popular* of all the gods."[67] Few white visitors to Chinatown failed to notice his existence. One even referred to him simply as "the Chinese god."[68] A number of temples, which were often "the most elaborate" of all temples, were erected exclusively for his worship.[69] Although white Americans usually described him as the god of war, Chinese sought out Guan Gong for many different things, including good fortune.[70] In 1868, when the Burlingame delegation came to

San Francisco, its high-ranking Chinese officials went to worship in the temple of Guan Gong before visiting huiguan leaders.[71]

Guan Gong remained popular over time. Liang Qichao noted in 1903 that every huiguan had a temple for Guan Gong.[72] In an essay about the Sanyi Huiguan's newly completed temple for Guan Gong, Liang Nianfang noted in 1902 that "this great man," who worshipped "in and out of China," set an example for Chinese immigrants for devotion to friendship. Liang also pointed out the Chinese identity of the immigrants: "Although the Chinese in America belong to different clans and are from different districts, [they] are all the descendants of the Yellow Emperor."[73] The popularity of deities such as Guan Gong that had had a national constituency in China bears testimony to the immigrants' memory of Chinese history and to the cosmic nature of their cultural heritage. That memory and heritage laid a foundation for their conscious Chinese-ness.

Chinese San Franciscans did not confine their religious practices to the temples but carried them loudly into the streets. During an annual parade held by the Yanghe Huiguan in honor of Hou Wang, a god of medicine, as Masters reported, there were "a thousand gaily dressed Chinamen in line. . . . Immediately in the rear of the idol came an enormous dancing dragon, one hundred and seventy feet long, supported by sixty actors." Masters continued his description of this "animated scene": "The whole street was one mass of color and glitter. The tinseled banners and trappings, burnished spears and halberds, the gorgeous robed attendants, the boom of gongs, roll of drums and roar of firecrackers made up a show of oriental splendor that, it is safe to say, was never before seen on the streets of a civilized city."[74] The dancing dragon, the Chinese dress, and the roaring gongs, drums, and firecrackers—all long-standing customs across China—represented a public expression of the immigrants' Chinese identity in an American city.

"A Grand Beat of the Heart": The Expression of Identity

For the immigrants, cultural identity was not just a state of mind. They publicly displayed and celebrated it. During the Chinese New Year, in particular, "gorgeous lanterns were suspended in front of doors or hung in rows from the numerous balconies," and the air was filled with the crackle of firecrackers and the thunder of gongs and drums.[75] Such celebration, as a newspaper article noted perceptively in 1855, helped "the heart of the old empire to give another grand beat and heave the tide of life for another year."[76] The immigrants displayed their distinctive identity with persistence and tenacity. During the Chinese New Year of 1876, when Chinese San Franciscans violated the city's ban on fireworks, more than a dozen people were arrested, and each was fined five dollars.[77]

The exhibition of cultural distinctiveness was by no means only a festive activity. It was deeply imbedded in everyday life. By wearing their "queer looking" clothes and queue, Chinese immigrants made a constant statement of their ethnic identity.[78] The historian Daniel Boorstin points out the social significance of the manner of dress in his discussion of the connection between "the American democracy of clothing" and the American democracy of politics: "If as the Old World proverb went, 'clothes make the man,' the New World's new way of clothing would help make new men."[79] In like fashion, we can say that the old style of dress helped the Chinese maintain and announce their identity.

The prevalence of Chinese-style dress made a deep impression on Chinese visitors to the city. In 1868 a Chinese official in the Burlingame delegation asserted that less than 1 percent of the Chinese in San Francisco had changed their style of dress.[80] Another Chinese observer noted in 1878: "In the streets, the decoration and sign-boards of all stores were in Chinese style. Chinese [here in general] do not change dress style, do not go to church."[81] Upon his first arrival in San Francisco in August 1879 as China's minister to America, Chen Lanbin noticed that the Chinese coming to welcome him were all dressed in Chinese-style clothes.[82] In 1886 Minister Zhang Yinhuan reported that many Chinese did not change their way of dressing after decades of residence in America. "This is quite commendable," he wrote.[83]

The queue was another cultural symbol, and its cultural meaning was well known. Originally imposed on the Chinese by the Manchus, the queue had long "ceased to be the symbol of the victory of the Mantchurians [*sic*]" by the late nineteenth century, as a contemporary noted.[84] In a simple analogy one American stated that the queue "is what our Star-Spangled Banner is."[85]

The cultural symbols of clothing and the queue usually went hand in hand. The Rev. Otis Gibson remarked: "So long as the queue is retained the

Chinese fashion of dress will be retained." He summarized their cultural significance: "These two things will forever make them a distinct and peculiar people."[86]

Unlike Ah Quin, during the second half of the nineteenth century most Chinese Christians did not abandon the queue, and they also maintained the Chinese way of dressing. Countering a widely held assumption that they had discarded the two traditions, Gibson wrote: "That is a mistake. Some two or three Chinese Christians have adopted the American dress and have discarded the queue, but the Chinese Christians generally have not done so."[87] This reveals that conversion did not signify fundamental assimilation. For one thing, wearing the same attire as their countrymen helped the converts mingle with others in the community. In reference to the presence of the Chinese Christians, Chin Fong Chow stated: "I would not know one if I should see him."[88] At the close of the nineteenth century Frederick J. Masters noted that "it is true that every Christian Chinaman does not cut off his queue or adopt American costume."[89]

These Chinese customs came under attack by Sinophobes, who viewed them as a statement of nonconformity.[90] As early as 1855 an article in *The Oriental* stated: "The Chinese in this city have often been made fun of, humiliated and bullied, because [they] do not dress the American way." At the 1876 congressional hearing on Chinese immigration, when the Rev. A. W. Loomis testified that a Chinese named Yung Wing "has been gathering up facts [concerning anti-Chinese discrimination]," the representative of San Francisco, Frank M. Pixley, interjected promptly and irrelevantly: "We will cut off his queue." Loomis responded: "He is an American citizen." "Then he will not want a queue," Pixley insisted.[91] Pixley's arrogance exemplified widespread hostility toward the queue. In the same year the city of San Francisco passed the Queue Ordinance, declaring that "every male person imprisoned in the county jail . . . should immediately upon his arrival at the jail, have the hair of his head 'cut or clipped to an uniform length of one inch from the scalp thereof.' "[92]

The Chinese resisted white San Franciscans' pressure to conform, indicating again that the persistence of their cultural identity was not just a result of oppression. They held dear their way of dressing and the queue because both represented Old World sentiments and sensibilities that were too deeply rooted in their life to be easily discarded. Moreover, many were unwilling to cut the queue, because they believed, as a newspaper editorial stated, that "the body and hair are inherited from parents to which [they] must not do any damage."[93] The queue was also part of each individual's cultural identity and dignity, and for it to be cut by white officials meant "a grave humiliation." If that happened, the editorial asked, "how can [one] face the hometown fellows and relatives?"[94]

The community made conscious and sometimes concerted efforts to uphold its cultural identity. The few who went astray were punished. According to Loomis, a youth "provoked wrath of his relatives and brought upon himself a fearful torrent of abuse and castigation," because he exhibited "symptoms of forsaking the customs and traditions of his fathers" by discarding the Chinese style of dressing.[95] In 1868, when the Burlingame delegation arrived in San Francisco, a notice was posted in front of the hotel where the delegation stayed: "No Chinese who wears Western-style clothes should see the Imperial Commissioners dispatched by the Emperor."[96] The huiguan, in particular, acted as guardians of tradition and cultural identity. The constitution of each huiguan stipulated that those who adopted Western-style clothes could not join it, nor would they enjoy its protection.[97]

Chinatown became a highly contested battlefield between two cultures. In an attempt to counter Western influence, in 1876 the Zhonghua Huiguan sponsored a lecture series, the subjects of which included the Emperor Kangxi's edicts on education from the early Qing Dynasty. In a public announcement, the Zhonghua Huiguan explained the significance of the lectures. In order to preserve the Chinese way of life in a land "not under the influence of [the Chinese] civilization," it stated, "we must listen to the Imperial Edicts."[98] The lecture series ran from 11 A.M. to 3:00 P.M. every day for several months. In the course of the series the lecture site was moved from the Zhonghua Huiguan's building to a theater in order to accommodate the increasing audience.

This event did not escape the attention of the missionaries. Gibson reported: "During the last few months the Chinese have employed a teacher or preacher from China to read and expound the teachings of Confucius, and the ceremonials of heathen worship."[99] Gibson understood that it represented the Chinese "cultural counterattack" on Christian missions: "The constant preaching of the Gospel of Jesus has had the effect, at least, to excite the Chinese to take a little active effort to teach their own peculiar national doctrines."[100] Gibson continued: "While Christian Chinamen have been expounding the Gospel of Jesus in the 'Gospel Temple', a heathen Chinaman has been expounding the philosophy of Confucius and the ceremonial of idolatry in a heathen theatre, on the opposite side of the street."[101] Reporting on the popularity of this lecture series on May 30, 1876, the *Chronicle* estimated that six hundred to one thousand Chinese attended the lecture series.

In conclusion, immigrants' Chinese awareness constituted an important part of their identity. Needless to say, they adapted in various ways. Yet insofar as their identity is concerned they were not overwhelmed by white America's efforts to transform them. They preserved and proudly and publicly demonstrated their cultural distinctiveness. That distinctiveness was less a response to racism than an outcome of the trans-Pacific ties in their life.

Nonetheless, we should not mistake the immigrants' Chinese consciousness for political nationalism. During the nineteenth century such a consciousness was defined primarily by cultural and historical ties. The immigrants were not yet participants in national political events in China. Visiting Chinese San Francisco in 1903, Liang Qichao was deeply disturbed by what he saw as the lack of nationalism among Chinese immigrants and wrote critically that they had "the quality of the clansman, not that of the citizen," and "the village spirit, not the national spirit."[102] Liang's criticism reflected his perspective as the elitist, Western-influenced intellectual he was at the time, and his eagerness to Westernize Chinese society. It would soon become clear that the immigrants' traditions constituted a fertile ground in which political nationalism would emerge.

Ah Quin and his wife, Sue Leong, probably in the 1880s. Courtesy San Diego
Historical Society.

(*Above*) Ah Quin and his wife, Sue, with their twelve children. Courtesy San Diego Historical Society.

(*Opposite*) A page from Ah Quin's 1892 diary. The characters at the top indicate the date in the lunar Chinese calendar. Courtesy Dr. Thomas Kong.

光緒 十八 年 五 月 廿 四

JUNE　　FRIDAY 17　　1892

Woke up ... ... at 9:18.
then ... in ... till 10:38. go up to
the ... of Pacific ... and coal co.
want to ... Villon he ... in some
... Wing Seng Yuen hay
... he had ... in the office. then also
I walk up to 6-th ... see Fung Wing
and 2 ... ... 馮榮金 香山 譚和 ...
... ...
then ... get E.M. in 6 constable Monahan
office ... talk Billie ... ... 5 minute
then at 11:48 I ... walk ... toward
on fourth sty ... I can ... stable talk
a gentle ... about ... hay ... few
... heard ... China Town some
... ... to ... said ... house to see
... ... relief 譚根喜 ...
... 根 ... ...
I in ... ... to see it. it is
... Chinese and White people in the St.
Dr Stockton and Northrop have me for Interpreter
also Samuel Russell want me to inquire the matter
... at 2:40 P.M. Tom Gang Hi and Tom ...

廿五　　SATURDAY 18

woke up 6:35. the bro. is in 9:15.
Stay in home. ... say ... Sam
because Samuel Russell 亦 ... 國
... ... with ... reason. I ...
不 ... 他 之 ... ... 相 見. and about
Sing Hi. 譚根喜 is also treat me
bad again. he call him own attor
my ... and I in home
good deal. ... in bed ... ...
... not fell much good,
... gave me very bad
about Sing Hi ...

(*Above*) "The Street of the Gamblers (by Day)," ca. 1900. Photograph by Arnold Genthe. Courtesy California Historical Society.

(*Opposite, above*) Clay Street at Waverly Place, San Francisco, ca. 1900. Courtesy California Historical Society.

(*Opposite, below*) Interior of the Chinese Theater on Jackson Street, San Francisco, ca. 1885. Courtesy California Historical Society.

Interior of a Chinese restaurant in San Francisco, ca. 1900. Courtesy California Historical Society.

May 27, 1854, front page of *The Golden Hill's News*, the earliest Chinese-language newspaper published in the United States.

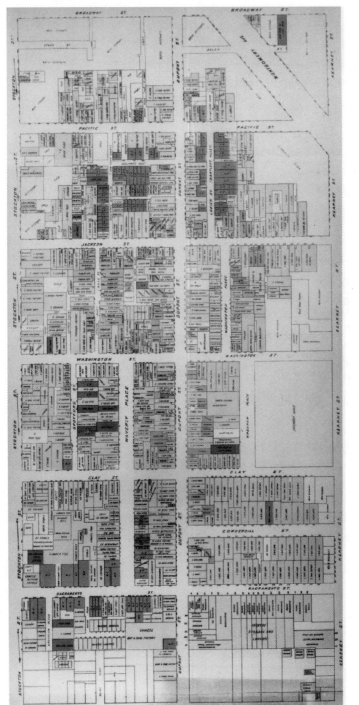

"Official Map of Chinatown in San Francisco, Prepared Under the Supervision of the Special Committee of the Board of Supervisors, July 1885," from San Francisco Municipal Reports for the fiscal year 1884–85. Courtesy California Historical Society, North Baker Research Library.

PART TWO

The Arrival of a True Trans-Pacific Community

Introduction

The first decade of the twentieth century began a new phase in Chinese American history. The decades-long anti-Chinese crusade finally reached a successful conclusion. The administration of the exclusion laws was placed in the safe hands of the U.S. Bureau of Immigration, ending the possibility of challenges from local federal courts.[1] In 1904 Congress reenacted and perpetuated these laws. The Chinese issue no longer commanded the same centrality in the public discourse of race relations as it had assumed in the earlier period. The public debate over the issue between 1901 and 1904 lost much of its earlier vehemence. In reference to Consul General Ho Yow's earlier article "Chinese Exclusion: A Benefit or a Harm?" James D. Phelan, mayor of San Francisco, wrote: "The people most familiar with the subject were disposed to regard the question as not wholly serious."[2] Even in California politics the issue no longer aroused the same heated public debates as it had before. "In 1904," Coolidge wrote, "for the first time in the history of the Democratic party in California, its platform contained no Chinese plank and the Republicans dismissed it with a line."[3]

The Chinese, however, did not disappear from the racial consciousness of the dominant society. Ideologically, a "scientific" way of accepted racial thinking emerged to define the proper place of the Chinese in the racial hierarchy of an increasingly racialized society. Beginning in 1899 all immigrants coming to the United States were registered by their race, rather than by their birthplace.[4] Various racial images and terms, such as "white race" and "Mongol," that featured prominently in the earlier anti-Chinese rhetoric became standardized and officially sanctioned, as is evidenced by the *Dictionary of Races of Peoples* compiled by the U.S. Immigration Commission between 1907 and 1910. "The Chinese physical type," it stated, "is well known—yellowish in color, with slanting eyes, high cheek bones, black hair, and a flat face."[5] Such stereotyping also took place in the movies and in various kinds of popular writings during this period. Creating stereotypes was but a part of the anti-Chinese discrimination that persisted in different forms and places. Government officials, in particular, continued their discriminatory practices, as is illustrated by several publicized incidents that occurred at the beginning of the twentieth century.

The Chinese did not accept the position the dominant society designated for them but carried their struggle against discrimination to a new level. In 1905 they joined hands with their compatriots in China and in the Chinese diaspora in a large-scale economic boycott of the United States. Coinciding with the devastating 1906 earthquake, the effects of the boycott were far-reaching and significant.[6] It signified a new era in Chinese San Francisco history, marked by the rise of political nationalism.

Articulated in Social Darwinistic rhetoric, the new nationalistic sentiments engendered an impulse to modernize and Westernize China and Chinese America as a way to combat discrimination. Like their compatriots in China, Chinese San Franciscans appropriated Western ideologies to comprehend the new situations facing China and Chinese America that traditional Chinese thinking was unable to explain. They also rationalized their struggle against racial prejudice using the ideological framework invented by their oppressors, rather than the principle of universal racial equality. Such ideological limitations help explain not only the contempt that Chinese Americans showed African Americans but also their reaction to the incarceration of Japanese Americans during World War II.

Most of all, it is during this period that Chinese San Francisco became a truly trans-Pacific community: while it reinforced and even expanded its ties with China the community also acquired an increasingly nontraditional, Western outlook. For neither Chinese nor white Americans at the time could the new outlook be construed as evidence of "assimilation." White neighbors continued to exoticize the new Chinatown into a spectators' sensation. Across the nation, Chinese Americans in general were regarded as "the most foreign of our foreigners."[7] On the other hand, Chinese Americans increasingly participated in national political events in China. Such participation did not make the Chinese American story less "American," for they hoped to improve their situation in the United States by strengthening China first. After 1931, when Japan began its aggression in China, they became "double warriors," fighting both racism in America and Japanese imperialism in Asia. As it turned out, the war in Asia significantly aided Chinese Americans in the end: shortly after the bombing of Pearl Harbor the United States abolished its long-standing Chinese exclusion policy as a gesture of goodwill to its wartime ally, marking the dawn of a yet another new era in Chinese American history.

A Time of Anger and a Time of Hope:
The 1905 Boycott

During the 1905 boycott of American goods, Chinese Americans' grievances and anger that had accumulated over the years erupted explosively.[1] A time of anger, it was also a time of hope. Immigrants found new hope in an alliance with their compatriots in China, where the protest originated and where it quickly spread across the nation. The movement demonstrates that the tightening political ties between Chinese America and China existed on substantive and meaningful grounds, rather than in the imagination. The struggle against racial hostility, once given voice by a solitary cry of Chinese Americans, now became a chorus that included the people of China, who took the mistreatment of the Chinese in the United States as an insult to the entire Chinese nation. Chinese Americans understood more clearly than ever before that their fate was linked to that of China.

After discussing the scope of the boycott in China, section two of this chapter takes a look at its origins, especially at the rise of modern Chinese nationalism. Much of the section is devoted to analyzing that nationalism, because it not only stimulated the waves of protest in 1905 but would also significantly influence the future development of Chinese San Francisco. The last section returns to Chinese San Francisco to investigate Chinese American participation in the movement and the movement's far-reaching impact.

A landmark event in Chinese American history, the boycott signaled the fact that Chinese Americans' national consciousness, once defined primarily culturally and historically, had achieved a new political dimension. They reinforced their ties to China by embracing its emerging nationalism. Increasingly articulated in a Western ideological framework, however, this new brand of nationalism would help accelerate the acculturation of Chinese San Francisco.

A Tidal Wave

Debates over whether to renew the expiring 1894 Sino-American treaty touched off the 1905 protest against the U.S. government's anti-Chinese policies.[2] This treaty sanctioned the exclusion of Chinese labor immigration and acknowledged the right of the United States to deny naturalization to Chinese immigrants. Characterized by the historian Zhang Cunwu as a "tidal wave," this spontaneous mass movement of protest started in Shanghai and soon expanded elsewhere.

The magnitude of support that Chinese people across the country showed for Chinese Americans enables us to understand why the movement strengthened political ties between China and Chinese America.[3] Geographically, it spread from north to south, and from coastal to inland areas, including even cities such as Beijing, Hankou, Tianjin, Suzhou, Nanjing, and Qingdao that had no direct ties with Chinese America.[4] In Guangdong, the province of origin for most Chinese Americans, the protest reached rural areas. In Xinning County, for instance, activists displayed imports from the U.S. in temples to show people what to boycott.[5]

In social terms, the movement included diverse classes and groups. Merchants were active participants almost everywhere, financing and organizing various activities. Intellectuals comprised another major element. While energetic students ran up and down the streets, organizing rallies and distributing leaflets, others resorted to writing.[6] Newspaper editorials urged readers to join the boycott. Plays were staged to dramatize the mistreatment Chinese Americans received. Novels, such as *Kushehui* (Bitter society), offered moving depictions of their plight under racism.[7] There were also many other kinds of boycott materials: folk songs in various dialects, cartoons and posters, flyers and pamphlets written in the vernacular.

Various political factions tried to establish some connection to this popular cause. The newly emerged women's movement hailed the boycott as "the first sign of national unity and the opportunity for women to recover their rights."[8] Reformists, too, joined the movement. In February 1906 Liang Qichao filed a complaint with the U.S. Bureau of Immigration.[9] In hopes of advancing their own cause, anti-Manchu revolutionaries blamed the Qing Court for its failure to protect the Chinese in America. A well-known nationalist, Hu Hanmin, contended that the Qing Court was indifferent to the suffering of the Chinese in America because "it was the government of the Manchu not of our Han people."[10]

The support provided by numerous high-ranking officials also proved quite instrumental.[11] In July the director of the Normal College at Wuchang asked educator W. A. P. Martin before his departure for America to advise the American government to terminate its discriminatory immigration policy.[12] Of particular importance was the Chinese minister in Washington, Liang Cheng. Having spent a considerable amount of time in America as a young pupil and later as an embassy employee, he harbored a strong aversion toward Chinese exclusion. In a memorial to the emperor upon his arrival in America in 1903 as Chinese minister, he pledged: "I will do my best . . . to alleviate the hardship of the immigrants, and to glorify the nation's dignity on the basis of justice."[13] When he learned about a Chinese diplomat who had committed suicide after being humiliated by San Francisco police, the indignant minister urged the consul general and Chinese San Franciscans to "fight hard" for justice.[14]

When the 1894 treaty was about to expire, therefore, he openly expressed firm opposition to its renewal. In a telegram to the Chinese Foreign Affairs Ministry on January 12, 1904, Liang declared that it was "too unfair to be renewed."[15] Realizing how difficult it would be to fight exclusion through diplomatic channels, in another memo to the Chinese Foreign Affairs Ministry a year later Liang in fact suggested that an unofficial boycott would be more effective.[16] Although no evidence proves that he was directly involved in igniting the boycott, the publicity surrounding his position undoubtedly encouraged it. Copies of his memo were circulated among Chinese Americans. Liang had reportedly collected evidence from "Chinese in this country and others who had been deported relative to the execution of the exclusion law."[17]

The working classes participated, too. Members of a Canton labor union, for instance, collectively swore in front of the god Guan Gong on July 25, 1905 (allegedly his birthday), that they would not use American goods until the United States changed its exclusion law.[18] A flyer distributed in Shanghai asked prostitutes not to use American soaps. The American public was duly informed about the boycott in China. An American official reported upon his return from Asia: "In the ports the hands who unload imported goods have been taught to leave untouched the merchandise brought from our country."[19]

As the movement progressed, more and more people demanded the abolition of Chinese exclusion laws rather than a modification of restrictions on the exempt classes. The Renjing Society of Shanghai suggested that the movement should address the needs of laborers.[20] The protest reached a climax when the sacrifice of Feng Xiawei became known. Feng, an immigrant laborer in the Philippines who was believed to have been to America and Mexico, committed suicide in front of the American consulate in Shanghai on July 26, 1905.[21] Feng's sacrifice, an act known as *sijian* (remonstration by death), which had been greatly revered throughout Chinese history, touched many hearts. Memorial services, including two in Canton alone, were held in numerous cities.

Chinese San Francisco closely monitored the development of the protest in China. Never before had the immigrants' plight been the object of so much concern and generated so much support. A close examination of the origins of the 1905 movement will shed more light on its significance for Chinese in America.

The Roots of the Boycott

An immediate cause of the boycott was persistent anti-Chinese hostility in America that, along with noisy mass anti-coolie meetings, did not vanish. A number of incidents that occurred between 1902 and 1904 illustrate a continued pattern of institutionalized discrimination exercised by the authorities. What made these incidents flammable is that the victims included the so-called exempt classes, such as merchants and even officials, demonstrating once again the racist nature of Chinese exclusion. If exclusion had targeted only the laboring classes it probably could never have provoked a nationwide protest in China.

Police represented a constant hazard for Chinese communities across the nation. On October 11, 1902, police and immigration officials raided Boston's Chinatown, and as John W. Foster, former U.S. secretary of state under the Harrison administration, recounted the event later: "Every Chinese who did not at once produce his certificate of residence was taken in charge." The police arrested 250 people without warrant, treating "merchants and laborers alike."[22] In what the *New York Times* called a "wholesale" raid of the city's Chinatown in April 1905, the police apprehended two hundred members of two literary societies for gambling.[23]

Across the nation in San Francisco, a Chinese diplomat named Tan Jinyong was severely beaten by two policemen in September 1903.[24] Adding insult to injury, the policemen tied him by his queue to a light pole before taking him to the police station. Even after his diplomatic status and innocence came to light, Tan would still have to stand trial—for allegedly assaulting an officer. Humiliated beyond what he could bear, he committed suicide.[25]

A more widely publicized case involved Chinese exhibitors invited by the American government to take part in the 1904 Louisiana Purchase Exposition in St. Louis. The Chinese team, headed by Prince Pu Lun, put up a large exhibit at the exposition, including a garden that was praised for being "artistic."[26] But Chinese participation in the event gave American authorities an opportunity to display their anti-Chinese hostility, rather than to "promote commerce and enhance diplomatic relations" as the Chinese government had hoped.[27] Some of the Chinese participants were interrogated and detained en route to the fair site. Immigration officials adopted extremely stringent regulations to insure their departure after the fair.[28]

These inflammatory incidents provoked protests from Americans and Chinese alike. In a widely noticed article published in the *North American Review* in 1904, Wong Kai Kah, the vice commissioner of the Chinese exhibition team, issued a warning of possible Chinese retaliation to "the business men and statesmen of the West and of the Pacific coast, whose growth and prosperity will be measured by the extent of American trade with the Orient."[29]

After their return to China, the exhibitors, especially the officials, used all their influence to expose not only the harshness of Chinese exclusion but also its racist nature. Others criticized it in nationalistic terms. In a popular book, Liang Qichao discussed at length how the Bertillon system, a body-measurement method designed to control prisoners, was applied to Chinese laborers coming to America "as if they were criminals." This, Liang concluded, "is an insult to our nation's dignity."[30]

We would fail to fully appreciate the historical significance of the 1905 boycott, however, if we regarded it only as "a reaction to American immigration regulations and procedures."[31] After all, anti-Chinese violence and other forms of discrimination had existed for decades. For quite some time white Americans had discussed the possibility of a Chinese reprisal. In 1902 O. O. Howard, a retired army general, called American mistreatment of the Chinese in America "suicidal."[32] Earlier, the Rev. Gilbert Reid expressed the same concern: "That China will declare war as a mode of retaliation, no one of sense has even suggested, but Chinese mandarins have enough of ingenuity and finesse to adopt other methods of retaliation which will hamper all foreign interests in China."[33]

It is also important to remember that China did not harbor a particularly strong anti-American sentiment prior to 1905. Even in the midst of a controversy over the Canton-Hankou railroad, the United States was still regarded as a lesser evil than other Western powers.[34] Some newspapers openly expressed gratitude to America for criticizing those who desired to divide up China.[35] This gratitude was echoed in Chinese San Francisco. Even before such a policy was explicitly promulgated, *The Chinese-Western Daily* published a news report entitled "America Protecting China," praising America's proposal not to violate China's territorial integrity.[36] Wong Kai Kah acknowledged in his 1904 article that the United States had "no desire of seizing Chinese territory," causing "a feeling of sincere friendship both in the Chinese officials and people."[37] Besides, many saw the United States as a model for China in its effort to modernize itself. A Chinese reformer wrote in 1903: "Perhaps she can help us most in the future by . . . educating our youths in her colleges and guiding China along the rough road that leads to true reform."[38]

For these reasons the beginning of the boycott caught even Chinese San Franciscans by surprise. Unprepared, the Zhonghua Huiguan's initial response was slow. In early June unhappy residents in another town wrote a public letter to the Zhonghua Huiguan, complaining—albeit politely—about its delayed reaction:

> If [people in] Hong Kong and Canton are willing to initiate the struggle, the Chinese in America should follow suit immediately. . . . But for such an important task as the protest against exclusion, quite some time had lapsed without seeing the huiguan make a proposal. If [they] ignore [the movement], do they not ignore their duties? . . . We plead, respectfully, with the leaders of the huiguan to gather and consider a strategy concerning how to raise money and conduct the movement.[39]

As eyewitness Thomas F. Millard recalled, the boycott movement itself had "a more far-reaching significance than the issue raised by this question [of the mistreatment of the Chinese]."[40] The *Outlook* regarded it as a sign of "a new national spirit and a new sensitiveness in China."[41] Indeed, the boycott marked an important step in the development of the new Chinese nationalism.[42] That nationalism is key to understanding not only the 1905 movement in China but also the transformation of Chinese San Francisco in subsequent years.

A number of elements set the new nationalism apart from previous nationalist movements such as the Boxer Rebellion of 1899. First, it was led by an urban elite and relied on civic organizations as well as on modern news journals that were experiencing phenomenal growth at the time.[43] Second, instead of preaching a blind anti-foreignism, the new nationalist movement embraced Western ideas in the hope of building a new China after the pattern of Western nations. In the lexicon of the day, therefore, the word "civilized" became the equivalent of "Westernized." A profound cultural change had apparently occurred since the mid-nineteenth century when, as we have seen earlier, Westerners were called "barbarians." This change is evident in the thought of Zou Rong, one of the most radical and influential nationalists at the time. In inciting an anti-Manchu revolution, he dismissed "barbaric revolutions" such as the Boxer Uprising and called for "a civilized revolution." He hoped that such an uprising would purify China and turn every Chinese into a George Washington.[44]

Western ideas, especially Social Darwinism, were gaining currency in China. In his study of its impact on modern China, James R. Pusey has written perceptively: "It was Darwin, not Kant, Hegel, or Marx, who revolutionized the Chinese concept of history."[45] "Revolution," Zou Rong declared, "is the universal law of natural evolution."[46] In explaining the meaning of the name of *Shi Bao* (meaning "times" and "newspaper," respectively), the newspaper that he founded, Liang Qichao said that the key to "the survival of the fit" was keeping up with the trend of the current times.[47]

Social Darwinism intensified the sense of national crisis. Using a Chinese proverb metaphorically, Liang warned that for China "this is a moment of a hundredweight hanging by one hair."[48] Influenced by a sense of crisis and the new nationalism, a powerful, enduring mentality emerged, which called for a break with tradition and the building of a new China.[49] This trend would soon be echoed in the Chinese immigrant community in America.

The rise of nationalism enabled the people of China to demonstrate nationalistic solidarity and a willingness to embrace Chinese Americans as members of one national community. Many people joined the boycott with a sense of mission, hoping to save China at a time of crisis. An impassioned author exclaimed: "We should be aware of the impending disastrous crisis. We should work with one heart to save [our country]. Save [our country]!"[50] A play produced during the movement, entitled *Bitter Journey*, used the history of modern Poland as a warning about what could happen to China. A poster in Canton stated: "The boycott movement concerns the life or death of our people's spirit."[51] Through the voice of a fictional character in *Tales of the Boycott*, a novelist called the beginning of the boycott "the Number One day in the struggle for survival."[52] In like fashion, a female writer appealed to Chinese women in a public statement: "Oh! In the racial competition of today's world, the universal law of the victory of the superior and the defeat of the inferior is inescapable."[53]

Activists consciously emphasized that theirs was "a civilized" boycott, not a "barbaric" one. From a Westerners' perspective, the Presbyterian missionary Joseph F. Griggs noted that the boycott was in sharp contrast to "previous movements, such as the Taiping rebellion and the Boxer movement [which] have been chiefly the outcome of unreasoning race hatred and fanaticism."[54] " 'China for the Chinese', which is the motto of the national agitation now under way," wrote another author, "is decidedly different from 'root out the foreigners', which was the slogan of the Boxers."[55]

Finally, the 1905 movement took place because of Chinese America's increasingly close connection with China. By that time many Chinese in

China were aware of Chinese Americans' contributions to the Chinese economy.[56] A flyer circulated by boycott participants reported that remittances from Chinese America in a period of less than five years amounted to 50 million Chinese dollars, money that would help strengthen China.[57]

For the same reasons, the Qing Court had adopted a more benevolent policy toward immigrants. In March 1903 it issued an order prohibiting the harassment of returned immigrants by government officials and local thugs.[58] This was a meaningful gesture because it addressed a common concern shared by a lot of Chinese Americans, whose financial resources had long been coveted by many. *The Chinese-Western Daily* noted later: "The returned immigrants were called Gold Mountaineers and envied by everyone."[59] Even those in the United States could not totally escape such harassment. After Liyi, a village in the emigrant region, was robbed by armed local thugs, a group of villagers placed an announcement in *The Chinese-Western Daily*, demanding that fellow Liyi expatriates donate at least five dollars to help pay for the damage done. It warned that those who refused would be forced to pay twice as much upon their return to China.[60]

Rival political factions in China also tried to tap into the pockets of Chinese Americans.[61] Liang Qichao and other Constitutionalist reformists such as Kang Youwei established reformist associations in San Francisco and other cities. One reported in 1903: "I have since met the Chinese of half a dozen large American cities and find them devoted to the cause and willing to work for and give money to it."[62]

Similarly, the revolutionaries developed close relations with the Chinese communities in America, as we can see when we examine the career of Sun Yat-sen, the founding father of the Chinese Republic. Sun had long-standing personal ties to the Chinese community in Hawaii, which he extended to the mainland.[63] He even joined the Zhigong Tang, Chinese America's most powerful secret society, in San Francisco in an attempt to promote his cause.[64] Competition between Constitutionalist and revolutionary factions to win support in Chinese America soon turned into a "bitter battle."[65] It was so bitter indeed that Sun allegedly plotted to kill Kang Youwei.[66]

Chinese Americans' growing involvement in politics in China heightened their nationalistic consciousness. While Chinese politicians crossed the Pacific Ocean to seek assistance, Chinese Americans increasingly turned to China for moral support from the late nineteenth century onward. In

October 1903 they sent a long petition to the Chinese authorities, recounting the history of Chinese exclusion and requesting the use of protective tariffs as a measure of retaliation. The petition was signed by Chinese residents from dozens of American cities.[67] Around the same time the editor in chief of a major Honolulu Chinese newspaper, the *New China Daily*, appealed directly to people in China to take the protest into their own hands, suggesting: "Buyers do not buy American goods; users do not use American goods."[68]

A sense of national solidarity evolved to connect the two Chinese communities across the ocean. The Chinese in China identified their American compatriots' struggle against racial discrimination with their own. "Although most Chinese laborers in America today are Cantonese," a popular pamphlet stated during the boycott, "they are like our brothers." "If we do not fight [against the mistreatment they now receive]," it concluded, "it will come to all of us."[69] The *New York Times* summarized the situation well: "The question of Chinese exclusion from the United States continues chiefly to occupy the attention of the Chinese. The extent and depth of the feeling manifested astonish foreigners and are regarded as an evidence of the growth of a national sentiment and public spirit which five years ago would have been inconceivable."[70]

In a word, the 1905 movement represented a serious challenge to America's anti-Chinese immigration policy. It announced the arrival of a new Chinese nationalism. And it intensified the ties between China and Chinese America.

The Impact of the 1905 Boycott

If we look at its short-term results, the 1905 boycott was basically a failure. It had little if any economic effect. As economist Charles F. Remer assessed, "trade between the United States and China reached an unprecedented peak in 1905."[71] Such an economically ineffective movement naturally did not achieve its political goal: the abolition of the exclusion acts.

The spontaneous movement lacked clear leadership and was further weakened by internal divisions. Under pressure from the American government, and fearful of the growing influence of anti-Manchu revolutionaries, the Qing Court quickly dealt the movement another mortal blow by turning against it. In August the court declared in an edict that the boycott was no longer necessary because of America's promise to improve its treatment of the exempt classes. If the boycott continued, the edict stated, it would harm China's diplomacy and "allow trouble makers to take advantage of the situation."[72] The movement lingered into 1906 before tapering off, and the exclusion acts remained in place.

In terms of its long-term and psychological impact, however, the boycott achieved a great deal. It increased Chinese Americans' willingness to identify with their compatriots, especially their supporters. A case in point was Chinese Minister Liang Cheng. The Chinese government's apathy on the issue of Chinese exclusion had long been well known, and Liang does not seem to have commanded much respect among Chinese Americans. But their attitude changed after they learned about his staunch opposition to the renewal of the 1894 treaty and, later, his support for the boycott. In 1905 *The Chinese-Western Daily* reported: "Public opinion towards Minister Liang is now changed. People are saying: I had cursed the Minister because I did not know the Minister well."[73] During the Chinese New Year season of 1906 the newspaper paid special homage to the minister by publishing a large photograph of him, with these respectful words of introduction: "H. E. Sir Chien-tung Liang Cheng, Chinese Minister in Washington."[74]

Chinese San Franciscans and others elsewhere joined the movement in various ways. They publicly voiced their objection to Chinese exclusion. One of the most vocal Chinese who worked to further the movement was the founder and editing manager of *The Chinese-Western Daily*, Ng Poon Chew, who toured several cities as a public speaker to seek support for the boycott. Fluent in English, he also spoke to white Americans, sometimes debating with white speakers over the issue of Chinese exclusion.

To support the movement Chinese Americans donated large amounts of money, their most powerful weapon. Despite its initially slow reaction, the Zhonghua Huiguan soon assumed a leadership role and in June 1905 helped to form the General Boycott Committee, which became the movement's most important organ in America. The vigilant Chinese inspector of San Francisco, John Endicott Gardener, dutifully reported the committee's activities and its monthly statements of account. According to his reports, from June 9 to July 19 it collected $6,347 from various cities. From July 20 to August 17 the amount increased to $9,611.[75] The committee mailed such contributions to the movement in China at different times.

Chinese San Franciscans communicated and cooperated closely with the boycott movement in China. Its development filled the headlines in Chinatown newspapers. Flyers and other materials published in Chinese cities were also distributed in San Francisco. Upon receiving the news in mid-June that newspapers in Tianjin refused to advertise American goods, employees at the three major newspapers in Chinatown sent a telegram to their colleagues to express support. Organizers in China traveled to Chinese communities in America. On July 31 Wang Maochai came to San Francisco to speak on the boycott movement in Shanghai. Hundreds of people packed a Chinese theater to listen to his long speech. The barrier of dialect was breached by the spirit of solidarity and by an interpreter who simultaneously rendered his remarks into Cantonese.

The 1905 movement stimulated Chinese Americans' cultural pride. They saw it not as a failure but as a show of the strength of the Chinese when they unified. While America's exclusion policy persisted, the Roosevelt Administration publicly acknowledged that its enforcement must be softened. After the outbreak of the boycott, President Roosevelt, a staunch supporter of the anti-Chinese movement, adjusted his position. In mid-June he declared to members of the American Asiatic Association, who came to discuss with him the unfair treatment of the Chinese: "[I am] personally in favor of making this administration [of Chinese Exclusion] just as little offensive as it can be made."[76] The White House held a prolonged cabinet meeting to discuss the boycott and decided to improve the treatment of Chinese in spite of the objection of Secretary of Commerce Victor Metcalf, an ardent anti-Asianist from California. In a letter to the acting secretary of state in late June that was immediately made public, Roosevelt ordered American consular representatives in China to show "the widest and heartiest courtesy."[77] As early as May, Frank P. Sargent, commissioner general of the immigration bureau, issued a directive to every Chinese inspector, expressing his "desire" that "the administration of the law shall . . . be stripped of all harshness of word or action." The directive specified: "When suspicion is entertained as to the lawfulness of the residence in this country of any Chinese person every proper and reasonable opportunity should be afforded him to satisfy the officer by whom suspected before placing such person under arrest."[78] American authorities were so concerned about the boycott in China that Secretary of War William Taft canceled his plan to visit Canton during his trip to Asia.

White America was increasingly willing to improve its treatment of Chinese Americans. In August the *Outlook* summarized the mood of the media: "If newspaper editorials are taken as a sign, popular feeling seems strongly to be inclined towards sympathy with the Chinese demands."[79] Several writers compared the 1905 Chinese movement to the Boston Tea Party. Chester Holcombe wrote: "Our ancestors of Revolutionary memory understood the boycott and applied it against British-owned Chinese tea in 1773; why should not the Chinese make use of it now?"[80] The Pacific Mail S. S. Company carefully disassociated itself from Chinese exclusion during the movement. It published a testimony, allegedly signed by 64 Chinese passengers who came to San Francisco on the company's ship *China*, that stated: "The owner and captain of the ship were hospitable and had no intention of discrimination. . . . We are very satisfied."[81] Minister Liang reported in a telegram to the Chinese Foreign Affairs Ministry in 1906, "in general, the situation [concerning the entry of Chinese immigrants and transits] is much better than before."[82] This change was clearly noticed by Chinese San Franciscans. *The Chinese-Western Daily*, for instance, reported in great detail on the new directive issued by the U.S. Bureau of Immigration and highlighted the changes therein.[83]

The movement and its achievement entered the collective memory of the community. In 1906, when Chinese San Franciscans openly challenged the segregation of San Francisco's public school system, they recalled the 1905 boycott with great pride. That challenge occurred after President Roosevelt, under pressure from Japan, pushed the San Francisco School Board to reverse its decision to place its 39 Japanese pupils in the segregated Chinese School—a reversal that further clarified for the Chinese the importance of their ancestral land's support in their efforts to better their situation. In response to attempts by the city's white merchants to boycott Chinese businesses in 1914, businessmen in Chinatown planned to appeal to their counterparts in China to rekindle the 1905 movement.[84]

Chinese Americans were aware of the link between their situation and the fate of China, and they hoped that a strong China would come to their rescue. "The wakening sound of the sleeping lion shocked the whole world,"

The Chinese-Western Daily proclaimed in 1906 in reference to the 1905 boycott.[85] "Since the start of the boycott last year," the newspaper noted on another occasion, "foreigners suddenly changed their perception [of the Chinese], saying the Chinese had awakened from their dream, and their spirit was re-vitalized."[86] This newspaper commentary effectively summarized the historical significance of the 1905 movement. It reinforced Chinese Americans' trans-Pacific connections and increased their pride in being Chinese. The boycott did not end discrimination, but it gave them hope that it might end some day. They realized more clearly than ever that only a strong China could help them succeed in the struggle to achieve racial justice.

SEVEN

A Changing Mentality, 1906 to 1913

The Chinese entered 1906 with jubilation and hope. The front page of the Chinese New Year's edition of *The Chinese-Western Daily* carried a reproduction of a large painting: rising on the horizon is the shining sun, cruising in the sea are war and cargo ships on which the Yellow Dragon flags flutter, greeting the ships in a fortification on the coastline are soldiers standing in line under the same flag, nearby are railroads and factories. Three English words tell the reader that this is "THE COMING CHINA." Another line says, in Chinese, "Long live China in the world to come."[1]

A celebration of a new future for China on the most important traditional holiday, the painting offered a visual articulation of the community's changing mentality. The message in this straightforward black-and-white painting is not difficult to decode. The ships, railroads, and factories under the rising sun represent important new icons of an emerging nationalist ideology; they embody the immigrants' wish for a militarily and economically strong China that would deliver Chinese Americans from racial oppression. That ideology is key to comprehending the social and cultural changes taking place in Chinese San Francisco. Under way since the turn of the century, they were not disrupted by the catastrophic earthquake of 1906 that totally destroyed San Francisco's Chinatown along with much of the rest of the city. In fact, Chinese San Franciscans quickly turned the tragic event into an opportunity to rebuild and renew their community.

During the years from 1906 to the outbreak of World War I, the trans-Pacific ties that connected China and Chinese San Francisco became increasingly reciprocal. In 1906, a year after challenging America's exclusion policy with the nationwide boycott, China once again extended a helping hand, this time reaching out to assist the earthquake victims. For their part, Chinese Americans heeded and even participated in national affairs in China with greater interest. They embraced China's new nationalism. "The awakening of China," a catchphrase of the American press at the time, captured the imagination of Chinese Americans and underscored the essence of their nationalist sentiments. Like their compatriots in China, they regarded the West as the model for a new China and internalized Western concepts that had Social Darwinistic flavors, believing that China must follow the path of "progress" paved by Western nations.

This re-imported Western outlook became a predominant mentality, prompting the community to reevaluate old traditions that it had once held so dear. The call to rejuvenate China accompanied an effort to renew their own community. As Chinese San Franciscans restored Chinatown, they took the opportunity to implement a number of social reforms.

The Aftermath of the Earthquake

The catastrophic 1906 earthquake and the ensuing fires toppled Chinatown, as it did almost the whole city, which had once been, in the words of a grieving contemporary, "wealthier and more prosperous than Tyre and Sidon of antiquity."[2]

The first issue of *The Chinese-Western Daily*, lithographed in reduced size, that appeared after the earthquake vividly conveyed the devastating aftermath of the catastrophe. A front-page story recounted the nightmare that had started at dawn on April 18: "At 5:15 in the morning of the 26th day of last month an earthquake hit the Gold Mountain. . . . Then, buildings collapsed, tiles and stones flew wildly in the sky. The saddening sound of cries was heard all over the city. . . . Soon the fire started . . . and reached Sacramento and California Streets by eight o'clock in the evening until ten o'clock the next morning when Chinatown was burned into ashes."[3]

Two hundred thousand San Franciscans spent the night in parks and other open areas. Many, including over twenty thousand Chinese, fled to nearby Oakland. The death toll was 435, and another three thousand five hundred were injured.[4] Others escaped bodily injury only to face a desperate situation. Mary Austin recalled: "I remember the night of rain, and seeing the grown man sitting on a curbstone the morning after, sobbing in the final break-down of bodily endurance."[5] The quake sent a shock wave across the nation. A *New York Times* headline read: "Over 500 Dead, $200,000,000 lost in San Francisco Earthquake."[6] Relief aid poured in from various sources. The mayor of Boston pledged twenty-five thousand dollars on April 18. The next day Congress voted to send one million dollars, and New Yorkers added about half a million.

The earthquake did not bury anti-Chinese sentiments. Numerous newspaper reports of the Relief Committee's serious discriminatory practices prompted President Roosevelt to inquire into the situation. Acts of violence against the Chinese persisted as well. In one incident a Chinese who went back to his former residence on Sacramento Street was stoned to death "by Western rascals."[7]

Incidents of discrimination such as these made Chinese San Franciscans appreciate the help they received from their compatriots in China and elsewhere, who donated cash, ranging from $10 to $3,800 in amount.[8] For China to provide such financial assistance was as unprecedented as its offer of moral support in 1905. Chinese Americans, who had been sending money back to China for years, were being repaid.

Particularly important was the Qing government's concrete assistance and direct expression of concern. Chinese officials in America worked with the Zhonghua Huiguan to organize the relief effort. Soon after the earthquake, consulate and Zhonghua Huiguan officials held a number of meetings in Oakland and issued a series of commands in an effort to bring order and relief to the chaotic and hungry community. Prices of food, clothes, and other basic goods were frozen. Four relief units of 50 people each were organized to search for missing persons, distribute food, manage relief camps, and register the victims.

On May 22 Chinese Minister Liang Cheng arrived in Oakland to lead the relief effort. Under his instruction a project was started to build 112 cabins for the homeless. When they were nearly completed strict regulations were adopted to insure the proper use of the dwellings. Orphans and widows received first priority. No opium would be allowed, and any man who did not go to work within about a month of moving in would be removed.[9]

While quickly providing food and housing, Chinese officials also made a valiant effort to address victims' other needs. With the cooperation of authorities in China Liang made special arrangements for widows and the extremely poor or elderly to return to China. The consulate general would give each of them a free ticket and five dollars in cash. The plan drew hundreds of applicants. In addition, the minister issued guidelines to help people deal with insurance companies. In response to rumors of individuals fleeing from debts, he posted another order, threatening to confiscate the property in China of anyone who tried to do that. These actions provided vital relief and helped restore order to the community. They were also indicative of a genuine empathy. As fellow Chinese and, in many cases, fellow Cantonese, the immigrants' compatriots back in China personally gave large sums of money. Donations made by officials at the Chinese embassy alone amounted to $4,800.[10]

Donations also came from officials in China and, as was previously mentioned, from the Qing government. Soon after the disaster Chinese San Franciscans learned that the Empress Dowager had sent fifty thousand dollars to help the victims. In a edict reprinted in *The Chinese-Western Daily* she ordered the immediate dispatch of the funds and expressed her "deep concern" about the victims.[11] Such an unprecedented move signaled a radical change in the Qing government's anti-emigration policy, a change that also reflected the increasing attention Chinese America commanded in China.

The natural disaster gave Chinese haters a chance to make the city hazardous for Chinese San Franciscans, and again Chinese diplomats came to their aid. Because the disaster ruined Chinatown and forced most Chinese out of the city, some white San Franciscans, as Jerome A. Hart recalled later, "congratulated themselves that Chinatown was gone."[12] They renewed the effort to move what they had long considered a major inconvenience because of its location in the center of the city.

Just a few days after the quake San Francisco mayor E. E. Schmitz promptly told the police chief that all Chinese should be placed at Hunter's Point on the southern end of the city. A special committee was formed to examine the relocation issue. The idea of removing and reconstructing Chinatown as a tourist site enraged Chinese residents. *The Chinese-Western Daily* editorialized: "This proposal treated us Chinese like toys. . . . To rebuild the old Chinatown was the right of us Chinese."[13] In the aftermath of the earthquake, however, the angry Chinese seemed particularly vulnerable, and *The Chinese-Western Daily* noted pessimistically: "It is predictable that the old Chinatown cannot be restored."[14]

The city's ever greater need for the revenue that Chinatown would generate represented a powerful argument against removal. Also instrumental in defeating the relocation plan was the Chinese government's intervention in the matter. "Arrival of a delegation from the Chinese Legation to the United States," reported Gladys Hansen and Emmet Condon, "changed the tone and the tenor of the 'relocation of Chinatown' rhetoric."[15] Chinese diplomats' intervention served as a reminder that the removal of Chinatown could become an international incident. Further, the consulate general building was unmovable because it was the property of the Chinese government; this made it practically impossible to fully implement the proposed removal.

China's aid did more for Chinese San Franciscans' pride as Chinese than it did to win any particular loyalty to the Empress Dowager's court. In November 1908 Chinese San Francisco went into mourning over the death of Emperor Guangxu; shops closed and flags were lowered. Grief for the deceased pro-reform emperor who had once symbolized China's hope and who had been the Empress Dowager's political foe underscored the community's growing concern about China's future.

Chinese San Franciscans were soon given a chance to express their gratitude to their compatriots in China when a severe famine hit a vast area north of the Yangtze River in central China in the spring of 1907. *The Chinese-Western Daily* urged its readers to help their fellow Chinese there. Moreover, it reminded them of the assistance they had received in 1906: "Those who receive help but do not repay are not gentlemen. . . . As we may recall, last year [after the earthquake] people in inland China generously helped with frequent remittances."[16] Another editorial, reporting the effects of the famine in detail, pleaded emotionally: "Fellows! Fellows! Think about it with your heart. Can you still remain aloof?"[17] Many did not and acted quickly and generously. A relief committee was formed and collected $19,878.14 by early July.[18]

After 1906 the Qing government's interest in Chinese America continued to grow. In 1907 the Ministry of Civil Administration started, for the first time, to collect data on the Chinese abroad, including the Chinese American population. Meanwhile, the Ministry of Agriculture, Industry and Commerce announced that it would award official titles to overseas Chinese investing in China.

Numerous people in China proposed the establishment of Chinese schools in Chinese America, thereby displaying a desire not only to help Chinese Americans but also to reinforce their national awareness, especially that of the younger generation. In 1908 the Ministry of Education dispatched a high-ranking official named Liang Qinggui, a native of the emigrant county of Panyu, to set up schools in Chinese communities in North America. The purpose of his education mission, as Liang stated in his 1909 official report, was to win the affection of the Chinese in America and to protect the nation's dignity. Learning Chinese, Liang hoped, would enable Chinese Americans to avoid the kind of acculturation that had occurred in Poland as a result of Russia's influence and in India as a result of the influence of the English.[19]

The idea of promoting Chinese education in the United States did not trickle down from China's elites. In the late nineteenth century, before the schools that Liang helped establish in Chinese San Francisco and five other U.S. cities had opened, Chinese San Francisco had already set up educational institutions—the most impressive among them being the Great Qing Academy. Some of its graduates had reportedly returned to China to continue their studies and had passed high-level civil examinations.[20] Often impeded by a lack of funds, however, the old-fashioned academy was unable to meet the growing needs of the community.[21]

Before 1908 such needs had already given rise to calls to establish a regular Chinese school. It is necessary to note that efforts to promote Chinese education paralleled the community's protest against segregation in San Francisco's public schools.[22] The desire to pass on Chinese cultural heritage did not lead to a de-emphasis on American education. In fact, Chinese Americans fought for an equal, integrated American education for their children. Wanting both a Chinese and an American education represented no paradox at all, because both were considered important in the trans-Pacific community.

A major goal associated with the promotion of Chinese education was the preservation of the language, which, as it was for members of many other ethnic communities, was a high priority for Chinese Americans in the United States.[23] After criticizing the city's school-segregation policy, *The Chinese-Western Daily* emphasized the importance of Chinese-language teaching in an editorial: "Even if it turned out unexpectedly, that is, they repealed the policy and allowed our children to enter the public school to receive the same education as the Western children, it is still not perfect for the education of our children. Why? Because it is not a complete education for our Chinese children to study only the Western language and not to learn Chinese." The editorial went on to explain the significance of a Chinese education for Chinese children: "Now that they are Chinese in blood, no matter in which country they grow, they always have many connections with their fellow countrymen [in China]."[24]

In light of the importance they placed on the acquisition of the Chinese language and a Chinese education, we can understand why Chinese San Franciscans warmly received Liang Qinggui in 1908 and worked with him closely. When he left, leaders of Chinese San Francisco provided funds to cover his travel expenses, and some accompanied him to help him set up schools in other cities. On his way back to China in February 1909 Liang must have been happy to see a hundred or so students streaming into San Francisco's Chinatown's new Chinese school, the Zhonghua School.[25] A true Chinese school, it emphasized language learning and adopted the curriculum issued by the Qing Ministry of Education.

The Awakening of China and the Mission of Chinese America

In the special 1907 Chinese New Year's issue of *The Chinese-Western Daily*, the editors replaced what they called "the clichéd auspicious greetings" with wishes for a strong China in the future and for the welfare of famine victims in the provinces north of the Yangtze River.[26] The editors communicated two familiar trends: Chinese Americans' broadened national consciousness and their hope for the emergence of a new China. Their optimism that China could change came about as a result of increasing evidence of modern Chinese nationalism.

Signs that China was rejuvenating began to capture America's imagination in the late nineteenth century. "The awakening of China" became a popular expression in the press.[27] In April 1905, shortly before the outbreak of the boycott, the *Independent* proclaimed: "China has been asleep; she is now waking up."[28] More convincing than any other event, the 1905 boycott stood as "a portentous sign of the awakening of a great people."[29] In an article titled "The New China," Thomas F. Millard declared: "The Western world has waited so long for China to rouse from her sleep of centuries that an impression has obtained she would never awake." But after the outbreak of the boycott, he contended, there were plenty of "internal evidences of the awakening of China."[30] In the eyes of the medical missionary Joseph F. Griggs, the 1905 movement was "a miracle of [China's] national resuscitation."[31] The *Outlook* noted in like fashion: "America should take notice that a special symptom of the reawakening of a spirit of nationalism in China is the protest by the boycott of American products against the unjust application of our Exclusion Act."[32] After 1905 the "the awakening of China" continued to fascinate Americans. Theodore Roosevelt declared in 1907: "The awakening of China is one of the great events of our age."[33] This was also the new image of China that Chinese diplomats and other officials visiting the United States tried to publicize. In one public speech, for example, Minister Liang Cheng announced China's new nationalistic economic policies, which constituted evidence of "the awakening of China," as the *New York Times* put it.[34]

Chinese Americans readily and enthusiastically embraced the idea that China was awakening. It gave them hope and made them proud. In 1909 *The Chinese-Western Daily* proclaimed: "Today the lion is awakening from sleep."[35] In accepting the notion of "the awakening of China," Chinese San Franciscans linked their destiny with China's future. "When China perishes," a newspaper editorial stated, "the immigrants too will perish because rejected in the foreign land, they would have no home to return to."[36]

The community adopted the task of renewing China as their own responsibility. The purpose of Chinese schools in America, *The Chinese-Western Daily* stated, was to prepare Chinese American children to assume that responsibility "when the Chinese government calls upon them to go back and make a useful contribution. . . . One more Chinese child attending the school," it concluded, "means one more useful citizen for the homeland in the future."[37]

Residence in the United States gave Chinese Americans a special sense of mission. *The Chinese-Western Daily* noted the unique historic role of Chinatown newspapers: "[While in China] the press cannot say what it wishes to say. . . . Chinese newspapers in San Francisco are free from the baneful influence [of tyranny]. Operating in the foreign country and enjoying the freedom of speech, [these newspapers] would absorb civilization and transfer it to the homeland."[38] In welcoming the publication of another Chinese newspaper, *Young China*, in 1909 *The Chinese-Western Daily* expressed the hope that China would be rejuvenated. The hope, it emphasized, lay in the youth "living overseas" who did not have "the poison of slavery implanted in their minds."[39]

In order to fulfill their special mission, Chinese Americans resorted to their most powerful weapon: sending money back to China. If in the past their remittances went primarily to support their loved ones, now they contributed more and more toward the building of a new China. Their investments in the country, especially in its manufacturing industries and railroads, significantly increased in the years after 1906. A prime example of a project that benefited from their contributions was the building of the Ningyang (Xinning) Railroad in Guangdong between 1906 and 1920, orchestrated by an immigrant, a Xinning native named Chen Yixi.[40] The 36-mile railroad has been seen as reflecting "the role of emigrant capital and nationalism in the development of enterprises in the emigrant motherland."[41] The historian Liu Pei Chi called it "one of the most successful enterprises built with the investment from Chinese immigrants in America."[42] Encouraged by the success and significance of such investments, *The Chinese-Western Daily* called on the "Gold Mountaineers" to "explore a gold mountain in China."[43] Because in America they faced not only discrimination but also diminishing economic opportunities, it concluded, their real future lay in China.

Their economic leverage enabled Chinese Americans to get involved in Chinese politics. Sometimes they intervened assertively in local politics in the emigrant region. The transfer of Enping County to the control of another district prompted the protests of Enping natives in San Francisco and Los Angeles in late 1906, and the governor had to explain his decision to appease them.[44] In another case, when a popular magistrate of Xinning County was forced to resign in 1908, expatriates from the county sent telegrams to the governor demanding that he retain the magistrate.[45]

Chinese Americans also demonstrated a growing interest in Chinese national affairs. In 1907 the Zhonghua Huiguan in San Francisco sent telegrams to China to protest Britain's infringement upon China's sovereignty. And when Chinese San Franciscans heard about Russia's attempt to annex Outer Mongolia they set up a bureau to collect money, planning to sponsor an expeditionary army to fight the Russians.[46]

Consistent with their wish to strengthen China in accordance with Western models, Chinese Americans continually asked the Qing Court to form a national assembly. In 1911 many embraced the Republican revolution with great enthusiasm because it seemed to signify that their hopes and dreams were coming true. Just days after its outbreak *The Chinese-Western Daily* saluted the revolution exultantly: "Cheers! Ruled by dictatorial monarchy for thousands of years, our country has finally become a democratic Republic."[47] Later the newspaper declared the revolution to be "the opening of a new era for our country."[48] It was also seen as a historic event in world history. In celebration of the first anniversary of the Wuchang uprising, the beginning of the revolution, an editorial in *The Chinese-Western Daily* compared it to the French and American Revolutions.[49]

The revolution, it was believed, would bring equality to everyone, including women. In July 1912 Ng Poon Chew told Mary Coolidge in a letter that "soon after the Provisional Assembly convened at Nanking women's suffrage was unanimously granted." Chew went on to assure Coolidge hopefully: "I believe when the [official] National Parliament convenes it will estend [*sic*] the suffrage to women."[50]

The revolutionaries tried to capitalize on the strong support for their cause. They issued bonds in Chinatown that they promised would be redeemable after the Republic was established. In late 1911 the Zhonghua Huiguan formed an agency to raise money for the Republican government in Canton. Using his skills as a public speaker, Ng Poon Chew publicly appealed to the American government to recognize the new Republic of China.[51]

The American government's recognition came as a pleasant surprise, because many Chinese, in and out of China, had expected Japan to be the first to act. "Unexpectedly," an editorial in *The Chinese-Western Daily* remarked, "the first to recognize our Republic, by remarkable morality, compassion and resolve . . . is the great Republican U. S. government in this magnificent new continent."[52] The lavish expression of gratitude reveals how much Chinese Americans valued the endorsement of another Republican government. Numerous organizations in Chinatown sent telegrams to Washington to express their thanks.

Initially, there was some resistance to the revolution, as is evidenced by the Constitutionalists' effort to organize a counterrevolutionary parade in November 1911. But such resistance quickly evaporated, and the revolution instantly became a memorable historic event. The owner of a new hotel that opened on November 11, 1912, chose the word "Republic" as its name. In January 1912 a parade was held in San Francisco in celebration of the newly formed Republic. Later in the year the anniversary of the Wuchang uprising was declared a holiday in Chinese San Francisco. Thereafter, the commemoration of the revolution remained one of its most important holidays.

New symbols also came along, one of which was the flag of the Republic. Soon after the revolution Mow Wo and Company, located on Grant Avenue, sold the new national flag alongside photographs of leaders of the revolution. The new symbol was quickly accepted by the entire community. In November 1911 the influential Ningyang Huiguan adopted the flag of the Republic. By then the Zhonghua Huiguan, along with various clan associations and the twelve big tongs, had all done the same.[53] Even visitors who did not know what the new flag signified could see that a change had taken place. In 1912 Mary Bamford commented that "there was noticeable in San Francisco's Chinatown a new flag, with crimson field, having on a blue background in the upper left-hand corner, a sun with twelve rays."[54]

Chinese Americans also wanted to take part in the revolution. In 1912 they elected their own representatives to the national congress in China. Primary elections were first conducted among individual huiguan, and eventually Kuang Yaojie, president of the Ningyang Huiguan, was elected to represent the West Coast Chinese population. In fact some people, especially members of the Zhigong Tang, which had supported Sun Yat-sen, felt that they had been part of the revolution from the very beginning. At a meeting in February 1913 this powerful secret society adopted a new name, the Mingguo Gonghui (the Republican association). Speakers at the meeting praised and congratulated the society—organized originally by anti-Manchu nationalists—for having achieved its own longtime goal.[55]

A New Mentality

A contextual analysis of editorials in *The Chinese-Western Daily* will help us catch a glimpse, however limited, of the new mentality that came to prevail in Chinese San Francisco. Making no pretense of journalistic objectivity, these editorials, which bluntly expressed opinions about every important issue concerning the community, always appeared in the front pages. They were written not just by the newspaper's editors but also often by other contributors, making the editorial section a kind of community forum.

Founded in 1900 and managed by Chinese Americans, *The Chinese-Western Daily* or "Chung Sai Yat Po" (the official transliteration of its Chinese title based on Cantonese pronunciation) represented the community more than did the other major papers established in close connection with different political factions in China.[56] The Nationalist Party in China started the *Chinese Free Press* (its first Chinese title was "Datong ribao"; 1903–27) and later on *Young China* (its Chinese title was "Shaonian zhongguo"; 1910–70s?). And *Chinese World* (its Chinese title was "Shijie ribao"; 1909–69) was established by the Constitutionalists who wanted to preserve the Qing Dynasty. Just as *The Chinese-Western Daily* often proudly pronounced its detachment from China's partisan politics, the other major papers made no effort to disguise their political affiliations and agenda.[57] *Young China*, for example, stated on its first anniversary that its purpose was to serve the Nationalists in China.[58] The individuals running the other papers were members of these factions who had come to the United States to promote their causes. In contrast Ng Poon Chew, founder of *The Chinese-Western Daily*, had deep roots within the Chinese American community. He came to America from Guangdong as an immigrant in 1881 at the age of fifteen. His community involvement and influence are indicated by the different roles he assumed as a Christian minister, a merchant and, most important of all, managing editor of *The Chinese-Western Daily*. Like most Chinese San Franciscans he was not totally detached from China. In fact he was also a member of both the Zhigong Tang (a powerful anti-Manchu organization) and the Ningyang Huiguan. In 1912, when the Ningyang Huiguan held a primary election of representatives to China's first national congress, Chew was nominated along with other prominent members of the huiguan.

The significance of *The Chinese-Western Daily*, which remained the largest Chinese newspaper in America during much of its existence (1900–51), was widely recognized by white Americans. As managing editor of this paper, therefore, Ng Poon Chew became the best-known Chinese of his day and acted as a spokesman for Chinese Americans on many different occasions.[59] The Chautauqua, which sponsored several of Chew's lectures across the country, called him the "Father of Chinese Journalism in America" in a flyer it published to promote him.[60] In private as well as in public the newspaperman Chew consciously took up a spokesman's role. In February 1909, right before the publication of Mary Coolidge's *Chinese Immigration*, a work he had helped research, Chew wrote to thank her "in behalf of the Chinese people . . . for your efforts in bringing the facts concerning the Chinese question before the American public." Interestingly, Chew also offered her protection: "when the book is out, in case you need a body guard, we can furnish you a select company of *Highbinders* for your protection."[61]

It is inevitable that questions remain about the size and nature of the newspaper's audience, about reader response to the editorials, and even about some readers' possible "deviant decoding" of the intended messages. We can no longer answer these questions with precision. But there is no doubt that the newspaper did not always speak for all Chinese San Franciscans all the time. In fact, in early 1911 members of the mighty Ningyang Huiguan even launched a boycott against it because an editorial allegedly showed contempt for Xinning people. Even as it provides evidence of disapproval, however, the boycott indicates that the newspaper was read and that the opinions it espoused mattered. In its more than fifty years of existence from 1900 on, its popularity and influence remained unrivaled in the community. And this self-supported newspaper stood as a leading voice to be reckoned with. In 1907, when businessmen in Chinese San Francisco planned to establish the Canton Bank, they came to the editors for their endorsement.

The Canton Bank was the largest enterprise Chinese Americans had launched up to that point. It received considerable support from organizations and individuals within the community. The language that *The Chinese-Western Daily* and the merchants used to endorse and promote the bank allows us a glimpse of two themes that characterized the collective mentality of Chinese San Francisco, namely, strong nationalistic sentiments and a receptiveness to Western culture and ideas.

In an editorial, *The Chinese-Western Daily* embraced the bank by declaring that it would help "foster commerce and enhance national dignity." The editorial hailed this Western-style financial institution as a sign of the community's departure from its old mind-set. In the early years, it elaborated, "we were not ambitious, and had a contempt for the barbarians . . . and were unfamiliar with their language." That was why, it contended, Chinese Americans had failed to build "legitimate businesses with marked features."[62] On a later occasion the newspaper used the same nationalistic notions to promote the bank again. It began by stating that because of China's weakness "our fellow Chinese in this country received all kinds of harsh treatment." Therefore, it declared, "anyone who wants China to be prosperous and strong should invest in the bank," because doing so would help to "restore our rights and interests from within, and increase our nation's dignity from without."[63]

For Chinese Americans, nationalism and receptiveness to Western ideas did not represent two conflicting paths. In the particular history context, they went hand in hand. In fact, Social Darwinist concepts often served as a vehicle for articulating Chinese nationalism. In a lengthy public statement made to solicit investments, the bank's founders explained its political significance by relating commercial competition to the struggle for survival among nations, and national interest to that of individual Chinese Americans. The statement recounted the local situation:

> In the Gold Mountain, the Japanese . . . have three banks with large volumes of profits. Few merchants from other countries do not have banks in this city. After six decades of trade between China and America, the Chinese in the Gold Mountain have not had a bank yet. Our rights and interest have therefore been lost to outsiders. They must laugh at our stupidity. Even if we do not care for profit, we should not lose the right and the convenience in monetary exchange and remittance.

Moreover, the statement continued, "banks are the basis of [a nation's] strength and prosperity." Therefore, the new Chinese American bank would help "protect national dignity, uphold our rights, significantly promote business, and improve China's foreign relations." Finally, the statement reminded potential investors of their political responsibility by asking: "If we are unable to raise money to establish a bank and continue to lose our rights, how can we then strengthen the homeland and avert foreigners' ridicule?"[64]

We do not know how many people read such newspaper endorsements and announcements or accepted the political message communicated therein. What we do know is that many individuals invested their personal savings in the Canton bank. By early June 1907 about 87 people had already deposited more than $75,000 in it.[65]

Evidence shows that in America, as in China, Social Darwinism became quite popular among Chinese.[66] Among the authors that numerous book dealers promoted, Herbert Spencer featured prominently. In newspaper articles and public speeches vulgarized Social Darwinistic notions were prevalent. Advertisers showed their understanding of the currency these notions had gained in the community by using them frequently. In one advertisement, for example, the Canton Hotel on Sacramento Street adopted Social Darwinistic rhetoric to appeal to customers' nationalist feelings by urging them not to stay in non-Chinese hotels because it would mean a "loss of rights and benefits" for Chinese people. All Chinese should do their share to restore the lost rights, the advertisement declared, "at a time when China has started to reform and to compete with foreign countries."[67]

The prevalence of Social Darwinism among Chinese Americans did not, however, stem from a blind, wholesale internalization of Western thoughts on their part. Rather, its usage reveals their efforts to appropriate the elements of Western thought that they deemed helpful. They selectively adopted what B. Semmel calls "external Social Darwinism" because it offered an explanation for China's current weakness, conveyed a clear sense of national crisis, and served as a stimulus for modernization.[68] It also provided a framework in which Chinese Americans could contemplate their own situation and their future. Furthermore, Social Darwinism gave them hope and enabled them to reject nineteenth-century racist notions of inherent white superiority and Chinese inferiority. By taking "the survival of the fittest" to mean "the survival of strongest" among national groups, they believed that a transformed China could change their present status.

The editorials in *The Chinese-Western Daily* exemplify Chinese Americans' appropriation of Social Darwinistic concepts. Explaining Social Darwinism, one editorial noted that "the law of evolution is the victory of the superior and the defeat of the inferior. The superior survives because of his victory;

the inferior perishes because of his defeat." The editorial then adapted Social Darwinism to Chinese cosmology by saying: "This is the competition of species under the heavenly mandate."[69] Social Darwinism, another editorial noted, was the law that governed "the competition among the nations on the five continents."[70] No individual or class could escape the consequence of such competition, as a different editorial put it: "In such a world of racial competition, no scholar, peasant, worker, and merchant can avoid the elimination of selection."[71]

The "survival of the fittest" concept was applied to every significant issue. Education was important because, one editorial averred, "a nation uneducated will face the risk of destruction," and "in the competition for survival, nothing but education can save the dying."[72] Physical education, which received more and more attention in the community, especially at the Chinese school, was labeled a significant element in "human evolution."[73]

Individual Chinese were urged to follow the example set by Americans and Europeans in order to strengthen China and their community. In February 1908 Chinese Methodist ministers from several cities gathered in San Francisco and proposed to establish an independent Chinese American church. Praising the proposal for showing the "spirit of independence," *The Chinese-Western Daily* concluded: "The civilized countries in Europe and America have been able to become strong on their own because their citizens do not have the character of dependency."[74]

The Western nations stood as points of comparison and models for China. The newspaper explained that while the Western powers had been victorious "over the land and in the sea" since the eighteenth century, "China has been in decline and its people have been suffering from poverty."[75] Another editorial called on people to support the Chinese school in San Francisco, stating that "Western countries' political institutions, scholarship, technology, customs, and morality are progressing every day as a result of their educational systems."[76]

The United States, in particular, was the object of much praise. According to the newspaper, "The United States, born in the new continent, is the youngest of all nations. Yet it is much better in government and more prosperous in wealth than its homeland."[77] Neither those who wrote these remarks nor those who read them had forgotten about racial oppression, however. Throughout Chinese American history, they never have.

We need to recognize the fact that in tackling the problem of racial injustice Chinese Americans adopted different approaches in different contexts. When dealing with white American legal, social, and political institutions they directly challenged discrimination and asserted their rights. Written in Chinese for internal consumption, the editorials in *The Chinese-Western Daily*, however, represented a different discourse within the Chinese community. As these editorials illustrate, internal discussions of discrimination were always conducted in connection with conditions in China. Self-examination and self-improvement constituted dominant themes. Chinese Americans critically reflected on problems within their own community in an effort to strengthen it. What is more, they looked for ways to rectify China's weakness, which they viewed as the ultimate origin of the racial oppression of the Chinese.

Chinese Americans had ample evidence to support that view. In April 1906 the San Francisco School Board sent Japanese students to the segregated school attended by Chinese pupils, thereby carrying out a resolution it had adopted a year before. Japan, a new world power that had defeated Russia in the 1904–5 Russo–Japanese War, protested vigorously, forcing Theodore Roosevelt to intervene. The school board rescinded its decision.[78] This incident stood as convincing evidence of the importance of a strong homeland. *The Chinese-Western Daily* noted: "the reason why Japan could win in the case, as our people know, is because of the national strength that the [Japanese] government has in protecting its people."[79] Immigrants saw the outrageous motion to relocate Chinatown as being similarly connected to China's powerlessness. Referring to this motion, an editorial remarked: "Before the fires [during the earthquake], Westerners had already proposed [the relocation] for several times. . . . The reason behind it . . . is because China is too weak."[80]

The ideas discussed above generated a yearning for progress and change. In fact, words such as "new," "progress," "reform," and, later on, "revolution," all of which defied the notion of tradition, bespoke a hope for the regeneration of China and the immigrant community and became extremely fashionable. China had fallen behind the West because, *The Chinese-Western Daily* editorialized, having suffered under tyranny for centuries, it "has been closed for internal intercourse and has not sought progress."[81] The enfeebled homeland needed to be revitalized with youthfulness. In 1909, in reference to the appearance of the aforementioned new daily, *Young China*, *The Chinese-Western Daily* proclaimed: "Youth is the time when the human spirit is at the fullest."[82]

On another occasion the newspaper declared: "The world is opening up, and the new trend is pressing us like the wind."[83] People could certainly feel this longing for renewal blowing through Chinese San Francisco. On Dupont Street stood the New Canton hotel. In mid-August 1912 theater-goers could enjoy performances by the New Stage, a Chinese opera troupe. Book dealers advertised books that were classified as "new-trend." *The Chinese-Western Daily* itself advertised over three hundred "new-trend" titles on a wide range of subjects, including world history, medicine, Chinese and world geography, literature, and social and political theories.[84]

Social evolution and Westernization constituted important subjects of these books, which were quite affordable. Another newspaper, *Chinese World*, also promoted "new-trend" books, including *The New Book of Western Etiquette and Customs*, which sold for 75 cents, and *Questions and Answers Concerning the Reproduction and Improvement of Species*, which was priced at 35 cents.[85] Ordinary residents did not have to buy books or go to the theater to absorb the effects of this ubiquitous trend, however. A cooking oil company, the Nam Mow Company, advertised its product, which was sold at four stores in San Francisco, by stressing that its philosophy was in accordance with the intellectual tenor of the day: "Today's world is one in which everything is being renewed and advanced. Therefore all kinds of food, even including a daily necessity like cooking oil, require constant improvement in order to survive."[86]

Tradition Versus Reform

The new mentality turned many Chinese San Franciscans into antitraditionalists and readied them for the task of building a new community. The post-earthquake reconstruction of Chinatown provided a catalyst for change. It intensified the community's self-criticism of its old social customs, which it identified as an important cause of past racial injustice. It also provided an opportunity to implement social renovation in order to achieve racial equality for the Chinese in America.

Less than a month after the earthquake, when talk of restoring China-town was still in the air, *The Chinese-Western Daily* called for social trans-formation in an editorial entitled "After Restoration, Chinatown Must Be Reformed." The editorial proposed the elimination of a long list of tradi-tional customs seen as "the causes of humiliation." On the list were faction-alism, the notorious tong wars, gambling, opium smoking, queues, and foot binding. It also urged the community "to sweep away idols." Extremely wasteful, the worship of "these senseless idols represents a most savage act," the editorial declared. Lamenting that some people still stuck to such cus-toms after many years of being exposed to the "civilization" of America, it exclaimed: "What a pity and how stupid!"[87] The pungent tone of self-criticism reflected an ardent desire to renew and regenerate.

One important area of social renovation was that of women's rights. Judy Yung points out that the impetus came not only from the women's move-ment in China but also from immigrant women's experiences in America, namely, their contact with Protestant missionary women and their entry into the economy.[88] The call to improve women's social status received support from the community. *The Chinese-Western Daily* advocated women's educa-tion and criticized the social oppression of women, including oppression by their husbands, in both the community and in China.[89] On one occasion the newspaper encouraged young people to choose their own spouses and at-tacked parent-arranged marriages as a legacy of tyranny.[90] At another time it criticized the mistreatment of maids, applying Social Darwinistic rhetoric and racial terms: "Even animals, unless they lose their natural instincts, cher-ish their own species. . . . At an age when racial war is the most intense, our people should unite and care for one another in order to survive in the world of evolution."[91]

Indeed, such rhetoric was constantly invoked to justify social reform. "Old customs," *The Chinese-Western Daily* editorialized, "are the obstacle to evolution," and "imprisonment by old customs will destroy a nation."[92] An earlier editorial viewed community renovation not only as a way to end anti-Chinese discrimination but also as part of global racial competition: "In the twentieth century [the world] has become a great stage of competition be-tween the yellow race and the white race." Connected to that competition, "the construction of a new Chinatown," the editorial concluded, would en-able Chinese San Franciscans to "rectify the old way, revitalize our spirit, sweep away the corrupt customs, and create a new world."[93] Such passages clearly show the extent to which Chinese Americans had internalized America's racial terms and the accompanying ideological framework. As we will see later, this constrained their battle against discrimination, especially their ability to form coalitions with other minorities.

The call for a departure from traditional customs represented not just an intellectual exercise performed by a few members of the elite but a practical effort that took place during the reconstruction of Chinatown. First of all, the community declared war on opium smoking, a deeply ingrained habit. Various medical remedies were made available for addicts who were willing to quit. This social evil was also viewed as being politically harmful. In an advertisement, one pharmaceutical store called opium "a big evil for our country." If the Chinese could "purge themselves from the obsessive sin," the advertisement promised, "the nation will be strong and the country will be prosperous in the near future." The store's effort was recognized by Minister Liang, who awarded it a horizontal board inscribed with the words: "Great contribution to the preservation of the [Chinese] race."[94]

Activists formed an organization to launch an anti-opium campaign in the spring of 1907. The group adopted the name of a similar one in China, Zhenwu (promoting martialism) Society—a name indicative of the influence of the prevailing ideology described earlier, because opium use was seen as having weakened the spiritual and physical strength of the Chinese. The organization's twelve regular members, all unpaid volunteers, distributed free medicine to opium addicts every day, and helped to disseminate prescriptions to assist them in making their own medicine.[95] Similar societies were soon established in New York and other cities. In 1908 San Franciscans formed the General Organization to Stop Opium Smoking (Jieyan zonghui). Associating their products with this new popular anti-opium crusade came to constitute a marketing strategy for some merchants. Store owners in Oregon and British Columbia posted a joint advertisement for "the first-class ginseng" as a cure for the addiction.

Also coming under attack was the queue. Once a symbol of their national identity and filial devotion, Chinese Americans had treasured it with so much pride that they fought hard against hostile white authorities' attempts to remove it. Under the influence of the new mentality, however, more and more people cut their queues voluntarily, making haircutting a profitable business. A growing number of advertisements for queue-cutting services appeared in Chinese newspapers. In one case a barber noted that queue cutting had become "a social trend." He stated that from the store's opening to "the fifteenth day of the fifth month last year," it had cut 1,986 queues.[96]

Claims like this cannot be construed solely as marketing schemes, however. It is clear that the new mentality had a significant social impact. Later on, the community designated special dates for queue cutting in San Francisco and elsewhere.[97] On one designated date in New York, community leaders were the first to cut their queues.[98] Queue cutting transformed Chinese Americans' physical appearance and revealed their resolve to renew China and their own community. At a public meeting in San Francisco on the day of the Mid-Autumn Festival, a date set for community queue cutting, one speaker attacked the queue as an obstacle to political progress.[99] Before long the queue had totally disappeared from the community.

The huiguan, once guardians of tradition, became vanguards of the reform mentality. The Ningyang Huiguan, the largest and most powerful of all the huiguan, was the first both to move back to San Francisco's Chinatown and to institute new social practices. It announced several times that to celebrate the opening of its new building, it would hold a new-style ceremony that would include speeches made by guest speakers rather than worship of the gods. In an editorial published on October 15, 1907, *The Chinese-Western Daily* hailed this idol-free huiguan as a "pioneer in the evolution of our overseas Chinese" and the new-style ceremony as "a significant step towards the enlightenment of the people."[100]

The ceremony attracted several hundred people. The progress of China and of Chinese America constituted the dominant theme of the eight speakers' speeches. A Chinese Christian minister, praising the huiguan's decision to discard idols, spoke of the Jewish people, who had prospered after discarding their idols. Speakers associated the innovations implemented by the Ningyang Huiguan with China's future. Deng Yiyun, a frequent contributor to *The Chinese-Western Daily*, declared: "The glory of China in the future shall shine over the five continents of the world."[101]

Other institutions soon followed suit. In July 1910 the Shaoqing Huiguan voted against placing idols in their rebuilt building.[102] On December 17, 1911, the Longgang Association, a clan association, had a "civilized" opening ceremony.[103] The trend spread to other Chinese communities as well. In 1912 the

Chinese in New York decided that idols would not appear in public places.[104] The new mentality and the drive toward community renewal achieved what the missionaries had not been able to accomplish.

Pleased by the fact that an increasing number of organizations were rejecting idols, an editorial in *The Chinese-Western Daily* joyfully declared as early as September 1907 that "today's Gold Mountain takes on an entirely new look after the earthquake." It used the example of Western nations to justify the abandonment of idolatry: "Today's world is the arena of an intelligence contest among nations. . . . Look at the civilized American and European nations, which one worships idols? Look at the nations that did, which one has not vanished?"[105] After its formation in September 1906, The Chinatown Chamber of Commerce resolved to regularly invite "Western" merchants to its annual meetings. *The Chinese-Western Daily* welcomed the resolution as "a sign of progress of the civilization of our Chinese people" and as a necessary adjustment in "the struggle for survival."[106]

The 1911 revolution in China further stimulated the process of social change in Chinese San Francisco.[107] A Society of Custom Reform formed shortly after the revolution. At its monthly meeting in July 1912, one speaker told an audience of about two hundred people that "a nation declines because of corrupt social customs."[108] The Chinese YMCA followed suit by inviting guest speakers to talk about changing customary practices.[109]

In its challenging of old traditions the Chinese revolution gave rise to new ones, such as the new calendar adopted by the recently formed Republic of China in Nanjing at the end of 1911. Designed to mark a new era in Chinese history, this calendar was truly revolutionary: not only did it change the way each year was named—1912 was to be the first year of the Republic—but the old lunar calendar was also replaced by a solar one. The latter change made the new calendar difficult for some Chinese San Franciscans, who had long been accustomed to the lunar system, to accept immediately. On New Year's day *The Chinese-Western Daily* defended the solar calendar on the grounds that it was used by "all the [Western] powers."[110] Later it labeled people's unwillingness to adopt the new calendar as a violation of the law of the Chinese government. Moreover, it stated that since the old calendar had nurtured fortune-telling and witchcraft, continuing to use it would promote superstition and hinder "social evolution."[111]

The reform minded eventually had their way when the new calendar was officially endorsed by one organization after another. By the beginning of 1912 the newspaper *Chinese World*, established originally by the Constitutionalists, had adopted the new calendar.[112] At the end of that year the Zhonghua Huiguan declared it the official calendar of the community, thereby changing the way the community marked time and beginning a new chapter in its history.[113]

As the preceding analysis illustrates, the stimulus for social reform came about as a result of Chinese Americans' own comprehension of how to improve their situation, instead of as a result of the pressure created by mainstream assimilationists. Few members of the dominant society had any interest in making Chinese Americans similar to themselves. In fact, most white Americans believed that the Chinese were "unassimilable." Inattentive to how dramatically the Chinese American community's collective mentality had been transformed and "Westernized," white Americans continued to seek and even recreate the old Orient through the Chinese community's physical appearance. In a passage about reconstructed Chinatown, an old-time San Franciscan recalled: "The result has an outward appearance of the Orient."[114] Before Chinatown was rebuilt tour guides had already revived the old practice of taking white tourists to staged scenes, such as opium dens in Oakland, that supposedly captured the alien-ness and immorality of the Chinese. Chinese San Franciscans resented this "act of deception" that "defamed the Chinese," and urged the consul general to find a way to stop it.[115]

The ideologically and socially transformed community did not lose its trans-Pacific ties. Increasingly nationalistic Chinese Americans maintained their parochial identity and connections to the ancestral places. Remittances continued to flow to loved ones; Guangdong scholars and pastors kept coming to San Francisco to head the huiguan and churches; periodicals published in the emigrant region arrived regularly in Chinese San Francisco with the latest news about events on the other side of the Pacific Ocean. China-bound ships also continued to carry the remains of the dead to their birthplaces for final rest. Early in 1912, right after the revolution, the Ningyang Huiguan started another massive operation to transport the bones of the dead to China. Hundreds of individuals joined numerous organizations across the nation in donating amounts ranging from $1 to $25 for the project.[116] By late 1913 fourteen hundred bodies had been excavated and shipped to Xinning County.

The social and cultural transformation that we have described did not amount to a thorough cultural revolution. The adoption of the new calendar did signal the end of the Chinese New Year celebration of other traditional festivals. Although diminished in influence, some severely criticized customs, including opium smoking, lingered on. In August 1911 *Young China* reported that the police had found large quantities of opium at six different places in Chinatown.[117]

What is more, the strong China that Chinese Americans had longed for did not emerge, and their eager hope soon dissipated as harsh reality set in. A Chinese American representative to the Chinese national assembly, Kuang Yaojie, found out that the dates and procedure for the assembly had not even been set upon his arrival in Shanghai. In frustration, Kuang told his fellow San Franciscans that instead of heading to Beijing he had decided to proceed to Guangdong first. He also reported that Shanghai was plagued by poverty and unemployment—apparently he found no sign of the prosperity that the revolution had promised.[118]

News of political realities in China soon reached Chinese San Francisco. *The Chinese-Western Daily*, once most enthusiastic about the revolution, quickly began criticizing political corruption in China. One editorial declared: "The corruption in politics is all the same all over the world. But the corruption in China was worse than any other place. And it is the worst in China today. . . . [It is] republican in name but dictatorial in reality."[119] Although they were disappointed by the failure of the 1911 revolution and by the corruption of political factions, Chinese San Franciscans did not abandon their effort to help China, or their nationalistic sentiments. As we shall see in the coming chapters, the struggle against the Japanese invasion in China, in particular, enhanced their nationalist spirit to an extraordinary degree.

EIGHT

The American-ness of the Trans-Pacific Community Between the Wars

In spite of a corruption-plagued city government, by the outbreak of World War I San Francisco had rebuilt itself. One element of its recovery was Chinatown's reemergence as a tourist site. The San Francisco Chamber of Commerce's tour guide devoted seventeen long pages to Chinatown, calling it "this most fascinating city of America."[1] It also assured visitors of their safety there: "Avoiding trouble is a Chinese national habit, and nowhere is the white visitor more secure in property or person."[2] As Jerome A. Hart pointed out before the war began, decades of exclusion had "relieved" Californians of their "fear concerning the Chinese," enabling the former to promote Chinatown as a safe attraction in an effort to bring more attention, tourists, and money to the recuperating city.[3]

The 1915 Panama Pacific International Exposition announced San Francisco's resurrection. The $25 million extravaganza added to the city's glory and prestige, bringing millions of visitors (nearly nineteen million had been admitted by December 4). The fair was also a celebration of ideas that had become popular in American society and that had influenced Chinese Americans. An important theme of the event was "the Progress of Man," of which the big Column of Progress, standing next to the centerpiece of the exposition, the Court of the Universe, provided visitors a visual reminder.[4] The exposition was a glorification of Western civilization. Non-Western cultures were displayed as objects of curiosity and as students of Western material and intellectual progress. In what Gray Brechin has called "a final flourish of Social Darwinism," an architect wrote prior to the opening of the exposition: "How grandly it would grace this farthest western frontier of the civilization of the Anglo-Saxon, where it faces its anti-type, the oriental."[5]

Capturing the fair organizers' idea of Orientalism was a re-creation of a Chinese opium den in the Joy Zone. Called Underground Chinatown, it employed Chinese individuals to demonstrate "the fate of the opium smoker and the drug fiend" and became a popular attraction at the fair.[6] Following a protest from the Chinese Exposition Commission, the exhibit was renamed Underground Slumming, and the Chinese actors were removed. But its popularity continued. This episode illustrates the public's desire to display and see the inferiority and vices of Chinatown and Chinese life.

Returning to the reconstructed Chinatown in increasingly large numbers, nostalgic non-Chinese tourists came in search of its exoticized past, which had been embedded in their minds for decades. Capitalizing on this nostalgia, the ex-missionary Mrs. Clemence Wong (formerly Ella May Clemens) and her husband made an exhibition of relics that they had rescued from the ruins of the old Chinatown into a highlight of their guided tour, "Wong Sun Yue Wong Chinatown Trip." The relics were housed in a tea garden, where the tour began. Mrs. Wong proudly called it "the greatest attraction, not only of Chinatown, but of all California" in the brochure she wrote to promote the tour in 1915.[7] Over the door of the tea garden was a big carved wooden arch taken from a temple in Canton, which took spectators further back to the community's pagan past.

Tour guides did much to make Chinese life into a commodity by highlighting its foreignness and reinforcing its image as "mysterious" and perennially stagnant.[8] But they offered little insight into the community that was fast becoming the opposite of its projected image. In early 1915 the Chinatown Chamber of Commerce hosted a banquet in honor of the Chinese envoy to the exposition. All members wore American-style attire and found ways to enjoy the individually served dishes with knives and forks instead of with chopsticks, turning the event into a display of how modernized or Westernized the revived Chinese community had become.

An event even more revealing of Chinatown's newfound modernity began to unfold in August 1915, when the community received the news that it would lose the service of the Pacific Mail S. S. Company, which had been the trans-Pacific passenger carrier for years. In 1911, for instance, it had trans-ported 38,467 passengers, far more than any of its competitors. For the in-creasingly anti-Japanese community the news also represented the frighten-ing prospect that "all trans-Pacific transportation would come under Japanese control."[9] The *Toyo Kisen Kaisha*, which had become by 1911 the second largest trans-Pacific passenger carrier since it began operations in the 1890s, later announced its intention to double the size of its fleet.

On August 25 the *Mongolian* began what was believed to be its last voy-age eastward, departing to the sound of firecrackers set off by its Chinese crew. It was the restriction on employing Chinese sailors like these, imposed by the widely criticized La Follette Act, that killed the Pacific Mail S. S. Company.[10] Three days later Chinese merchants decided to establish a ship-ping company, the China Mail S. S. Company. In about two months, on October 30, its first ship, *China*, set sail for Hong Kong with 355 passengers on board.[11] The formation of this company marked a defining moment in Chinese San Francisco's history. The company represented the beginning of the struggle against accelerating Japanese aggression in China—a struggle that remained the dominant issue within the community for the next three decades, as we will see in the next chapter. Japan's infamous Twenty-one Demands that threatened China's sovereignty had triggered an organized boycott against Japan in Chinese America early in the year. The impetus to create a Chinese American shipping enterprise arose out of a zealous desire to boycott Japanese ocean liners. Emphasizing its political significance, the company's founders promoted their enterprise as a means to "protect our na-tional interest and rights."[12] Supporting it thus became a moral obligation. The few merchants who had not invested in the company by early October were publicly identified and humiliated.

Furthermore, the emergence of the China Mail S. S. Company under-lined the transformation of Chinese San Francisco that had started a few years before. Made possible by Chinese American investments of as much as ten thousand dollars in some cases, its creation stood as an indicator of the community's growing economic strength and stronger desire to control its own destiny. In just the next few years, a number of similarly large Chinese companies appeared in San Francisco.

Changes took place in every aspect of life, illustrating how American the trans-Pacific community had become. The changes were social, cultural, and political. Reflecting greater social stratification and class conflict, labor unions and radical ideologies came on the scene. Chinese San Franciscans entertained themselves with newly adopted non-Chinese traditions like the Miss Chinatown Pageant. Beginning with their support for America's war efforts, a growing number of Chinese San Franciscans participated in American politics in various ways. More and more Chinese American citizens voted in national and local elections, and they emerged as a visible social force within the community. Many Chinese San Franciscans came to regard the United States as their adopted country. On July 4, 1927, *The Chinese-Western Daily* noted that celebrating this American holiday had become a "usual practice" in the community. It went on to say that "We Chinese people have lived in the United States for a long time and have come to regard it as our second homeland."[13] By then the huiguan had begun to abandon the practice of selecting scholars from China to be their presidents. Gradually, the new ones all came to be elected from within Chinese America.[14]

Socioeconomic Changes

The establishment of the China and Mail S. S. Company was followed by the creation of a number of other large companies: a cigarette-manufacturing company established in 1916 that produced "The China Beauty Cigarettes," the Chinese and American Trunk Manufacturing Company founded in 1916, and the Tool Kwong Aviation Corporation founded in 1918.[15] It became so fashionable to establish large-scale companies in these years that a criminal formed a phony shipping company in an attempt to swindle clients out of their money. In 1919 Chen Chunrong founded the Chinese American Agricultural Company. His ambitious purchase of a 3,437-acre farm near Stockton immediately attracted hundreds of investors. A Chinese San Franciscan named Chen Jiyao, owner of Kwong San Wo and Company, invested ten thousand dollars. By early October $105,275 had been raised. Investment money continued to come in for quite some time. As late as March 1920 the twelfth list of investors published in *The Chinese-Western Daily* still included more than 110 people.[16] The extraordinary popularity of this agricultural company best symbolized the willingness of many Chinese to put their money into and settle permanently on American soil.[17]

In addition, those business ventures testify to the rise of a small yet growing group of Chinese who had accumulated not only considerable wealth but also useful economic and legal knowledge about America. Chen Chunrong of the Chinese American Farms, for instance, had worked for the Italian American Bank in San Francisco. He was also one of the first Chinese lawyers to represent Chinese clients in courts. By the early 1940s the Chinese community had not only its own legal and banking experts but also accountants, opticians, dentists, and insurance counselors.

While well-to-do Chinese San Franciscans undertook the building of large companies, workers started to unionize. At a meeting in May 1919, 29 "noble-minded" men proposed the organization of a Chinese labor union.[18] They sent out 70 copies of the proposal to solicit support from workers in clothing and garment factories and received over a hundred favorable responses, exceeding their expectations. On May 18 the League of Labor was established. It soon afterwards delivered to employers nine demands, which included a nine-hour work day. In October the expanding league, which some agricultural workers had by then joined, was renamed the American General League of Labor. On October 5 more than two hundred people, among them the president of the Yanghe Huiguan, attended a ceremony at the elegant Xinhua Lou restaurant.[19]

From the beginning the Chinese labor movement faced an array of difficulties. First of all, it had limited financial resources. In 1919, according to the annual financial report published later in its organ *Kung Sing* (the voice of the workers), the League of Labor's total revenue amounted to a modest $496.15, and its total expenditure stood at $535.50.[20] Second, the movement in general did not command much support from established organizations in Chinese American communities across the nation.[21] In early January 1919 several major organizations in New York's Chinatown, including merchants, clan associations, and secret societies, jointly declared that "labor union members, joined by some Westerners, harassed [Chinese] restaurants, which had a negative impact on business and the image of the Chinese." They urged all organizations to restrain their members from enlisting in labor unions and making trouble.[22] In a community meeting held on October 5 the city's leading Chinese organization prohibited young

Chinese from joining labor unions. Those who did not comply, it warned, would lose the protection of all other organizations.[23]

Nevertheless, new labor unions continued to emerge, and they organized numerous strikes. Sponsored by the Xifu Union in San Francisco, Chinese laundry workers went on strike early in 1929, demanding that the more than eighty-five hours per week that they worked at the time be reduced.[24] The scale of the large strike propelled community leaders to act as mediators. The Chinese employers did not budge, instead trying to replace Chinese workers with African Americans.[25]

The Zhongxing Company (Joe Shong Company, Inc.; later National Dollar Stores), one of the largest and most successful Chinese American companies, was involved in serious labor disputes during this period.[26] A flyer distributed by a radical organization during one strike reported that long work hours had cost several female employees of this company their lives. The savage cruelty of the owner, the flyer charged, "is many, many times worse than that of a Western capitalist."[27] In a strike in January 1938, about two hundred workers walked out of the company's factory on Washington Street. By then about three fourths of the company's workforce, including its factory workers and retail-store employees, had been unionized by the Congress of Industrial Organizations (CIO) and the American Federation of Labor (AF of L), respectively.[28] In economic relations, evidently, Chinese San Francisco was becoming more and more like white American society.

Anarchism, which had been part of the European immigrants' political heritage and had commanded a great deal of attention in American society since the late nineteenth century, also reached Chinese San Francisco.[29] In March 1928, seven months after the electrocution of Bartolomeo Vanzetti and Nicola Sacco, two Chinese anarchists were arrested by the police. They were members of the Equality Society, an anarchist organization founded in Chinese San Francisco in the 1910s. The society published the journal *Equality* as its organ and distributed anarchist and revolutionary books to the community.

Like its counterpart in white American society, Chinese anarchism was closely connected with the labor movement.[30] That connection was embodied by Zhong Shi, an officer of the American General League of Labor and an editor of *Equality*. Like many other Chinese, he had come to America as an immigrant laborer. His experience in the New World, nonetheless, transformed him into a stern critic of capitalism rather than making him a Horatio Alger.

As is evidenced in a letter that he wrote to his parents in 1921, Zhong Shi's criticism stemmed from his personal experience. The militancy and the strong political language that characterizes his letter portrays an informed radical who happened to be Chinese. Referring to the photographs he sent along with the letter, he wrote:

> You can see the hardship in my life. I suffer from hardship because in order to live [we] have to sell our labor to the vicious capitalists, planters and landlords, and work as slaves of wages. This is forced on us by the private ownership of capitalism. Under capitalism, most of us common people do not have the control of our own labor. I think capitalism and the dictatorial private ownership will eventually be destroyed.

It interesting to note that Zhong Shi shared the community's desire to change the Chinese way of life, a desired revealed by his attacks on traditional social customs, such as rites and religious idols. These customs, he declared, "fetter the free development of human beings, hinder social progress and must be eradicated." As he mentioned, rather ironically, at the end of the letter, this critic of American capitalism remembered to send his parents "a big piece of gold."[31]

The transformation of Chinese San Francisco also involved cultural adaptation. In August 1915, while the merchants were planning to launch a shipping company, Chinatown conducted a Miss Chinatown Pageant, a new and traditionally non-Chinese event, as part of a carnival. In fact, the idea came from what *Young China* called "an association of Western women citizens."[32] Using the pageant as an occasion for charity fund-raising, organizers sold raffle tickets for the "election" of a beauty queen. The novel event created a great deal of turmoil in the community and turned out to be an almost complete fiasco. The "election," in particular, was more anxiety-provoking than entertaining. Many Chinese were particularly outraged by the last-minute "votes" cast by a wealthy white man that helped to claim the victory for the winner. Some individuals became restless, cursing in front of "Western women" and tearing down an American flag. The Zhonghua

Huiguan had to hold a special meeting to find a solution, and several hundred people showed up uninvited, anxious for clarification. Its explanation that a beauty queen contest was different from the election of officials could hardly calm them. The controversy forced the pageant winner to concede her title, and the crown went to Rosie Lew (she had a Chinese name, Liu Yin, as it was spelled in pinyin). The main coronation ceremony was moved out of Chinatown, and a scheduled parade was canceled. It is difficult to determine to what extent Chinese Americans' anger toward the wealthy man represented a conscious political outburst against racial oppression. It seems clear, however, that the strong reaction to what was billed as entertainment cannot be seen as purely apolitical.

The beauty pageant that was subsequently held many times and became an important public event was never pure entertainment. Called the Lion-Awakening Fair, the 1927 pageant featured a lion parade. Organizers of the nine-day extravaganza used the lion theme to communicate a political message. They published an official "declaration" at the opening of the event. "The lion has wakened with its power and majesty to inspire and awaken our fellow Chinese from dreams," it proclaimed.[33] The purpose of the pageant was to raise money for the Chinese Hospital. The popular event was widely supported within the community, and it also attracted non-Chinese visitors to Chinatown. Different organizations nominated their own contestants and deployed their members to sell raffle tickets. At the coronation ceremony on November 4, Mayor James Ralph Jr. placed the crown on the elected queen. Colorful decorated floats, representing various organizations, schools, and stores, then paraded through Chinatown. The 1927 pageant exemplifies how Chinese San Franciscans turned a non-Chinese tradition into a vehicle to mobilize, benefit, and empower their community.

Women's highly visible role in such public events served as evidence of their rising presence. It signified improvement not only in the community's sex ratio but also in women's status. At a time when all leading social institutions remained fraternal organizations, the pageants increased Chinese American women's access to the public sphere. In the nineteenth century the most important public space that women occupied was within the confines of the theaters, where actresses performed together with men and female patrons sat in segregated sections. By comparison, the pageants took place out in the open and were directly connected to the welfare of the community.

Furthermore, at pageants women were the center of attention. Even the Chinese newspapers devoted space to their life stories.

As the newspaper reports show, beauty pageant contestants possessed more than physical beauty. Many of them went to school or even to college. A few had their own careers. They represented a new generation of Chinese women who were able to explore opportunities that had recently started to become available to them. The eighteen-year-old queen of the 1915 pageant, Rosie Lew, for instance, had graduated from a high school in Oakland. Ella Dong, the 1927 contest winner, was then a junior at the University of California. The 1925 Miss Chinatown, Liang Suling, had studied business after graduating from the Oriental School and was at that time working for a Chinese company in San Francisco. More and more women were participating in various other public events, in addition to the pageants.

An increasing number of women also followed the same educational and career path that these beauty queens did. A brief resume of Ng Poon Chew's four daughters provides an additional index to the life of this growing group of women. The eldest sister, Jingping, a musician by profession, worked as a secretary for *The Chinese-Western Daily*. Yuqing, the second sister, had been a teacher in Oakland's Lincoln School after 1918; she was reportedly the first Chinese, except for those hired as Chinese-language instructors, ever to have taught in a public school.[34] The third sister, Dongmei, a college graduate, became executive secretary of San Francisco's Chinese YWCA. Qionglan (Caroline), the youngest, had once worked for the Chinese YWCA. Also known as "Dancer Caroline Chew," she learned to dance from American and Chinese teachers after graduating from Mills College, where she studied piano and composition.

"The striving for equal rights between men and women [was] under way," as a Chinese American poem went.[35] The change was gradual, but it was clearly occurring. With better opportunities for education, more and more women enjoyed greater personal freedom as well. Divorce cases, for one thing, seemed to be on the rise. While some women filed their requests with the Zhonghua Huiguan, others, especially those outside San Francisco, simply took them to court. In early 1918 a Chinese woman in Oregon successfully divorced her husband. She reportedly hired a lawyer and accused her husband of abusing her. Women's increased assertiveness on the individual level and their influence on community affairs as a group were undoubtedly attributable to the socioeconomic and demographic transformation of Chinese America as well as to the influence of the mainstream culture.

Chinese newspapers' coverage of women and of issues concerning them also increased over time, which helps to reveal the community's changing mentality regarding gender relations. Let us take a look at some examples that appeared in the *Chinese Times* toward the end of this period.

In February 1942 the daily paper published an article that described what it considered to be an ideal woman. She was first and foremost a housewife whose world centered around her husband and her domestic responsibilities: "She desires to marry a man. . . . She can take only half of the credit for her husband's career but all the credit for building a successful family. She knows when her husband needs a hair cut but does not notice when he gets it." Meanwhile, however, the article suggested that the ideal woman must be mentally strong; she "loves a man who comes home with fatigue more than with the news of a job promotion."[36] Furthermore, it recognized her independence. "She once regarded some man as perfect. She has had more than one chance to get married." It is important to note what is explicitly communicated here: it was a virtue for a woman to have dated more than one man and even to have made some mistakes. Clearly, the ideal woman prescribed here was different from the one Ah Quin and the Xianzhi writers envisioned back in the late nineteenth century.

An earlier article reported the achievements of a young woman, a sixteen-year-old opera singer named Liu Jinlan, using language that conveyed much respect. It called her *nushi* (meaning "lady"), a term usually reserved for high-status older women. The last paragraph states: "When asked if she wanted to perform in China some day, she nodded with a smile. . . . When she does that . . . people in China would understand that we [Chinese Americans] have other merits besides donating money."[37] The author clearly saw Liu Jinlan as someone who was well qualified to represent Chinese Americans and their achievements. The last sentence of the quote also expessed an awareness of a distinctive Chinese American identity.

In part seven of a long commentary series entitled "On Love," a female writer encouraged women to "develop critical eyes." Then she gave her own assessment of the elevation of women's status: "As the old saying goes: 'nothing is more unfortunate than existing in the female body, and [if you are a woman] your joy and sorrow are determined by other people.' This is a reflection of the past, when women's free will was restricted, and they had to obey the elders and men. But modern women have much more room to act freely."[38] Comments such as this indicate that people in the community were aware of changes in gender relations. These changes were certainly part of the social and cultural transformation that had been under way beginning early in the century.

Indeed, acculturation became visible in many aspects of social life. The use of the telephone had become commonplace by the beginning of the century. As early as 1915 there were already eleven hundred telephone subscribers in Chinatown, served by bilingual Chinese operators.[39] If the many prominent advertisements posted by mainstream clothing and shoe stores in Chinese-language newspapers are any indication, white American fashions had established a noticeable presence in Chinatown by the 1930s.

In the community that had remained predominantly Cantonese speaking for decades, the English language became increasingly important. In fact, English proficiency was required of 1930 Miss Chinatown Pageant contestants. Moreover, those who purchased the 50-cent raffle tickets in the pageant could win various prizes, first prize being a car—a staple and an important symbol of America's material culture. Called "liberty vehicles" by the Chinese, automobiles had already become commonplace in Chinese San Francisco. As early as 1920 a New Republic Garage advertised "exclusive service to Chinese customers."[40] Those who could not afford their own cars could use the rental and lease services. In the early 1940s driving schools conducted aggressive advertising campaigns in the Chinese community in an effort to capitalize on the growing interest in cars. The Empire Auto School had branches in San Francisco, Oakland, and Berkeley.[41] The Original Chinese Driving School, which opened a new office in Chinatown early in the 1940s, promised that customers would be able to get a driver's license within 24 hours of completing their lessons.[42]

As early as the first decade of the twentieth century books appeared that described what was considered standard American social etiquette at the time. That etiquette became a newspaper topic by the early 1940s. In November 1941 the *Chinese Times*, the newspaper run by and for Chinese American citizens, published a series of articles on "manners." It stated:

> When drinking milk and coffee, [you] should remove the small spoon from the cup. When not using the knife, hold the fork in your right hand. If you

hold the knife in your right hand, use the left hand to hold the fork and take the meat to your mouth. As a host, you must understand your guests' interest. Depending on their interest, you can talk about poetry and novels, or movies. Do not force your guests to talk about the things that only you are interested in.[43]

While few actually practiced the etiquette regarding forks and knives regularly in their family dining rooms, many could talk about American movies, which became increasingly popular in Chinese San Francisco. In the late 1930s and early 1940s movie theaters outside Chinatown ran extensive advertisements in all Chinese newspapers, especially the *Chinese Times*. Such advertisements often simply printed the names of Hollywood stars in English, along with their pictures. In one 1941 advertisement, the Liberty Theatre, a strip club that also showed films, offered Chinese customers special coupons. Another establishment, the Verdi Theatre, had Tuesday specials that promised not only free admissions but also "plates and bowls" for women.[44]

Those who wanted to practice American table manners could do it in a growing number of clubs and taverns that provided American-style food services and entertainment, which Chinese businessmen began to set up from the late 1930s on. One of them was the Forbidden City, a nightclub owned by Charlie Low, a native of MacDermitt, Nevada. In it, young Chinese customers could have an American-style drink and Western food that was advertised to be "delicate and delicious." They could also dance with girls who had "great beauty and skills," as the club bragged in an advertisement.[45] The shrewd businessman Low reportedly retained his former wife as a singer at the club after she divorced him. The Forbidden City was just one of numerous such Chinese-run bars and nightclubs in San Francisco. By 1940 the San Francisco Chinese Tavern Association had ten members.

Many of these places catered primarily to a non-Chinese clientele, and their emergence also marked a new trend: one in which the Chinese American food industry was expanding into the non-Chinese market, and the accompanying acculturation of Chinese (Cantonese) food. The trend began in the late 1920s, when Chinese merchants opened full-service restaurants (not the traditional chop suey shops) outside Chinatown. One of the pioneers was the New Shanghai Terrace Bowl, which began to distribute coupons in department stores to solicit non-Chinese customers. In 1938, eleven years after it first opened, it expanded its service, adding a bar and a stage for performances in an attempt to satisfy its non-Chinese customers. The 12,500-square-foot restaurant also provided space and music for dancing. The owner tried to maintain its Chinese flavor: he served both Chinese and Western foods and hired Chinese performers. In 1941, for example, he brought an acrobatic troupe from China to perform in the restaurant, making dining a cultural as well as a culinary experience. In its 1943 advertisement that attempted to attract the Christmas crowd, the acrobatic troupe topped all the listed features.[46] Chinese culture became a marketing tool.

Examining the development of Chinese food helps us recognize that acculturation has always been a two-way street. While Chinese restaurateurs made changes to accommodate their white clientele, they also helped to change the palates of their non-Chinese customers and to influence the visibility of Chinese culture. The New Shanghai Terrace Bowl's formula was adopted by other Chinese restaurateurs, who expanded their services in an attempt to tap the non-Chinese market.[47] The Shanghai Cafe in Chinatown stated on its menu, "Please visit our cafe, it is equal to a trip to China."[48] The restaurants' efforts to educate non-Chinese patrons on how to order food are interesting. The following is a standard passage printed on menus at different restaurants:

> Suggestion is offered dining parties that all Chinese dishes are served in very generous portions, almost any order except soups, being sufficient for two or three persons if supplemented by some other order. For instance, instead of individual orders, if a party of four orders a variety of single dishes to be served to all on individual plates after being brought to the table, a really portentious [*sic*; this was spelled "pretentious" on menus elsewhere] spread may be secured at a trifling expense. Try it. If you experience difficulty in making selections the management or waiter will be more than happy to assist you.[49]

The increasing popularity of Chinese food coincided with mainstream society's changing perceptions of it. The *St. Louis Post-Dispatch* regarded it as "among the best in the world." It then listed a number of Americanized Chinese dishes that had become widely recognizable, including pork cooked in a bland sweet-and-sour sauce and chicken with chestnuts.[50]

Those Chinatown restaurants that continued to rely primarily on the Chinese market did not remain unchanged. A menu from Mary's Cafe in

December 1940 offered "7 up" along with Chinese dishes. Printed beside the logo for the soft drink on the otherwise Chinese menu, an English line invited customers to "fresh up with '7 Up.' "[51] The many advertisements for this soft drink suggest that demand for this non-Chinese beverage was high in Chinatown.

The influence of the dominant society on Chinese San Franciscans was so pervasive that the decades-long struggle for racial equality did not make them immune to infectious and hegemonic racism. Numerous derogatory reports about African Americans appeared in *The Chinese-Western Daily* in the late 1910s and early 1920s. Those reports, which were often direct translations from English sources of stories about African Americans attacking white women, are examples of the transmitted racial bias against African Americans. One report stated: "It is believed that blacks have no self-respect and often assault whites." The report was scornfully entitled, "What Will the Blacks Do Next?"[52] Another report of a rape case had an even more scornful title, which adopted a Chinese idiomatic expression: "A Toad Lusting After a Swan's Flesh."[53] Reporting on a lynch mob's attempt to kill three African Americans for attacking white women in North Carolina, the newspaper commented: "Black loose animals sparked public anger."[54] There is no indication that these reports endorsed lynching or other kinds of violence perpetrated against African Americans. Nor is there much indication of an open denunciation of such acts, either. An account of social life in Mississippi showed no respect for either whites or African Americans. The whites, it remarked, "ignorant in isolation, domineer over local affairs and commit physical violence by willfully beating and plundering people." Even worse, "the black are brutal by character and prone to commit murders."[55]

We must note that while the bias manifested in these reports was not a result of their heritage, the Chinese did not have a tradition that called for equal treatment of African Americans. There had been blacks in South China. The gazetteer of Zhongshan County reports that in 1809 the Portuguese in Macao had 365 black slaves. It cites a passage from Qu Dajun's *Guangdong Xinyu* of the early eighteenth century that describes them thus: "Their body was as dark as [Chinese] lacquer, with disheveled beards and hair, reeking an offensive smell. These are the ghost slaves."[56] Chinese minister Zhang Yinhuan noted in his diary that "blacks are the zhong [species] of Africa and are as dark as [Chinese] lacquer . . . mostly performing cheap labor. But they are lazy by nature and unable to endure hard work."[57] The mentality expressed in the passages cited above certainly did not help Chinese Americans resist the dominant society's anti–African American attitudes. Similarly, many African Americans strongly disliked Chinese immigrants.[58] Such mutual disdain between different minority groups, still evident in the 1990s, has significantly weakened their solidarity in the struggle for social justice.

Antagonism also existed between Asian American groups. Another good example of Chinese immigrants' racism is the troubled, often hostile relationship between the Chinese and the Japanese, both targets of the anti-Asian movement in America. Reflecting what happened between China and Japan in Asia, their conflict reveals the complicated nature of ethnic relations in American society, which were also intertwined with class and gender issues. Most important of all, it shows that race consciousness and relations in America were also affected by events that occurred in a transnational context.

The Chinese-Western Daily mirrored Chinese San Franciscans' animosity toward the Japanese. Displaying a keen awareness of the two groups' shared predicament, one editorial stated: "In the beginning, Californians were hostile to the Chinese. . . . After Chinese exclusion, California's mentality changed from anti-Chinese to anti-Japanese." Yet the editorial showed no empathy toward the Japanese and commented on the anti-Japanese mentality rather approvingly: "The Japanese in California are now besieged on all sides."[59]

Often the Japanese were blamed for the increase in anti-Asian racism. Referring to California's alien land acts, which were aimed primarily at the Japanese, another editorial first acknowledged that "the anti-Japanese issue in California" was caused by white Americans' bias against the yellow race. But the bias was in turn caused by "the shameless greedy nature of the Japanese who, regarding California as a good place for colonization, seized land . . . and swindled for any profit."[60] In an earlier report that also blamed the Japanese for increased anti-Asian discrimination, *The Chinese-Western Daily* concluded straightforwardly: "The Japanese are most loathsome."[61]

Animosity toward the Japanese was obviously widespread in Chinese San Francisco. On January 24, 1920, when a Japanese was arrested for gambling, Chinese spectators "clapped with satisfaction," according to a report in *The Chinese-Western Daily*.[62] Even the harsh treatment of the Japanese during

World War II, which culminated in their forced relocation, aroused little sympathy on the part of Chinese San Franciscans. A March 4, 1942, report on the arrest of Japanese Americans in Seattle in *Young China* described them as "enemy residents in violation of the law."[63] On March 3 the *Chinese Times* printed a photograph of federal agents searching suspected Japanese immigrants. Above the photo was a line that read, in Chinese: "[They] do not look innocent."[64] The *Chinese Times* published photographs of Japanese being relocated and noted: "The relocated 'Wo' people reluctant to depart."[65] The word *wo*, a pejorative Chinese term for the Japanese that conveyed strong antipathy, belied any compassion for these victims of war and racism. A report of white Americans physically attacking Japanese Americans in the *Chinese World* was entitled " 'Wo' people provoked objections from Americans everywhere."[66]

Direct and unpleasant confrontations occurred between Chinese and Japanese in the city. In May 1919 some Chinese broke into a Japanese-owned dye house and forcefully took more than two hundred pieces of clothing. Condemning the incident as "uncivilized," *The Chinese-Western Daily* stated that such violence "does not serve the general cause."[67] The "general cause" that *The Chinese-Western Daily* spoke of was the ongoing protest against Japanese aggression in China. An issue that inspired increasing passion in Chinese America, the protest inevitably enhanced the tension between Chinese and Japanese Americans. In 1942 a Chinese daily reported that a Chinese laundry in New Mexico refused to serve Japanese American customers.[68] On July 7, 1943, the anniversary of the Japanese invasion in China, 47 Chinese engaged in a violent fight with Japanese detainees while awaiting deportation at San Francisco's detention center. Chinese newspaper reports of this incident did not bother to clarify whether the individuals that fought with the Chinese were Japanese nationals or Japanese Americans.[69] Probably the reporter saw no need to make such a distinction.

Increased Political Participation

Increased participation in American politics represented another marked change in the Chinese community. Chinese Americans demonstrated a keen awareness of the significance of political rights long before the outbreak of World War I. In 1901 Chinese residents in Philadelphia formed an organization the purpose of which was to help the Chinese gain the right to become American citizens. The organization published a public statement in *The Chinese-Western Daily* to solicit financial support, in which it declared that its main goal was to abolish laws that prohibited citizenship. Once the right to obtain citizenship had been granted, it went on, "it would be easier to fight against other discriminatory acts." At the same time, the statement recognized internal cultural obstacles facing the struggle for justice: "Coming from a land of ancient civilization, we must find it hard to conform to the customs of this country."[70]

Over time, as more and more people became aware of the importance of political participation, the Chinese community increasingly encouraged Chinese American citizens to vote in elections. The 1908 presidential election in Chinese San Francisco was a case in point. *The Chinese-Western Daily* repeatedly urged eligible Chinese to vote as a way to ward off discrimination, and articulated the significance of political participation. It attributed the increase in anti-Chinese sentiments to the Chinese people's own neglect of political rights in the past, calling that a regrettable mistake.[71] A later editorial noted that because the early immigrants had not fought for political rights, those rights had been taken away one after another. The right to vote, it reminded readers, "is the foundation of all other rights."[72]

"The presidential election," *The Chinese-Western Daily* announced in 1908, "greatly concerns us Chinese."[73] Between the two major candidates, William Taft and William Jennings Bryan, it openly endorsed the former, who was believed to be friendlier toward Chinese. An editorial noted: "Bryan is the one who the workingmen's party will vote for and he appeals to voters by advocating the exclusion of our yellow race." Turning to Taft, the editorial went on, "Although he was not willing to contradict public opinion by particularly protecting us Chinese people, he would take into consideration Sino-American relations."[74] On October 30, 1908, days before the election, *The Chinese-Western Daily* once more urged Chinese to vote for Taft. If Bryan won, it stated, "there would be no place for the Chinese to lay their feet on."[75] On November 1, 1908, the Zhonghua Huiguan held a community meeting to discuss the election of the president and other officials, and all Chinese were invited to attend the discussion. The invitation announcement noted that because the coming election "concerns the future of all Chinese and is of great significance, the opinions of all in the community must be consulted."[76]

With World War I came another opportunity for political participation. After the United States joined the war, many European immigrants eagerly showed their loyalty to their adopted country. The Irish, for example, combined Catholicism with Americanism. Similarly, Chinese San Franciscans supported America's war effort in an attempt to improve their status.

Having suffered greater injustice than European ethnic groups had, however, the Chinese community did not show wholehearted support for the war effort, at least in the beginning. In July 1916 when the preparedness groups in San Francisco invited the Chinese community to take part in their parade, the Zhonghua Huiguan decided to send a musical band in order to "enhance the image of the Chinese." The decision faced noticeable opposition in the community. The opponents argued, as reported by *Young China*: "the participation of the Zhonghua Huiguan will be ridiculed by Westerners because Chinese immigrants did not even have the right to become citizens."[77] Later on, in response to news that the government would draft noncitizens, the Zhonghua Huiguan itself expressed similar grievances in a December 1917 letter to the Chinese minister in Washington. The letter suggests that the Zhonghua Huiguan apparently did not share Wilson's idea of "universal liability to service":

> Denied their rights, [the Chinese] should not be drafted. . . . The United States declared war on Germany for justice. But why are all kinds of exclusion acts and regulations applied to the Chinese, not to [the people of] other countries? Is it justice? Knowing that our country is weak, we Chinese immigrants have been trying to muddle along. Yet, as the discrimination [against us] goes on, conscription is jumping in. . . . When not needed, we are cruelly oppressed and treated like meat on somebody's chopping board. When needed, we are forced to toil like oxen and horses. We have responsibilities but no rights. We may be ignorant, but we are not so foolish as to tolerate this.[78]

These grievances were undoubtedly shared by members of the community. In 1917 at least thirty-six people in Chinatown failed to answer draft calls. Before long, however, the community changed its position, realizing that other ethnic groups had displayed their enthusiastic support for America's war effort in order to improve their own status. In late November 1918 the Zhonghua Huiguan publicly appealed to all Chinese not to "be left behind" in buying war bonds. Buying bonds, it explained, would help to "protect our interest, rights, and dignity."[79] There was another justification—China had become America's ally after declaring war on Germany and Austria in August 1917. Calling for the purchase of liberty bonds, *The Chinese-Western Daily* stated: "Our country and the United States are both on the side of the Allies, and are bound by a common cause. Our Chinese fellows . . . have the responsibility to provide assistance . . . for the motherland and for the United States."[80]

Calling again upon its readers to purchase war bonds, *The Chinese-Western Daily* gave a number of reasons. First of all, "our country had joined the war. Therefore, financial assistance to the United States . . . is, in fact, beneficial to China." "Since immigrants from other countries are very active in buying public bonds," moreover, "the apathy of some of our fellows would impair the reputation of us all." Besides, "we Chinese immigrants are living in the United States and our incomes are earned in the United States. Therefore, assisting the American army to defeat its enemy is our obligation."[81] By then this had become a commonplace argument for American patriotism. By October 1918 Chinese San Franciscans had bought forty thousand dollars' worth of liberty bonds. More and more Chinese men joined the armed forces. One of them was Ng Poon Chew's son, who became a lieutenant after graduating from a military academy.[82]

For the Chinese, however, the war was no "public school" for democracy or Americanization, as Theodore Roosevelt proclaimed. Nor did Chinese servicemen benefit from the war as much as others did. In 1918 the government loosened naturalization restrictions for servicemen. Yet the Chinese soon learned that the new policy applied only to white men.[83]

The war was nonetheless a significant event within the Chinese community. For the first time a sizeable number of Chinese joined the armed forces of the United States.[84] In 1918, when their support for America's war efforts increased, Chinese San Franciscans celebrated Independence Day with unprecedented enthusiasm. In the July Fourth parade, marching along with white Americans and other immigrant groups were several hundred Chinese, including a band, schoolchildren, and members of different huiguan. National flags of the United States and China flew side by side in Chinatown, and for the first time the day was declared a holiday.

Increased participation in American politics also arose as a result of Chinese Americans' realization that the Chinese government was both unable and unwilling to protect them. This realization strained Chinese San Franciscans' relationships with the Beijing government in the 1910s and 1920s. In 1914, for example, the condescending Beijing government dispatched a commissioner to "console" the Chinese in America. In sharp contrast to the warm welcome that other visiting envoys had received in the past, he met with open resentment in San Francisco. A scheduled speech by the commissioner at the Zhonghua Huiguan was canceled because of widespread objections. Later, on July 24, 1914, the Zhonghua Huiguan held a meeting to discuss the issue, and an unusually large crowd of several hundred people showed up. One man raised his voice to complain that because the Beijing government showed no interest in fighting against the exclusion laws, there should be no official reception for its representative. The president of the Yanghe Huiguan, Wu Wenbin, concurred: "The Zhonghua Huiguan is the public forum of all Chinese in America. Now that people have objections, [the commissioner] should not speak here."[85] Earlier, Wu and other community leaders had rejected in person the consul general's mediation, and Wu indicated that he would not even be afraid to sign a written objection. The community's blunt rejection of the commissioner conveyed a deep disappointment in the outcome of the once-promising revolution of 1911.[86] Instead of delivering a new China, it had been followed by political corruption and devastating civil wars, and the newly established Republic soon fell prey to aggravated foreign aggression.

Later the Chinese government spent a great deal of money to participate in the Panama Pacific International Exposition, where it placed extensive exhibits in different locations. Its intention was to show the Western world a modernizing China, best revealed by its massive school exhibit in the Palace of Education. At the exposition Commissioner General Chen Chi also gave and attended numerous parties to entertain non-Chinese as well as Chinese guests. At one luncheon he praised President Yuan Shikai's achievements in his effort to "elevate [China] to a Western standard."[87] Present at the event were numerous American politicians, judges, and merchants, including Judge William B. Lamar, chairman of the U.S. National Commission; George W. Guthrie, ambassador to Japan; and Joseph E. Davies, chairman of the Federal Trade Commission.

Contrary to its goal, the Chinese government's participation in the exposition magnified its weakness, incompetence, and corruption in the eyes of

Chinese San Franciscans. It subjected itself to the same humiliating insult that it had received during the 1904 Louisiana Purchase Exposition in St. Louis. U.S. immigration officials treated Chinese construction workers— who arrived in 1914 to prepare the Chinese exhibits—harshly; three were detained and one beaten. At the fair site these workers wore ragged clothes and lived in dirty quarters, showing the Chinese government's insensitivity toward the need to maintain national dignity. On the opening day the main Chinese exhibition remained closed because it was not ready. Only the two tea houses at the entrance were open, and they served Japanese tea cakes in American-made containers. *The Chinese-Western Daily* criticized the delegation's incompetence and its disregard for cultural authenticity by pointing out that what remained Chinese about the pavilion were "the clothes that the waitresses wear and the yellowish faces of the manager and cashiers."[88]

One scandal followed another. The Chinese commissioner general arbitrarily granted to two men the privilege of opening a food booth at the fair site. This apparent indication of corruption aroused intense discontent among many Chinese, and the incensed Zhonghua Huiguan demanded an explanation from the commissioner "in order to clear up people's doubts."[89] Frustrated by the Chinese delegation's performance, *The Chinese-Western Daily* suggested sarcastically and angrily that the Chinese government "should not participate in expositions any more."[90]

Frustration about what happened at the exposition illustrated the deep disillusionment of more and more Chinese San Franciscans with regard to the state of post-revolution China. Early in 1915 an editorial in *The Chinese-Western Daily* elaborated on this feeling: "The Republic has been founded for four years. In the beginning, people were passionately excited, and cheers resounded like rolls of thunder. With a grand promise, it stirred the world. . . . Before long, however, the spirit of innovation deteriorated, and the essence of the Republic is fading away. The [new] government and social customs, like the redness of flower and the greenness of willow, after flourishing for a few days, now appear lifeless."[91]

Looking back at the decade following 1911, a New Year's editorial in 1921 stated gloomily: "The revolution only changed the signboard of the Manchu Dynasty. Everything else, including former Qing officials, have remained in place." The revolution, the editorial complained, only created more and more warlords "who in these years have scrambled for power and profit and harmed the people by launching numerous wars."[92] In 1924 the Beijing government refused to issue promptly the new Ningyang Huiguan president the customary diplomatic passport. Chinese Americans perceived the delay as more evidence of the corruption and incompetence of Chinese officials and of the government itself.[93]

Disillusionment with the Beijing government bolstered a sense of independence and self-reliance. Using the American Revolution as an analogy, an editorial in *Young China* argued that if the government continued to fail to provide proper protection, the Chinese in America should break away from it. "Because of their government's failure to provide protection," the editorial went on, citing history rather freely, "the English immigrants in North America declared independence in 1775."[94] Clearly, Chinese San Franciscans had realized that they would "have to rely on themselves" in the struggle against discrimination.[95]

It is no accident, therefore, that in 1914, when the community's relationship with the Beijing government was especially strained, the willingness to partake in American politics became popular among Chinese Americans. In March the Zhonghua Huiguan held a special meeting to discuss how to mobilize the resources of the entire community in order to encourage eligible Chinese to vote in elections. At a banquet in commemoration of Confucius in October, speakers spoke on political participation as a way to restore lost rights and fight racism.[96] The number of Chinese who voted in various elections noticeably increased during this period.[97] More and more state and local politicians took note and started making efforts to win Chinese votes. In the 1939 mayoral election, for example, the two major candidates both posted advertisements in Chinese.

During this period Chinese San Franciscans' increasing enthusiasm for aiding China's resistance to Japanese aggression did not reduce their appreciation of the importance of political participation, and especially of electoral politics. Their assertiveness in defending and exercising their rights as Chinese Americans was a natural development of their increasing rootedness in American society. It also reflected demographic changes in the community, that is, the rise of a younger generation of Chinese Americans with the political rights attached to citizenship. In March 1937 *The Chinese-Western Daily* published another editorial urging Chinese American citizens to "collectively exercise [their] legal rights and protect our interest." The editorial first stated that the two thousand Chinese voters constituted a significant force in the city, where political opinions were often divided. It then summarized the significance of the voting right: "Legally, the right to vote is the most important of all natural human rights; politically, the right to vote is every citizen's responsibility; for the Chinese community itself, this is the most powerful weapon."[98]

Chinese American Citizens and the Struggle for Justice

No group of Chinese Americans took part in American politics more directly than the one whose members were American citizens. Many of them were native-born and educated in American schools, and were thus more familiar with American society than the rest of the community was. What is more, as American citizens they enjoyed political rights denied to immigrant Chinese, which enabled them to become an increasingly visible group in the Chinese community.[99] They were the only Chinese who could enter the United States without being subjected to humiliating physical examinations. Back in 1907 an editorial in *The Chinese-Western Daily* recognized that "this is an important right."[100]

Even more important were their political rights. *The Chinese-Western Daily* pointed out: "While [the rest of] our Chinese people are unable to become citizens, American-born Chinese enjoy the same rights and bear the same responsibility as [white] Americans."[101] Of course, "the most significant right," as a Chinese from Chicago wrote at another time, "was the right to vote."[102]

The formation of their own associations announced the arrival of Chinese American citizens as a social force in Chinese America. The first such association, the Native Sons of the Golden State, was founded in 1895 in San Francisco's Chinatown. Later it forged a federation with similar organizations in Oakland and Los Angeles, becoming in 1915 the Chinese American Citizens Alliance.[103] The alliance experienced significant growth during this period. From the early 1910s to the mid-1920s the number of local lodges increased from three to nine. By September 1925 membership in the San Francisco lodge—the largest and most important one—had reached about two thousand, and more than a fourth of them, or 592 people, were recruited between 1923 and 1925.[104] Completed in August 1921, the alliance's new building on Stockton Street stood as a reminder of the presence of Chinese American citizens. On August 10 numerous celebrities joined the crowd at the grand opening ceremony. Their presence provide evidence of "the recognized significance" of this rising social group, as the governor of California put it in his congratulatory speech.[105] In July 1924 the alliance launched its own organ, the *Chinese Times* (Jinshan Shibao), which soon became an established institution in Chinatown.

The growing visibility of the citizens' group paralleled Chinese America's changing demography. Federal census figures suggest that the number of American-born Chinese grew from 18,532 in 1920 to 40,262 in 1940, which made them a majority within the community.[106] In San Francisco, toward the end of the period under discussion, Albert K. Chow was elected president of the Zhonghua Huiguan. He was the first native-born man to hold the position.

The formation of the alliance, which was titled "Tongyuan Hui" in Chinese (meaning "association of common origin"), reflected Chinese American citizens' distinctive group consciousness. Consisting of "American male citizens of Chinese ancestry, who are 21 years of age, of good character, and capable of self support," this organization also functioned as a mutual-aid fraternity.[107] Stated in its 1927 constitution, the mission of the alliance included the following: "To inculcate the principles of charity, justice, brotherly love and fidelity among the members, to promote the general welfare and happiness of its members."[108]

Membership brought benefits. In the early years the Native Sons of the Golden State in Chinese San Francisco provided financial assistance for its poor members, including 25 cents for the burial of a deceased member.[109] In the early 1920s the alliance set up a large life-insurance fund that generously compensated the families of deceased members; for example, a member of less than six months received $250, a member of over a year received $500, and a member of over two years receive $1,000.[110]

Chinese American citizens in San Francisco showed an awareness of their distinctive status. During the Boxer Rebellion that took place at the turn of the century, they asked the American government whether it would protect individuals with citizenship if white Americans were to seek revenge on the Chinese in America.[111] Some even used their special status as American citizens to evade Chinese laws after they returned to China. As early as 1908 the Chinese government sought the U.S. government's cooperation in dealing with such people.[112] In one case an American-born Chinese American citizen living in China injured a native person in a brawl and was sentenced to three months' imprisonment. He managed to get American consulate officials to force his release on the grounds of his American citizenship.[113]

Cases like this serve to illuminate the fact that the Chinese American identity was also constructed in an international context in relation to a host of complicated issues. The action of American consulate officials in the case should not be seen as an effort to protect Chinese Americans, whom their government had long tried to disfranchise domestically. Rather, it represented an imperialist power's attempt to assert the extraterritoriality that it had imposed on China after the Opium War. The imprisonment of the Chinese American suspect, on the other hand, was not only a challenge to imperialism; it also underscored the unwillingness of the Chinese government, whose nationality law was based primarily on the principle of jus sanguinis, to regard the Chinese American man as simply American.

An event even more revealing of Chinese American citizens' consciousness occurred in August 1925, when members of a Chinese students' association met with teachers of the Zhonghua Chinese school and other Chinese San Franciscans to discuss educational issues concerning Chinese America. Among the guiding principles adopted by the student group at the meeting, one that included a statement about "devoted patriotism to the Republic of China" provoked the protests of Chinese American citizens. At the tenth convention in Chicago the Chinese American Citizens Alliance resolved to issue the student association an official protest.

The pronounced Americanism of the protest represented a new voice in the community. However, it did not signal rejection of cultural identity as much as it did fear of discrimination. In a written statement, the alliance objected to the clause on the grounds that a pledge of allegiance to China would endanger the citizenship of Chinese Americans.[114] The fear was based on harsh realities. By then Chinese American citizens were already engaged in a campaign to defeat a constitutional amendment, introduced a little earlier in Congress, to deprive them of their citizenship.

Just as the community's transformation did not make the dominant society more accepting of it, the legal status of Chinese American citizens did not exempt them from racial prejudice. In an article explicitly expressing his consciousness as a native-born Chinese American, Walter Kong pointed out: "Even American-born Chinese have their difficulties when leaving and returning to this country."[115]

The struggle for racial justice, therefore, remained a priority that Chinese American citizens shared with the rest of the Chinese community.[116] In fact, an important purpose of San Francisco's Native Sons of the Golden State was to mobilize eligible Chinese to vote in elections so that white Americans "would not be as contemptuous [of the Chinese] as before."[117] According to the alliance's constitutions, taking part in the struggle was every member's duty. In the 1910s each member was required to report to the organization's "law department" his "contribution to protecting the rights of Chinese American citizens."[118] A resolution adopted at the tenth convention of the alliance in 1925 reiterated that in fighting against increasing discrimination, "the Alliance should educate the American-born, their children and grandchildren . . . about their rights and responsibilities as American citizens."[119]

Chinese American citizens' right to vote, in particular, became a political asset for the entire community. Thus the alliance assumed a pivotal role in the struggle for racial equality. A Chinese person pointed out in a newspaper article that in the struggle against Chinese exclusion the Chinese government was unable to do anything. "The Zhonghua Huiguan," he continued metaphorically, "can only provide some temporary remedies but cannot take out the firewood from under the cauldron and stop the water from boiling." With the ability to influence policymakers through its members' votes, the author concluded, the alliance was "the most reliable" in such a struggle.[120] Because of the importance of the voting right, the alliance did everything possible to encourage the members to exercise it. During election seasons it posted public statements to inform Chinese voters of each candidate's position, assigned officers to answer questions concerning the election, and set up classes to teach eligible voters how to register and vote.

In their common struggle the alliance worked side by side with the Zhonghua Huiguan and other leading organizations. In an effort to block another discriminatory bill late in 1915 the alliance sent lobbyists to Washington. While there they wrote to the Zhonghua Huiguan for "instructions."[121] The lobbying effort illustrates that Chinese Americans battled discrimination the American way. The alliance lobbyists noted in 1915 that such an effort "is imperative because once it [the bill] is passed and becomes law it will be extremely difficult to do anything about it."[122]

The passage of the 1924 immigration law exemplifies America's continued hostility toward both Chinese American citizens and immigrants. It also offers a case study of how closely the two groups worked together in the struggle for equality. Let us first take a brief look at this landmark piece of legislation, which represented an official attempt to define the racial nature of American society. By far the most comprehensive of all immigration laws, it standardized immigration control measures and finalized an evolving restrictive policy that had started with the 1882 Chinese exclusion act. Most important of all, it codified and openly endorsed a racist ideology that had become a systematic and dominant social way of thinking. Characterized by a "bold expression of Nordic preference,"[123] the law was designed to curb the so-called "new immigrants" from Eastern and Southern Europe, the "un-assimilated and unassimilable peoples."[124] In reference to how easily Congress passed this extraordinarily important bill, H. H. Powers wrote: "At a time when the American Congress seems incapable of mustering a majority on any subject, it has with practical unanimity passed upon an issue probably the most momentous upon which it has ever taken action."[125] Supporters hailed it as a measure to "save the nation."[126] In a public speech he made in New York, Rabbi Stephen Wise, one of the most vocal critics of the law, denounced the quota system in the pending bill, saying that Jesus and his twelve disciples "would have to cast lots as to which one of them could have the privilege to come to the United States."[127]

Indeed, Jesus would not have been able to enter the country because he would have been considered both poor and Asian, as Rabindranath Tagore reportedly pointed out after his short and unpleasant trip to the United States in 1929. Known also as the Oriental Exclusion Act, the 1924 bill virtually barred immigration from all Asian countries by excluding those ineligible for citizenship. Oliver P. Stidger, the attorney of the Chinatown Chamber of Commerce, pointed out that its passage occurred as a result "of the so-called 'menace' to American institutions, economic conditions, etc., involved in Oriental immigration."[128] Abrogating the earlier Gentlemen's Agreement, the bill legislated the exclusion of the Japanese, though they were widely viewed as more assimilable and desirable than the Chinese and Indians.

The passage of the law became an international incident, eliciting furious protest from Eastern and Southern Europeans. The Japanese reaction was extremely strong.[129] People in Japan boycotted American goods, and militant groups even wanted to declare war on the United States. Newspapers in Chinatown reported on Japanese protests in great detail.[130] By comparison, the Chinese government remained silent, even though the 1924 act tightened Chinese exclusion. *The Chinese-Western Daily* criticized that silence, calling it "cowardly and shameful."[131] Both citizens and immigrants within the Chinese community were affected by the new law: under it, merchants and the native-born could no longer bring their wives into the country, and Chinese-born children of U.S.-citizen fathers faced the danger of losing their citizenship.[132]

For several months Chinese newspapers in San Francisco devoted much space to publishing and analyzing key clauses of the proposed bill. On May 22 the Zhonghua Huiguan held a public meeting to discuss how to respond. Both the Zhonghua Huiguan and the Chinatown Chamber of Commerce instructed their respective attorneys to focus on the issue. Working for the latter, Oliver P. Stidger published a long analysis of the new law.

Early in the year the alliance sent its chief to Washington to lobby on behalf of the Chinese. On July 26 it formed a "Committee to Protect the Rights of Citizens" to challenge the law's constitutionality in the courts. At the 1925 convention in Chicago, the committee reported that the law "has been upheld by the Supreme Court. . . . There is no room to fight [against it] in the courts. . . . " The report concluded that the only way to abolish it now was through congressional action.[133]

Resorting to a different strategy, the Chicago convention of the alliance resolved to establish five "departments" to conduct a massive public relations campaign in order to change the law. Two departments were in charge of mobilizing the resources of the Chinese community in America. An "English Propaganda Department" was to get "articles published in English magazines and newspapers . . . to remind the Americans of the instructions of their ancestors." Two other departments bore the responsibility of selecting representatives to communicate to the American public directly. These representatives were to have been articulate in English and to have made "significant contributions" to America, for example by serving the country in wartime.[134]

Dr. Walter Lewis Treadway of the U.S. Public Health Service, which had been responsible for the mental and physical examinations of new immigrants since the end of the nineteenth century, endorsed the new law by arguing that the effort to exclude "undesirable elements" had long been an American tradition. The medical doctor was also pleased to report that the restrictive law of 1924 improved the United States' ability to exclude people with the following diseases: "idiocy, insanity, imbecility, feeble-mindedness, epilepsy, constitutional psychopathic inferiority, chronic alcoholism, tuberculosis in any form, or a loathsome or dangerous contagious disease."[135] As Chinese Americans knew from firsthand experience, the issue of public health had always been associated with efforts to control immigration and ethnic communities. In fact, in early April, just shortly before the 1924 bill became law, the Supreme Court affirmed a lower court ruling that denied the wife of a San Francisco native named Zhong Fu the right to enter the United States because she was allegedly a carrier of clonorchiasis.[136]

Identified as one of the excludable "Oriental diseases,"[137] immigration and health officials had used clonorchiasis (an infestation with or disease caused by a liver fluke that invades the bile ducts of the liver) to exclude Chinese from the United States for several years beginning in 1917, when the U.S. Public Health Service listed clonorchiasis as an excludable disease. In 1921 the agency declared it incurable and decided to refuse to admit any person infected with it. In that year 53 Chinese merchants were ordered to return to China as soon as they arrived in the United States. This state of affairs posed a serious threat to the trans-Pacific community.

As we can see when we examine Chinese Americans' concerted campaign to overcome this new type of discrimination during the next few years, the increasingly important alliance did not replace the Zhonghua Huiguan as the leading organization in the community. Under the Zhonghua Huiguan's leadership, the alliance succeeded in effecting the removal of clonorchiasis from the list of Class A (dangerous contagious) diseases, to Class C diseases in 1927. In the process it employed the service of fourteen lawyers and consulted numerous medical scientists across the country, spending thousands of dollars. As the organizer of the campaign, the Zhonghua Huiguan enlisted the help of Chinese diplomats and coordinated the activities of various organizations in Chinatown. Leaders of the alliance were actively involved in the campaign. Acting as an organization, the alliance appealed to President Coolidge directly and lobbied on Capitol Hill.

On December 5 the Zhonghua Huiguan hosted a big banquet at the Xinhua Lou restaurant to celebrate the victory and thank those who had made significant contributions. Among the one hundred and fifty or so in attendance were numerous white lawyers and health experts and officials, as well as Chinese consulate officials and leaders of all the seven huiguan. Noticeably absent from the event was Dr. Fred K. Lam (his Chinese name, as spelled in pinyin, is Lin Ronggui), a Chinese Hawaiian and an important character in the story. The medical doctor had done "considerable work" on clonorchiasis and was one of the first to learn that it was curable.[138] He had conveyed this to Dr. H. S. Cumming, surgeon general of the U.S. Public Health Service, during a conversation at a Honolulu hospital in the spring of 1926.

When the news of the reclassification of the disease reached Chinese American communities, Dr. Lam became a hero. The *Chinese World* (a daily mentioned in the preceding chapter) credited him in large part for the victory.[139] Chinese communities on the East Coast also honored him and donated money to him. White attorneys and health experts, however, quickly reacted to discredit him in the public's eyes. Some apparently did so for egotistic reasons. Dr. H. S. Cumming, for instance, claimed that the reclassification was based solely on "scientific and epidemiological investigation instituted" by himself.[140] As a few suggested, the event's successful outcome was not the result of one individual's effort. It is evident that Lam received, and apparently enjoyed, more credit than he deserved. What is interesting, nonetheless, is how quick many whites were to simultaneously and publicly attack him and to emphasize their own (and each other's) contributions, once they realized that he had become a hero in Chinese America. It appears likely that at least some of them had another motive as well—that is, they wanted both to prevent the creation of a Chinese hero and to avoid allowing the event to turn into a Chinese victory.[141]

On the other hand, supporting a Chinese hero and seeing the clonorchiasis episode as a Chinese American triumph seemed to be exactly what Chinese Americans wanted to do. Chinese communities in cities such as New York, Chicago, and Sacramento invited Lam to visit and presented him with gifts. In New York, for example, Chinese Americans raised $2,730.35 to honor him, over $1,800 of which was given to him as a present. Despite the controversy, in early December Chinese San Franciscans joined others in welcoming him. On December 4 Chinese San Franciscans filled the

Dazhonghua (Great China) Theatre to listen to his speech. The place was packed so full that latecomers couldn't get in. The speech was followed by a reception held by the Lam (Lin) clan, and later by a 30-table banquet hosted by the chamber of commerce. The introduction delivered by the chamber of commerce president, Li Lisheng, helps reveal the nature of Chinese Americans' mentality.

Li recounted how much the Chinese had suffered under the "harsh liver-fluke regulation" by saying that in the past few years many had been forced to return to China, "losing huge amount of transportation expenses." And their emotional pain was "beyond description." Li declared the reclassification a victory for all Chinese Americans, "who were greatly encouraged and overjoyed." Then he explained that "although Dr. Lam does not claim credit for himself and attributes the success to the Surgeon General [H. S. Cumming], the Chinese all welcome Dr. Lam because of feelings they have deep in their hearts."[142] Despite the criticism of Lam, of which they were aware, Chinese Americans still hailed him as the most important hero in this victory. This must have reflected a desire to create their own hero in one of the few battles they had won in the war against anti-Chinese discrimination. For a community that strived to catch up with the West's scientific and social progress, no one was better suited to being such a hero than was Lam, a Hawaiian-born Chinese American and an expert on Western medicine who successfully challenged anti-Chinese discrimination through his own scientific research.

This chapter has described how culturally, politically, and socioeconomically rooted Chinese San Francisco became in America during the early twentieth century. The transformation did not signify a total departure from the past. Though it was gradually improving, an unbalanced ratio of men to women remained a marked feature of Chinese San Francisco. Fighting discrimination, which did not vanish, continued to be a priority for all Chinese American groups. Furthermore, as we will see in the next chapter, Chinese San Francisco maintained its cultural distinctiveness and its multilayered ties with China. Its participation in China's resistance to Japanese aggression, in particular, illustrated how profoundly such connections influenced Chinese America.

(*Above*) Detention buildings on Angel Island. Courtesy California Historical Society.

(*Below*) Refugees in Chinatown after the 1906 earthquake. Courtesy California Historical Society, Virginia M. Storti Collection.

本樓分設兩層餐房陳設華美五光奪目幽雅超倫
四壁所懸盡是中國名勝畫景而地又附近花園草
木芬芳餐房之內常能引吸新鮮空氣使在坐者悅

意快然故中西人士無論用宴及請謙無不如意週
到且招待殷勤所有器具及用具極其潔淨仰各界
君子幸祈留意光顧焉
上海樓主人謹識

SHANGHAI LOW

532 GRANT AVE., SAN FRANCISCO

We serve finest kind of Chinese dishes. Excellent service at
moderate prices, private rooms for parties.
Dining room overlooking Park and San Francisco Bay.
Please visit our cafe, it is equal to a trip to China.

Advertisement for the Shanghai Low restaurant in San Francisco.

San Francisco's Chinatown ca. 1900. Photograph by Arnold Genthe. Courtesy California Historical Society.

(*Above*) Chinese Americans participating in the public parade to welcome Mme. Jiang in San Francisco, 1943.

(*Below*) San Francisco welcomes Mme. Jiang in 1943.

Mme. Jiang during her public tour of the United States, 1943.

FEBRUARY 17

茅家用文宝戏布局建議十
十五代（民前宣統十月十九元）
搭上五町速號浣编船四回
PRESIDENT PIERCE.

那怎傳譽十月十日（元計
四号十九月七回到誰兮年哇
卖喽左遷船中还屬隔雪
隆光伯去行島這滿之り
茶有差问波喜.

FEBRUARY 18

茅元囲家傳三月五衮碾程
民囲式拾年正月拾日三拾
本月未宝月六號来約兮兮香
觀老人己巳邦程救左鄉師
任身不囲勝儶三鄉招
六人間大十六篷風浪天天上
偁由未帮忙如参飯外共报
都速村護持元收结求業报
好速次米有惶念器报

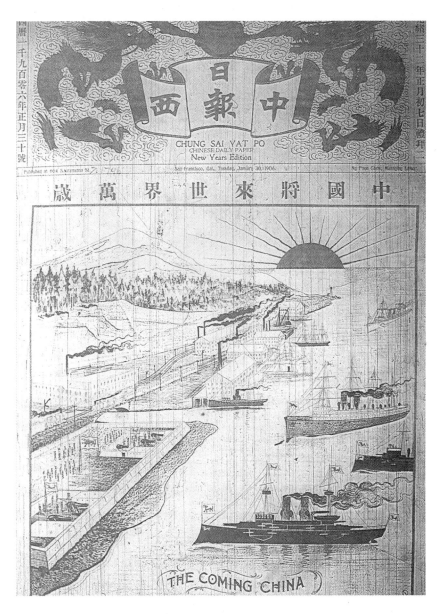

(*Opposite, above*) Chinatown decorated to welcome Mme. Jiang (Chiang Kai-shek) in March 1943.

(*Opposite, below*) Recollections by Wah-chung Leung of his first and second trips to China in 1924 and 1931.

(*Above*) A page from the 1906 Chinese New Year's issue of Chung Sai Yat Po. The Chinese characters at the top of the picture read "Long live the world of the future China."

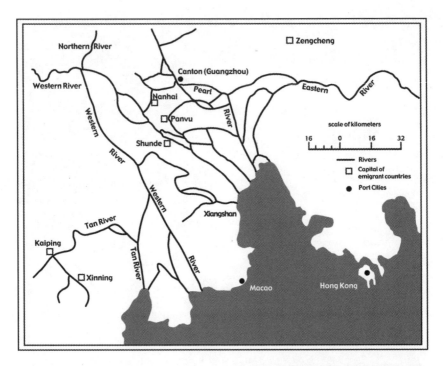

(*Above*) The Pearl River Delta region showing port cities and major emigrant areas.

(*Right*) Receipt of the departure fee ($3.00) imposed by the Chinese American Citizens Alliance on its members before they returned to China. March 3, 1931. Courtesy Sandy Yee Man Leung.

美洲同源總會
離美益壽費收條

本總會爲美籍華人團體最高機關對于美籍同尺公有之權利素負維持與保護之責諸凡辦事經費端賴同人鼎力義助凡未加入本會之華裔籍民每次出離美境例助公益費叁元

茲收到 11638

樂助公益費三元

經收銀人

一九卅一年三月六日

NINE

Persistence of Trans-Pacific Ties

While Chinese San Francisco was becoming increasingly "Americanized," it remained at heart a trans-Pacific community, invigorating a multitude of ties to China. Individuals stayed in touch with their loved ones in the Pearl River Delta Region, and many traveled back and forth across the ocean. Cultural institutions such as Chinese schools multiplied, reflecting the community's efforts to maintain and nourish collective memories of its cultural identity.

The community also stayed tuned to political events on the other side of the ocean. Nothing generated more attention and anxiety than the acceleration of Japanese aggression in China after the outbreak of World War I, which tied the hands of the European powers elsewhere. In 1915, a year after taking the port city of Qingdao from Germany, Japan issued the infamous Twenty-one Demands, unveiling its desire to make China a Japanese protectorate, an ambition that eventually led to military invasion. For three decades thereafter, Chinese Americans in San Francisco and elsewhere actively took part in the struggle against Japan. In 1937, six years after Japan invaded the Chinese northeast, its troops crossed the Marco Polo Bridge north of Beijing and started an all-out war with China. Arguably the most important event in twentieth-century Chinese history, the Chinese Pacific War was a defining moment in Chinese American history as well.

The enormous effort and sacrifice that Chinese Americans made in assisting the resistance helped them, also, demonstrating how closely their lives were connected with China. The war significantly improved the image of the Chinese and paved the way for the repeal of the Chinese exclusion acts. Meanwhile, Chinese Americans consciously grasped the opportunity that presented itself during the war to combat racial bias and win the friendship of white Americans.

Social Memories and Continued Trans-Pacific Ties

Chinese life between the two world wars demonstrated a great deal of continuity. The cultural transformation described earlier did not erase memories of China from individual minds. As we have seen before, most vivid were the memories of personal experiences that had taken place in the emigrant townships. In a 1943 essay titled "The Motherland in Hunger," Huang Dingchong, an immigrant laborer and student at the Zhonghua (Chinese) School, devoted a great deal of space to articulating what he remembered about the village where he grew up:

> In front of the small village spread a pond. Further away were the rice fields where seedlings of cereal crops waved in the soft and cool breeze. Nearby was a small limpid creek. Flowing water in the creek patting the rocks sent a whispering sound into the air. Above the creek hung the weeping willow. Behind the village were evenly spaced woods. Children enjoyed playing under the trees. To the right of the woods was a piece of grassland, the playground of shepherd boys.[1]

Whether it was real or imagined, this detailed and evidently passionate re-creation of village scenery bespeaks enduring personal memories. Another Chinese San Franciscan laborer, Wah-chung Leung, also nurtured similarly vivid memories of the scenery around his "home village." In 1939 he composed a poem in his diary:

> ...
> chase after the birds amidst green bushes,
> then rest under the cool shadow of pine trees;
> down the creek flows water leisurely,
> as the autumn breeze stirs up the heart;
> without time for the wild flowers and grass,
> On the way home, shepherd boys' singing brought much joy.[2]

These two pieces, one public and the other private, together reconstruct the Pearl River Delta Region's physical environment, which stood in stark contrast with highly industrialized America. It was an environment close to nature, where life was leisurely, peaceful, and pastoral. While it undoubtedly contains romanticized elements, the memory truthfully reveals the authors' keen awareness both of their changed relationship to natural space and of the different pace of work and existence in their urbanized community in America, as compared to that in the emigrant region. Huang Dingchong's essay began with a brief account of his busy life as a laborer: "After a day of hard work, I finally have a moment to rest." Taking advantage of that moment he looked through the window at a view of San Francisco and Oakland. "The high rises tower into the sky. The lights on the Oakland and San Francisco bridges are especially magnificent."[3]

Wah-chung Leung's private writings also enable us to appreciate immigrants' memories of the Pearl River Delta's social environment, as well as their attachment to that area. His writings contain reminiscences of festive activities he attended during the holidays when he was a child. In a poem composed in May 1939 he recalled, with "tears wetting clothes," the emotional moment of his departure from China.[4]

Individual recollections like these were also a part of the community's collective memory of life in the Pearl River Delta Region.[5] Folk songs from that region, for example, persisted in Chinese America, helping to keep it alive. In one song parents were advised not to marry their daughters to *dushujun* (the man who reads), bakers, or peasants. "If you have a daughter," it went, "marry her to a Gold Mountaineer."[6] As one of these highly desirable "Gold Mountaineers," Wah-chung Leung had gone back to get married before returning to America to resume his bachelor life. His writings unveil a lonely man's bonds to his hometown and loved ones. Such feelings were undoubtedly shared by many in Chinese America, which long retained characteristics of a "bachelor society."[7] Over the years Chinese Americans learned to laugh away this predicament occasionally. In 1930 a New York–based Chinese newspaper reported a dialogue between a judge and a Chinese defendant in a Seattle court:

The judge asked: "How long have you been married?"
"For thirty-eight years," the defendant responded.
"Do you fight with your wife?"

"Never."

"Where is your wife?" the puzzled judge asked.

Making everyone in the courtroom laugh, the 64-year-old defendant replied: "My wife has always been in China."[8]

Intended to make readers laugh as well, the newspaper story reflected a bitter experience that many shared. In fact, Wah-chung Leung himself remained physically separated from his wife for nearly four decades after his last departure from China. No quantitative data are available to help us fathom the impact of this state of affairs on the mind and body of the Chinese American bachelor. But we can catch a glimpse of the ramifications of the situation by taking a look at the medical advertisements, mostly of the more than twenty Chinese pharmaceutical stores and practitioners that persisted in spite of long-standing hostility, in Chinese newspapers.[9]

First, a word about newspaper advertising in Chinese San Francisco. Far less inclusive than the various business directories, the advertisement sections in newspapers do not give us a comprehensive picture of the scope of the Chinese American economy. They nonetheless constitute a very precious collective narrative that offers unique in-depth insights into the community. They not only took up far more space than the regular news reports and commentary but also appeared on every page, including the front page, of all the newspapers. Moreover, it is clear that individuals and organizations used the advertisement sections as a social bulletin, because they also published various important announcements there.

The commercial advertisements that appeared in the major Chinese American dailies were not brief "classifieds." Instead they were individually designed and often contained elaborately worded passages. The newspaper advertisers did not include manufacturers or businesses with exclusively non-Chinese clientele, such as laundries. They tended to be commercial establishments that needed to reach individual Chinese American customers. To promote their products or services they used language that was easy for ordinary customers to understand.

Of all the commercial advertisements, medical ones remained the most numerous and elaborate. Many directly addressed the medical as well as the psychological needs of the bachelor by promising both treatment for venereal diseases and measures to "increase masculinity." An analysis of three randomly selected issues of *The Chinese-Western Daily* illustrates the prevalence

of such ads.[10] In the February 15, 1916, issue, 29 of the 87 commercial advertisements were medical, and of those, 22 were related to sexuality. Among
the 69 commercial advertisements in the December 8, 1925, issue, 29 were
medical, and 23 were explicitly associated with sexuality. Of the 61 commercial advertisements in the January 5, 1940, issue, 22 were medical, and 15 were
related to sexuality.[11]

If the large number of medical advertisements bespoke an undiminished
trust in traditional Chinese medicine, the numerous sexuality-related ones
offer an intimate portrait of many sexually active bachelors. A good many
advertisements promised cures for syphilis, a widespread disease that resulted
from lonely bachelors' frequent visits to brothels, as is often emphasized in
the testimonials contained in the text of the advertisements. Advertisers also
promoted preventive measures, as customers could tell from the extremely
descriptive names of the pills. One pill was called "[the medicine] to take before sleeping with a whore." While prostitutes disappeared from the 1920
census, as Judy Yung points out, they clearly maintained a visible presence in
the community throughout the period.[12]

Despite the risks, bachelors continued to seek sexual pleasure, not only
because they thought there were remedies for the diseases they might get as
a result of doing so, but also because it gave them a chance to prove their
manhood. In fact, manhood was a prominent motif throughout the medical
advertisements, many of which vowed either to restore energy and masculinity to those exhausted from excessive sex, or simply to enhance the
pleasure of sex. One advertisement promoted a medicine that could
"strengthen . . . the penis so that [one could] freely enjoy the joy [of sexual
intercourse] and endure it without feeling tired at all."[13] Another one targeted people who "have had excessive sex . . . and developed regretful conditions such as impotence or premature ejaculation."[14] An advertisement for
"semen-production dew," a medicine supposedly able to increase the
amount of men's semen, exemplified how elaborate some medical advertisements were. "There is semen in a man's body," it stated philosophically, "just
as there are rain and dew on earth and water in the river and sea. Without
rain and dew, grass and plants cannot grow; if there is no water in the river
and sea, fish and shrimp cannot survive; if there is no semen in a man's body,
there would be no life."[15]

Other Chinese newspapers ran similar and even identical advertisements.

The Jiaan Company advertised in the *Chinese World* three medicines supposed to enhance men's sexual potency. One of them was called the "Pill to Strengthen Masculinity for Extended Battles." The advertisement asserted that lustful people shared the same desires, but most were "defeated after only one battle. . . . All brothel-goers should take this medicine," the advertisement prescribed, "[three hours] before visiting a prostitute."[16] An advertiser in the *Chinese Times* promoted a "secret prescription" that promised to help "older men" satisfy their sexual desire. The advertisement defended such desires by quoting a famous saying of the sage (Confucius): "The desire for both food and sex is human nature."[17]

Book dealers also catered to the bachelor's sexual needs. Along with medical advertisements, there were advertisements for such books as *New Book on Sexual Intercourse Between Men and Women* and *Secret Records of Activities Behind the Bed-Curtain from Ancient Times to the Present*.[18] A book entitled *Syphilis-Prevention Measures* was so popular that a number of book dealers kept it in stock for quite a long period.[19]

As they had in the past, all the books and advertisements primarily targeted men, addressing male desires and problems. The community remained quite tolerant of men's heterosexual activities. There existed no severe public condemnation of such activities, or any open suggestion that men should abstain. The previously mentioned "sperm-production dew" was publicly endorsed by the presidents of two huiguan.[20] Some community leaders even had a financial interest in certain drugstores that sold such medicines. Ng Poon Chew, for instance, was on the board of trustees of one of the largest pharmacies, the Republic Drug Company. Nevertheless, public tolerance did not exempt Chinese men from various problems associated with prostitution. Besides exposing them to the danger of venereal disease, frequent brothel visits could also exhaust a bachelor's small savings, jeopardizing his ability to fulfill family responsibilities. Such problems often aroused a deep sense of guilt. In 1939 Wah-chung Leung, a brothelgoer, admonished himself metaphorically: "The rose is beautiful. . . . But [it is also] thorny and poisonous when touched."[21] Unable to resist the persistent temptations of the brothel, the guilt-ridden Leung later condemned houses of prostitution as "a trap of smoky flowers."

The brothels could not meet the deep psychological needs of the lonely men. Many people who had American citizenship or another status that allowed them to travel back and forth journeyed to China to see their families, usually going more than once. The 32-year-old Wah-chung Leung, for example, returned to China twice by 1939 (he had arrived in the United States in 1922), but after that he never went back again because of the war in China. In crossing the Pacific he followed the path established by his father and other Chinese long before him.

Wah-chung's father, On Leung, was born in San Francisco in 1877 (which made Wah-chung a citizen as well). Soon his parents passed away. At the age of three On Leung went back to his native Zhongshan County with his adoptive parents. In 1889, when On Leung's adoptive father died, the mother was forced to take him to live in another village. When On Leung grew up he continued the family's trans-Pacific heritage by going back to America—his native land. In 1922 it was Wah-chung Leung's turn to carry on that heritage. Upon his arrival in San Francisco on January 17 he could only wave to his father, who came to greet him at the harbor because Wah-chung had to spent the next seventeen days on Angel Island for interrogation. The reunion of father and son illustrates the significance of Chinese San Francisco for trans-Pacific Chinese American families.

In 1924 Wah-chung Leung went back to his village, where he married a woman of his own age from another village in 1926. A year later he returned to America, leaving his bride behind. In 1931 he traveled to China with his father, taking the money he had saved. As he recalled in 1939, in the next seven years he simply "fooled around," gambling and visiting prostitutes. As I have noted earlier, many returned "Gold Mountaineers" found it particularly meaningful and enjoyable to spend their American money in their Chinese home communities. Wah-chung Leung did not just spend but "squandered money like dirt."[22] Subsequent financial needs forced him to take another trip across the Pacific Ocean in 1938.

Leung's story is not at all unique. In fact, as a Cantonese author noticed in 1936, sailing back and forth across the Pacific Ocean was a regular occurrence for many people: "American Chinese . . . after saving some money in ten years . . . return to China at about the age of 35 to get married. Less than half a year after marriage, they spend all their saving and must go overseas again for another ten years. They come back to China at the age of 45 to buy land and houses."[23] For these Chinese Americans cross-Pacific travels served as markers of major milestones in their lives, such as marriage, family growth, and even death.

Those who did not have an able body with which to earn the fare could now receive assistance from various charity organizations that had previously focused on transporting the dead. In 1911 the Nanhai Charity House (Nam Hoy Fook Yum Benevolent Society) decided that once a year it would finance a return trip back to Canton for those who "are over sixty and truly without any support."[24]

Because of the continuing flow of passengers leaving for China, the departure fees collected from them remained a major source of revenue for almost all major organizations in Chinese San Francisco.[25] During this period the Zhonghua Huiguan regularly dispatched officers to make sure that every passenger had a "departure ticket." The new bylaws that the Zhonghua Huiguan adopted early in 1930 required every Chinese American traveler over eighteen years of age to pay the departure fee. Soon the organization imposed a ten-dollar fine on those attempting to dodge the fees and a fine of one hundred dollars on each huiguan officer assisting them.[26] When a special need arose, additional fees would be collected. In 1914 the Zhonghua Huiguan added another 50 cents to the required fee to help the Peace Association, which was formed to deal with internal violence.[27] During the Great Depression dutiful collectors sometimes collided with uncooperative passengers. After such a collision turned violent in 1931, the Pacific Mail S. S. Company had the collectors arrested. The Chinese consulate had to instruct the organizations involved to restrain their fee-collecting officers "in order to avoid the criticism of outsiders."[28]

Many native-born Chinese Americans too maintained close connections to the emigrant region. First of all, it remained part of their identity within the community. Let us consider the announcements that individuals posted to renounce their tong membership in order to escape violence during every major tong war. In thoroughly specifying the ex-tong members' identity in order to insure their safety, these announcements reveal that a significant number of American-born Chinese had joined the tongs. What is more, their ancestral community in China constituted an important part of their identity. In the tong war of October 1921 that spread to several cities, more than 30 people renounced their tong membership in *The Chinese-Western Daily*. Among the 4 explicitly identified as American-born, Huang Chang-fu's statement declared that "[he] also styled himself Kunqiu, of Huang-chong village of Xinhui County, born in America, now working in a restaurant on Clay Street in the Big City."[29]

Like their Chinese-born counterparts, the native-born men also had families, even wives, in China. This is why the 1924 immigration act that barred their wives from entering the country gave rise to an extraordinary and lasting protest on the part of Chinese American citizens. The record of the Chinese American Citizens Alliance's life-insurance fund from October 1923 to July 1925 serves as further concrete evidence of the citizens' family ties in China. About 50 applications were filed by the relatives of deceased alliance members. Of the 37 cases that were approved, 25 recipients were in China, and 12 were in America. Twenty-nine recipients were the wives of the deceased members. Twenty-four of them were in China, and only 5 were in America.[30]

Evidence shows that many native-born Chinese traveled to China themselves, not only as children but also as adults. In the 1920s the bylaws of the alliance's life-insurance fund expressly stipulated that members should pay their dues in advance before they made a trip to China. Starting in 1907 the alliance collected departure fees from its members, many of whom were native born. The alliance even levied such fees on nonmember Chinese American citizens. On March 2, 1931, Fong Chung paid the alliance three dollars before leaving for China. On his receipt appears the following statement: "Upon each departure, every Chinese American citizen who has not joined our association must make a contribution of three dollars for public welfare."[31] The large number of Chinese American citizens traveling westward to China generated much revenue for the alliance.

Reunions with loved ones remained a perennial theme of Chinese life. In a song titled "Xiyang Honglei Siqin" ("Missing the family under the setting sun with tears in red eyes"), a female performer named Li Xuefang described a heartbreaking scenario: when they returned home too late, Chinese Americans could pay respects to their deceased parents only at the graves. Its lyrics went: "I dream and dream. I dream of returning to my hometown. Dreaming of returning to the hometown worsens the wound in my heart. . . . I am waiting for the day of my return. I will go to the graveyard, rush to kneel down, and burn paper money to pay my delayed respects to my dear parents."[32] Li Xuefang was one of the most famous performers of Cantonese opera in Guangdong Province, and "Xiyang Honglei Siqin" was the title of one of her most popular shows. She was the guest star at the

Mandarin Theatre on Grant Avenue in 1927, and her popularity kept her in Chinese San Francisco for an entire year. Li was still performing in San Francisco when Wah-chung Leung returned from his marriage trip to China. Though we do not know whether or not he went to listen to her singing, we do know that he would have understood the lyrics printed above. In his diary entry for the Qingming festival (the holiday designated for the sweeping of the graves of deceased loved ones) in 1943, he wrote sorrowfully that he had "not swept the grave of his mother for five years," calling himself "an unfilial son."[33]

Li was but one of many performing artists from China who visited Chinese San Francisco during this period. In fact, her presence coincided with that of another performer from Canton at the Great China Theatre on Jackson Street. The familiarity of the music and performances of visiting Cantonese opera singers like Li undoubtedly offered homesick Chinese San Franciscans some consolation. They also had the opportunity to enjoy Beijing opera in 1930 when Mei Lanfang, the foremost star of Beijing opera, came to town. His visit generated much excitement in Chinese San Francisco. During his first show on April 24 as *The Chinese-Western Daily* reported, "the theater had a full house."[34]

In an article included in the promotion pamphlet for Mei Lanfang's Pacific Coast tour, the theater expert George Leung proclaimed in dramatic language: "To know their theater is to know, in no small degree, the Chinese people."[35] Indeed, the Chinese American theater can offer some insight into the change and continuity in Chinese American life. Having recovered along with Chinatown after the earthquake, by the 1920s Chinese drama had entered another period of prosperity, "a renaissance" in the words of Ronald Riddle.[36] Like the rest of the community, the theaters were being modernized. Electric lighting was used more often, and the orchestras adopted a few Western instruments.

As it had in the nineteenth century, however, the audience remained primarily Chinese. Tickets were still affordable: the cheapest seat cost only 50 cents in the 1920s, while the rich could get the best seats by paying three times as much. More important, the theater remained a cultural institution, as we can tell from surviving program flyers of dramas staged in the Mandarin Theatre, known among Chinese simply as Dawutai (great stage).[37] Serving to reinforce historical memories, it produced shows that re-created events and figures from Chinese history and folklore. Moral instructions represented another major theme. A drama entitled Meihua Zan (Plum-blossom hairpin) that opened on June 8, 1920, was reportedly based on a true love story that occurred in Guangdong Province. According to the program description it was also about "women's virtue of chastity and men's virtue of loyalty and filial piety, and the sinful evils caused by lust." On March 29, 1925, the theater presented another drama about a widow who refused to remarry after her husband's death and who devoted the rest of her life to the education of her son. Intended to "set a model for family education," the show reportedly "had been popular for more than ten years."

Theatrical productions also reflected and promoted the ideological and social transformation of the community. One 1925 program flyer emphasizes the educational significance of theatrical productions by explaining that the popularity of the show came from "its ability to reform social customs and to awaken common people." The flyer for another show in 1927 states that "the principle of the survival of the fittest and the law of the strong eating the flesh of the weak" were universally true. It then says that the show was meant to "awaken our fellow countrymen to defend against the insult from outsiders."

We need to note that all four stars prominently featured in that 1927 show were women, illustrating the important role that female artists played in helping to fulfill the theater's cultural and social responsibilities. Indeed, Chinese theaters in San Francisco had always preferred to use real women stars rather than female impersonators. The use of such impersonators, a long-standing tradition in mainstream Chinese theater that was perfected by Mei Lanfang, reflected China's unequal gender system. The pamphlet promoting Mei Lanfang's Pacific Coast tour admitted that "in the old social system of China . . . the appearance of women on the stage was absolutely forbidden by public opinion." In his piece included in the pamphlet, George Leung expressed his preference for impersonators:

> The emperor Chi'ien Lung (1736–1795) banished women from the professional stage; and although they have gradually returned since the Republic (1911), they have, with rare exception, proved no match for men in the highly stylized acting and singing of feminine roles. Women in order to hold the public are obliged to imitate the leading male exponents of feminine art who in the beginning, devised the falsetto and conventional manner to imitate real women.[38]

Preferring to watch real women performing on the stage, San Franciscans clearly disagreed with Leung's aesthetics. At least in terms of the theatrical world, Chinese San Francisco had a less rigid gender hierarchy than China did.

If the theaters served to popularize historical memories and cultural heritage, the Chinese schools represented the community's conscious, organized efforts to bolster ties to the Old World. The growth of these schools made it possible for more and more children to receive a Chinese education within the community. Urging people to make financial contributions to the Zhonghua School, *Young China* associated education with the community's survival: "In the world, those with education have prospered, and those without education have become weak and declined. Among settlements within a foreign country, those with education . . . have multiplied generation after generation." To save China and make Chinese San Francisco prosper, the newspaper declared that "nothing is more important than supporting the [Zhonghua] School and perpetuating the education of Chinese children in the foreign land."[39]

Education was also regarded as a guarantee of cultural continuity. In an article about the importance of education, Lin Shihen, former principal of the Zhonghua School, stressed the necessity of teaching the Chinese language to the younger generation:[40]

> For Chinese, however, it is also important to learn the Chinese
> language. . . . If Chinese people only know Western Learning and
> do not learn Chinese, they would be ignorant of the state of the
> [home] country and unable to communicate [with the Chinese
> in China]. A longtime influence by the West will weaken [their]
> affection toward the ancestral land. This is especially true of Chinese
> children who were born and grow up abroad.[41]

Many parents shared Lin's desire to pass Chinese cultural identity on to children. Regarding his reason for sending his children to a Chinese school, one parent stated: "I hope my children will be able to write simple letters in order to communicate with non-English-speaking relatives in the United States and China." Another said: "I don't want my children to become so Americanized that they forget the good qualities of a Chinese."[42]

During this period the Zhonghua School remained the most important and the largest Chinese school and was under the direct supervision of the Zhonghua Huiguan. Setting a pattern for other schools to follow, it imported both its textbooks and its curriculum from China. It also hired scholars from China as teachers.[43] The school experienced significant growth during the years under discussion. In July 1916 the number of school hours was increased. By 1918, when enrollment reached about one hundred and forty, the school implemented an effort to build a sports ground for its pupils. In 1920 female students were admitted. In 1925 the expanding school built new facilities for a junior high school section, becoming "the highest educational institution of all Chinese in America."[44] By 1927 the number of students had increased to two hundred.

With support from different organizations, the number of Chinese schools multiplied over time to meet the community's growing need. The Chenzhong (morning bell) Society, a theatrical group, established a school early in 1919 and supported it for many years. According to a report in *Young China*, by August 1919 there were 126 students in the school, with a few more on the waiting list.[45] In August 1920 the school's enrollment rose to 159. The famous Nanhai Charity House founded the Nanqiao (southern immigrant) School in 1920 when its leaders realized that educating the younger generation was as important as its mission of shipping the bones of the dead to China, which it had been doing for decades.[46] The school had 30 students when it opened, and its enrollment went up to about two hundred late in the 1920s, by which time a new building had already been completed to accommodate the growing number of students. Its enrollment reached a record high of over four hundred in 1932, when there were nine teachers.[47] During its expansion the school added a junior high in 1926. The Yanghe Huiguan set up the Yanghe School in 1924. The Confucius Society established the Confucius School in 1930. In the 1920s the Chinese in nearby Oakland set up a Chinese school for women. Even Christian churches, which were interested in converting Chinese, catered to the needs of the Chinese community by establishing Chinese schools, including the Xiehe School founded by the Congregational and Presbyterian churches in 1924.

Coming to study America's educational system in 1937, a Beijing University professor named Wu Junsheng made an inquiry into the state of education in Chinese American communities. Wu found that almost all of them had a Chinese school. In San Francisco more than two thousand students attended the ten or so Chinese schools, seven of which had junior high school sections. Based on data collected from Chinese American educators, Wu reported that 90 percent of all school-aged children living in San Francisco's Chinatown attended a Chinese school.[48]

These schools, at which the Chinese language was an important subject, played a major role in reinforcing cultural identity.[49] As Wu Junsheng noted in his report, "The textbooks used in the Chinese schools are the same as the ones used in China."[50] Let us take a brief look at some of the textbooks used at the Xiehe School.[51] The content of the language textbooks enables us to appreciate the cultural significance of language acquisition. In such textbooks, for example, students learned linguistic categories particular to the Chinese language that helped codify intricate relations within the extended family—relations that were of paramount importance in Chinese culture. Titled "Relatives," Lesson 18 in the *New Chinese Language* textbook introduced a long of list of terms, including the following:

> "Father's elder brother is 'bofu,' father's younger brother is 'shufu.' "
> "Elder brother's wife is 'sao,' and younger brother's wife is 'difu.' "
> "Mother's elder and younger brothers are 'jiufu,' and parents' sisters are 'yimu.' "
> "Sons of 'yimu's are 'biaoxiongdi.' "[52]

These were very useful terms in the context of the Chinese American community, where kinship constituted the most fundamental basis for social relations. Extended families represented coherent social circles, which were often quite large in size, as we can tell from obituaries. A 1930 obituary was signed by about sixty family members.[53] About fifty relatives signed a 1943 obituary.[54] In both cases the obituary used special terms clearly to specify each signer's precise position in the extended family.

The textbooks also incorporated lessons in morality, teaching the students not only to respect parents but also to be courteous to others. Lesson 33 of the *Chinese Language Textbook* told the following story:

> [I] came home and told my mother that while I was playing in the hills, someone of the village who hid behind the hills insulted me by imitating what I said. I then cursed him. And he cursed back. But [I] do not know who he was. Having heard what I said, my mother burst out laughing and

said: "that was the echo, or the sound response. There was no one there to insult you. Whatever comes to your ears goes out of your mouth. You heard the curse and were enraged [by it]. In fact, you should not have cursed in the first place. Now you should apply this principle not only to what you say but also to how you treat people. Be kind to others, and they will be kind to you. If you do not treat others nicely, they will treat you accordingly."[55]

Most important of all was the infusion of nationalism into language teaching. Lesson 12 of a conversation textbook contained a well-known story about an event that had happened more than two thousand years before. In order to preserve the unity of the country a civilian official sacrificed his personal dignity and interest to win the friendship of a hostile general. The lesson ended with the official's own words: "The country comes before anything else."[56]

Lesson 17 in the *New Chinese Language* textbook is titled "Patriotism." It is straightforward about the subject: "A country is a ship that carries its people [over water]. The country's interest concerns its people's weal and woe. If everyone only cares about himself and does not set the country's interest above everything else . . . the country can rarely survive."[57] In history textbooks, especially those on Chinese history, patriotism was a dominant theme. The *New Chinese History Textbook* included America's exclusion acts as one of the national humiliations China had suffered in modern times.[58]

All the schools strived to teach students to remember their cultural identity. In transformed twentieth-century Chinese San Francisco this did not mean a rejection of Western learning. In fact, many people believed that one could serve China better by mastering Western technology and science. In his speech at the Zhonghua School's graduation ceremony of 1920, the president of the Shaoqing Huiguan advised the graduates that "Western and Chinese learning are equally important."[59] He hoped that with the knowledge of both they would help save China when they returned there after completing their education.

On its anniversary on November 11, 1921, the Zhonghua School announced that the student journal, *Great China*, would be restored, and it officially adopted a new school song, which was sung at the ceremony by all the students in chorus: "Brothers and sisters . . . make known the honored name of our school, let the glory of our Republic rise. The name of our country is China, the name of our school is China. China! China! Bright-colored in full blossom is the morning flower. . . . I love China. I love China."[60]

The mission of the Nanqiao School included "the inculcation of the culture of the homeland, the growth of children's minds and bodies, and the development of a healthy character."[61] These schools were successful in achieving their declared purpose, as we can see from the data collected in 1944 by Yi Ying Ma, who was an opponent of Chinese schools. At the time 1,909 students attended the ten Chinese schools in Chinese San Francisco. According to Ma's survey these students received even better grades in public schools than did their peers who did not go to a Chinese school. Furthermore, over 63 percent of the Chinese-school students said that they often read books in Chinese, and over 23 percent read Chinese periodicals often. Naturally, they were more proficient in Chinese than their counterparts who did not attend Chinese school.[62] It is evident that these schools did a great deal to maintain the Chinese language among immigrants' children.

Most significant of all, the Chinese schools helped to reinforce the community's cultural identity. During his 1937 visit Wu Junsheng was impressed by Chinese Americans' nationalistic sentiment, which he thought was sometimes "stronger than that of the Chinese in China." He concluded that the nationalism of Chinese in America, especially of the younger generation, "should be attributed, at least in part, to the education" they had received in the Chinese schools. Because they were taught "the motherland's language and history," Wu stated, "they still do not forget their homeland."[63]

As one indication of their nationalism, students in the Chinese schools actively took part in the struggle against Japanese aggression. As a school assignment, they practiced translating into English stories published in Chinese newspapers about the resistance war in China. They wrote essays on topics such as "By the Marco Polo Bridge," where Japan started the all-out war with China in 1937. In November 1934 about two thousand students from the Chinese schools joined other Chinese San Franciscans in a grand parade to welcome General Cai Tingkai. A native of Guangdong, Cai had emerged as a hero in China's resistance to Japan during the defense of Shanghai in 1932. San Francisco was part of the retired general's global tour. Cai's vocal criticism of Jiang Jieshi's nonresistance policy not only inspired Chinese America, it also generated unprecedented respect and receptiveness on the part of white America. If the retired general made remarks insulting to Chinese San Francisco during his visit, as one old-timer recalled him doing, they did not enter public Chinese-language records.[64] Nor did they cool Chinese San Francisco's fervor for aiding China.

Participation in the Resistance to Japanese Aggression

Japan's Twenty-one Demands of 1915 prompted the first wave of anti-Japanese protest in Chinese San Francisco. In March 1915 a Chinese Patriotic Society was formed to organize a boycott of Japanese goods.[65] The society mobilized the entire community. Individuals posted statements in Chinese newspapers, urging all Chinese in America to join the movement. Organizations sent telegrams to China, asking the government to reject "Japan's unreasonable and greedy demands."[66] Merchants formed the China Mail S. S. Company to fight the Japanese economically. Chinese San Franciscans were so enthusiastic about the boycott that the Chinese Patriotic Society had to remind the public that the boycott was aimed only at Japan, not at other countries.[67] Thereafter Chinese San Franciscans launched continuous anti-Japanese campaigns in response to a chain of events: the postwar peace conference in 1919, when Japan adamantly insisted upon maintaining its holdings and other privileges in Shandong Province; the 1928 Jinan Incident, when Japanese soldiers killed innocent Chinese in the capital of Shandong Province; the September 18 Incident of 1931, when Japan invaded Manchuria; and the July 7 Incident of 1937, when Japan started an all-out invasion of China.

To support the campaigns, all segments of the Chinese American community made sacrifices. In a 1919 boycott the Guangzhen store on Jackson Street publicly burned Japanese-made cosmetics and embroideries in stock. The boycott spread throughout Chinese America. Chinese in Chicago imposed heavy fines on those who violated the boycott: two thousand dollars for a seller and one hundred dollars for a buyer of Japanese goods. In 1919 the Chinese American Citizens Alliance joined other organizations in sending telegrams to China in protest against Japan's demands at the peace conference.[68]

Over time nationalistic sentiment became so prevalent that it influenced all manner of groups. Such sentiment is found in advertisers' language. Hong Hop Company of Los Angeles promoted a "masculinity-strengthening" medicine by stating: "If you want to strengthen your nation, you have to strengthen your species first."[69] After the September 18 Incident of 1931 even the antinationalist anarchists in Chinese San Francisco publicly condemned "The invasion of Manchuria by Japanese imperialists."[70]

Chinese San Franciscans linked their fate with that of China and regarded resisting Japan as their duty. Calling on Chinese Americans to break away from regionalism and clannism, *Young China* noted in 1918 that they had an obligation to help "restore national sovereignty."[71] In 1934 the daily newspaper published a series of editorials on General Cai Tingkai's visit. In reference to the strong patriotic feelings Cai helped generate, it concluded: "The spirit displayed at that moment is very precious. If we are able to maintain it, we can defeat Japan and save our country."[72]

If the Japanese aggression created a national crisis, the formation of a united front of resistance in China rekindled the Chinese Americans' hope. After the 1936 Xian Incident that forced Jiang Jieshi (Chiang Kai-shek) to terminate the civil war with the Communists, Jiang emerged as the supreme national leader of a reunited China. The persistent internal political discord that had prevailed ever since the 1911 revolution seemed to have come to an end. Chinese San Franciscans embraced Jiang. Stores competed with one another in selling his photographs. In 1939 the Zhonghua Huiguan in San Francisco placed one in its meeting hall. An owner of a pharmaceutical store renamed his store "New China" to mark the encouraging development in China. During the Chinese New Year season of 1939, the owner called on fellow Chinese to "carry on the anti-Japan war until the final victory and support the Supreme Leader in solidarity."[73]

The struggle against Japan became a "public school" for nationalism. In support of China, Chinese schools in San Francisco participated in rallies and marches and helped raise funds. In 1941, at the tenth anniversary of the September 18 incident, the Zhonghua School held a commemorative meeting. Students sang the Chinese national anthem, made three bows in front of the Chinese national flag, and observed three minutes of silence for Chinese soldiers who died during the war. Speakers encouraged the students to do what they could for China. The chairman of the student association announced the establishment of a Save the Country Savings Fund.

China's vigorous spirit of resistance enhanced Chinese Americans' nationalistic pride. On June 25, 1942, *The Chinese-Western Daily* published an
editorial on "the national character of the Chinese." It defined national character as "a nation's essential attitude towards life, that is . . . a nation's unique
spirit in dealing with a particular situation." In the competition for survival
among nations, the editorial noted, "national character has a decisive influence." The Chinese national character based on Confucianism, it asserted,
was "courteous and all-encompassing" and included the spirit of "sacrifice
for a just cause." At the end the editorial proudly declared that the great national character of the Chinese people, long suppressed by the Manchu
tyranny, "will brightly shine" on the day of victory over Japan.[74]

Chinese San Franciscans' financial contribution to China's resistance is the
best indication of their nationalism. From the 1920s to the 1940s numerous
drives—sometimes more than one at a time—were conducted to raise
money for China in the struggle against Japan. For a mid-1928 drive, for
example, six contingents traveled from San Francisco to other locations to
raise money. Each had a one-character name that combined to mean "the
earnest patriotism of the Chinese in America."[75]

After the July 7 Incident of 1937, Chinese Americans "pledge[d] full support" for China, starting a new phase in fund-raising efforts.[76] By August, 21
individual Chinese in San Francisco had already sent five thousand dollars to
China.[77] On that day community leaders formed the Association to Save
China to coordinate and lead all the fund-raising activities taking place
throughout the American West.[78] It became the most visible and effective of
all similar organizations that emerged across Chinese America during these
years. By the end of 1937 it had sent donations worth more than two million
Chinese dollars to China.[79] Donor lists filled the news sections of Chinese
newspapers. So many donated that giving money became a public honor.
Contributions kept pouring in, forcing the Association to Save China and
the five major Chinese newspapers to issue a joint announcement in mid-
November 1937 stating that any donation of less than one hundred dollars
would not be publicly acknowledged.

Economic difficulties that came about as a result of the Great Depression
did not cool individuals' desire to contribute generously. In March 1938
The Chinese-Western Daily reported that Huang Yuanzhan, a Chinese in
Arizona, had been donating five hundred dollars each month since the

beginning of the war.[80] Various organizations also raised money independently. On July 31 a theatrical research institute in Chinese San Francisco raised $4,741.15 to purchase gas masks for Chinese soldiers.[81] By mid-December 1939, when a year-long "war-contribution" campaign ended, the Association to Save China had collected $630,000. Coming primarily from Chinese San Franciscans, this was a "very impressive" amount to have collected in just one year, as an editorial pointed out.[82] During the eight years of the Sino-Japanese War (1937–45), the Association to Save China sent at least five million American dollars to China.[83] During these years there was hardly a time when no fund-raising campaign was being conducted in the community.

Chinese San Francisco was never an economic and political monolithic bloc. Even China's national crisis failed to inspire every single Chinese San Franciscan to make personal sacrifices for the resistance against Japan. Some must have contributed money because of the enormous social pressure that existed in the community. During a 1932 campaign to raise money to buy war planes for China, everyone over the age of eighteen, except for the extremely poor, was required to contribute. In 1936 the Zhongxing Company ordered its managers to give a month's salary to China, and every employee to give ten dollars.[84] During another fund-raising drive for the purchase of war planes two years later, the Association to Save China imposed a fine on those who did not make the minimum contribution. It also advised those who had already done so to wear a badge as a certificate of compliance.[85] One person who participated in several fund-raising activities in 1937 recalled that all stores were required to pay the monthly contribution at the time. Those who refused to comply would be boycotted. People would even throw eggs at their stores, or break the windows.[86]

It cannot be said, however, that the community's high degree of financial and moral support for China's resistance war was the result of coercion on the part of a hegemonic power elite. Rather, the mandate to apply social pressure in these campaigns came from a widespread, genuine concern about the development of the Chinese Pacific War. While struggling against the lure of opium and prostitution in his personal life, for example, the laborer Wah-chung Leung remained concerned about the war in China. In 1943, as he recorded in his diary, he went to a temple and "kneeled down to ask the Buddha when the armed conflict would end."[87] Such anxieties are easy to understand. The war was not only about China's future; it also directly affected Chinese Americans. The Chinese American economy was closely tied to the China market. Many goods that Chinese Americans consumed came directly from China—either from the south via Hong Kong or from Shanghai. Fighting on the other side of the ocean drove up the prices in Chinatown, as the *Chinese Times* noted in 1942.[88] Japanese military action in South China, in particular, brought much hardship to the emigrant communities and made it difficult for Chinese Americans to visit their loved ones.[89] In response to this situation the Chinese government established new routes for those returning from overseas to their native communities.

Chinese Americans' nationalism served to shorten the distance between themselves and China. In 1937, following the July 7 Incident, an unprecedented number of Chinese Americans participated in the election of representatives to China's Congress. Within the jurisdiction of the Chinese consulate general in San Francisco, fifteen voting stations administered by 134 people were set up. In San Francisco 24 people supervised the election.[90] According to a Chinese consulate report in August 1937 the three elected candidates commanded 2,697, 2,497, and 1,686 votes, respectively.[91] It is clear that many more Chinese Americans cast their votes in this election than in American elections.

Chinese San Franciscans had evidence that their compatriots in China deeply appreciated their generous support. In March 1941 Kuang Bingyao, the chairman of the Association to Save China, visited China and was received by Chinese leaders, including Jiang Jieshi and his wife.[92] A Chinese encyclopedia published in 1940 included an entry for the "Bowl of Rice Movement." Inaugurated late in the 1930s, this movement marks a new level of Chinese Americans' support for China, as we will see later.

In conclusion, the socially and ideologically transformed community maintained its ties to the emigrant region in South China, and its cultural identity. That identity did not remain important on its own. Development of Chinese schools exemplified community leaders' and ordinary individuals' conscious and organized efforts to reinforce collective memory and cultural heritage. Participation in the resistance against Japanese aggression in China was the most effective school of Chinese nationalism for the entire community. The full-scale Sino-Japanese War that began in 1937, in particular, became a monumental event in the lives of Chinese Americans. They devoted a great deal of energy and many resources to fighting that war, which threatened not only China but also their families' safety. Aiding the resistance to Japanese aggression in China also became a powerful weapon with which to combat anti-Chinese prejudice in the United States.

The Road to 1943

The Chinese Pacific War and Chinese Americans' participation in it paved the way to the repeal of the Chinese exclusion acts in 1943, demonstrating once again that Chinese American history must be understood in the context of the trans-Pacific world. China's role in World War II as America's ally after the bombing of Pearl Harbor explains the genesis of the repeal movement. This movement received a significant boost when Mme. Jiang (her maiden name was Song Meiling, which was sometimes spelled Soong Mayling at the time), the wife of Generalissimo Jiang Jieshi, took a tour of the United States. Investigating events leading to the end of Chinese exclusion helps us appreciate how Chinese San Franciscans and their counterparts elsewhere actively combined efforts to aid China and efforts to fight anti-Chinese prejudice. Such an investigation also affords us an opportunity to discuss the nature of changes regarding Chinese Americans' position in American society.

Reshaping the Image

For Chinese Americans, reshaping their image had always been an important part of the struggle for racial justice. After all, their communities that stood as isolated islands in metropolitan centers had been under constant and close

239

public scrutiny: they had been investigated and even raided by authorities, and had been gazed upon by curious, sometimes trespassing, visitors. As Chinese Americans knew, anti-Chinese forces had always exploited negative perceptions of Chinese life. In reference to a violent tong war that broke out in 1905, the *New York Times* commented that the Chinese, who challenged Chinese exclusion, should first find a way "to restrain lawlessness among their own race."[1] From the late nineteenth century onward the Chinese had made significant efforts not only to curb the notorious tong wars but also to eliminate everything else that served to smear their image. They had tried to stop tour guides and, later, filmmakers from perpetuating the stereotype of a dirty and immoral Chinatown. They had renovated the streets and stores to make it clean. During the pre-war period they also tried to publicly display their political and cultural Americanism as much as possible. Urging the Chinese to join in the celebration of the anniversary of California's statehood, *The Chinese-Western Daily* editorialized: "We Chinese people must take part in the big celebration in order to enhance the affection between Chinese and Americans."[2] Joining the rest of the community in the public relations campaign, the Chinese American Citizens Alliance resolved at its tenth convention in Chicago that "at the opening ceremonies of national conventions and at public banquets, officers of the Alliance and representatives from local lodges should all wear tuxedos in order to enhance the image [of the Alliance]."[3]

Twentieth-century mainstream society inherited much of the anti-Chinese prejudice that nineteenth-century writers had propagated. Citing Arthur H. Smith, a longtime China missionary who wrote late in the nineteenth century on the Chinese national character, Ralph Townsend stated in 1934: "Nobody trusts anybody else in China, for the excellent reason that he knows that under similar circumstances he could not be trusted himself."[4] With the anti-Japanese war, however, came an excellent opportunity to create a new and positive image for China. As the Association to Save China noted in a public announcement soliciting donations to be used to purchase winter clothes for Chinese soldiers, the war "raised the international status of China."[5] It aroused a great deal of sympathy from white Americans, who formed numerous organizations to aid China, such as the American Bureau for Medical Aid to China and the American Committee for Non-Participation in Japanese Aggression. As Fred W. Riggs has noted, after 1937 the image of the Chinese was raised "to an abnormally high level in popular esteem, facilitating the implementation of a pro-Chinese policy, of which the repeal of the exclusion laws constituted one segment."[6] Gradually, a long-standing social trend reversed, and in the white American consciousness Chinese Americans became a "superior" and "more desirable" race than their Japanese counterparts.

Partly as a response to post–Pearl Harbor attacks on Chinese Americans mistaken for Japanese, mainstream periodicals published photographs that had been analyzed in detail to help readers understand the "anthropological conformations that distinguish friendly Chinese from enemy alien Japs."[7] Using carefully chosen adjectives, *Life* magazine drew a laudatory portrait of the Chinese man: he was relatively tall and slender, "his face long and delicately boned, his nose more finely bridged." The Japanese man, by comparison, "betrays aboriginal antecedents in a squat, long-torsoed build." Clearly, new stereotypes were in the making. The magazine also stated that "Chinese wear rational calm of tolerant realists. Japs, like General [Hideki] Tojo, show humorless intensity of ruthless mystics." *Time* magazine carried similar comparisons of the two groups: "Those who know them best often rely on facial expression to tell them apart: the Chinese expression is likely to be more placid, kindly, open; the Japanese more positive, dogmatic, arrogant."[8] The anthropologist Dr. Ales Hrdliska of the Smithsonian Institute informed the public that while the Japanese had a "psychological expression" that reflected "their materialistic and commercial interests," the Chinese faces were "mild and friendly and interesting."[9] It is hard to imagine that such descriptive words actually helped people distinguish Chinese from Japanese Americans, but they did reveal the way white America looked at Asian American groups.

Chinese San Franciscans seized the wartime opportunity to reshape their public image. A case in point was what Chinese Americans called the Bowl of Rice movement, a campaign to raise money for China's war refugees that was conducted many times in San Francisco and elsewhere from 1938 to 1941. The name of the movement had been decided upon by its non-Chinese sponsors. In an article that was translated into Chinese, the head of the Bureau for Medical Aid to China explained its meaning. First, "bowl of rice" alluded to an ancient Chinese story about a general named Han Xin, who helped to found the Western Han Dynasty (206 B.C–A.D. 220). According to the story, Han had once been fed and saved by a female stranger, who did not want to be repaid. Second, rice was the staple of the Chinese diet. Third, the "bowl of rice" notion had the "unbelievable power to draw attention" because it invoked curiosity. Fourth, the name allowed the movement to be conducted any time and any place, whereas names such as "Mooncake festival" and "Mid-Autumn Festival" were restricted to a certain time period.

The "bowl of rice" image clearly enabled white sponsors of the movement to view themselves as culturally and materially superior, and as altruistic. The image characterized China as a helpless, impoverished, and victimized nation waiting to be saved. But while the "bowl of rice" notion had been adopted to stimulate curiosity, the movement itself served to promote, more than exoticize, Chinese culture. It also embodied the increasing Sinophile sentiments that were beginning to influence the dominant society.

Independent of white Americans' intentions, the Chinese had their own agenda, that is, to aid China and to improve their relationship with white Americans. As we can see by observing San Francisco, Chinese Americans became main organizers of events related to aiding China. In early June 1938 the Chinese embassy asked Chinese communities across the United States to hold a parade to mark "the Day of Grand Chinese Solidarity" during the nationwide Bowl of Rice event. Chinese San Franciscans decided to put on a festival-like "Chinatown Night." Preparing for the event, Chinese San Franciscans sought the cooperation of white Americans in order to, as a reporter put it, "achieve a great effect." The reporter called on all Chinese to make the event successful so that it would "draw the attention of the entire United States."[10]

On the night of June 17, white San Franciscans came to Chinatown to join their Chinese neighbors in a wide variety of attractions and activities including games, dancing dragons, Chinese plays, and Cantonese music. All the Chinese put on their most beautiful clothes. Chinese women in traditional dress were a particular focus of attention. Adding a comic and joyful air to the occasion, a kangaroo court was set up. Paul Smith, general manager of the *Chronicle* and an organizer of the event, was found "guilty" of giving the event so much publicity that traffic in Chinatown became jammed. Snarling up traffic was a crowd consisting of about three hundred thousand people, all of whom attended the event. As *The Chinese-Western Daily* noted, the event's success demonstrated "sufficient evidence of Westerners' sympathy towards us," and marked "an unprecedented cooperation between Chinese and the Westerners."[11]

"Chinatown Night" was historic. For the first time, white San Franciscans displayed their friendliness toward the Chinese on a large scale during a Chinese American occasion centered in Chinatown. Their unprecedented show of friendship stood in striking contrast with their earlier hostility. Just three years earlier, in 1935, hostile policemen had blockaded Chinatown for two days over an unfounded rumor that a tong war might break out, forcing Chinese San Franciscans to celebrated their lunar New Year under siege.

The 1940 "Bowl of Rice Party," as the event was called, started with a parade on February 9. Leading the parade, an open car carried American and Chinese dignitaries, including the city's chief of police William Quinn, who had ordered that roadblocks be placed around Chinatown five years earlier. What a change the anti-Japanese war had brought about! Cosponsored by the regional committee of the United Council for Civilian Relief in China, the three-day event took place during the Chinese New Year season. It turned out to be a festive party characterized by good feelings—feelings that were manifested far beyond the confines of Chinatown. The *Chronicle* reported that "San Francisco celebrated that New Year in a manner especially neighborly—it was almost a family affair. For that celebration in which joined the entire city and even the State was The Bowl of Rice!"[12] Politicians and judges showed their support for the event in different ways. Paul Smith served as the general chairman. The mayor of the city, Angelo J. Rossi, was an active supporter and participant. The governor of California sent his congratulations.

Various government officials openly expressed their respect for the Chinese. On the first day the district attorney of San Francisco, Mathew Brady, faced a trial at the popular kangaroo court on Grant Avenue and Washington Street. A white reporter described this scene that took place at the court: "Brady, dragged from behind the bars to face justice, declared he had the greatest respect for the Chinese member of the court, but couldn't say so much for the other two members."[13] Then "Brady said he would be glad to pay a fine for whatever charges except that he was lacking in sympathy for the people of China."[14] The kangaroo court was a part of the entertainment program, but the sentiments expressed there could not be dismissed as insincere. "In a generous, happy mood," white San Franciscans communicated what they felt with donations amounting to eighty-five thousand dollars.[15]

In a conscious effort to "propagate Chinese culture," organizers put on Chinese fashion shows, Chinese concerts, acrobatics exhibitions, Chinese dramas, Chinese art exhibitions, lion dances, and dragon dances—all made possible by the efforts of over fifteen hundred Chinese San Franciscan volunteers.[16] A contemporary, William Hoy, vividly described the Chinese flavor of the event: "Through the narrow streets and by-ways of Chinatown float the delicate narcissus. . . . In the shops and homes you see the tall, rugged branches of plum blossoms. . . . At intervals firecrackers detonated here and there . . . the happy cries of children, the laughter of carefree adults. . . . The air resounding with greeting of 'Kung Hay Fat Choy [wish you rich]!'. . . . The native music of the south, pervading everywhere." This was, Hoy concluded, "the setting of the Bowl of Rice pageant in Chinatown, a setting as colorful as old Canton."[17]

The event received overwhelming support. In an effort to capitalize on its popularity, a white gold refiner store, S. B. Gracier & Sons, reworked its advertisement, asking Chinese San Franciscans to sell their gold for cash "to aid Chinese refugees."[18] It is necessary to note women's significant roles in the 1940 Bowl of Rice party. During the parades held on February 9 and 11 a very visible several hundred women carried a gigantic Chinese national flag. A female painter raised $239.11 by selling her work. Long before the Bowl of Rice movement took place, women had established a substantial presence in various nationalist activities. In 1934, for example, women in some cities played a more prominent role than men in representing their communities to welcome General Cai Tingkai.[19]

In the preceding chapter we saw how women's visibility and status increased as a result of the influence of mainstream culture. We must also remember two other sources of the change: certain unorthodox traditions in the emigrant region and, as Judy Yung points out in her recent work, the rising women's movement in China.[20] Chinese American women knew very well where the roots of their movement lay. In one newspaper article a Chinese American woman summarized the Chinese American women's movement. "It has reached a new stage with the struggle against aggression," she began. She then traced it back to Guangdong Province: "The women here are mostly from Guangdong. And they inherited Cantonese people's energetic, adventurous and militant character." As evidence of the development of the women's movement, she declared rather radically, "In the past few years many have come out of the kitchen and from the entanglement of children." She emphasized that the campaign to aid China offered a new forum "for Chinese American women to demonstrate their ability."[21]

Raising money to aid China also made it possible for Chinese Americans to work toward increasing Chinatown's tourist popularity. At the 1940 Bowl of Rice pageant, Humanity Legion badges were sold to raise money. The Chinese organizers assured people that the badges would give them free entrance into Chinese "clubs and temples and special entertainment features."[22] Bringing thousands of visitors to Chinatown, such fund-raising events in turn undoubtedly enhanced its visibility.

Chinese Americans throughout the nation realized that in helping China they were also helping themselves.[23] Chinese San Franciscans organized the 1940 Bowl of Rice event not only to aid China but also to improve the Chinese American economy. Over three thousand five hundred people were mobilized to prepare for the pageant, decorating the stores and improving the streets. Such efforts, the *Chinese Times* noted, "were also essential to the prosperity of Chinatown and can help to promote business." It concluded that creating an environment in which white visitors could have a good time would make them "happy and willing" to spend money in Chinatown as consumers.[24]

The Bowl of Rice movement became memorable for both Chinese and white San Franciscans. A 1943 city guide included a passage about it in the "Chinatown" section, calling it "a real party."[25] A member of the Bureau for Medical Aid to China summarized its achievements. Citing Hu Shi (Hu Shih), the incumbent Chinese ambassador to America, the author stated that the movement represented "the best opportunity to increase friendship between the Chinese and Americans." He went on: "Organizers of the movement everywhere all tried to praise Chinese culture through the programs, an effort that enhanced [Americans'] affection for China. . . . During the movement, Chinese and Americans gathered and freely chatted after dinner and drink. An earnest friendship was therein forged."[26] Making all this possible was China's war against Japan. Visiting Chinatown late in April 1941, shortly before another Bowl of Rice party, Eleanor Roosevelt donated five dollars and received a Humanity Legion badge. She said: "I think all of us want to support this particular effort because China had made such a re-markable effort of resistance."[27]

In the course of World War II, especially after Pearl Harbor, China emerged as one of the "Big Four." In early 1943 the United States and Britain abolished their extraterritorial rights in China, now their ally. The news came to Chinese San Francisco during the Chinese New Year's season, adding to the holiday joy. On February 7, 1943, Chinese Americans cele-brated the occasion in the rain by marching in a parade with both Chinese and American national flags before holding a rally. Of this historic develop-ment, *Young China* editorialized: "Judging from history . . . those nations that can sustain hard struggles are able to overcome any difficulties."[28]

China's new international position elevated the status of Chinese Americans as well. After Pearl Harbor the War-Time Committee of the Association to Save China distributed badges to Chinese residents in the Bay Area to identify them as Chinese, not Japanese. This was in part a response to the fact that Chinese Americans were sometimes victims of intensified anti-Japanese feelings. It also gave the Chinese a way to express pride in their Chinese identity. Printed on these badges were Chinese and American na-tional flags and the words "China" and "the United States" in English.[29] Demand for the badges was high. By the end of 1941 about ten thousand had been sold at around five cents apiece.[30] Chinese-owned stores and cars car-ried equally affordable signs, which helped protect businesses and allowed Chinese individuals to pass through check stations without difficulty. Chinese newspapers more explicitly communicated Chinese Americans' ap-preciation of their new status. *The Chinese-Western Daily*, for example, noted a board of supervisors' decision that restrictions on foreigners working in the ship-manufacturing factories did not apply to Chinese.[31] Indeed, the Pacific War created job opportunities in defense-related industries that had long been closed to Chinese Americans. In an advertisement that ran in May 1943, a labor recruiter named Albert K. Chow publicly announced "precious opportunities" in the "important national defense industries."[32] According to the advertisement, each worker could earn $225 a month, including room and board. The wage was significantly higher than what Chinese laborers could make in other areas, such as domestic service and restaurant work.[33] The wartime shortage of labor also increased work opportunities for Chinese American women. Butler Brothers, a company owned by whites, sought

Chinese women "to be typists and take care of documents and calculating machines." It also promised a "comfortable environment" along with health insurance, paid vacations, and time-and-a-half pay for overtime.[34]

The good feelings did not render Chinese San Franciscans oblivious to social realities. They carefully safeguarded their fragile new image that was beginning to be established in white consciousness. During the successful Bowl of Rice event in 1940, organizers did their best to prevent disorderly activities, especially the use of fireworks beyond the designated hours (8:00–9:30 A.M. and 3:30–4:30 P.M.) and the harassment of women, particulary white women. Disciplinary officers were employed to maintain public order.

More important, Chinese San Franciscans did not forget the exclusion laws. The improved relations between China and the United States and between white and Chinese San Franciscans fed the hope that these laws would be repealed. The beginning of 1943 gave Chinese "an infinite new hope," proclaimed the New Year's editorial of the *Chinese Times*. The editorial put the changes that began to transpire late in the 1930s into a historical perspective. "In the past," it noted, "we Chinese people were not at an equal position with whites because of racial bias, and racial bias resulted from the language barrier and different social customs. Without any interaction, there was not any affection [between whites and Chinese]. . . . Since the United States entered the war," however, "most of the barriers between the white and the yellow [races] have been broken down." Clearly, this line did not accurately characterize race relations in America, where Asians ("the yellow race"), especially the Japanese, still faced serious legal and social discrimination. The characterization was not indicative of naïveté about the reality but reflected an optimism generated by the wartime atmosphere. The editorial emphasized that during the resistance war the Chinese demonstrated "our excellent national character," and as a result various unequal treaties, including those affecting extraterritoriality, would soon be abolished. Turning to the existing Chinese exclusion acts, the editorial encouraged people to continue their long struggle: "We should take advantage of this moment when Sino-American friendship is at its best . . . to win the affection of Americans by assisting the war effort of the United States and by increasing contact with American officials and people."[35]

Indeed, Chinese San Franciscans aggressively exploited the amicable Sino-American relationship. During the 1941 Bowl of Rice party, organizers put on a fireworks show called "figures in flame," which included a staged scene of Generalissimo Jiang Jieshi shaking hands with President Roosevelt under American and Chinese flags. Mme. Jiang's visit to San Francisco during her tour of the United States prior to Generalissimo Jiang's meeting with President Roosevelt at the Cairo Conference in November, was one of the most memorable events in the city's history.[36]

Mme. Jiang's American Tour: Prelude to Repeal

She "came, saw and conquered," wrote a contemporary reporter upon Mme. Jiang Jieshi's arrival in San Francisco during her 1943 whirlwind tour of the country.[37] A symbol of a nation resisting aggression, her tour marked a climax in the improvement of Sino-American relations. The extraordinarily warm reception accorded her by people from all over the country, from Washington to San Francisco, illustrated China's new position in the American public perception. It also put her name in history books. At Capitol Hill, following her address to the Senate, she delivered a nationally broadcast speech at the House of Representatives, becoming "the first private citizen and the second woman (Queen Wilhelmina was the first) to address the Congress," as *Current History* magazine reported.[38] Creating momentum for the repeal of the Chinese exclusion laws and boosting the national pride of Chinese Americans, her tour clearly manifested the significance of their connection with China.

Mme. Jiang was no stranger to San Francisco. Even before her name became a household word after her official visits to Americans cities such as Washington, D.C., New York, Boston, and Chicago, it was featured in some city fund-raisers. On December 6, 1940, for example, the city's Committee to Aid China and China Aid Council, together with Chinese Americans, held a "A Night for China" to raise money to "benefit Madame Chiang Kai-Shek's War Orphans."[39]

On March 25 Mme. Jiang came to San Francisco, a city prepared to give her the same royal welcome she had received elsewhere. With twenty-five thousand people in the plaza at the Civic Center below the balcony of the city hall on which she stood, Mme. Jiang watched a parade that lasted an hour and a half. Marching in the parade were uniformed soldiers representing the navy, the army, and the American Women Voluntary Service, together with civilian groups and Chinese Americans from different parts of California. Standing by Mme. Jiang's side were Chinese officials and a platoon of American military and civil notables, including Admiral John W. Greenslade; Major General and Mrs. William P. Upshur; Governor and Mrs. Earl Warren; and the mayors of San Francisco, Oakland, and Berkeley, and their wives.

Calling her "Missimo" fondly and "Madame" formally, newspaper articles, radio broadcasts, and public speeches showered China's first lady with the most lavish praise, characterizing her as one of the world's greatest women, the symbol of women's power and achievement, a symbol of free humanity. Carolyn Anspacher of the *Chronicle* dubbed her "China's Joan of Arc."[40] Describing the city's warm welcome on the day of her arrival, Fred Duerr wrote: "Dainty, queenly Madame Chiang Kai-shek, who commands the devotion of 450,000,000 people in her native right, yesterday added San Francisco to her domain."[41]

The city was indeed overwhelmed. During her public speech on Saturday, March 27, the big civic auditorium was jammed to capacity. Behind the platform hung a huge Chinese flag, and under the flag was a large sign that read, "Welcome to Mme. Jiang," written in Chinese. Her address was also broadcast live by radio stations—KPO, KGO, and KQW—throughout the day. Denied the right to broadcast her speech, an Oakland radio station, KLX, protested furiously.

Virtually everyone, it seems, wanted to share the privilege of honoring Mme. Jiang. The board of supervisors proposed in a resolution that a planned Chinatown low-rent housing project be named after her. A newly manufactured ship launched during her visit was named after Sun Yat-sen, the spiritual founder of the Chinese Republic and her brother-in-law. The state legislature decided to adjourn so that its members could pay tribute to her.

White Americans' enthusiastic reception of Mme. Jiang also tells us a great deal about them. It served as a mirror of their wartime emotions and of the fact that China was America's most important ally in the Pacific theater. It reflected their positive perceptions of China. We need to look beyond the obvious factors contributing to their reaction, however. First of all, her American education and her ability to communicate with mainstream society in its own language and within its cultural frame of reference made it easier for white Americans to relate to her. Born to a Christian family, she first came to the United States in 1908 at the age of eleven and later graduated from Wellesley College, where she majored in English. Such details about her personal background were constantly mentioned and praised in the news during and before her U.S. tour.

Second and more important, Mme. Jiang's appeal also stemmed from her attributes that appeared to set her apart from white Americans and that embodied the imagined "orient" in their minds. Many reports represent her as having an American education and American values and manners, but remaining distinctively Chinese. After relating how she took her husband to Christianity before being taken by him to the altar, an article in *Scholastic* offered the following depiction: "[At the wedding] Mayling wore a beautiful white veil and carried a sheath of lilies, like any Western bride. But unlike any Western bride, from that day on Mayling Chiang seldom knew the comforts at home of home."[42] In an earlier feature article, the *New York Times Magazine* noted: "Her manner is a combination of American directness and the self-effacing modesty of the Chinese." It noted her physical beauty as a Chinese woman: "She is also the prettiest of the famous Soong sisters. She has the cream-colored complexion of a Chinese gentlewoman." Her marriage afforded her political power, but she looked fragile: "She is small and dainty of figure."[43] In 1943 *Life* magazine depicted her as a "small, well-proportioned, birdlike woman."[44]

Clearly, in Mme. Jiang the dominant society found not only a representative but also a personification of China. Indeed, who else could better embody a weak nation waiting to be rescued and enlightened than a nonthreatening and injured female? In an explanation of her effectiveness and popularity that revealed white Americans' perspective on the Chinese, the *New York Times* emphasized two "extraordinary facts." "One is that a woman from China, only partly by virtue of her American education, seems less 'foreign' to ordinary Americans than most visitors from abroad. The second is that a woman from the Orient occupies a position of such special influence in her country, and now as its spokesperson."[45]

The *New York Times* commentary raises a question. Could a non-Westernized, masculine figure from China have engendered the same level of enthusiasm? While history will never be able to answer such hypothetical questions with any degree of certainty, a look at General Cai Tingkai's 1934 visit offers some clues. The differences between the two cases are evident. Cai came to America during a different period in history—he arrived long before Pearl Harbor. Further, the retired general came as a private citizen who had no official affiliation with the Chinese government. At the same time, however, there were significant similarities between the two figures. During the 1930s Japanese aggression in China had already captured a great deal of public attention, and the news media reported on it frequently. Like Mme. Jiang, Cai was seen as a symbol of China's resistance to Japanese aggression. Also like her, Cai made visible appearances in numerous American cities. Wherever he went, Cai generated excitement among Chinese Americans. In late August, when he arrived in New York following his European tour, thousands of Chinese Americans came out to show their support for what he represented. On November 4 over three thousand Chinese San Franciscans, along with the mayor and other city officials, came in three hundred cars to meet him at the train station. Later the Chinese community held a massive parade, and Chinese American pilots dropped leaflets out of aircrafts. Mainstream society was keenly aware of Cai's stature as a Chinese national hero. In both New York and San Francisco he was invited to meet the respective mayors and other politicians.

The relative absence of non-Chinese media interest in Cai's 1934 visit, however, stood in stark contrast to its extensive coverage of Mme. Jiang. The major journals ran no feature articles covering Cai's tour. Placed alongside other insignificant news items, the brief mentions of him in local newspapers duly noted his inability to speak English.[46] Indeed, Cai had none of the qualities that fascinated the public in Mme. Jiang. Here was a male figure, "tall" and "ascetic," who could not communicate with the mainstream society directly.[47] It appears likely that the news media slighted him largely because it was unable to relate to the Chinese general.[48]

There is therefore reason to believe that Mme. Jiang's popularity can be credited in part to her Western education and to her nonthreatening, fragile image that fit white Americans' gendered perception of the Orient. This is no reason, however, to underestimate the historical importance of her tour. It reinforced the emerging friendly relations between white and Chinese San Franciscans. At receptions, banquets, and mass meetings, Chinese and white San Franciscans joined hands to honor Mme. Jiang. The San Francisco Press

Club, for example, cordially invited their Chinese colleagues to attend a banquet in her honor.

If white San Franciscans were thrilled, the Chinese in the city were inspired. In a letter to the *Young China* daily, a Chinese school student called her "the greatest woman of the world."[49] The Zhonghua Huiguan and the Association to Save China had formed a committee to prepare for her visit, which included 135 Chinese San Franciscans and representatives from 38 other Chinese communities throughout the American West, as well as two individuals from Mexico. In colorfully decorated Chinatown, photographs of Mme. Jiang along with American and Chinese national flags were everywhere. Most noticeable was an arch at Grant Avenue and Clay Street, on which "Welcome Mme. Jiang" was written in large Chinese characters. The arch was surrounded by plum blossoms, a traditional symbol of purity and determination.[50]

Mme. Jiang brought special messages to Chinese America. Her monumental tour itself embodied China's new international status. In a Chinese-language address, she proudly declared to the nine thousand Chinese San Franciscans who packed the civic auditorium: "China has become one of the four greatest nations of the world."[51] Thanking them on behalf of China, she said that the people "want to tell you of their appreciation for your patriotic efforts shown since the start of resistance."[52] She encouraged them to cherish and preserve the essence of China's five-thousand-year-old civilization.

In her speech to the city Mme. Jiang hailed the virtue of patriotism by citing the story of Guan Gong and his two sworn brothers. As we have seen, it was a household story among Chinese San Franciscans, and they had been worshipping Guan Gong, in particular, in their temples for decades.[53] Earlier, on March 2, she reminded Chinese Americans in New York of longstanding anti-Chinese prejudice by saying that "people have looked down upon us, calling us Chinaman."[54] But China's war of resistance had restored Chinese dignity. Her message undoubtedly resonated with Chinese Americans. In one letter to a Chinese newspaper a reader urged his fellow Chinese Americans to adopt her "patriotic spirit as the guidance for us to save our country."[55]

Chinese San Franciscans appreciated the historic significance of Mme. Jiang's visit. On March 25, 1943, *Young China* commented that Mme. Jiang's journey was a landmark event in Sino-American relations.[56] In early 1943 the

Tim Yat Herb Company published a long public statement titled "On Diseases." The one-thousand-word statement was not a commercial advertisement but a metaphorical piece that elaborated on a wide range of political and social diseases plaguing China and Chinese America. The most important was "a wide-spread mental disease among the Chinese in America," resulting from their anxieties about the future of China. Mme. Jiang's arrival, the statement declared, had generated much support for the Chinese and thereby cured this mental disease.[57] Chinese San Franciscans did not express their feelings through words only. Upon her arrival they gave Mme. Jiang various presents intended to help China, including $44,193.60 in cash.[58]

Chinese San Franciscans hoped that Mme. Jiang's visit, in the words of a *Chinese-Western Daily* editorial, "will help to eliminate all [anti-Chinese] bias."[59] Needless to say, her trip did not effect the elimination of all racial bias. The Sinophile feelings she helped to stimulate, however, helped the movement to repeal the Chinese exclusion acts gain momentum. On December 17, 1943, one day after he had returned from conferences in Cairo and Tehran, President Roosevelt signed into law the bill to repeal Chinese exclusion.

1943

Our story ends with the 1943 act. Some critics have dismissed it as merely "a token gesture of goodwill."[60] Ling-chi Wang concludes that it "did little to liberate Chinese Americans from racial oppression."[61] Needless to say, we must not overestimate its impact. Mainstream newspapers in major cities such as New York, St. Louis, San Francisco, and Los Angeles apparently did not treat it as front-page news—the few that mentioned it did so tersely and inconspicuously.

It was no secret that from the point of view of the Roosevelt administration the bill represented "one safe and inexpensive move" to evade having to provide substantive aid to China.[62] Like the Chinese in China, Chinese Americans had also become increasingly critical of the Chinese administration's lack of sincerity about supporting China. The New York-based *Chinese Nationalist Daily* stated early in 1941 that "we the Chinese are not content with the beautifully worded promises and the cheers and applause for China by those congressmen. What we need is assistance in substance."[63] Repealing Chinese exclusion, state department officials hoped, would result in the lessening of such criticisms. For the American government, the repeal also served as a strategic move with which to refute Japanese propaganda in China about America's anti-Chinese discrimination. Widely reported in the American news media, such propaganda was known to the American public and resulted in politicians' concern.[64] As the historian John W. Dower has noted, "A retired Navy officer told the congressional hearings inquiring into the issue that the anti-Chinese legislation was worth 'twenty divisions' to the Japanese Army."[65]

From the vantage point of the late twentieth century, and knowing what has happened since 1943, we can confidently say that the repeal act did not signify an end to anti-Asian racism. After 1943 only 105 Chinese—up to 75 percent of them from China and the rest from elsewhere—were allowed to enter the United States each year under the existing discriminatory quota system. Apparently this was a racial quota applied to the entire Chinese race. The fact that individual whites were friendly toward China and the Chinese does not mean that America abandoned its racial bias. For example, General John DeWitt, who joined many others in welcoming Mme. Jiang to San Francisco at Pier 14 on March 25, 1943, once commented: "The Japanese race is an enemy race." Furthermore, all other Asian exclusion acts remained in effect.[66] Nothing is more revealing of the racism of wartime America than the Japanese American experience.[67] After Pearl Harbor, shortly before Congress passed the repeal act in 1943, the entire Japanese population in California, Oregon, and Washington—over half of them U.S. citizens—was incarcerated by the U.S. government. Roger Daniels writes: "The legal atrocity which was committed against the Japanese Americans was the logical outgrowth of over three centuries of American experience, an experience which taught Americans to regard the United States as a white man's country."[68] Finally, as Lisa Lowe points out in her recent, masterfully crafted book, "the promise of inclusion through citizenship and rights cannot resolve the material inequalities of racialized exploitation."[69]

To fully appreciate the significance of the repeal act we must consider it historically. First, we need to look at it from the point of view of its own times. What is more, we must view it from the perspective of Chinese

Americans so that we can understand their response to it and respect their feelings. After all, as the *China Daily News* pointed out, it was they who were "most directly affected by the repeal of Chinese exclusion."[70]

As has been previously mentioned, American society's increasing Sinophile sentiments during the late 1930s and early 1940s created an environment in which the Chinese exclusion acts could finally be abolished. The proposal to repeal the acts was endorsed in unlikely quarters. At its national convention on November 2, 1942, the Congress of Industrial Organizations (CIO) adopted a resolution in favor of repeal. In San Francisco the California chapter of the American Legion dissented from the national convention's official position by following in the CIO's footsteps in August 1943. The display of support by this and other influential California groups, including San Francisco's chamber of commerce and board of supervisors, was critical, because the state had traditionally been the focal point of the anti-Chinese movement. Such new developments were attributable not only to the wartime Sino-American alliance but also to Chinese San Franciscans' successful public relations campaign.

White America's change of attitude toward the Chinese reached a watershed during Mme. Jiang's American tour. Activists in the repeal movement recognized that "full advantage should be taken of the presence of Mme. Chiang [Jiang] for strong agitation."[71] Following Mme. Jiang's arrival in Washington, Congressman Martin Kennedy of New York introduced the first repeal bill, which "was hastily whipped up to catch the tide of enthusiasm which followed the visit of Madame Chiang Kai-shek to Congress," as the *Christian Century* reported.[72]

Furthermore, the challenge to Chinese exclusion coincided with Americans' realization that racism practiced in Nazi Germany had resulted in horrify ing and inhumane consequences. While, for Roosevelt, the repeal was effected for reasons of military expediency, many critics of the exclusion laws took the opportunity to denounce the racial prejudice they represented. Oswald Garrison Villard wondered how, given their discriminatory immigration policy, "can we Americans continue to denounce the abominable racial doctrine?"[73] In like fashion, Charles Nelson Spinks wrote: "We condemn the Axis challenge to the fundamental principles of mankind . . . [but] we ourselves are today violating two of the essential principles."[74]

Others took the opportunity to raise Americans' awareness of the country's racist policy affecting all Asians. In an article focused on Chinese exclusion, Harry Paxton Howard wrote in June 1942 that the "racialist Exclusion Act still stands" against not only the Chinese but also other Asians.[75] The *Christian Century* stated more bluntly: "The sole issue of moment is racial justice. A whole series of American laws and court decisions based on those laws has singled out Asiatics as ineligible for American entry or citizenship."[76] Bruno Lasker expressly attacked the racist ideological basis of the exclusion policy: "Recent educational activity in every part of the United States has just been effective enough to make most people realize the absurdity of branding whole nations and races as unassimilable." He favored an immigration policy that "has nothing to do with color or blood, and expresses no racial discrimination." Therefore, he concluded, "there is a strong case for removing from our statute book not only the Chinese Exclusion law of 1882, but all legal provisions by which any racial group . . . are marked out for distinct treatment in the matter of either immigration or naturalization."[77] The postwar period, he hoped, would bring changes to the quota system itself.

If America's exclusion policy stood as its "Great Wall against the Chinese,"[78] the repeal clearly punched a hole in it by abolishing or modifying sixteen different pieces of legislation. No matter how small that hole was at the time, it invited future challenges to Asian exclusion, challenges that weakened the wall and eventually caused it to crumble.[79] This was what the repeal bill's opponents, such as Congressman A. Leonard Allen, feared most. Shortly after its passage, Anup Singh demanded on behalf of Asian Indians what the Chinese had just achieved by using the same argument: "When the Chinese were made eligible to American citizenship and Chinese immigration was placed on a quota basis, the United States took the wind out of the sails of Japanese propaganda and earned the good will of the Chinese. The arguments that prompted Congress in the case of the Chinese are equally pertinent in the case of Indians."[80]

Improving their image and their relations with white Americans represented an indirect way for Chinese Americans to combat Chinese exclusion, but some of them preferred to launch a direct assault on the exclusionary policies. Recounting the injustice that all Chinese American groups had suffered under Chinese exclusion, Walter Kong wrote in 1942: "It is no exaggeration to say that the Chinese regard our immigration officials with as much fear as if they were the Gestapo." Despite his pungent criticism, however, Kong was pragmatic in his demands: "Grant the Chinese the same fair treatment that immigrants from other countries receive."[81]

Mme. Jiang's U.S. tour injected new energy into Chinese Americans' struggle for racial justice. Undoubtedly, that struggle was not the priority of the Chinese government that Mme. Jiang represented. In fact, in all her public speeches across the United States, she focused on urging Chinese Americans to support China's war effort, and never confronted Chinese exclusion explicitly.[82] In a discussion of the politics surrounding the repeal, Professor Ling-chi Wang portrays China as another "oppressive" force that "exploited the repeal politics and reinforced" its "domination of Chinese America."[83] Many Chinese Americans, however, did not share this view at the time. They identified with China and its war effort, which they believed would liberate both China and Chinese America. It was particularly clear to them that Mme. Jiang bolstered sympathy not only for China's resistance war but also for the repeal movement. *The Chinese-Western Daily* noted that while past struggles against exclusion had all failed, Mme. Jiang's presence in Washington quickly prompted Martin Kennedy to introduce his repeal bill.[84]

In March 1943 the New York–based *China Daily News* published an editorial entitled "To Struggle for Abolishing the Harsh [anti-Chinese] Immigration Laws." It placed that struggle in an international context by arguing that the exclusion laws would "hinder the further development of Sino-American relations, the victory of the United Nations and post-war world cooperation and peace." These laws, it went on, had not only barred Chinese immigration but had inhumanely forced those in America to live the bachelor life, which constituted "both the ultimate source of many Chinese immigrants' problems and an insult to the Chinese nation." In the end, it suggested four specific tactics, including directly voicing opinions to politicians and to the public.[85] Many Chinese Americans were already doing just that. In an earlier editorial, the newspaper pleaded with Mme. Jiang to use her "prestige and diplomatic skills" to help put an end to the exclusion acts.[86] In February, when she was in Washington, the Chinese Women's Association in New York sent a letter to her and Mrs. Roosevelt, urging the abolition of the exclusion laws and the establishment of a quota for the Chinese. The publicized letter simply and realistically asked for "token recognition of our equality in the newer, freer order of democracy."[87]

Noticeably absent was a vocal, organized repeal movement in Chinese

America that directly targeted the exclusion laws. This is in part because Chinese Americans did not choose protest as their main strategy for fighting discrimination. Rather, for the most part they resorted to moral persuasion and to emphasizing Sino-American friendship. On October 28, 1943, the *Chinese Times* published an article about how to deal with discrimination, in which the author suggested being humble and praiseful. The article engendered a number of reader responses, nearly all in favor of its view.

In his lengthy response, a reader named Deng Wentao first identified three sources of anti-Chinese prejudice. The first was China's weakness. "Weak nations made their citizens cheap," he stated. The second was "white people's negative impression" created by the Chinese. Third, "at the heart of racial discrimination" were the anti-Chinese laws designed to protect the interest of whites. Reiterating two themes that had long prevailed in the community, he proposed strengthening China and self-atonement as the cure for discrimination. Collectively, he noted, Chinese Americans must do more to help China and to eliminate their community's opium and gambling problems in order to raise China's international status and win white people's respect. Individually, "we must get rid of all bad habits and criminal activities in order to show the noble character of the Chinese." He did not totally agree with those who promoted the "being humble and praiseful" tactic, arguing that this response was effective only when the discriminatory party was willing to act reasonably. If the other party acted unreasonably and behaved like a bully, he said, "you have to be strong and firm."[88]

While an increasing number of Chinese Americans discussed and challenged exclusion with greater candor, individual Chinese Americans did not ask for more than the 1943 repeal act eventually granted them. Their expectations were realistic because they recognized that American society was not ready to eradicate the racism that was so deeply embedded in people's minds.

We have already seen that Chinese Americans also had racial biases, as Lin Ruochong, another participant in the discussions of how to deal with racism, acknowledged in the *Chinese Times*. Racial discrimination was the most difficult kind of prejudice to deal with, he stated, because of the "fundamental conflict" between races. "White people view yellow people the same way as yellow people view black people." "Look at the young men and women in Chinatown," he asked, "who would be willing to go out publicly with a black person of the opposite sex?" The unwilling party "is always the yellow person, not the black person." While they apparently strived to eliminate racism, "the Chinese still maintained this tradition."[89]

The news that President Roosevelt had signed the repeal bill did not generate the same kind of public outpouring of excitement in Chinese American communities as Mme. Jiang's tour had. This is in part because the community was aware of the bill's limitations. Besides, Chinese America had widely anticipated its passage before it became official. Their extended and extensive attention to the event suggest its importance for them. Throughout almost all of 1943 Chinese America closely followed every development concerning the repeal with great interest and some anxiety. These developments were reported on and analyzed in great detail in all Chinese newspapers across the country, and at public meetings community members were informed about the bill's progress. As *The Chinese-Western Daily* noted on June 1, 1943, the "repeal of the Chinese exclusion acts in the lower house" was one of the events of most concern to the Chinese. "The new bill may not become law," it continued, "but its significance is extraordinary."[90]

In response to the passage of the bill in the house of representatives, the *Young China* daily first pointed out its limitations: "It is not the ideal measure because it does not give to the Chinese the same equal treatment as the Europeans receive." The newspaper nonetheless acknowledged its historical importance by saying that "it undoubtedly signifies that they begin to treat us equally" as a result of the Chinese Pacific War. Anticipating the final passage of the bill, it declared that "a new era is about to arrive."[91] In like fashion, the *China Daily News* editorialized that soon Chinese immigrants would be able to apply for citizenship and thereby to obtain "the right of political participation that all taxpayers deserve." They would be able to bring their families to the country, and their children would have a brighter future in America.[92]

For most Chinese Americans, the repeal of the Chinese exclusion acts marked a triumph in their long struggle against anti-Chinese discrimination. As Chinese San Franciscans knew well, that triumph was related to China's elevated status during the Pacific War and to Chinese America's participation in it. The repeal bill that went into effect at the end of 1943, therefore, provided conclusive evidence that Chinese Americans' lives were closely related to events in the trans-Pacific world, rather than existing solely in the American context.

After Franklin Delano Roosevelt addressed Congress regarding the abolition of Chinese exclusion, the editor of *Young China* noted: "Before the United States declared war on the Axis countries, those sympathetic to our country in this land had advocated repeal of the Chinese exclusion acts but had not received much endorsement." He went on: "President Roosevelt stated [in his address]: 'While it would give the Chinese a preferred status over certain other people, their great contribution to the cause of decency and freedom entitles them to such preference.' Apparently, the American people respect us because civilians and servicemen in the motherland have been fighting strenuously for the freedom of human beings."[93]

Repeal also announced the beginning of a new era. Despite all its apparent flaws, it recognized the right of Chinese immigrants to be naturalized for the first time in American history. Although Sino-American relations changed after the establishment of the communist government in China in 1949 and after the outbreak of the Korean War in 1950, the old exclusion laws were never reinstituted. In addition, the 1943 act led to the gradual collapse of legal restrictions on Asian immigration and on Asian immigrants' eligibility for citizenship.

Conclusion

In this book I have tried to describe and comprehend the formation and transformation of Chinese San Francisco, and its varied meanings in different contexts. As the most visible Chinese community in the United States, it loomed large in American society's discourse of race. It became a focal point of the anti-Chinese crusade against Chinese immigration late in the nineteenth century. The crusade was not solely economic; it also represented a cultural war against the Chinese way of life. While anti-Chinese crusaders did not succeed in eliminating Chinatown or Chinese American culture, they helped create lasting stereotypes of Chinese Americans. As we have seen in the case of Chinese women, such stereotypes have tampered with our knowledge of Chinese American history.

My main objective, however, has been to uncover what Chinese San Francisco meant for Chinese Americans themselves. It was the first permanent urban settlement that Chinese pioneers established in the New World. Standing as the "capital" of Chinese America for a long time, it housed key social institutions that coordinated individual lives and provided various opportunities and services. It also existed as a gateway to the social and cultural spaces that Chinese Americans created and occupied across the ocean.

The story of Chinese San Francisco demonstrates that the Chinese American experience was formed by New World as well as Old World forces. I have tried to shed light on how Chinese Americans lived, organized, and comprehended their lives in the United States, based on their historical memories and other trans-Pacific ties. My primary goal has been to show how these ties formed the foundation of their community and identity and how they constituted significant sources of strength from which they could draw in order to endure the various difficulties they encountered in the New World. In a word, this book represents an attempt to reenter the world of Chinese Americans as they knew and experienced it. It was a world quite different from that of their non-Chinese contemporaries, and also from our own.

To demonstrate further the significance of the trans-Pacific spaces for understanding Chinese Americans' experiences and cultural identity we must reevaluate the dichotomy of "sojourner" and "settler." Invented as early as the 1850s, that dichotomy became a dominant framework in which to explain the Chinese American experience. It was first used by the anti-Chinese forces in order to put the Chinese and white immigrants in two opposite categories, namely that of sojourner and that of settler. It was designed to identify the Chinese as un-American and undesirable. The sojourner thesis has since been embraced by several scholars of Chinese America. One of them is Paul Siu, a product of the Chicago School of Sociology. In his study of Chinese laundrymen in Chicago, which was completed early in the 1950s, Siu argues that Chinese immigrants were not only "temporary residents in this country" but also that they remained sojourners over time within their "static" community.[1] Therefore, he concludes, these people constituted a "deviant type" of immigrant.[2] Echoing Siu's argument, Gunther Barth contends that "the vast majority of arrivals from the Middle Kingdom were merely sojourners" and, therefore, were set "apart from other immigrants who came to America as permanent residents."[3] He revives the nineteenth-century anti-Chinese rhetoric by suggesting that it was Chinese immigrants' sojourner mentality that gave rise to the hostility toward them. To characterize the "sojourner" mentality as a uniquely Chinese phenomenon ignores basic historical facts, however. As Roger Daniels has pointed out, that mentality prevailed among many non-Asian groups as well.[4]

Other Chinese Americanists have challenged the "sojourner thesis" by claiming that early immigrants from China were indeed settlers. Some have even tried to show that the immigrants had a desire to "assimilate." Sandy Lydon, for example, asserts in a study of the Chinese in California's Monterey Bay Region that "the Point Alones village, with its families and children, testifies to the desire of many Chinese to remain in this country." Lydon also suggests that they embraced Americanism: "The Chinese . . . demonstrated loyalty to their new country even in the face of crippling discrimination."[5]

Lydon's critique clearly represents a political defense of Chinese Americans against persistent stereotypes that depicted them as perpetual aliens. "The term *sojourner*," Lydon notes, "implicitly defined Chinese immigrants as less loyal than other immigrants, less willing to make a commitment to the United States."[6] Pro-Chinese individuals adopted the same defense decades ago. Mary Coolidge proclaimed in 1909 that "a comparison of the Chinese with other aliens, particularly with the Italians, Mexicans and Greeks in San Francisco, disclosed the fact that they are being Americanized quite as rapidly, and in some respects, make better citizens because of superior intellectual capacity."[7] The problem with this argument is that it does not satisfactorily explain Chinese Americans' experiences historically.[8] The small number of Chinese families at Point Alones village constitutes nothing but an "exception," as Lydon concedes.

Moreover, as long as we focus on proving that Chinese immigrants had a "settler" mentality and that they wished to assimilate (anglicize), we remain trapped in the bipolar paradigm that originated in the hegemonic ideologies of the nineteenth century. That paradigm fails to recognize the flexibility of individual immigrants' mentality and intentions. What is more, it suggests that Chinese immigrants must be either "Chinese" or "American," as if these were static and mutually exclusive entities.

In order to understand the early Chinese American experience historically, we must remember that the meaning of being "American," "Chinese," and "Chinese-American" changes over time and across social space. The now-obsolete vision of America prescribed by the dominant society in the nineteenth century had no place for Chinese Americans. Furthermore, just as their Chinese-ness was not a duplicate of their compatriots' mentality in China, their identity bears significant differences from the Chinese American identity that prevails in various academic and political forums late in the twentieth century.

Recognizing that the world of Chinese Americans transcended national boundaries offers an alternative to the bipolar paradigm. Their cultural identity was constructed in the different contexts in which they were situated at different times, rather than in the U.S. setting alone. Let us first take a look at the American context. Chinese immigrants did not come to America to "assimilate." As I have suggested in chapter 1, their departure for America represented a calculated attempt to fulfill family responsibilities and individual aspirations. Over time Chinese Americans acquired new language and work skills and built new communities. But the changes that occurred in their lives and the roots they planted in America do not constitute evidence that they accepted the hegemonic ideology of assimilation. As I have shown in this study, they maintained personal, socioeconomic, and political ties to China, as well as their distinctive cultural identity. Instead of weakening their attachment to America, their trans-Pacific ties empowered them to face various difficulties and hostilities.

The persistence of cultural distinctiveness in Chinese life, therefore, simply meant that Chinese immigrants did not become the kind of "American" articulated by the dominant blocs in the late nineteenth and early twentieth centuries. While there was no organized movement seeking to "Americanize" the Chinese, strong social pressure demanded that they conform culturally. Ah Quin was evidently under such pressure when he cut his queue in a public act to please the whites around him in 1878. He was not alone in feeling that pressure. "The Chinese in San Francisco are often bullied," a Chinese newspaper editorial concluded in the 1850s, "all because we do not dress the same way as 'Flower-flag' people do."[9] Chinese immigrants could alter their outward appearance, but they could not change their legal status as noncitizens. Even those individuals who had citizenship remained socially disfranchised in many ways.

Racial antagonism in America undoubtedly helped reinforce early Chinese Americans' connections with China, but it never succeeded in eradicating the roots that they had collectively planted in America. A large number of those Chinese Americans who went back to their ancestral communities did so with the intention of returning to the United States. In 1888, when the Scott Act nullified the return certificates of those Chinese who had gone to China, it came to light that as many as twenty thousand people had obtained them. For these people the trip to China clearly did not signal an end to their American experience. Throughout the period under discussion, many people came back to the United States after making such trips. Although hundreds of Chinese Americans returned to China to retire, in numerous cases their offspring grew up to carry on their disrupted American journey.

If within the U.S. setting Chinese Americans remained and were seen as "Chinese," in China their "American-ness" was increasingly recognized, and it served to distinguish them from the people of China. The term "Jin-shanke" or "Gold Mountaineers," as they were called in the Pearl River Delta, indicates that their American experience had become part of their identity. It signified a distinctive status, one that was often revered and sometimes envied in the local communities.

At the national level, another term, "*huaqiao*," emerged, probably late in the 1880s. It had gained currency in Chinese society by the beginning of the twentieth century. "*Hua*" means Chinese, and "*qiao*" refers to those who have left their hometowns to settle in other places, either within China or abroad.[10] The emergence of this term underscored an attempt by the people of China to define the identity of the Chinese, including Chinese Americans, in the diaspora. After abandoning its long-standing hostile policy toward overseas immigration, the Chinese government acknowledged and codified the special status of ethnic Chinese in the United States and other parts of the world. The change undoubtedly represented a financially motivated move to woo overseas Chinese investments.[11] But it also signified that the government could no longer ignore the growing influence of the Chinese diaspora and the new legal and political issues it posed.

A central issue concerned the construction of the national identity of ethnic Chinese overseas. In 1909 the Qing Court issued the first nationality law in Chinese history. It defined "Chinese" as anyone born to Chinese parents. It also stipulated that those who acquired foreign citizenship without notifying the Chinese government would continue to be regarded as citizens of China.[12] During the Republican period China's nationality act was rewritten several times. All the new laws were nonetheless still based primarily on the principle of jus sanguinis and tolerated dual citizenship of overseas Chinese. These two features did not merely embody the Chinese government's desire to assert its hegemony over Chinese communities overseas. They also reflected the wishes of many people in the diaspora. In fact, the call for enacting the 1909 law came first from Chinese residents in the Dutch East Indies who did not want to be forced to become Dutch subjects.[13] Before the passage of the 1912 nationality act, a proposal to adopt the principle of jus soli met strong opposition from ethnic Chinese in Southeast Asia because such a proposal would not allow foreign-born Chinese to be citizens. In the effort to legally define the concept of "huaqiao," the Chinese nationality laws recognized the differences between the people of China and ethnic Chinese in the diaspora.

Chinese Americans themselves became more and more conscious of their special status as huaqiao or "Gold Mountaineers," which was constructed in Chinese contexts beginning late in the nineteenth century. Some even deliberately manipulated this status for personal gain. As a New York–based newspaper noted in 1928, some individuals tended to "show off" or improperly "take advantage" of their huaqiao status when traveling to China.[14] As testimony to the collective consciousness of their group identity, Chinese Americans also started to record their collective experience and history. In 1934, for example, several Chinese San Franciscans participated in writing a book about Chinese America.

In Chinese newspapers Chinese Americans articulated their understanding of "huaqiao." One editorial series stated in 1928 that " 'Huaqiao' has now been used frequently." It then explained that the notion included all overseas Chinese who were born either in China or overseas and who were with or without citizenship in their country of residence.[15] In an earlier editorial series on the relationship between the Chinese government and huaqiao, *The Chinese-Western Daily* proclaimed, "Huaqiao are also citizens [of China]." In 1941 an article published in the *Chinese Times* embraced the identity of huaqiao and called it "a glorious name."[16] The author proudly noted the contribution made by Chinese Americans to China's ongoing war with Japan and, especially, their vital support for the 1911 Chinese revolution. The author cited Sun Yat-sen, who once said that "huaqiao are the mother of the [Chinese] revolution."[17]

Disfranchised in America, Chinese Americans found and cherished the opportunity for social and political participation in China. Such participation did not blur the differences between them and the native Chinese, but it afforded them frames in which to fathom and appreciate the meaning of their American-ness. Clearly, for Chinese Americans their "Chinese-ness" and their "American" affiliation did not represent contradictory consciousnesses. Rather their association with both China and the United States helps us understand the coherence of the experiences of Chinese Americans or

"Gold Mountaineers," experiences that transcended national boundaries. By maintaining that association, they maximized the value of their position as Chinese in the United States.

The trans-Pacific spaces discussed in this book offer a perspective from which we can comprehend not only the commonalties but also the differences among individual Chinese Americans in terms of gender, economic interest, dialect, geographical origin, religion, and age. Such differences explain the conflicts within the community, and they also affected the degree of individuals' affiliation to China or America.

In short, this book is about the process that reflected developments within Chinese San Francisco and in the Pacific region. It is the story of one Chinese community at a particular moment in Chinese American history, a moment that came to an end during World War II. The historical circumstances in which Chinese Americans created their trans-Pacific community changed shortly thereafter. The Communists' victory in China in 1949 severed the physical connections between Chinese Americans and their ancestral land. In the United States the political climate during the McCarthy era increased their eagerness to disassociate themselves from the Chinese Communist government. Within Chinese America, meanwhile, the demographic structure underwent additional transformation, a transformation marked most notably by women's and the younger generation's increasing influence and growth in number.[18]

During the postwar years the Civil Rights Movement emerged to replace political Chinese nationalism as the main source of inspiration and strength in Chinese Americans' struggle for justice. This movement significantly undermined institutionalized racism and, as Michael Omi and Howard Winant point out, "radically transformed" the discourse of racial identity and the nature of racial politics.[19] The 1965 immigration reform act, a product of the Civil Rights Movement, finally ended Asian exclusion by abolishing the racist quota system.[20] Since 1965 new waves of Chinese immigration from origins more diverse than ever before have regenerated and profoundly transformed Chinese America. The new immigration has also revitalized and expanded the trans-Pacific socioeconomic, cultural, and political spaces in which early Chinese Americans were pioneers.

Notes

1. Hall, p. 222.
2. Dobie, pp. vii–viii.
3. *New York Times*, Aug. 8, 1906, 6: 4.
4. *The Chinese-Western Daily*, Aug. 14, 1934. Editorial.
5. This book relies primarily on written sources because of its nature and scope, not because of any inclination to blindly privilege such sources over oral-history data. Several scholars have already used and made available such data about Chinese San Francisco. For example, Nee and de Barry Nee's *Longtime California* contains numerous lengthy oral histories.
6. Glazer and Moynihan, xxii.
7. As early as 1940 John A. Hawgood wrote that "the Germans used their language as a weapon to ward off Americanization and assimilation, and used every social milieu, the home, the church, the school, the press, in the fight to preserve the German language, even among their children and grandchildren." It must be noted that non-English mother tongues have historically played an enormously important role in the lives of millions of immigrants and their children. In 1910 nearly three million of the thirteen million immigrants over ten years of age in the United States could not speak English. Half a century later, in 1960, about nineteen million people, or 11 percent of the entire U.S. population, possessed a non-English mother tongue. See Hawgood, p. 39; P. A. M. Taylor, p. 212; and Fishman et al., p. 392.

8. German-language newspapers were of particular significance: before their number began to decline partly as a result of anti-German sentiments during and after World War I, they constituted at least two-thirds of all non-English newspapers published in the United States in the years after 1880. The presence of the German-language press, which had its origins in colonial America, went back further than the Chinese-language press. But in both cases an important source of energy and vitality came from the respective "homeland." Numerous Chinese newspapers published in San Francisco and New York early in the twentieth century had close connections to politics in China. Similarly, the German-language press was revitalized by the coming of the 48'ers. We must note, however, that the impact of the ethnic press was not monolithic. As Fones-Wolf and Shore have argued in their essay on the German press, in some cases ethnic newspapers assisted immigrants in the process of assimilation and, in other cases, they encouraged ethnic solidarity. See Fones-Wolf and Shore, "The German Press," p. 63. For discussions of the German-language press, see Wittke.

9. The 1790 naturalization act stipulated that only free white men could be naturalized. After the Civil War the fourteenth amendment gave African Americans citizenship. The 1870 naturalization act clearly indicated that the amendment did not make the Chinese eligible for naturalization.

10. "The Race Problem—An Autobiography by a Southern Colored Woman," which originally appeared in the *Independent* 56 (Mar. 17, 1904): 586–89. The passage is cited in Holt, p. 220.

11. Various forms of anti-Chinese racism have long been a principal topic of Chinese American history. While earlier studies tend to focus on discrimination itself, more recent ones have attempted to show Chinese resistance as well. See for example S. Chan, *Entry Denied*; Courtney, *San Francisco's Anti-Chinese Ordinances*; McClain; Low; Sandmeyer; and Saxton, *The Indispensable Enemy*.

12. For example, Benson Tong discusses Chinese prostitution in his *Unsubmissive Women*. Analyses of prejudiced perceptions against the Chinese are found in J. S. Moy, and S. Miller; R. Yu's *To Save China*, a political history focused on a labor group in New York, also discusses Chinese American support for China during its war with Japan.

13. Judy Yung's well-crafted *Unbound Feet*, for example, focuses on women in Chinese San Francisco, especially those who were relatively acculturated. Those acculturated individuals are also the subject of several articles in Wong and Chan.

14. Such words have appeared, for example, in the titles of numerous books, including Thomas W. Chinn, *Bridging the Pacific: San Francisco Chinatown and Its People*; Hune et al., *Asian Americans: Comparative and Global Perspectives*; and

Ong et al., *The New Asian Immigration in Los Angeles and Global Restructuring*.
The emerging trend is not confined to Asian American Studies. See for example
Schillar et al.

CHAPTER 1: REVISITING THE PRE-EMIGRATION OLD WORLD

1. Rasmussen, 1: 110.

2. An ancient Chinese document records the fifth-century journey of a Chinese monk, Hui Sheng, to a place called "Fusang." Since the eighteenth century
Western and Chinese scholars have been debating whether that place was America.
For a recent Chinese perspective on this issue, see Luo Rongqu, "Fusangguo
Caixiang Yu Meizhou De Faqian" (The Fusang country hypothesis and the discovery of America), which first appeared in the second issue of *Lishi Yanjiu* (Historical Studies) in 1983. The debate is not my concern here, because even if Hui Sheng
had been to America, this isolated incident did not have any lasting impact on
China's geographical awareness.

3. This area maintained its significance in Sino-Western contact after the
Opium War. In January 1847, for instance, a majority (543) of the 711 foreigners
in China still lived in Canton and Hong Kong, according to the list of names of
foreigners in the *Chinese Repository* 16 (Jan. 1847): 3–9. The list did not include
the foreigners' wives, or British military personnel stationed in China then. The
Chinese Repository, published in Macao from 1832 to 1851 by Elija Coleman Bridgman, is an invaluable source of information about early relations between China
and the Western countries.

4. The prevailing interpretation that dominates not only Chinese American
histories but also general studies of Asian America views the emigration primarily
as an act of desperation to escape poverty and other socioeconomic difficulties,
which were aggravated by certain new developments, especially the arrival of
Western imperialism, marked by the Opium War (1840–42). See for example
Mei, pp. 229 and 235; Chinn et al., p. 12; S. Chan, *This Bittersweet Soil*, p. 16 and
pp. 18–20; and J. Yung, *Unbound Feet*, pp. 17–18. Also see Hyung-chan, *Legal
History*, p. 44; and Takaki, *Strangers*, pp. 32–33. I have offered a critique of the
overemphasis on the adversity faced by the emigration community in "The
Internal Origins of Chinese Emigration."

5. *Oriental*, Feb. 8, 1855. The article appeared in the English-language section
of this bilingual newspaper without clear indication of authorship. On page 6 of
his *An Humble Plea*, Speer makes it clear that he wrote it.

6. The number is based on Chinese arrivals at the San Francisco Customs

House. See Coolidge, p. 498. Other estimates are more conservative. According to Gall and Gall, p. 411, for instance, slightly over forty thousand Chinese arrived in the United States between 1850 and 1860.

7. There were one hundred and fifty thousand Chinese in Java at the time, according to Coppel (p. 2). Based on membership figures of the home-district associations, the Chinese population in the United States by the mid-1850s was around forty thousand (probably less than one thousand did not join those associations), a slightly larger number than the census figure. The membership figure is also consistent with Mary Coolidge's estimate. See Coolidge, p. 498. According to federal census materials, the number of Chinese in America was 63,199 in 1870 and 105,465 in 1880.

8. *Shunde Xianzhi (1853)*, 3: 35.

9. No records are more systematic and extensive than the local gazetteers, a special genre in China's centuries-old historical literature. The most common and important are those written at the county level, called "xianzhi" (meaning "county gazetteer"). They used both written and oral data and covered a wide range of subjects, from economy, demography, and natural environment to history, literature, social customs, and biographies. Over the years, especially during the Qing Dynasty (1644–1911), continuous efforts were made to revise or recompile the xianzhi in order to bring them up to date.

10. *Nanhai Xianzhi (1836)*, 5: 21.

11. The dialects in the region belonged to the Cantonese dialect group, which is one of the three dialect groups of Guangdong Province. The other two are Hakka and Chaozhou. Discussions of the origins of certain words or pronunciations of words in various local documents suggest that people in the region were aware of the roots of their dialects. See for example *Panyu Xianzhi*, 6: 50.

12. *Zhongshan Xianzhi*, 26: 57.

13. *Nanhai Xianzhi*, 26: 57.

14. Fan, p. 238.

15. Ibid.

16. There is no need to exaggerate the development of such an economy in the Canton area at the time. By today's standard or even by the standard of nineteenth-century industrializing western Europe it was rather underdeveloped. And it was not totally free of the Chinese government's restrictive intervention. While the government imposed, not always successfully, various restrictions on the trade between China and the West, local merchants' access to the domestic market remained more open.

17. Qu, p. 431.

18. Some of the characteristics of the emigrant communities discussed above

have been mentioned elsewhere by other scholars of Chinese America. But the significance of these characteristics in effecting nineteenth-century emigration to California has not been fully recognized. Several studies have referred to the development of commerce in the Pearl River Delta, for example. Yet that development is too often seen as merely an indication as well as a result of economic disadvantages. Betty Lee Sung argued, for instance, that people turned to trade because they "were forced to look for nonagricultural means of subsistence." See Sung, *The Story of the Chinese*, p. 14. Similarly, June Mei wrote that people "turned to nonagricultural jobs because there was too little land to sustain them." Mei, "Socioeconomic Origins," p. 235.

Such a view fails to capture the dynamic nature of the economy in the Pearl River Delta Region. In other words, the development of a market-oriented economy in the region cannot be interpreted simply as a manifestation of its problems, such as the shortage of grain or land.

19. *Chinese Repository* 2 (Nov. 1933): 292. For detailed discussions of Guangdong's rice importation during the eighteenth century, see Marks, "Rice Prices," pp. 64–116.

20. *Nanhai Xianzhi (1836)*, 12: 32.

21. *Zengcheng Xianzhi*, introduction, p. 8.

22. Ibid.

23. *Nanhai Xianzhi (1836)*, 5: 19.

24. *Zengcheng Xianzhi*, introduction, p. 10.

25. See Jiang, pp. 342–43.

26. Fan, p. 54.

27. Hunter, pp. 13–14.

28. *Panyu Xianzhi*, 6: 4. Panyu's long-standing significance as a center of trade is also noted in *Guangdong tongzhi*, 91: 1779.

29. *Guangdong tongzhi*, 92: 1768.

30. Different versions of the Nanhai gazetteer include many biographies of well-connected rich merchants. See for instance *Nanhai Xianzhi (1836)*, 19: 2 and 5; and *Nanhai Xianzhi*, 20: 9–10, and 11–12. People in Nanhai, especially its rich residents, were known for their affluent lifestyle. See *Nanhai Xianzhi (1910)*, 4: 20.

31. *Nanhai Xianzhi*, 5: 13 and 14.

32. Fan, p. 360.

33. *Shunde Xianzhi (1853)*, 2: 46.

34. Ibid., 3: 45.

35. *Guangdong tongzhi*, 92: 1789.

36. Fan, p. 33.

37. *Chinese Repository* 17 (Aug. 1848): 428.

38. *Shunde Xianzhi (1853),* 3: 35.

39. *Xinning Xianzhi,* 8: 5; 29: 3.

40. *Enping Xianzhi,* 4: 1, 12.

41. Ibid., 4: 12; and *Xinning Xianzhi,* introduction.

42. *Xinning Xianzhi,* 21: 12. The authors of this and other gazetteers simply stated that these men had gone overseas, without identifying their specific destinations.

43. Faure, p. 202.

44. Bodnar, pp. 13 and 20.

45. Bailyn.

46. S. W. Williams, *Chinese Immigration,* p. 45.

47. Tea, especially green tea, remained Americans' major beverage until the 1830s. Contemporaries, such as C. Toogood Downing, knew well the American habit of drinking green tea. See Downing, 3: 127. In the later part of the 1840s millions of tons of tea were exported to the United States. And most of it was green tea, including the famous Imperial, Gunpowder, and Hyson teas. See *The China Mail,* Nov. 8, 1849.

48. Johnson and Supple, p. 24.

49. For Americans' involvement in the opium trade, see Stelle, "American Trade in Opium to China Prior to 1820," pp. 425–44; and Stelle, "American Trade in Opium to China, 1821–1839," pp. 57–74.

50. Studies of Americans in late Qing China usually discuss a third group, the diplomats. I do not include them here because in the early years American diplomatic positions were usually held concurrently by merchants or missionaries. For instance, the first American consul in China (Canton), Major Samuel Shaw, a revolutionary veteran, had originally come to China as supercargo on the *Empress of China.* The Rev. David Abeel, one of the first two American missionaries to China, was the first American consul ever appointed in a place north of Canton—in Xiamen (Amoy). Another missionary, Dr. Peter Parker, became the American charge d'affaires. For more information about the first two men, see Quincy, and Abeel. Parker will be discussed later. For a discussion of the relationship between American missionary work and diplomatic activities, see Varg. The first chapter of his book deals with the years between 1830 and 1900.

51. Long before American China traders established their presence, European merchants had come to South China, including the Spanish (1574), the Portuguese (1514), the Dutch (1601), the English (1637), and the French (1600).

52. "Description of the City of Canton," in *Chinese Repository* 2 (Nov. 1833): 300. In 1847, shortly before the beginning of Chinese emigration, the number of

American ships coming to Canton increased to over 60. *Chinese Repository* 16 (June 1847): 134.

53. See the Liang and Fang's estimate in Hu and Wang, 1: 848. In 1834 and 1845 two other officials made similar estimates; see *Daoguangchao Chouban Yiwu Shimo*, 68: 24 and 74: 18. This 260-volume series includes diplomatic documents from the reigns of three emperors of the Qing Dynasty.

54. Wei, 39: 26. After its first publication in 1844 in Yangzhou in 50 volumes, the book was republished and enlarged to 60 volumes in 1847. It was reprinted in facsimile in 1967 by the Sheng-wen Publishing Company, Taipei.

55. Hunter, p. 27.

56. Downing, 1: 147.

57. *Chinese Repository* 2 (Nov. 1833): 290.

58. Zhang Guiyong, p. 1.

59. At that time, thirteen such "factories" existed, constituting a part of the famous Canton system. That system was designed to deal with foreign trade and was later replaced by the treaty system after the Opium War. Although both sometimes shared the same name of Thirteen Hang, it is nonetheless important for us to recognize the difference between the foreigner-run "factories" and the co-hong, which referred to the Chinese security merchants as a group. The co-hong had a long history, and the number of hang actually varied from time to time. For further discussions of the Chinese Thirteen Hang see Fairbank, *Trade and Diplomacy*. For a contemporary account, see Liang Tingnan's "The Thirteen Hang," in Liang and Fang, 7: 181–88. According to Frederic Wakeman Jr., almost all members of the co-hong lost their wealth and influence by 1900. Wakeman Jr., p. 100.

60. Although the crowded and damp factories offered little physical comfort, Americans and other foreigners stayed there, rather than returning to Macao, during the winter season, even before that stay became legal. *Zhongshan Xianzhi*, 8: 28–29. For a description of factory conditions see F. Williams, *Life and Letters*, p. 56.

61. Hunter, pp. 53–54.

62. Suzanne Wilson Barnett discusses Protestant missions in China during this period in "Protestant Expansion and Chinese," pp. 1–20; and "Practical Evangelism."

63. In fact it was a New York merchant named D. W. C. Olyphant who first suggested that missionaries be sent to China and provided passage and one year of support for Elija Coleman Bridgman and Rev. David Abeel, the first American missionaries to China. Olyphant and his business partners later rented a house for

American missionaries for about thirteen years. See Baird, p. 362; F. Williams, *Life and Letters*, p. 78.

64. Boone.

65. The missionaries also played an important role in shaping Americans' perceptions of China and the Chinese. See S. Miller, pp. 57–80.

66. For a discussion of this organization, see Phillips. Founded in Boston between 1810 and 1812, the American Board of Commissioners for Foreign Missions was one of the numerous missionary organizations formed in America early in the nineteenth century. Some others were the American Baptist Missionary Union, which formed in 1814, the Board of Foreign Missions of the Presbyterian Church, which formed in 1837, the Board of Foreign Missions of the Protestant Episcopal Church, which formed in 1835, and the Methodist Episcopal Missionary Society, which formed in 1836. Many such organizations were involved in missionary work in China. The American Catholic Church did not start its missionary work in China until the twentieth century. For discussions of U.S. Catholic missions there, see Breslin.

67. For a history of American missionaries' Christian predecessors, see Legge. Of particular importance were Jesuits, who had a close relationship with the Chinese government during the late Ming (1368–1644) and early Qing dynasties. Many Jesuits, such as Matteo Ricci, Sabbathen de Ursis, and Jean Adam Schall von Bell, were well versed in Chinese, and they wrote and translated many books on mathematics, astrology, geography, and so on. See Rowbotham, and Ronan and Oheds. Also see Jonathan Spence's fascinating study of Matteo Ricci, *The Memory Palace of Matteo Ricci*.

68. Coming to China in 1807 by way of New York, Morrison was the first Protestant missionary to China, and he also received financial support from American merchants. In China he compiled a six-volume Chinese dictionary, founded the Anglo-Chinese School at Malacca, and translated the Bible into Chinese.

69. *Minutes of the Annual Meeting of the Medical Missionary Society in China; and the Fifteenth Report of its Ophthalmic Hospital at Canton, for the Years 1848–1849* (Canton, 1850): 20. For a full discussion of Parker's various activities in China, see Gulick.

70. Stuart C. Miller has shown that American merchants generally regarded the Chinese as a "peculiar" people with bizarre tastes and habits, who were characterized by vices and social backwardness. S. Miller, pp. 26–27.

71. Parker's diary entry of May 10, 1834, in Stevens and Markwich, p. 80.

72. Ibid., p. 85.

73. *Chinese Repository* 17 (Mar. 1848): 133.

74. Downing, 2: 202.

75. The Ophthalmic Hospital, *Thirteenth Report of the Ophthalmic Hospital*, p. 3.

76. Ibid., p. 7.

77. See Swisher, p. 821. This book includes translations of more than five hundred official Chinese documents from *Daoguangchao chouban yiwu shimo*. The book that Parker helped translate was Emer de Vattel's *Le droit des gens ou, principles de la loi naturelle appliques a la couduite & aux affaires des nations & des souverains* (A Leide: Aux depens de la compagnie, 1758). Its Chinese translation, *The Public Laws of Ten Thousand Countries*, was later included in Wei.

78. The Medical Missionary Society. *The Fifteenth Report of the Ophthalmic Hospital, in Minutes of the Annual Meeting of the Medical Missionary Society*, p. 24.

79. The Medical Missionary Society, *Address with Minutes of the Medical Missionary Society in China*, pp. 10 and 13.

80. Wei, 39: 7.

81. *Chinese Repository* 16 (Jan. 1847): 12–14.

82. *Statement of Reasons in Favor of Larger Contributions for the Support of the Missions* (Boston, 1848): 18.

83. See *Daoguangchao Chouban Yiwu Shimo*, 72: 3; F. Williams, *Life and Letters*, pp. 181–82.

84. Fairbank, *Missionary Enterprise*, pp. 2–3.

85. Methodist Missionary Society, p. 10.

86. Pre-emigration Chinese visitors to the United States are discussed at some length in Fessler, chap. 1.

87. *Chinese Repository* 14 (May 1845): 247.

88. Published in 1849, shortly after he returned to China, *Xihai youji cao* consisted of several different parts, including a poem and a long introduction. When the book was published, it won praise from numerous people, including Xu Jiyu. Discovered by a Chinese scholar in 1980, it was reprinted in 1985, together with a few other documents, by the Hunan Publishing House, Changsha, China.

89. Ibid.

90. Xie Qinggao. Xu Jiyu's *Yinghuan zhilue* is included in Hu and Wang. Lin Zexu's *sizhou zhi* was later included in Wei.

91. Xie Qinggao's work was noticed by Westerners and read by numerous Chinese at the time, including Lin Zexu. As we will see later, the other two pieces were even more popular.

92. For further discussions of the subject over a longer period of time, see Arkush and Lee.

93. The actual writing was done by someone else—Xie had lost his sight, which forced him to give up his long career as a sailor that he had started in 1783 at the age of eighteen.

94. Xie Qinggao, p. 75.

95. Ibid.

96. Ibid.

97. Ibid.

98. *Chinese Repository* 9 (May 1940): 22 and 25.

99. Back in 1806, when a ship from "Luchen" arrived in Canton, it took quite some time for a customs official to figure out that "Luchen" was Russia or "Eluosi." Wang Yanwei, 1: 37. John King Fairbank also shows some examples of the confusion regarding other European countries in his *Trade and Diplomacy*, p. 10.

100. *Daoguangchao chouban yiwu shimo*, 74: 17.

101. The Chinese title of Xie Qinggao's book, *Haiwai fanyi lu*, includes these two words. Lin Zexu used the word "yi" when mentioning Westerners in his diary in the late 1830s. See his diary entry for June 16, 1839, in Lin Zexu. *Lin zexu ji: Riji*, p. 343.

102. Dikötter, pp. vi and 6.

103. In ancient times, "yi" was designated to categorize the minorities in the East, and "fan" the minorities in the South and Southwest. *Ciyuan* (Origins of words), 4 vols. (Beijing: Shangwu yinshugan, 1979), 1: 713–14 and 3: 2121–22. First published in 1915 and revised several times, this is one of the best Chinese dictionaries.

Although the two terms were identical in meaning and were used interchangeably during the nineteenth century, "yi" appears to have been a more literary and formal term and was used more frequently in official documents, whereas "fan" was a more colloquial term, used more often by commoners. The two terms are herein translated as "barbarian."

104. C. Downing, 1: 145.

105. Wei, 30: 73 and 75.

106. There have been two erroneous assumptions about this book since its publication. The first is that Lin was the translator. See for example Jian Bozhan, *Zhongguoshi gangyao* (An outline of Chinese history) (Beijing, renmin chubanshe, 1964), 4: 14; and Drake, "A Nineteenth-Century View," p. 47. It is clear that this assumption is incorrect, because Lin did not know English. Numerous people, including contemporaries, have noted that several young interpreters worked for him.

According to the second assumption, *Sizhou zhi* was a translation of Hugh Murray's *An Encyclopaedia of Geography*. See Lin Chongyong, pp. 342 and 629; Guo Tingyi, "The Import of Modern Western Culture and China's Understanding of It," in Guo, p. 32; Ssu-yu Teng and Fairbank, *China's Response*, p. 29. A close comparison of the section on the United States in Lin's *Sizhou zhi* and the corresponding section in Murray's book reveals that while a significant portion of the *Sizhou zhi* is translated from Murray's book, the former contains much information, as well as conspicuous misinformation, which is not in Murray's book. For instance, the former includes statistics about America's population, national revenue, and so forth not found in the latter.

107. Sir J. F. Davis, 1: 309–310.

108. Wei, p. 22.

109. See a review of Lin's book in *Chinese Repository* 16 (Sept. 1847): 423.

110. Leonard, p. 203. Wei Yuan acknowledged that his *Haiguo tuzhi* was based on Lin Zexu's *Sizhou zhi*. See Wei, 1: 1. Also see Sir. J. F. Davis, 1: 310–311. Among other Chinese influenced by *Sizhou zhi* was Xu Jiyu. See Drake, "A Nineteenth-Century View," p. 47.

111. Wei, 39: 2.

112. Fairbank, *Trade and Diplomacy*, p. 20.

113. Xu, 1: 736.

114. Ibid., 1: 527.

115. This quotation is found in the manuscript version of Xu's work. The manuscript was reprinted by Wen-hai in 1874, p. 210.

116. Review of Xu's book, *Chinese Repository* 20 (Apr. 1851): 170.

117. Lengthy excerpts of the book, for example, appeared in the gazetteer of major emigrant counties. See for example *Zhongshan xianzhi*, 22: 12. Zhang Yinhuan, who was Chinese minister to the United States (1886–89) and a native of Nanhai, mentioned Xu's work. See Zhang Yinhuan, 1: 27 and 2: 28. Later on, scholars like Liang Qichao also mentioned Xu's work.

118. Xu, 1: 530.

119. Ibid., 1: 526.

120. Hastings, p. 133.

121. Brown, p. 26.

122. Rasmussen, 1: 110.

123. *Daily Alta California*, Aug. 5, 1850.

124. Barry and Patter, p. 100.

125. Soule et al., pp. 414–15.

126. *The China Mail*, Dec. 26, 1850.

127. Ibid., Jan. 18, 1949. Mary Coolidge incorrectly cited Helms and asserted that the news of gold might have reached China in 1848. See her *Chinese Immigration*, p. 17.

128. F. Williams, *Life and Letters*, p. 169.

129. Helms, p. 74.

130. *The China Mail*, Sept. 26, 1850.

131. Morison, p. 274.

132. S. Williams, *Middle Kingdom*, 2: 559–60. Williams believed, rather inaccurately, that Houqua himself came from Amoy, Fujian. The gazetteer reports only that the family's ancestors came from Fujian. If the findings Hosea Ballou Morse published in his *The Chronicles of the East India Company* are to be trusted, one member of the Wu family, also named Houqua, had already started doing business with foreigners as early as 1778. See Morse, 2: 28. Morse identified four Houquas in his book.

133. *The Oriental*, Feb. 15, 1855. Chinese section.

134. *Nanhai Xianzhi*, 14: 46. It is interesting to note that a vessel engaged in the China trade that carried tea and other goods between San Francisco and China was named "Houqua." See *Daily Alta California*, Aug. 5, 1850. Also see *The China Mail*, June 13, 1849.

135. Johnson and Supple, p. 24.

136. See Liu Pei Chi, *Meiguo huaqiao shi*, p. 36.

137. *The Oriental*, Feb. 15, 1855.

138. *Chinese Repository* 19 (June 1850): 344.

139. F. Williams, *Life and Letters*, p. 177.

140. *Shunde Xianzhi (1996)*, p. 1172.

141. Condit, pp. 91–92.

142. Yung Wing, pp. 13 and 20. Yung Wing was one of the three who went to America in 1847. He was the first Chinese student to graduate from an American college (Yale). Later he became a prominent figure in modern Chinese history.

143. Transliterated names of early Chinese emigrants often took more than one form in English. For example, Lee Kan was also spelled "Li Kan" and "Lee Ken," and Tong K. Achick appears as "Tong Chik" and "Tong Achick" in different places. The letter "A" in "Achick" is actually an informal prefix (more often spelled "Ah") that people in South China used together with the first name but that was almost always mistaken by U.S. officials to be a permanent part of their name, as we will discuss further later. Such misunderstanding is one significant reason for the lack of consistency in Chinese (actually Cantonese) transliterations, which makes it extremely difficult to track the same individuals through different sources.

144. It is necessary to note that people like him and his classmates did not leave China because they feared religious persecution. The three who left China with Brown came to America for their education. Lee Kan was not converted to Christianity until late in his life.

145. Langley, p. 905.

146. S. Chan, *Asian Americans*, p. 104.

147. Skinner, p. 275.

148. Lo, *Yuedongzhifeng*, pp. 268, 274, and 278. There is no indication of when the song first appeared.

149. There were also local gold mines in the region, as numerous documents report. See for instance *Zhongshan Xianzhi*, 5: 31; Qu, p. 402; *Enping Xianzhi*, 5: 48, and Fan, p. 242.

150. Sanchez, p. 38.

INTRODUCTION TO PART I

1. Countering the long-standing myth that Chinese were initially welcomed by white America, in chapter 1 of his *The Unwelcome Immigrant* S. Miller shows that an unfavorable image of China and the Chinese preceded Chinese immigration by a long time.

2. Soule et al., p. 378.

3. The Chinese were one of many groups who took part in the Gold Rush. From October 1849 through September 1850 43,618 passengers were recorded as having arrived in San Francisco, making it the second-largest passenger-receiving port in the United States. Between 1850 and 1860 California's population more than quadrupled, increasing from 93,000 to 379,994. Many of the newcomers were immigrants, who accounted for over 23 percent of the state's population in 1850 and over a third of it in both 1860 and 1870. See Cong. Docs., U.S. serial set no. 598, 31st congress, Dec. 2, 1850–Mar. 3, 1851, House ex. document., pp. 42–43.; Francis A. Walker, Superintendent of Census, comp., *A Compendium of the Ninth Census* (Washington, D.C., 1872): 28–29; and Joseph C. G. Kennedy, comp., *Population of the United States in 1860* (Washington, D.C., 1864): 33.

4. Browne, appendix, p. iv. Although Southerners such as William Gwin had some impact on the convention, their overall influence must not be exaggerated. Of the 48 delegates, Southerners did not constitute a majority. William Gwin, a disciple of John C. Calhoun, chaired the committee to draft the constitution at the 1849 convention. For further discussions of William Gwin, see Quinn.

5. For an analysis of the subject, see Pitt, pp. 23–38.

6. Helms, p. 79.

7. Saxton, *The Indispensable Enemy*, p. 261.

8. Many white ethnics had experienced much prejudice on the East Coast. While such prejudice also existed on the West Coast, as Burchell points out in his *The San Francisco Irish* (p. 4), it declined significantly, in general. Micaela Di Leonardo writes: "The significant presence of racial minorities, largely Chinese

and Japanese . . . clearly acted to displace white racial animosities from white ethnics." See Leonardo, p. 56.

9. *New York Times*, Mar. 4, 1882, 4: 3.

10. Peffer, "Forbidden Families," pp. 28–46; S. Chan, "Exclusion of Chinese Women," pp. 94–146.

11. See also the statistics concerning the regional distribution of Chinese in California from 1860 to 1900 included in S. Chan, *This Bittersweet Soil*, p. 43.

CHAPTER 2: THE "FIRST CITY"

1. *San Francisco Chronicle*, Dec. 13, 1878, p. 3.

2. Ibid., p. 2.

3. *San Francisco Chronicle*, Dec. 9, 1878, p. 3.

4. Ah Quin is one of the few early Chinese immigrants whose life we know about in some detail, thanks to the diary he kept. We will discuss his life and diary at greater length in later chapters.

5. Ah Quin's diary entries for Oct. 5 and 9, 1879.

6. U.S. Congress, Joint Special Committee to Investigate Chinese Immigration, *Report of the Joint Special Committee to Investigate Chinese Immigration*, 44th congress, p. 1196; hereafter cited as *Report of the Joint Special Committee*.

7. Chen Lanbin, in Wang Xiqi, book 44, p. 59. This book was first published in twelve parts, which were followed by two twelve-part supplements.

8. *The Chinese-Western Daily*, Apr. 17, 1906. Advertisement section.

9. *Report of the Joint Special Committee*, p. 513.

10. Her projection is based on a wide range of sources. For her figures and an explanation of her computation, see Coolidge, pp. 498–503.

11. Coolidge, p. 498, and note 3 on p. 499. Alfred Wheeler estimated Chinese arrivals at ten thousand before 1852; this figure is similar to figures cited by Coolidge. His number was based on his own research of the customs-house records. As he testified before the 1876 Congressional Committee on Chinese Immigration, he had published his research results in a few articles. See *Report of the Joint Special Committee*, pp. 513 and 1196.

12. After 1882, when Congress passed the first Chinese exclusion act, the number of Chinese coming to America fell.

13. The census figures for the Chinese population are 105,465 for the year 1880, 107,488 for 1890, and 89,963 for 1900. For a summary of the Chinese American population between 1860 and 1950, see U.S. Bureau of the Census *Historical Statistics of the United States*, p. 9.

14. *The Golden Hills' News*, July 29, 1854. The Chinese section.

15. *Oriental*, Jan. 25, 1855. English section. As we will see later in the book, the huiguan were based on the immigrants' social relations formed in the Old World.

16. Coolidge, p. 498.

17. Li was then en route to Philadelphia for the 1876 exposition in celebration of the centennial of independence, to which he had been sent by China as an observer. The cited figure is from his diary in Chen Lanbin, book 45, p. 94.

18. Coolidge, p. 498.

19. Liang Qichao, 10: 380. An important intellectual and political figure in modern Chinese history, Liang was then in political exile. Numerous studies of Liang's life, including Levenson's *Liang Ch'i-Ch'ao*, have been published in both Chinese and English.

20. Estimates of the Chinese American population from Chinese and other sources:

year	Chinese numbers	source	Coolidge Census
1854	40,000 to 50,000	*The Golden Hills' News*	37,447
1855	about 40,000.	Huiguan membership	36,557
1860	46,897		34,933
1870	71,083		63,199
1876	160,000	Li Gui	111,971
1878	148,600	Huiguan membership	110,664
1879	140,000 to 150,000	Chen Lanbin	108,827
1880	104,991		105,465

21. Wang Xiqi, book 44, pp. 59–60.

22. The figures are from the testimonies of the presidents of the huiguan before a California Senate committee. See California State Legislature, Senate, Special Committee on Chinese Immigration, *Chinese Immigration: The Social, Moral, and Political Effect of Chinese Immigration* (1876): 44. Hereafter cited as *The Social, Moral, and Political Effect of Chinese Immigration*.

23. *Report of the Joint Special Committee*, p. 12.

24. The seemingly "scientific" task of gathering and organizing official statistics has never been totally objective. The federal census, in particular, has been of special political importance because it offers official assessments of the population, which have served as the basis of the distribution and redistribution of economic and political resources. The restrictive and racist immigration quota system (also known as the national origins system) that was designed in the 1920s was also based on census numbers. For a detailed discussion of the census, see Anderson.

25. See for example the census manuscripts of Rattlesnake Bar, Sutter County, California.

26. *Report of the Joint Special Committee*, p. vi.

27. Farwell.

28. Julian Ralph, "The Chinese Leak," *Harper's New Monthly Magazine* (Mar. 1891): 515–25.

29. *Report of the Joint Special Committee*, p. 253.

30. The 1868 treaty stipulated free immigration between the two countries and protection for Chinese immigrants. And the appointment of a minister was also intended to protect Chinese immigrants. His official title was Minister to America, Spain, and Peru; his responsibilities therefore also included the protection of many Chinese immigrants who resided and faced discrimination in Peru and other parts of Latin America. See Wang Yanwei, 4: 17–18.

31. See the memorials to the Emperor by Xue Fucheng and Yi Kuang, in Chen Hansheng, 1: part I, pp. 292–96.

32. In 1907 the Qing Court sent officials to conduct a census of Chinese America.

33. Soule et al., p. 381.

34. Speer, *An Humble Plea*, p. 411.

35. Francis A. Walker, Superintendent of Census, comp., *A Compendium of the Ninth Census* (Washington, D.C., 1872): 29.

36. These are the two earliest years for which federal census returns are available for San Francisco. The 1850 records were destroyed in a fire. Conducted under the supervision of a centralized census office with an expanded staff created by the 1850 census law, the 1860 and 1870 census returns contain important statistical information for these formative years of Chinatown. Other sources that have similar information, such as the extensive investigations of Chinatown by various government agencies, did not appear until after 1870.

37. My analysis is based on random samplings of the 1860 and 1870 census Chinese populations. The two samplings consist of 2,193 and 8,901 adults, respectively, from the population manuscript census. Five hundred and eighty-seven people from the 1860 sampling and 1,410 of those from the 1870 sampling were women. As I have noted before, the total Chinese population stood at 2,719 in 1860 and at 12,022 in 1870, according to the census. The two samplings do not include those who were identified by census takers as children or as pupils. Margins of error are less than 2 percent.

A few other scholars have used the census in their studies of different aspects of San Francisco. Lucie Cheng, for example, used it to discuss Chinese prostitutes in San Francisco. Her tabulation of the 1860 census, which yielded 2,693 Chinese residents, represents an incomplete count of the total Chinese population in the city. The 654 women represent 24 percent of the 2,693 residents, a percentage similar to the one I came up with (over 22 percent). See Cheng, pp. 402–34.

38. Most women of this age group were between 17 and 19 years old. But a few were under 17; and the youngest was 11 years old.

39. Only a few women in this age group in 1870 were under 17, and the youngest was 10 years old.

40. My calculation is based on figures in U.S. Bureau of the Census, *Historical Statistics of the United States*, p. 10. It must be noted that the nonwhite population in general was younger than its white counterpart during those two years.

41. Lucie Cheng's tabulation of the same census manuscripts turned out more children—52 for 1860 and 595 for 1870. Although we do not know how she defined the word "children," her figures clearly indicate the increase in the number of children in Chinatown. For her figures, see Cheng, p. 419.

42. One was born in Japan, a five-year-old girl named Giuy Ying.

43. In the census manuscripts, many children were listed together with women identified as prostitutes in brothels. Their relationship with the alleged prostitutes remains an interesting question. They could have been children of prostitutes, as Lucie Cheng has assumed in the previously cited article. But they could also have been children of parents who were busy making a living elsewhere. We will return to these and other issues pertaining to brothels later.

44. This is based on Lucie Cheng's figures for Chinese children in 1860 (52) and in 1870 (495).

45. *Report of the Joint Special Committee*, p. 611.

46. See for example *Report of the Joint Special Committee*, p. 19; *The Social, Moral, and Political Effect of Chinese Immigration,* pp. 46 and 59.

47. Lloyd, p. 236.

48. Farwell, part II, p. 3.

49. *Report of the Joint Special Committee*, pp. 10, 12, and 19.

50. Chen Lanbin, book 45, p. 94.

51. Ibid., book 44, pp. 59–60.

52. U.S. Census Office. *Census Reports*, vol. 1, *Twentieth Census of the United States*, p. 565. Hereafter cited as *Census Reports* (1901).

53. *Disturnell's Strangers' Guide*, p. 108.

54. Farwell, part II, pp. 6 and 7.

55. *Census Reports* (1901): 565.

56. U. S. Industrial Commission on Immigration, p. 763.

57. Liang Qichao, p. 380.

58. That percentage dropped from over 9 percent in 1880 to about 4 percent in 1900. See *Census Reports* (1901): 495 and 565.

59. Coolidge, p. 411.

60. Wang Yanwei, 15: 32.

61. For discussions of some of the numerous violent incidents perpetrated against the Chinese, see B. P. Wilcox, "Anti-Chinese Riots in Washington," *Washington Historical Quarterly*, 20 (1929): 204–12; J. A. Karlin, "The Anti-Chinese Outbreaks in Seattle, 1885–1886," *Pacific Northwest Quarterly*, 39 (1948): 103–29; and J. A. Karlin, "The Anti-Chinese Outbreak in Tacoma, 1885," *Pacific Historical Review*, 23 (1964): 271–83.

62. Coolidge, p. 412.

63. *The Chinese-Western Daily*, 1900. American News section.

64. Gibson, *The Chinese in America*, pp. 52–53.

65. Ping Chiu, pp. x, 110; Saxton, *The Indispensable Enemy*, p. 4.

66. *The Oriental*, Jan. 25, 1855. English section.

67. Ibid., Feb. 22, 1855. Chinese section.

68. *The Golden Hills' News*, July 29, 1854. Chinese section.

69. Ibid.

70. *The Oriental*, May 11, 1856. Chinese section.

71. "Chinese Directory" listed in *The Oriental*, Feb. 8, 1856. English section.

72. The 1878 directory lists 55 on Commercial Street, 31 on Washington Street, 28 on Clay Street, 17 on Pacific Street, 9 on Washington Alley, and 7 on Stockton Street. See Wells Fargo, *Directory of Principal Chinese Business Firms* (in San Francisco, Sacramento, Marysville, Portland, Stockton, San Jose, and Virginia City of Nevada).

73. Langley, pp. 1004–10.

74. *The Chinese-Western Daily*, Directory, 1902. The directory included not only economic establishments but also social organizations.

75. According to Ping Chiu, there were 34 such gardening businesses in 1860, 117 in 1870, and 135 in 1880. See Ping Chiu, p. 76. His numbers are based on his tabulation of the manuscript population census and include only farm operators. These figures do not seem to precisely reflect the total number of people engaged in the gardening business. According to the city assessor, in 1876 about twenty-five hundred people worked as gardeners and vegetable peddlers in San Francisco. See *Report of the Joint Special Committee*, p. 252.

76. By comparison, the English-language names of Chinese businesses were usually shorter, less specific, and sometimes less accurate. The English name of the same business sometimes appeared differently in different places.

77. The 1882 directory recorded 16 tailor and 12 barber shops, but no such shops appeared in the 1878 directory. These were by no means new kinds of busi-

nesses that suddenly emerged after 1878; they were clearly documented in the federal census schedules for 1860 and 1870.

78. One hundred and eighty-nine, or nearly 40 percent, of the 473 Chinese businesses in the 1878 city directory were not listed in the 1882 directory. See Langley.

79. These might include a few that had changed ownership.

80. *Report of the Joint Special Committee*, p. 622.

81. Alexander Badlam, the assessor of the city, and his associates spent four to five days surveying Chinatown in 1876. The following list of the numbers of Chinese engaged in different industries was compiled from their survey results (source: *Report of the Joint Special Committee*, pp. 252–53):

> cigar manufacturing: 2,800
> cigar box making: 350
> garment manufacturing: 3,450
> match-making: 100 – 150
> shoe/boot/slipper making: 3,000
> wool milling: 500 – 700
> fruit canning: 2,200
> tanning: 400

82. Farwell, appendix, "exhibit A," pp. 79–84.

83. Some of the factories were owned by whites, others by Chinese. See Mei, "Socioeconomic Developments," pp. 375 and 377.

84. *Report of the Industrial Commission*, p. 754.

85. *The Oriental*, Jan. 13, 1876.

86. "A Card to the Business and the Public in General: A New and Great Agitation in Which Everybody Should Join" by S. Klarenmeyer. (A merchandise list that came with the card suggests that it was printed in the 1880s, but it does not indicate the specific year of publication.)

87. The percentage of the city's inhabitants who were foreign born declined very slowly over the years thereafter. Over 34 percent of the city's population was foreign born in 1900. The percentages are based on U.S. census figures. See *Census Reports* (1901): 495.

88. U.S. Census Office, *Compendium of the Tenth Census*, part 2, pp. 1094–95.

89. Based on my 1870 sampling of the population census manuscripts, only one Chinese manufacturer had ten thousand dollars' worth of personal property (in most cases the value of their property ranged from eight hundred to a few thousand dollars). According to the early population census manuscripts, very

few Chinese residents possessed real estate property. My tabulation of the 1860 census manuscripts yields two individuals who owned both personal and real estate property: Chy Lung, 58 years old, possessed two thousand dollars' worth of real estate property and three thousand dollars' worth of personal property; Ah Low had two thousand dollars in real estate property and one thousand in personal property. It is possible that the Chinese capitalists underreported their property, however.

90. It was formed by a few individuals, usually friends, with each contributing periodically to a general pool. Members took turns using the money collected each time.

91. This case eventually went to the California Supreme Court. California Supreme Court, See *Chin Kem You v Ah Joan*.

CHAPTER 3: THE SOCIAL LANDSCAPE OF CHINESE SAN FRANCISCO

1. Coolidge, p. 411.

2. Liang Qichao, pp. 394 and 386–96.

3. William Hoy is one scholar who has stated that the Kong Chow Huiguan was indeed the oldest. See Hoy, *The Story of Kong Chow Temple*, p. 3.

4. These huiguan (called "houses" at the time) are identified as the Se-yup, Yaong Wo, Suwon, and Canton Huiguan in California State Legislature, Assembly, *Majority and Minority Reports*, p. 9.

5. *The Oriental* listed them as the Yeung-wo, Canton, Sze-yap, Yan-wo, and Ning-yeung Huiguan. They were transliterated according to the pronunciation of those words in Cantonese. The transliterations of Yeung-wo, Sze-yap, Yan-wo, and Ning-yeung according to the modern, standard method (the pinyin system) based on mandarin pronunciation are Yanghe, Sanyi, Renhe, and Ningyang, respectively.

6. *The Oriental*, Jan. 25, 1855. English section.

7. There was a Panyu Huiguan in Beijing, for example. In 1843 a rich merchant from Panyu County donated a large sum of money to maintain the huiguan house. *Panyu Xianzhi*, 16: 52.

8. The list is based on a document translated from Chinese. See *The Oriental*, Jan. 25, 1855. English section.

9. Ibid.

10. *The Social, Moral, and Political Effect of Chinese Immigration*, p. 44.

11. Culin, *China in America*, p. 13.

12. Lo and Lai, p. 2.

13. *The Golden Hills' News*, July 24, 1854. Chinese section.

14. *The Golden Hills' News*, July 29, 1854. Chinese section.

15. *The Oriental*, Jan. 4, 1855. English section. Also see *The Golden Hills' News*, June 10, 1854. English section.

16. *The Golden Hills' News*, July 29, 1854. Chinese section; *The Oriental*, Jan. 4, 1855. Chinese section.

17. *The Social, Moral, and Political Effect of Chinese Immigration*, p. 150. Also see Condit, pp. 95–96.

18. *The Golden Hills' News*, July 1, 1854.

19. *The Oriental*, Jan. 25, 1855.

20. Ibid., Jan. 4, 1855.

21. *The California China Mail and Flying Dragon*, Jan. 1, 1867, p. 10.

22. Unfortunately, not many issues of the early Chinese newspapers have survived. For holdings of these and other old Chinese-language newspapers published in America, see Lo and Lai.

23. *The Oriental*, Sept. 25, 1875. The original text is in English.

24. Lloyd, p. 268.

25. Recently, more and more studies of Chinese American women, who have long been rendered voiceless, have been emerging. For a summary of those studies, see Peffer, "From Under the Sojourner's Shadow," pp. 41–67. Also see J. Yung, *Unbound Feet*, and Benson Tong, *Unsubmissive Women*.

26. Sucheng Chan offers a brief discussion of white response to Chinese prostitution prior to the 1870s in her "Exclusion of Chinese Women," p. 97.

27. Cited from Barnhart, p. 47. The police also enforced laws selectively in terms of geography, forcing prostitutes to move away from certain streets, as Shumsky and Springer show in their study. See Shumsky and Springer, pp. 71–89.

28. Male-female ratio among the Chinese in the U.S. and California, 1860–1890:

	United States	*California*
1860	nearly 19:1.	nearly 19:1
1870	nearly 13:1	nearly 12:1
1880	over 21:1	over 18:1
1890	nearly 27:1	over 24:1

See Cheng, p. 404; and Daniels, *Asian America*, p. 69.

In his study of Chinese laundrymen in Chicago in the early twentieth century, Paul Siu wrote: "the Chinese community condones and excuses prostitution as natural and inevitable for the sojourners separated for long years from home and family." Siu, p. 270.

29. Those thought to be prostitutes represented a very high percentage of the

female population in Chinese San Francisco in 1860 and 1870, but that percentage declined in 1880. The following numbers pertaining to Chinese prostitution are taken from the work of two scholars and are based on their varying tabulations of the census schedules. The two sets of numbers are different, but they suggest the same trend and are based on similar assumptions about Chinese women in San Francisco.

	No. of prostitutes	*total population*	*percentages*
1860	556	654	85%
1870	1,426	2,018	71%
1880	435	2,058	21%

Source: Cheng, pp. 420 – 21.

	No. of prostitutes	*total population*	*percentages*
1860	583	681	85.6%
1870	1,456	2,499	62.6%
1880	305	1,742	17.5%

Source: Tong, *Unsubmissive Women*, p. 94.

30. Farwell, part II, p. 3.

31. *The Chinese-Western Daily*, Mar. 3, 1900. American News section.

32. Ah Quin's diary entry for Feb. 6, 1880.

33. Ibid., Jan. 25, 1880.

34. Ibid.

35. Asbury, p. 175.

36. *The Oriental*, Mar. 25, 1876. Big City News section.

37. Ibid., Dec. 18, 1875.

38. Ibid., Dec. 11, 1875.

39. In a recollection about prostitution in Canton during the late Qing Dynasty, Liu Guoxin discussed how brothel patrons established such relationships with prostitutes. See Liu Guoxin, 10: 201.

40. *The Oriental*, June 3, 1876. Big City News section.

41. Pascoe, p. 143.

42. Barnhart, p. 48.

43. Soule et al., p. 384. For the story of Ah Toy, see Asbury, pp. 172–73. In a recent study Benson Tong offers a rather detailed account of her life. See Tong, *Unsubmissive Women*, pp. 6–9, 11–12.

44. I identified 18 such women in a sample of 1,410 women in the 1870 manu-

script census. Two were in their twenties, six in their thirties, six in their forties, and four in their fifties.

45. Both parties hired white attorneys. Chin Kem You lost in the Superior Court of San Francisco and then filed an appeal in the California Supreme Court. See California Supreme Court, *Chin Kem You v Ah Joan*.

46. According to Andrew R. Griego, a family friend named Mrs. Buelah Rynerson indicated that Sue Leong had been imported to America as a slave girl. But in a letter to Andrew R. Griego, Dr. Thomas Quin Kong, a great grandson of Ah Quin, notes that Sue Leong was the daughter of a merchant. See Griego, p. 72, note. But Dr. Kong no longer holds that belief. In an interview with the author on February 23, 1996, he told me that he had learned from his aunt and grandmother that Sue Leong was bought by Ah Quin. In an article that mentioned Ah Quin's bribe, the *San Diego Union* reported (on Nov. 29, 1881) that Sue was from the Presbyterian mission home in San Francisco. If Sue was indeed a "slave girl" rescued by the missionaries, then Ah Quin did not pay for her freedom.

47. Edholm, p. 159.

48. J. Yung, *Unbound Feet*, p. 36.

49. *The Oriental*, Oct. 2, 1875. Big City News section.

50. For the story of Donaldina Cameron, see Wilson.

51. In 1871 Rev. Otis Gibson started the Women's Missionary Society of the Methodist Episcopal Church. In the same year anti-Chinese violence erupted in Los Angeles. Resulting in the murder of nineteen Chinese, the incident marked the beginning of a wave of large-scale violent acts of persecution, including mass massacres, of the Chinese that swept the American West. As S. Miller argues in his *The Unwelcome Immigrant*, p. 194, the early 1870s were also a critical time "in proselyting anti-Chinese sentiments on the East Coast."

52. The attacks on Chinese prostitution have been mentioned in numerous studies, ranging from Elmer Clarence Sandmeyer's *The Anti-Chinese Movement in California* to J. S. Moy's *Marginal Sights*.

53. Asbury, p. 167.

54. Sandmeyer, p. 34.

55. The congressional report contained testimony from 128 witnesses and included both pros and cons of Chinese immigration. In 1877 the senate committee of California prepared "An Address to the People of the United States upon the Evils of Chinese Immigration," which was published together with the committee's earlier report. At the beginning of the document the committee recognized the nation's increasing hostility toward the Chinese: "We note a marked change in the expressions of the Eastern press since the circulation of the testimony taken

by this committee." Special Committee on *Chinese Immigration: Its Social, Moral, and Political Effect* (Sacramento, 1878): 4. The testimony was taken just months before the congressional investigation.

56. *Report of the Joint Special Committee*, p. 229. In 1885 he said that he had served as a special police officer in Chinatown for a number of years.

57. Buel, p. 277.

58. Gibson, *The Chinese in America*, p. 134. His statements about the number of Chinese prostitutes are quite murky and sometimes even inconsistent, indicating his uncertainty about the subject.

59. Loomis, "Chinese Women in California," p. 344.

60. U.S. manuscript census, 1860.

61. *Enping Xianzhi*, 4: 3.

62. *Shunde Xianzhi (1853)*, 3: 45.

63. Cheng, p. 415.

64. "Official Map of Chinatown," in the San Francisco Municipal Reports for 1884–85.

65. *San Francisco Call*, July 23, 1885.

66. Discussing the 1860 census materials, Lucie Cheng said that among those women whose occupation was not listed, most were likely to be prostitutes, except for the following cases: "(a) those women living in households with a man with or without children, (b) those living in households with more than one man, and (c) girls under twelve years old." Cheng, p. 420. Benson Tong states such an assumption about women more clearly: "Single women living alone or with other females and not holding down any job in all probability provided commercialized sex." Tong, *Unsubmissive Women*, p. 94.

67. See Stockard. In an earlier article Marjorie Topley also discusses the long-standing tradition of resistance to marriage among women—especially those who belonged to women's semisecret organizations such as the Jinlan Hui (Golden orchid associations), in such emigrant districts as Shunde County in rural Guangdong. See Topley, pp. 67–88.

68. *Shunde Xianzhi (1853)*, 3: 42.

69. *Zhongshan Xianzhi*, 5: 18.

70. California Supreme Court, *Chin Kem You v Ah Joan*, p. 26.

71. *Report of the Joint Special Committee*, p. 194.

72. *The Social, Moral, and Political Effect of Chinese Immigration*, p. 73.

73. The newspaper also reported another point that the senate report failed to record: that Ah You never saw any houses of prostitution or of gambling remain in business for a long period of time. In addition, the newspaper revealed that Ah You's last name was actually Li. *The Oriental*, Apr. 22, 1876.

74. J. S. Moy, p. 36.

75. Conwell, p. 226.

76. Workingmen's Party of California, p. 24.

77. *Report of the Joint Special Committee*, p. 15.

78. Densmore, p. 22.

79. Farwell, part II, p. 21.

80. For another discussion of the subject, see Trauner, pp. 70–87.

81. U.S. Census Office, *Census Report of the Social Statistics of Cities*, p. 809.

82. *Chinatown Declared a Nuisance!*, p. 3.

83. Workingmen's Party of California, p. 12.

84. Joint Special Commission to Investigate Chinese Immigration, *Report of the Royal Commission on Chinese Immigration* (Ottawa: Printed by the order of the Commission, 1885), p. 198.

85. *The Oriental*, June 3, 1876. Big City News section.

86. Stout, p. 21.

87. *The Social, Moral, and Political Effect of Chinese Immigration*, p. 104.

88. Stout, p. 8.

89. Ibid., p. 21.

90. *Report of the Joint Special Committee*, p. 864.

91. Dr. Thomas M. Logan, permanent member of the city's board of health, asked Stout to make the document available in his 1862 pamphlet to the state legislature in 1871. The entire pamphlet except for one portion was subsequently also read before the Congressional Joint Special Committee on Chinese immigration in 1876. See *Report of the Joint Special Committee*, pp. 864–71. By 1876, although Stout still believed that the white race was superior, he had modified his views. Before the 1876 Congressional Special Joint Committee, he openly repudiated the view held by Toland and others that the Chinese were the source of various diseases. He went as far as to advocate the naturalization of the Chinese on the basis of the Fifteenth Amendment. By this time Stout had started renting his property to the Chinese and was making a 200-percent profit. But the demonstrated change in his attitude toward the Chinese does not appear to have been motivated purely by economic considerations. Ibid., pp. 652, 654, and 875.

92. Farwell, pp. 14–15.

93. Some have believed that opium was absent from the lives of the early immigrants. Citing other studies of Chinese immigration, for example, in his *Drugs and Minority Oppression* John Helmer asserted that "There is no record of its use among the first generation of immigrants in California" (p. 19). The word "record" here, however, refers only to English-language sources, where "there no mention of opium-smoking until the mid-1860s" (ibid).

94. *The Oriental*, mid-May issue, 1856. Chinese section.

95. Wells Fargo, *Directory of Principal Chinese Business Firms* (in San Francisco, Oakland, Los Angeles, Virginia City, Victoria, and Denver).

96. Usually *The Oriental* listed wholesale prices of different food items on the front page. The quoted prices are from the issue of June 10, 1876. The words "Li Yun" and "Fuk Lung" are the contemporary forms of transliteration for the two opium products.

97. Kane, p. 132.

98. Hubbard, p. 3.

99. Masters, "Opium and Its Votaries," p. 634.

100. Condit, p. 60.

101. *Report of the Joint Special Committee*, p. 133.

102. Lloyd, p. 261.

103. Masters, "Opium and Its Votaries," p. 638.

104. Brooks, *The Chinese in California*, p. 5.

105. *Report of the Joint Special Committee*, p. 60.

106. Kane, p. 137.

107. International Opium Commission, *Report of the International Opium Commission* (Shanghai, 1909), 2: 8. John Helmer has shown that the percentage figure was miscalculated and that it overstated the incidence of opium smoking among the Chinese. See Helmer, p. 27.

108. Condit, p. 61.

109. Kane, p. 135.

110. Gompers and Gutstadt, p. 19.

111. Masters, "Opium and Its Votaries," p. 641.

112. Hertslet, 1: 501.

113. In his *The American Disease*, David F. Musto notes that "Before 1800, opium was available in America," (p. 1). When Americans became increasingly aware of the opium question during the late nineteenth century, many knew of its earlier presence in America. In a book published in the 1860s an opium addict talked about how he picked up the habit during the 1830s in Brooklyn. Day, pp. 119–223.

114. Contemporary Chinese writers chronicled the development of opium use in China. The gazetteer for Nanhai reported that opium was recorded in Li Shizhen's *Benchao gangmu* (a medical classic written during the Ming Dynasty), and the number of smokers gradually began to increase in South China early in the nineteenth century. See *Nanhai Xianzhi (1836)*, 26: 5. Huang Juezi wrote in 1838 that during the early years of the Daoguang period (1821–51) opium smoking, which had earlier been confined mainly to "playboys of rich families," spread to

all groups, ranging from government officials and the gentry to merchants and servants and even including women, monks, and nuns. Huang Juezi, 1: 485. Also see Xiao Ninyu, 49: 8–11.

115. For discussions of America's involvement in the opium trade, see Stelle's two articles: "American Trade in Opium to China Prior to 1820," pp. 425–44, and "American Trade in Opium to China, 1821–1839," pp. 57–74.

116. Sala, p. 240.

117. Ibid., 2: 250–51.

118. Ibid., p. 250.

119. McDowell, *The Chinese Theater*, p. 31.

120. On Sept. 24, 1879, for instance, he wrote in his diary that some performers from China had recently played at the Wing Tin Pung Theatre.

121. *The Oriental*, Sept. 25, 1875. Advertisement section.

122. Langley, p. 1004.

123. The federal manuscript census.

124. Fitch, p. 189.

125. Lloyd, p. 265.

126. Sala, 2: 240 and 247. Years later, in 1903, another visitor to a Chinese theater also noticed its simplicity. See Green, pp. 118–25.

127. Brecht experienced and was influenced by the Chinese immigrant theater when he was in the United States during the 1940s. James K. Lyon writes of him: "With Karl August Wittfogel and Heinz Langerhans, this playwright who openly acknowledged his debt to Chinese theatre went to performances of the Cantonese Players in New York's Chinatown." Lyon, p 108.

128. Hardy, p. 165.

129. Carey, p. 199.

130. Green, p. 118.

131. Farquhar, p. 366.

132. Conwell, p. 267.

133. Ibid., p. 265.

134. There are numerous Chinese-language studies of the development of Cantonese opera. For a fairly thorough discussion of the subject, see Lai Bojiang and Huang Jingming.

135. Green, p. 118.

136. Ah Quin's diary entry for Nov. 19, 1879.

137. Sala, 2: 245.

138. Fitch, p. 190. For another discussion of the large audiences in the Chinese theater, see Arthur Inkersley, "The Chinese Drama in California," *The Strand Magazine* 15, p. 406.

139. Brace, p. 225.
140. McDowell, "The Chinese Theater," p. 28.
141. Lloyd, p. 265.
142. Sala, 2: 245.
143. McDowell, "The Chinese Theater," p. 34.

CHAPTER 4: "CHINA IN AMERICA"

1. Some, like Ah Quin's grandson, Joseph, have stated that Ah Quin first came to the United States in 1868. See Sharon Whitley's "Ah Quin—Father of San Diego's Chinatown," *San Diego Union*, Oct. 23, 1986. After researching his family history for years, Dr. Thomas Quin Kong, Ah Quin's great grandson, told me in a 1996 interview that his great grandfather came to the United States in 1863. Ah Quin's initial arrival clearly did not take place in 1868, because he made a trip to China in 1867. He might have returned to the United States in 1868. Helen Kong, the only daughter of Ah Quin's second son (Thomas), indicated in a letter of Jan. 19, 1977, to her niece Cynthia Soo that Ah Quin was fifteen years old when he came to the United States. Helen knew a great deal about Ah Quin and helped preserve many of his private documents, including his diaries. Her letter appears to suggest that Ah Quin first landed in America in 1863—in the old days, the Chinese were one year old upon the moment of birth and would become one year older at every Chinese lunar New Year, adding one or two years to what we would today consider their actual age. According to a brief note about family members that Ah Quin wrote himself sometime in the nineteen hundreds, he was born in 1850—not 1848 as others have assumed. All this demonstrates that 1863 was indeed the year of his arrival.

In addition, in his "Mayor of Chinatown" Andrew Griego states that Ah Quin was from Xinning County (p. 9). Information from my interviews with Ah Quin's descendants suggests, however, that Kaiping was his native county. One of Ah Quin's grandchildren who had gone back to Ah Quin's village can no longer pinpoint its location but remembers the word *hoiping*; this is how Kaiping is pronounced in the Siyi dialect. Another grandchild of Ah Quin also recalled that "Uncle Frank" (one of Ah Quin's children) used to tell him that "grandpa came from 'hoiping-chiangsha' "; Changsha is another name often attached to Kaiping. This is also confirmed by written records. On a large brown envelope among the documents collected by a great grandchild of Ah Quin there are a few Chinese words, indicating what used to be inside: "Kaiping, Midong, Tangmei, the genealogy of the Tan family." "Tan" (pronounced "Hom" or "Tom" in Cantonese dialects) is Ah Quin's original family name. Also on the envelope were three English words explaining that the first three Chinese words are the names of the "county, commune, village," respectively. In fact, in the Chinese parts of Ah Quin's diary, the word "Midong" appears quite often. The inscription on Ah Quin's tomb also states that he was from Kaiping County. It identifies Ah Quin's birthday as Dec. 5, 1848. More than once in his diary, however, Ah Quin stated that December 8 was his birthday.

2. This is what a grandchild of Ah Quin's told me during an interview conducted on Aug. 22, 1998.

3. Andrew Griego's "Mayor of Chinatown," a fine M. A. thesis, represents an attempt to produce such a biography. But Griego used only the English-language sections of Ah Quin's diaries. The thesis also contains a number of erroneous assumptions, as we will see. Besides the diaries and other documents at the San Diego Historical Society, I have used numerous additional written records from the private collections of Ah Quin's descendants, including a newly surfaced diary. I have also interviewed more than seven such third- and fourth-generation descendants.

4. Soule et al., p. 381.

5. Sala, 2: 220, and Mary Davison, "The Babies in Chinatown," *Cosmopolitan* 28, no. 6 (Oct. 1900): 606. For a discussion of similar notions, also see Carey, p. 136; Condit, p. 37; and McDowell, "A New Light on the Chinese," p. 3.

6. B. F. Taylor, p. 107.

7. Hardy, p. 154. Also see Buel, p. 276.

8. W. Doxey, p. 116.

9. *The Chinese-Western Daily*, Jan. 16, 1903. Advertisement section.

10. Stoddard, p. 2.

11. Ah Quin's diary entry for Nov. 30, 1877.

12. Ibid. The brother later came to America and died in Santa Barbara. Helen Kong, letter to Cynthia Soo, Jan. 19, 1977.

13. Ah Quin's diary entry for Dec. 7, 1877.

14. Ibid., Dec. 10, 1877.

15. Ibid., Jan. 29, 1878.

16. Ibid., Dec. 8, 1877.

17. List of correspondence, 1878–80.

18. Ibid.

19. Ibid.

20. Cui Guoyin, 1: 34.

21. W. Taylor, p. 260.

22. *A. W. Morgan & Co.'s San Francisco City Directory*, p. 72.

23. Warner, p. 63.

24. *The Oriental*, Apr. 13, 1898. Advertisement section.

25. *The Chinese-Western Daily*, Nov. 4, 1901. Advertisement section.

26. Ibid., June 16, 1903.

27. For these and other stories, see *Xinning Xianzhi*, vol. 21.

28. Hu Zhaozhong, pp. 67–68.

29. This is based on photos of Ah Quin and the rest of his family taken at different times, and on physical descriptions of George and Thomas taken from their passports and recorded by Ah Quin in one diary.

30. Sharon Whitley, "Ah Quin—Father of San Diego's Chinatown," *San Diego Union*, Oct. 23, 1986. The article is based on an interview with Joseph Quin, son of George Quin.

31. The figures are based on the records of San Francisco Customs House, which are cited by Coolidge in her 1909 study. For more statistics about Chinese reverse emigration, see Coolidge, pp. 498–500, appendix.

32. Brettel, p. 263.

33. *The Oriental*, June 24, 1854. Chinese section.

34. *The Chinese-Western Daily*, Apr. 1, 1907.

35. Condit, p. 35.

36. *The Chinese-Western Daily*, July 4, 1904. Advertisement section.

37. Liang Qichao, p. 388.

38. Loomis, "Chinese 'Funeral Baked Meats,' " p. 29.

39. In most cases, the bodies were buried in America first before being exhumed for transportation to China.

40. Huggins, part I, p. 43.

41. Loomis, "Chinese 'Funeral Baked Meats,' " p. 29.

42. Zhang Yinhuan, 2: 18.

43. The document is included in Ow et al., p. 252.

44. Ah Quin's diary entry for Dec. 10, 1877.

45. A comparison of the Chinese and English handwriting in the diary and the glossary confirms that the latter is indeed Ah Quin's work. The glossary also includes many technical terms that are apparently relevant to the book on assaying that he translated.

46. Certain Chinese herbal doctors in the immigrant communities compiled medical recipes, some of which have survived the passage of time. For a discussion of such recipes, see Buell and Muench, pp. 100–105.

47. Culin, *Chinese Drug Stores in America*, p. 1.

48. Loomis, "Medical Art in the Chinese Quarter," p. 506.

49. Ibid., p. 503.

50. *The Social, Moral, and Political Effect of Chinese Immigration*, pp. 95 and 97.

51. Gibson, *The Chinese in America*, p. 364.

52. See Trauner, p. 82.

53. Culin, *Chinese Drug Stores in America*, p. 4.

54. Loomis, "Medical Art in the Chinese Quarter," p. 496.

55. Federal manuscript census for 1870.

56. Tisdale, p. 412.

57. Ah Quin's diary entry for Nov. 26, 1891.

58. Ibid., 1892.

59. That system, first instituted in 587 during the Sui Dynasty (581–618), was abolished by the Qing government in 1905.

60. Hoy, *The Chinese Six Companies*, p. 11.

61. *The Social, Moral, and Political Effect of Chinese Immigration*, pp. 63, 70, 94, 95, 97, and 98.

62. Ibid., p. 63.

63. Liu Pei Chi, *Meiguo Huaqiao Shi*, p. 174. Also see *The Oriental*, Apr. 27, 1888. Big City News section.

64. *Jinshi, juren*, and *xiucai* were scholarly titles that those aspiring to be scholar-statesmen hoped to receive by participating in civil examinations at national, provincial, and prefectural levels, respectively.

65. Liang Qichao, p. 389.

66. Ibid., 10: 384.

67. Island Avenue and J Street and Third and Fourth Avenues were the boundaries of the now-vanished Chinatown in San Diego. Around the time when Ah Quin arrived there were less than two hundred Chinese in the city. Its Chinese population remained fairly small in comparison with those of major Chinese American communities elsewhere.

68. To a certain degree, the Japanese government had a similar influence on Japanese immigrants in America, especially the Issei or the first-generation Japanese. For instance, one of the most important Japanese social organizations, the Japanese Association, was a semiofficial agency of the Japanese government. See Ichioka, "Japanese Associations," pp. 409–38. For a discussion of the Issei, see Ichioka, *The Issei*.

69. The delegation toured America and Europe. England openly expressed its unhappiness and doubt about Burlingame's objectivity. The mission also included two Europeans.

70. Zhang Deyi, p. 54. Zhang was a member of the delegation, and *Hanghai Shuqi* is the diary he kept during the trip.

71. A native Cantonese, this Washington-based official was then in charge of the Qing Court's program to educate Chinese youth in America. Between 1872 and

1875, 120 students came to America under this program. Some of them later became diplomats. Liang Cheng, Chinese minister to America (1903–7), and Ouyang Geng, Chinese consul in San Francisco (1884–1908), were among these students.

72. *The Oriental*, Apr. 29, 1876. Big City News section.

73. Ibid., Sept. 8, 1875.

74. Zhang Yinhuan's diary entry for Aug. 15, 1886, in Zhang Yinhuan, 1: 75.

75. Numerous studies focus on Chinese ministers to the United States. See for example K. M. Chan.

76. The death toll is from Storti, p. 142.

77. In fact, the policy caught Chinese San Franciscans by surprise, as Zhang Yinhuan reported in 1888. See Zhang Yinhuan, 5: 68.

78. *The Chinese-Western Daily*, Feb. 17, 1900. American News section. As Chinese Minister to the United States in 1897–1902 and 1908–9, Wu was the best known and most respected, among Chinese as well as Americans, of all seven ministers. A British-educated gentleman, he also wrote a number of articles in American journals in defense of Chinese immigrants.

79. Zhang Yinhuan's diary entry for Apr. 7, 1886, in Zhang Yinhuan, 1: 10.

80. In 1889 a scandal occurred involving the Chinese consul general, who reportedly stole the indemnity the U.S. government paid to the victims of the Rock Springs Massacre. In conjunction with this incident, according to an article published in the *San Francisco Chronicle* on Aug. 26, 1889, Bee had "a terrible war of words in the consulate building on Powell Street." After that, the *Chronicle* reported, "Colonel Bee has not spent much of his time in the Chinese Consulate." Nevertheless, he continued to work for the consulate for some time, as is suggested by a letter written on consulate stationary that Bee sent to a judge on behalf of a Chinese merchant. Bee was not the only American appointed as consul by the Chinese government. Years later, at the beginning of the twentieth century, Stephen W. Nickerson served as consul at the Chinese consulate in Boston.

81. *The Oriental*, Apr. 27, 1888. Big City News section.

82. Chinese diplomats also began the effort to build such a hospital for the Chinese in New York City. On May 30, 1886, Chinese minister Zhang Yinhuan learned from huiguan officials that Chinese San Franciscans needed a hospital; they were reluctant to go to "Westerners' hospital" because it would force them to change their way of dressing. He immediately donated one hundred dollars to start a hospital fund. Zhang Yinhuan's diary, in Zhang Yinhuan, 1: 33.

83. Manuscript federal census for 1870.

84. *The Oriental*, Apr. 27, 1888. Big City News section.

85. See *The Chinese Hospital of San Francisco* (Oakland, 1899). Over ten whites pledged to make an annual subscription of five dollars. The Chinese hospital was

basically supported by the Chinese community. Individuals continued to donate, and the fee collected from departing Chinese passengers remained a constant source of considerable revenue.

86. *The Chinese-Western Daily*, June 30, 1905. American News section.

87. Ibid., Feb. 15, 1902.

88. Ah Quin's diary entry for June 1, 1878. An earlier photo, taken in 1873 when he was in Santa Barbara, shows Ah Quin wearing Chinese-style clothes and the queue.

89. *San Diego Union*, Dec. 14, 1881.

90. Cited from MacPhail, *Shady Ladies*, p. 14.

91. *Panyu Xianzhi*, 6: 15.

92. Ah Quin's diary entry for Sept. 4, 1879.

93. Ibid., Dec. 28–31, 1884.

94. Ibid., Aug. 15, 1891.

95. *The Oriental*, Sept. 18, 1875. Schedules of inland river ships. Advertisement section.

96. Nora, p. 19.

97. American historians have acknowledged in other contexts that people's conception of time constitutes an integral part of their culture. See for example Hareven.

98. *The Oriental*, Sept. 18, 1875. Big City News section.

99. Loomis, "Holiday in the Chinese Quarter," p. 152.

100. McDowell, "A New Light on the Chinese," p. 14.

101. *The Chinese-Western Daily*, July 5, 1900. Advertisement section.

102. Loomis, "Chinese in California, Their Sign-Boards," p. 154.

103. Loomis, "Chinese Occult Science in the Chinese Quarter," p. 162.

104. Culin, *Gambling Games*, p. 15.

105. *The Chinese-Western Daily*, Jan. 16, 1903. Advertisement section.

106. Ibid., Aug. 2, 1905.

107. Ibid., Mar. 2, 1900.

108. All the evidence cited in this section is from Ah Quin's 1892 diary. I am grateful to Dr. Thomas Quin Kong for allowing me to use this diary, which was recently discovered by a relative of Ah Quin.

109. Griego's assertion that Ah Quin's "diaries are remarkably free of mention of race prejudice" is rather problematic. Although not always in explicit language, Ah Quin showed a keen awareness of racial discrimination throughout the journal. Griego, p. 56.

110. Andrew Griego has incorrectly assumed that Ah Quin did not spend much time with his wife. Ibid., p. 73. Regarding Sue's age, one of her children

(we do not know which one) wrote a few lines in English in a document of Ah Quin's after his death that "Mamma" was "born in 1861."

CHAPTER 5: COLLECTIVE IDENTITY

1. S. Andrews, "Wo Lee and his Kinsfolk," *Atlantic Monthly* 25, (Feb. 1870): 224.

2. Helper, p. 91. In Charles Nordhoff's *California, for Health, Pleasure and Residence* the chapter on the Chinese in California is titled "John."

3. See Sarna, pp. 370–78; Nelli.

4. Handlin, *The Uprooted*, p. 186.

5. Vecoli, "Contadini in Chicago," p. 413.

6. Few white Americans were interested in making Chinese immigrants, who did not even have the right to become citizens, "Americans." We need to note that the persistence of cultural distinctiveness was not uniquely Chinese. Even some second-generation European ethnic groups displayed resistance to assimilation. In his study of the native-born Italians in Boston's West End, for example, Herbert J. Gans notes that assimilation, in terms of "the disappearance of the Italian social system," proceeded slowly. See Gans, p. 35.

7. Similar parochialism existed in other contexts as well. According to Theodore Saloutos, for instance, the Greeks formed many societies that "reflected the localism and provincialism of a naturally provincial people." Saloutos stated: "These traits were transplanted to the United States." Saloutos, p. 75.

8. "The Chinese Dead," *The Oriental*, July, 1855. English section.

9. Loomis, "Chinese 'Funeral Baked Meats,' " p. 29.

10. Lloyd, p. 367.

11. The regulations were included in Xian Ruiqi's 1914 report of the three charity houses' effort to renovate a Chinese cemetery. Ow et al., p. 164.

12. Liang Qichao, p. 394.

13. All Ah Quin's children had a non-Chinese first name. Contrary to Andrew Griego's claim, however, all Ah Quin's children also had a Chinese name. Griego, p. 87.

14. The Yellow Dragon Flag was first adopted as China's official national flag by the Burlingame delegation in 1868. A dragon was drawn in the middle of this yellow flag, which was rimmed with blue laces. See Zhi Gang, p. 39; Zhang Deyi, p. 89. Many people noticed the flag when visiting Chinatown. See for instance Chen Lanbin, diary entry for Aug. 14, 1879, book 44, p. 59.

15. Some have even asserted that China's national identity did not develop until the turn of the twentieth century. See for example Levenson, *Modern China*.

16. Ng-Quinn, pp. 32–61.

17. Duara, pp. 1–26.

18. "The Chinese Dead," *The Oriental*, July 1855, English section.

19. See the genealogy of the Lu Family (in Chinese) (1835).

20. Ah Quin's diary entry for Feb. 26, 1880.

21. Such notions appeared in a number of statements addressed to the American public and officials, including the president of the United States, members of Congress, and San Francisco city officials.

22. *Memorial of the Six Chinese Companies*, p. 2.

23. *New York Times*, Oct. 2, 1888; 1: 7.

24. Condit, p. 169.

25. Presbyterian Home Mission, p. 58.

26. Speer, *The Oldest and the Newest Empire*, p. 471.

27. Benjamin La Fevre, *Biographies of S. Grover Cleveland, and Thomas A. Hendricks, with a Description of the Leading Issues and the Proceedings of the National Convention Together with a History of the Political Parties of the United States: Comparisons of Platforms on All Important Questions, and Political Tables for Ready Reference* (New York: Baird & Dillon, 1884): 284.

28. Besides publicly speaking on behalf of the Chinese, the Rev. William Speer helped the Chinese in various other ways, making visits to newcomers and to those in the mines. He also opened a dispensary for the Chinese. The quote is from his *The Oldest and the Newest Empire*, p. 605. Bret Harte's poem, also known as "Plain Language from Truthful James," appeared in the *Overland Monthly* 5 (Sept. 1870): 287–88. This poem, Ronald T. Takaki writes, "helped to crystallize and focus anti-Chinese anxieties and paranoia." Takaki, *Iron Cages*, p. 223. For further discussions of Bret Harte, see Keim, pp. 441–50. A musician named Charles Towner set Harte's poems to music, and a collection of folk songs published in New York was titled "The Heathen Chinee Songster." See Towner; and *The Heathen Chinee Songster*.

29. Okihiro, *Cane Fires*, p. 130. The word "nisei" refers to second-generation Japanese Americans.

30. Speer, *An Humble Plea*, p. 4.

31. Gibson, *The Chinese in America*, p. 124.

32. Woo, "Chinese Protestants," S. Chan, *Entry Denied*, p. 214.

33. Other veteran China missionaries included the Rev. Ira Condit, who in 1870 left the church in Girard, Pennsylvania, to join the Presbyterian mission in San Francisco and, after Loomis's death in 1892, came to be in charge of the mission; the Rev. A. W. Loomis, who took over Speer's position in 1859 and worked at the mission for 32 years; the Methodist minister Rev. Otis Gibson; the Rev. J. L. Shuck,

a Baptist minister, who established a mission in Sacramento in 1854; E. Z. Simmon, who replaced the Rev. John Francis in 1875 as a Baptist missionary to the Chinese; Frederick J. Masters, who later, after Gibson's death, headed the Methodist mission in San Francisco; W. S. Holt of the Presbyterian mission in Portland; and J. C. Nevin, a Los Angeles missionary.

34. Pond, p. 128.

35. Other people's assessments of Christian missionary work were often contradictory and inaccurate. While opponents of Chinese immigration often attempted to show, in order to justify their prejudice, that the "cause of Christianity" was not advanced, others exaggerated the achievement of the missions. In a pamphlet entitled "the Chinese Problem," the Rev. L. T. Townsend of the Boston Theological School stated that the Presbyterian Mission school of San Francisco had as many as eight hundred students. The missionary Gibson pointed out that Townsend's statement was "considerably stronger than the facts will warrant." According to Gibson, "instead of eight hundred Chinese students in the school at any one session, the Mission House can not accommodate more than one hundred and fifty or two hundred scholars at any one time." Gibson pointed out that Townsend had never "*visited any of the Chinese* Missions in California," nor had he "made the acquaintance of a single missionary to the Chinese in this country" (emphasis in original). See Gibson, *The Chinese in America*, pp. 179 and 182.

36. Presbyterian Home Mission, p. 74.

37. *Report of the Joint Special Committee*, p. 325.

38. Condit, p. 115.

39. *Report of the Joint Special Committee*, pp. 1172 and 1173.

40. Ibid., pp. 414, 453, and 1173.

41. Masters, "Can a Chinaman Become a Christian?" p. 625.

42. According to U.S. census the Chinese population in California was 49,277 in 1870, and in 1900 there were 45,753 Chinese in California and 67,729 in eleven western states. Earlier I show that the census figures underestimate the size of the Chinese population. Even based on these figures it is safe to say that Christians represented less than 1 percent of that population by the 1870s and never exceeded 2 percent throughout the second half of the nineteenth century. Being Christian not only meant gaining access to the white American world and sometimes to greater economic opportunities; it also entailed certain privileges. Christians were the only Chinese who did not have to pay the passenger fees before voyaging back to China.

43. Presbyterian Home Mission, p. 59.

44. Gibson, *The Chinese in America*, p. 193.

45. S. Andrews, "The Gods of Wo Lee," *Atlantic Monthly*, 25 (Apr. 1870): 477.

46. *The Penn Monthly*, 3 (1871): 181–88.

47. Andrews, "The Gods of Wo Lee," *Atlantic Monthly*, 25, no. 150 (Apr. 1870): 477.

48. Gibson, *The Chinese in America*, pp. 183, 185, and 190.

49. Presbyterian Home Mission, p. 46.

50. *Report of the Joint Special Committee*, pp. 1178–1179.

51. Poole, p. 12.

52. Gibson, *The Chinese in America*, p. 192.

53. *The Penn Monthly*, Apr. 1871, pp. 186–88.

54. Condit, p. 36.

55. Masters, "Can a Chinaman Become a Christian?" p. 625.

56. Gibson, *The Chinese in America*, p. 158.

57. American Baptist Home Mission Society, p. 28.

58. Philip Schaff, "Progress of Christianity in the United States of America," *The Princeton Review* (Sept. 1879): 251.

59. Masters, "Can a Chinaman Become a Christian?" p. 623.

60. For more information about Chinese religious practices, see Armentrout Ma, "Chinese Traditional Religion," pp. 131–47.

61. Gibson, *The Chinese in America*, pp. 169–70.

62. Bamford, *Angel Island*, p. 47.

63. Shearer, p. 285. It is necessary to note that temples, especially the ones in smaller communities, assumed various social responsibilities as well. See for example the discussion of a temple in Marysville in Eberhard, pp. 362–71.

64. B. F. Taylor, p. 112.

65. The "official map of Chinatown" identified thirteen joss houses in Chinatown. But two of the structures so identified were not actually joss houses; one was the location of a famous secret society. The map is included in the San Francisco Municipal Reports for 1884–85.

66. Rae, p. 296.

67. Shearer, p. 287; Rev. A. W. Loomis, "Our Heathen Temples," p. 454.

68. Carey, p. 217.

69. Shearer, p. 287.

70. Stewart Culin recorded in detail how a Chinese laundryman in Philadelphia asked Guan Gong for good fortune in "Divination and Fortune-Telling," p. 166.

71. Zhang Deyi, p. 53.

72. Liang Qichao, p. 388.

73. Ow et al., p. 260. The Yellow Emperor (Huang Di) was the legendary ancestor of the Chinese.

74. Masters, "Can a Chinaman become a Christian?" pp. 733–34.

75. Catherine Baldwin, "The Sixth Year of Qwong See," *Harper's New Magazine* 62, no. 367 (Dec. 1880): 72.

76. *The Oriental*, Feb. 15, 1855. English section.

77. Ibid., Feb. 5, 1876, Big City News section.

78. Shearer, p. 279.

79. Boorstin, p. 92.

80. Zhang Deyi, p. 51.

81. Wang Yongling, number 11 of the diaries on the way back to China in *Xianfenghuzha: Yudichungchau*, book 42.

82. Chen Lanbin, diary entry for Aug. 14, 1879, book 44, p. 59.

83. Zhang Yinhuan, 1: 74.

84. M. von Brandt, *Chinese Pigtails and What Hangs Thereby* (New York: Tucker, 1900): 4.

85. *Report of the Joint Special Committee*, p. 640.

86. Gibson, *The Chinese in America*, p. 77.

87. Ibid., p. 76. See also Charles Wolcott Brooks's testimony of 1876 in *Report of the Joint Special Committee*, pp. 950–51.

88. *The Social, Moral, and Political Effect of Chinese Immigration*, p. 98.

89. Masters, "Can a Chinaman Become a Christian?" p. 625.

90. Loomis noted that even the Chinese manner of walking was "apt to provoke in many persons a scornful smile." Loomis, "The Oldest East in the New West," p. 363.

91. *Report of the Joint Special Committee*, p. 461. After graduating from Yale in 1854, Yung Wing became a Chinese diplomat in Washington from 1875 to 1881. According to Roger Daniels, Yung became a U.S. citizen in 1852, but in 1898 his citizenship was nullified. See Daniels, *Asian America*, p. 27.

92. *The Invalidity of the "Queue Ordinance" of the City and County of San Francisco: Opinion of the Circuit Court of the United States for the District of California in Ho Ah Kow v. Mathew Nunan, Delivered July 7th, 1879* (San Francisco, 1879): 3. In this case, which declared the Queue Ordinance invalid, the plaintiff was originally arrested and convicted in the same year for breaking another ordinance of San Francisco, the Cubic Air ordinance, which required that there be at least 500 cubic feet of space for each person who slept in a room.

93. *The Oriental*, June 10, 1876. Big City News section.

94. Ibid.

95. Loomis, "The Oldest East in the New West," p. 362.

96. Zhang Deyi, pp. 66–67.

97. Chen Lanbin, diary entry for Aug. 14, 1879, book 44, p. 60.

98. *The Oriental*, Feb. 19, 1876. Special announcement.

99. Gibson, *The Chinese in America*, p. 86.

100. Ibid.

101. Ibid.

102. Liang Qichao, pp. 378–79.

INTRODUCTION TO PART II

1. Chinese immigrants used the courts of law in their struggle against discrimination. After the deaths of Judge Ogden Hoffman of the U.S. District Court and Judge Lorenzo Sawyer of the U.S. Circuit Court in 1891, the Chinese lost two important, albeit somewhat reluctant, allies. Out of commitment to due process rather than because of any affection for the Chinese, these judges had heard many habeas corpus cases in California and often ruled in favor of Chinese petitioners. A detailed account of the judges is included in Christian G. Fritz's "Due Process, Treaty Rights, and Chinese Exclusion, 1882–1891," pp. 25–56. In 1894 a congressional act prohibited judicial review of Chinese immigration cases. By 1903 the enforcement of Chinese exclusion had been transferred entirely from the collectors of customs to the U.S. Bureau of Immigration—another major victory for the anti-Chinese forces. The bureau was headed by Terence V. Powderly until 1902, when he was succeeded by Frank P. Sargent. Both men had strong ties to the anti-Chinese labor movement—the former was the most prominent leader of the Knights of Labor and the latter was an associate of Samuel Gompers. In early May 1905 the Supreme Court ruled in the case of Ju Toy that the secretary of commerce and labor had the highest authority over Chinese immigration cases. Later, in October 1909, the government opened Angel Island as the station for arriving Chinese in an attempt to isolate them from the community. In October 1910 the commissioner of immigration on the island, H. H. North, was suspended when he was accused by anti-Asian forces of letting in too many Chinese and other Asians.

2. Phelan, p. 663. Ho Yow was Chinese consul general, and his article, "Chinese Exclusion" appeared in the *North American Review*.

3. Coolidge, pp. 252–53.

4. During the years before 1899, while most incoming immigrants were recorded by their country of birth, the Chinese were reported as a racial group.

5. U.S. Immigration Commission, p. 20.

6. Howard Schuman and Jacqueline Scott have shown the significance of

major historical events in defining the consciousness of a generation in their "Generations and Collective Memories," pp. 359–81.

7. *New York Times*, July 26, 1906, 6: 4.

CHAPTER 6: A TIME OF ANGER AND A TIME OF HOPE

1. There are a number of studies of the boycott that focus mainly on its significance for modern Chinese history, especially for modern Sino-American relations. In this study I have attempted to understand its significance for Chinese America. See Tsai, "Reaction to Exclusion"; Field; and Remer, *A Study of Chinese Boycotts*, which has one section on the 1905 boycott. See also Zhang Cunwu.

2. For further discussion of the renewal issue, see Paulsen, "The Abrogation of the Gresham-Yang Treaty," pp. 457–77.

3. As Daniel Bell has argued, "the question of what one is, is not only a matter of one's own choice, but the label of others as well." (Bell, "Ethnicity and Social Change," p. 159.) Nor was it determined solely in the U.S. context insofar as Chinese Americans were concerned. Equally important was their relation, both real and perceived, with the people of China.

4. The far-reaching movement was also echoed in Chinese communities in the Philippines, Panama, Canada, Singapore, Thailand, Australia, Vietnam, and Japan.

5. Ding You, p. 27.

6. The movement produced a vast literature. Some of the writings are included in A Ying's seven-hundred-page *Fanmeihuagongjinyue Wenji*.

7. Written by Wu Jianren, *Kushehui* came out at the height of the movement and has been called "the most profound and moving" account of Chinese Americans' suffering. A Ying, p. 11.

8. He Zuo, p. 82.

9. Another leader of the Reformist Movement, Kang Youwei, then in America, was also involved in the boycott. See Delber L. McKee, "The Chinese Boycott of 1905–1906 Reconsidered," pp. 178–80.

10. *Minbao* (People's newspaper), no. 1, p. 112.

11. These officials included Zhang Renfu, the interior minister of Shanxi Province, and Wu Tingfang, former Chinese minister in Washington and then deputy secretary of the Foreign Affairs Ministry, who was widely believed in America to be "the personality behind the boycott" (Remer, p. 31).

12. W. A. P. Martin, "The Awakening of China," p. 7127. Martin went to China in 1850 as a missionary and was later involved in education in China. He worked at the Tung Wen College and then became president of the Imperial

University until the turn of the century. In 1902 he became president of the University of Wuchang in Hubei Province.

13. Lo Hsiang-lin, *Liang Cheng*, p. 189.

14. Ibid., p. 248. Also see pp. 14–15.

15. Ibid., p. 259.

16. Zhang, *The Tidal Wave*, p. 30.

17. *New York Times*, May 19, 1905, 5: 1.

18. Ding You, p. 18.

19. *New York Times*, June 29, 1905, 4: 2.

20. Zhu Shijia, p. 152.

21. Zhang, *The Tidal Wave*, p. 220. In his "Reaction to Exclusion" (p. 97) Shih-shan H. Tsai states that Feng had been a victim of the 1902 Boston raid.

22. John W. Foster, "The Chinese Boycott," *Atlantic Monthly* 97, no. 1 (Jan. 1906): 118–127.

23. *New York Times*, Apr. 25, 1905, 8: 1.

24. The diplomat's name was spelled by contemporary Americans as Tom Kim Yung and is incorrectly construed as Yung Tom-kim by Shih-shan H. Tsai. See his "Reaction to Exclusion," p. 97.

25. Lo Hsiang-lin, *Liang Cheng*, p. 248.

26. Lowenstein, p. 127.

27. Zhu Shoupeng, p. 4977.

28. These regulations were included in Rule 44 of the 61 rules governing the entry of Chinese into the United States that were approved in July 1903. Under the new rules every exhibitor had to submit three photographs along with a bond of five hundred dollars and go through a physical examination upon entry. Each had to go directly to the exposition site after landing and return to China within 30 days after the event. During the fair anyone wishing to leave the fairgrounds had to obtain a dated card from American officials and to return within 48 hours.

29. Wong Kai Kah, "A Menace to America's Oriental Trade," *North American Review* 178, no. 568 (Mar. 1904): 414–424. Wong's article was mentioned in a number of places. See U.S. Congress, House, *Facts Concerning the Enforcement of the Chinese-Exclusion Laws*, pp. 47, 130, 147; C. F. Holder, "The Dragon in America," *Arena* 32, no. 177 (Aug. 1904): 113; *Journal of the American Asiatic Association* 5, no. 6 (July 1905): 180.

30. Liang Qichao, p. 456.

31. Field, p. 64. Some have emphasized the incident relating to the Louisiana Purchase Exposition, in particular. Of the origin of the 1905 movement, C. F. Remer wrote: "Irritation over the exclusion policy arose chiefly because of the harsh enforcement of the various regulations and acts by the Treasury Depart-

ment, in whose hands their enforcement was placed. One of the most flagrant cases of abuse was that in connection with the Louisiana Purchase Exposition at St. Louis in 1904." Remer, p. 30.

32. O. O. Howard, "Our Suicidal Chinese Policy," *The Independent* 59 no. 2783 (Apr. 10, 1902): 858.

33. G. Reid, "Chinese Views of Chinese Exclusion," *Forum* (June 1893): 407 and 415.

34. Some argued, incorrectly, that the boycott was launched in order to restore the concession on the Canton-Hankou railroad from the United States. See "America's Humiliation in 1905. How Roosevelt Won the Boycott but Lost a Railroad," *The Far Eastern Review* 28, no. 6 (June 1932): 257.

35. An article in the influential *Dong Fang Journal* stated: "At the end of the Russo-Japanese War, a war fought on Chinese soil and an obvious threat to China's territorial integrity, the United States . . . declared the policy of protecting China's territorial integrity, for which everyone in our country is grateful." *The Dong Fang Journal* 2, no. 3, pp. 68–71.

36. *The Chinese-Western Daily*, Mar. 3, 1900. Another report of America's stand on the issue of China's territorial integrity appeared in *The Chinese-Western Daily*, May 28, 1901. The issue was not directly mentioned in John Hay's first Open Door notes of September 1899. Only in the second notes of July 1900 did the United States explicitly express its position on that issue.

37. Wong Kai Kah, "A Menace to America's Oriental Trade," *North American Review* 178, no. 568 (Mar. 1904): 414.

38. Leong Kai Cheu, "The Awakening of China," *The Independent* 55 (May 28, 1903): 1268.

39. *The Chinese-Western Daily*, June 5, 1905. American News section.

40. Thomas F. Millard, "The New China," *Scribner's Magazine* 71, no. 4 (Feb. 1906): 244.

41. *Outlook* 80 (Aug. 26, 1905): 992.

42. Historians such as Zhang Cunwu and Shi-shan H. Tsai have pointed out the connection between the 1905 movement and Chinese nationalism.

43. Americans too took note of the new developments in the nationalist movement. Robert K. Douglas wrote in 1900: "Not only are they [the Chinese people] publishing on their own account translations of foreign works which they deem likely to be useful, but they are multiplying native newspapers at such a rate that if there existed a Chinese Imperial Library that establishment would before long be reduced to the present overcrowded condition of the British Museum. In 1895 only nineteen native newspapers enlightened the dark minds of the people. In 1898 this number was quadrupled." See Robert K. Douglas, "The Intellectual

Awakening of China," *The Nineteenth Century* (June 1900): 991. Among the influential news journals that appeared shortly before 1905 were the *Xing Ming Chong Bao* or the *New People's Journal* (Feb. 1902), the *Da Gong Newspaper* in Tianjin (June 1902), the *Dong Fang Journal* (*The Oriental Review*)(Mar. 1904) and the *Shi Bao* (*Eastern Times*) both in Shanghai (June 1904).

44. Zou Rong, *Geminjun* (The revolutionary army) (Beijing, 1958): 1 and 21. Published in Shanghai in May 1903, when Zou was under 20, it was an extremely popular political treatise. The book, which was printed in many places, including San Francisco, and which sold more than one million copies, called for the establishment of a republican government and proposed to kill all the Manchu. After its publication Zou refused to escape and was arrested. He died in prison a year later.

45. Pusey, p. 193.

46. Zou Rong, *Geminjun*, p. 2.

47. Ge Gongzheng, p. 150.

48. Ibid.

49. As a marked feature of this trend, the hope of "strengthening China" rose to the top of the nation's political and social agenda. Beginning in 1901 the Qing government itself adopted a series of policies under a modernization program called *xingzheng* (new government). It abolished the ancient civil examination system in favor of a Western-style education. In 1906 it assumed control of China's Maritime Customs Service, which had long been in the hands of the Briton Robert Hart. In the minds of those who desired to change the country more radically and more quickly, however, the Qing Court did not go far enough. Reflecting such a mentality, the word "new" became a most fashionable adjective in the political language of the day. Phrases like "new nation," "new army," "new learning," and "new youth" became idiomatic expressions. The eagerness for fast and radical renewal would be continuously pushed to higher levels until late in the twentieth century by groups who wanted more radical changes.

50. See A Ying, p. 656.

51. Ding You, p. 23.

52. A Ying, p. 230.

53. Ling Guan Hong, "To the 200,000,000 Fellow Sisters," in A Ying, p. 648.

54. Joseph F. Griggs, "China Awakened," *The Century Magazine* 73, no. 3 (July 1906): 393.

55. K. K. Kawakami, "The Awakening of China," *North American Review* 182 (Oct. 1906): 647–59.

56. In an essay on the 1905 boycott Delber L. McKee wrote: "the tiny community in mainland America had temporarily acquired a special leverage with

influential Chinese leaders and with groups both in and out of government." See "The Chinese Boycott of 1905–1906 Reconsidered," p. 169.

57. He Zuo, p. 16.

58. *Guangxuchao donghualu* (Records of the donghua in the reign of the Emperor Guangxu) 5: 5001–5002.

59. *The Chinese-Western Daily*, Jan. 15, 1908. Editorial.

60. Ibid., Feb. 29, 1912. Advertisement section.

61. L. Eve Armentrout Ma has discussed the activities of these political factions in the Americas before the 1911 revolution in her *Revolutionaries, Monarchists, and Chinatowns.*

62. Leong Kai Cheu, "The Awakening of China," *The Independent* 55 (May 28, 1903): 1268.

63. Two of Sun's uncles reportedly went to work in California's mines in the 1860s and later died there. Educated himself in Honolulu (1879–83), where his brother and another uncle were affluent entrepreneurs, Sun visited Honolulu six times between 1879 and 1910. In 1894 he helped form the Xingzhonghui (the Society to Strengthen China), a forerunner of the Chinese nationalist party, in Honolulu. The support of the Chinese in Hawaii was indispensable for Sun's cause.

64. It was originally formed by Ming loyalists after the Manchu overthrew the Ming Dynasty.

65. *Sun Zhongshan quanji* (Complete works of Sun Yat-sen), 11 vols. (Beijing: Zhunghua Shuju, 1981) 1, p. 240.

66. Huang Sande, *Hongmeng Geming Shi*. Hongmeng is another name of the secret society Zhigong Tang.

67. Liang Qichao, p. 487.

68. Ibid., p. 490.

69. *The Suffering of Our Fellow Merchants*, in A Ying, p. 546.

70. *New York Times*, June 28, 1905, 4: 1.

71. Remer, p. 35. Nevertheless, U.S. exports to China did decline between 1905 and 1906, falling from $55 million to $44 million. This trend continued over the next four years. But it does not seem to have been a direct result of the boycott. In terms of total U.S. exports to China, the figures for the second half of the first decade of the twentieth century are higher than those of the first. We need to remember that even in 1905 America's exports to China represented only a small fraction (slightly over 3 percent) of its total exports. My discussion is based on U.S. Bureau of the Census, *Historical Statistics of the United States*, p. 855.

72. Wang Yanwei, 190, p. 23.

73. *The Chinese-Western Daily*, May 6, 1905. Editorial. Chien-tung

("Zhendong" in pinyin) was his style (a name people took at the age of 20).

74. Ibid., Jan. 30, 1906.

75. U.S. Congress, House, *Facts Concerning the Enforcement of the Chinese-Exclusion Laws*, pp. 152–53.

76. *Journal of the American Asiatic Association* 5, no. 6 (July 1905): 168.

77. *New York Times*, June 26, 1905, 7: 1.

78. U.S. Congress, House, *Facts Concerning the Enforcement of the Chinese-Exclusion Laws*, p. 149.

79. *Outlook* 80 (Aug. 26, 1905): 992–93.

80. Holcombe, p. 1067. W. A. P. Martin also invoked the Boston Tea Party in his article about the 1905 event in his "The Awakening of China," p. 7124.

81. *The Chinese-Western Daily*, June 13, 1905. Advertisement section.

82. Lo Hsiang-lin, *Liang Cheng*, p. 310. "Transits" referred to those who traveled through the United States on their way from one place to another.

83. *The Chinese-Western Daily*, June 25, 1905. Editorial.

84. The white merchants' attempt was abandoned later as a result of the intervention of Chinese diplomats.

85. Ibid., Dec. 6, 1906. Editorial.

86. Ibid., Oct. 27, 1906.

CHAPTER 7: A CHANGING MENTALITY, 1906 TO 1913

1. *The Chinese-Western Daily*, Jan. 30, 1906.

2. Linthicum, p. 33.

3. *The Chinese-Western Daily*, Apr. 26, 1906.

4. Himmelwright, p. 23.

5. Mary Austin, "The Temblor: A Personal Narration," in David Starr Jordan, ed., *The California Earthquake of 1906* (San Francisco: A. M. Robertson, 1907): 359.

6. *New York Times*, Apr. 19, 1906.

7. *The Chinese-Western Daily*, June 15, 1906.

8. Ibid., Apr. 26 and 28, May 3, and Aug. 17, 1906.

9. Ibid., Aug. 14, 1906.

10. Ibid., May 10, 1906.

11. Ibid.

12. Hart, p. 593.

13. *The Chinese-Western Daily*, June 10, 1906. Editorial.

14. Ibid., Apr. 27, 1906.

15. Hansen and Condon, p. 114.

16. *The Chinese-Western Daily*, Apr. 18, 1907. Editorial.

17. Ibid., Apr. 8, 1907.

18. Ibid., July 4, 1907. American News section.

19. Liang Jiabin, "Biography of Liang Qinggui," p. 26. The biography includes Liang Qinggui's entire text. The author of the biography is a descendant of Liang Qinggui and also wrote a previously cited study of the "thirteen hong" in Canton.

20. Liu Pei Chi, *Meiguo huaqiao jiaoyu*, pp. 30–31. Also see Zhang Yinhuan, 5: 68.

21. Zhang Yinhuan's diary entry for Nov. 20, 1887, Wanqin Wenxuan (Selected [historical] writings from the Late Qing Dynasty), in Zhang Yinhuan, p. 145.

22. For discussions of the issue of school segregation, see Low, and F. Yung Chang.

23. A. Joshua Fishman points out in a study of language maintenance among non-Asian immigrant groups that "The *most* active language maintenance institution in the majority of ethnic communities in the United States is the ethnic group school." Fishman et al., p. 393.

24. *The Chinese-Western Daily*, Feb. 3, 1906. Editorial.

25. The school offered day and evening classes from 10:00 A.M. until 9:00 P.M., according to the school's *Modified Regulations. The Chinese-Western Daily*, May 22, 1909. American News section.

26. *The Chinese-Western Daily*, Feb. 15, 1907. Editorial.

27. See for example M. R. Davies, "The Awakening of China," *Eclectic of Foreign Literature, Science and Art* 62, no. 5 (Nov. 1895): 604, and Robert K. Douglas, "The Intellectual Awakening of China," *The Nineteenth Century* (June 1900): 991.

28. "The Awakening of China," *Independent* 58 (Apr. 20, 1905): 909.

29. W. A. P. Martin, "The Awakening of China," p. 7127.

30. Thomas F. Millard, "The New China," *Scribner's Magazine* 71, no. 4 (Feb. 1906): 240 and 249.

31. Joseph F. Griggs, "China Awakened," *The Century Magazine* 73, no. 3 (July 1906): 392.

32. *The Outlook* 81 (Dec. 30, 1905): 1025.

33. T. Roosevelt, "The Awakening of China," *The Outlook* 87 (Nov. 30, 1907): 666.

34. *New York Times*, Feb. 19, 1906, 8: 2.

35. *The Chinese-Western Daily*, July 7, 1909. Editorial.

36. *Young China*, Sept. 30, 1911. Editorial.

37. *The Chinese-Western Daily*, Feb. 3, 1906. Editorial. Many immigrants from elsewhere also believed that it was their obligation to promote religious and politi-

cal reforms in their home countries, either by setting a moral example or by direct participation.

38. Ibid., Aug. 21, 1906.

39. Ibid., July 7, 1909.

40. Chen invested in American railroads as well. He once loaned thirty thousand dollars to white Americans to build railroads. See Zhang Yinhuan, 3: 16; 5: 54; and 8: 14. Chen spent many years in Seattle. For his biography, see Jue, pp. 31–38. According to Chen himself, the railroad cost about three million dollars. See Xinning Railroad Company, *Shangban Guangdong Xinning Tielu Shiye Guzhi Tongjice* (Estimated property value of the Private Guangdong Xinning Railroad Company) (1928), introduction. According to the official rules it adopted for rewarding overseas Chinese investors, the Qing Court made him a second-class official. See *The Chinese-Western Daily*, Nov. 25, 1908.

41. Cheng et al., p. 60.

42. Liu Pei Chi, *Meiguo Huaqiao Yishi*, p. 265.

43. *The Chinese-Western Daily*, Apr. 11, 1913. Editorial.

44. Lo Hsiang-lin, *Liang Cheng*, p. 331.

45. *The Chinese-Western Daily*, July 26, 1908. American News section.

46. Ibid., Oct. 30, 1911. Editorial.

47. Ibid.

48. Ibid., Nov. 7, 1911.

49. Ibid., Sept. 27, 1912.

50. Ng Poon Chew, letter to Coolidge, July 17, 1912. Papers of Ng Poon Chew. AASL, U. C. Berkeley.

51. *The Chinese-Western Daily*, Sept. 9, 1912. American News section.

52. Ibid., Apr. 10, 1913. Editorial.

53. *Young China*, Nov. 25, 1911. City News section.

54. Bamford, *Angel Island*, p. 38.

55. *The Chinese-Western Daily*, Feb. 17, 1913. American News section. Huang Sande, a longtime head of the organization, later openly broke with Sun Yat-sen. Huang recounted his relationship with Sun in his *Hongmeng Geming Shi*.

56. In this book I have used the literal translation of the paper's Chinese title, namely, *The Chinese-Western Daily*, in an attempt to preserve the intention of the individual(s) who came up with that title, as well as the meaning it carried.

57. *The Chinese-Western Daily*, Aug. 4, 1910; Sept. 10, 1911.

58. *Young China*, Sept. 10, 1911. Editorial.

59. In 1965, 34 years after his death, Chew was included in the San Francisco *Examiner*'s Gallery of Great Americans—along with F. D. Roosevelt, Henry David Thoreau and, ironically, Samuel Gompers, an opponent of Chinese immigration.

The *Dictionary of American Biography* of the 1930s also includes a biographical sketch of Chew. The second part of Corinne K. Hoexter's *From Canton to California* includes a biography of him. His last name in Chinese is Ng (Wu). As often happened, the last part of his name, "Chew," became his last name in English.

60. Undated flyer.

61. Ng Poon Chew, letter to Mary Coolidge, Feb. 13, 1909. After the book came out Chew wrote Coolidge another letter from Oregon, in which he stated: "in behalf of the Chinese people, I want to thank you for the great service you have rendered to us, by your work." The word "highbinders" or "hatchetmen" was a term widely used for members of Chinese secret societies (tongs). See Asbury, pp. 185–86.

62. *The Chinese-Western Daily*, Apr. 1, 1907. Editorial.

63. Ibid., May 22, 1907.

64. Ibid., Apr. 4, 1907. Advertisement section.

65. *The Chinese-Western Daily*, June 8, 1907.

66. Beginning late in the nineteenth century Social Darwinism also became an influential social theory in American society. For a discussion of the subject see Hofstadter.

67. *The Chinese-Western Daily*, Apr. 17, 1906. Advertisement section.

68. In his *Imperialism and Social Reform*, (p. 30) Semmel argues that Social Darwinism had two variations, namely, "internal" Social Darwinism and "external" Social Darwinism. As a theory of international relations, external Social Darwinism was particularly appealing to many Chinese in both China and America, who used it to interpret their plight as victims of imperialism and racism.

69. *The Chinese-Western Daily*, July 7, 1909.

70. Ibid., Oct. 21, 1907.

71. Ibid., Sept. 28, 1908.

72. Ibid.

73. Ibid., Dec. 11, 1908.

74. Ibid., Feb. 25, 1908.

75. Ibid., Jan. 21, 1913.

76. Ibid., Sept. 28, 1908.

77. Ibid., July 7, 1909.

78. Soon afterwards Japan and the United States reached the "Gentlemen's Agreement," which allowed Japan to restrict immigration to the United States on its own in lieu of the United States passing an exclusion act. The wives of Japanese immigrants were allowed to continue to immigrate.

79. *The Chinese-Western Daily*, July 23, 1907. Editorial.

80. Ibid., May 5, 1906.

81. Ibid., Mar. 21, 1907. Editorial.

82. Ibid., July 7, 1909.

83. Ibid., Aug. 30, 1909.

84. Ibid., Oct. 13, 1909. Advertisement section.

85. *Chinese World*, Nov. 12, 1911. Advertisement section.

86. *The Chinese-Western Daily*, Aug. 13, 1912.

87. Ibid., May 5, 1905.

88. J. Yung, *Unbound Feet*, p. 55.

89. *The Chinese-Western Daily*, Aug. 30, 1909. Judy Yung analyzes discussion in this newspaper of issues concerning women in her article, "The Social Awakening of Chinese American Women," pp. 195–207.

90. *The Chinese-Western Daily*, Apr. 26, 1907.

91. Ibid., Apr. 5, 1907.

92. Ibid., Jan. 21, 1913.

93. Ibid., July 27, 1906.

94. Ibid., Jan. 15, 1907. Advertisement section.

95. See regulations of the Zhenwu Society for stopping opium smoking, in *The Chinese-Western Daily*, May 10, 1907. Advertisement section.

96. Ibid., Aug. 21, 1906. Advertisement section.

97. See *Young China*, Apr. 4, 1911.

98. *The Chinese-Western Daily*, Sept. 27, 1910. American News section.

99. Ibid., Sept. 28, 1910.

100. Ibid., Oct. 15, 1907.

101. Ibid., Oct. 21, 1907. American News section.

102. Ibid., July 28, 1910.

103. *Young China*, Dec. 18, 1911. American News section.

104. Ibid., June 8, 1912.

105. *The Chinese-Western Daily*, Nov. 11, 1907. Editorial.

106. Ibid., Mar. 2, 1909.

107. The 1911 revolution affected individual immigrants, as is evidenced by anecdotal accounts provided by scholars. Rose Hum Lee's *The Growth and Decline of Chinese Communities* includes the testimony of an old woman in Butte's Chinatown. The woman spoke about the influence of the revolution on her life: "Until the Revolution, I was allowed out of the house once a year," she recalled. "After the Revolution," she continued, "when the father of my children cut his queue he adopted new habits; I discarded my Chinese clothes and began to wear American clothes . . . Gradually the other women followed my example. We began to go out frequently and since then I go out all the time" (pp. 252–53).

108. *Young China*, July, 14, 1912. City News section.

109. Ibid., Aug. 30, 1912.

110. *The Chinese-Western Daily*, Jan. 1, 1912. Editorial.

111. Ibid., Sept. 18, 1912.

112. *Chinese World*, Jan. 1, 1912.

113. *The Chinese-Western Daily*, Dec. 24 and 25, 1912. Advertisement section.

114. Dobie, p. 311.

115. *The Chinese-Western Daily*, Oct. 10, 1907. American News section.

116. See the first list of donors in *The Chinese-Western Daily*, Jan. 3, 1912. Advertisement section.

117. *Young China*, Aug. 4, 1911. City News section.

118. Kuang Yaojie's letter from Shanghai, Nov. 1912, in *The Chinese-Western Daily*, Jan. 9, 1913.

119. *The Chinese-Western Daily*, Apr. 10, 1913. Editorial.

CHAPTER 8: THE AMERICAN-NESS OF THE TRANS-PACIFIC
COMMUNITY BETWEEN THE WARS

1. Todd, *The Chamber of Commerce Handbook for San Francisco*, p. 67.

2. Ibid., p. 68.

3. Hart, p. 598.

4. J. D. Barry, p. 114.

5. Cited from Gray Brechin, "Sailing To Byzantium: The Architecture of the Fair," in Benedict, pp. 96–97. The architect's statement is contained in a letter to a journal, which expressed objections to the exposition's Mission-style (Spanish) architecture. See *Architect and Engineer* 25, 1 (Aug. 1911): 102–3.

6. Todd, *The Story of the Exposition*, 2: 358.

7. Mrs. Clemens Wong, p. 6.

8. Ibid., p. 1. On page 2, Mrs. Wong wrote: "The Chinese of the present day differ very little in habit and customs which have descended from generation to generation." Frank Morton Todd wrote: "It is and always will be San Francisco's Chinatown, unique and outlandish, a foreign country of ten city squares, supposed to be a part of Canton, or a part of Tartary, as you please." See *The Chamber of Commerce Handbook for San Francisco*, p. 67.

9. *Young China*, Aug. 16, 1915. City News section.

10. The reorganized Pacific Mail resumed its trans-Pacific service a year later.

11. The company failed in 1923 as a result of poor management and of an internal power struggle within its board of directors. Its failure led to the fall of the Bank of Canton a few years later.

12. The Regulations of China Mail S. S. Co. Ltd. *Young China*, Oct. 8, 1915. Advertisement section. Also see *The Chinese-Western Daily*, Dec. 7, 1917. Advertisement section.

13. *The Chinese-Western Daily*, July 4, 1927. Editorial.

14. In May 1926 the Chinese government decided not to issue diplomatic passports to the huiguan presidents selected in the emigrant communities. They had to travel to the United States as ordinary travelers, subject to the same harsh treatment that other Chinese immigrants received. Thereafter the huiguan began to elect their heads from among the elite in America. This old practice did not disappear overnight, however. It was reaffirmed in the Zhonghua Huiguan's new constitution, Article 8 of which stipulated: "each huiguan should select and hire a well-respected and learned individual from the motherland to be the president." See *The Chinese-Western Daily*, Oct. 24, 1925, and May 4, 1930. The entire text was published in the newspaper. The Ningyang Huiguan continued this practice as late as 1930, when Zhu Yujie came from China to become its president.

15. Chinese in other cities established large enterprises as well, including a chemical company, the Wah Chang Company, founded in New York in 1915, and a China Motion Picture Company founded in Detroit in 1917. For another discussion of the subject see Armentrout Ma, "The Big-Business Ventures of Chinese," pp. 101–12.

16. *The Chinese-Western Daily*, Mar. 20, 1920. Advertisement section. Eventually, the enterprise failed on account of legal disputes over ownership of the land.

17. Chinese immigrants had been agricultural laborers since the nineteenth century, a topic discussed in great detail in S. Chan's *This Bittersweet Soil*.

18. *Kung Sing* 1 (Mar. 1924): 2.

19. *Young China*, Oct. 6, 1919. City News section.

20. Ibid., p. 8.

21. The unusually open endorsement of the League of Labor by the Yanghe Huiguan in 1919 should not come as a surprise. As I indicate earlier in the book, people from Xinning County (who founded the Yanghe Huiguan) were more likely to become laborers than were their counterparts from the Sanyi region.

22. *The Chinese-Western Daily*, Jan. 13, 1919. American News section.

23. Ibid., Jan. 21, 1919. Over time, however, the Chinese labor movement became quite influential in New York city. According to Renqiu Yu, leaders of the Chinese Hand Laundry Alliance were elected to key positions in nearly all clan and district associations. See Renqiu Yu, *To Save China, To Save Ourselves*, p. 85. Labor unions in Chinese San Francisco did not attain the same level of influence.

24. Long work hours were quite normal for Chinese immigrants. Chinese

laundrymen, for example, worked 10 to 16 hours a day, for six days a week, plus half a day every Sunday. See Siu, pp. 69–72.

25. *Chinese Nationalist Daily*, Feb. 14 and 15, 1929. Immigrants' News section.

26. The company was founded early in the twentieth century, and by 1921 it had operated garment-manufacturing factories in San Francisco as well as nine retail stores in different cities, including Sacramento, San Francisco, and San Diego.

27. Undated flyer of the Equality Society.

28. *The Chinese-Western Daily*, Jan. 13, 1938. City News section.

29. Writing of the political radicalism of European immigrants, particularly the Finns, Neil Betten concluded that such radicalism was rooted "in the political heritage that Finish immigrants brought from the homeland where socialism was respectable." Betten, p. 44. Anarchism arrived in China in the early twentieth century, but its influence remained confined to a small circle of intellectuals. Their translations of Russian anarchists' works were occasionally exported to the United States. It is possible that these works had some impact on Chinese American anarchists.

30. Paul Buhle wrote in a 1983 article: "Among German craftsmen of the 1880s, Jewish clothing workers of the 1890s, Italian clothing and garment workers of the 1910s, anarchist and syndicalist militants had an importance all out of proportion to their numbers. Without them craft and industrial unionism might not have happened for another generation." Buhle, p. 21. Within the Chinese community, the Equality Society had close ties with the labor movement and supported strikes by Chinese workers.

31. Letter of Nov. 25, 1921.

32. *Young China*, Aug. 21, 1915. City News section.

33. *The Chinese-Western Daily*, Oct. 27, 1927. City News section.

34. Ibid., Jan. 8, 1918. American News section.

35. Ibid., Oct. 8, 1919.

36. *Chinese Times*, Feb. 10, 1942.

37. Ibid., Apr. 4, 1941.

38. Ibid., May 2, 1941.

39. According to a 1927 report in the *San Francisco Chronicle* (Nov. 17, 1927), all the employees working at the telephone exchange were from the same family.

40. *Young China*, Mar. 20, 1920. Advertisement section.

41. *Chinese Times*, Apr. 24, 1942. Advertisement section.

42. Ibid., June 3, 1943.

43. *Chinese Times*, Nov. 12, 1941.

44. Ibid., May 2, 1941. Advertisement section.

45. *Chinese Times*, July 8, 1943. Arthur Dong's "Forbidden City," a documentary film made in the 1980s, offers a glimpse of the club, Charlie Low, and a number of former performers. See also Dong, pp. 125–48.

46. *San Francisco Chronicle*, Dec. 19, 1943. Advertisement.

47. While most of them continued to do business with Chinese customers, a few focused exclusively on serving a non-Chinese clientele. A Chinese restaurant named Sun Wah Kue, for example, was known for "serving only American menu." See Delkin, p. 58.

48. Menu of the Shanghai Cafe from the early 1930s.

49. Ibid.

50. *St. Louis Post-Dispatch*, Dec. 17, 1943, D-1.

51. Menu from Mary's Cafe, 1940.

52. *The Chinese-Western Daily*, Nov. 1, 1919. American News section.

53. Ibid., Jan. 30, 1918.

54. Ibid., July 21, 1920. We do not know from the Chinese words used whether more than one woman was believed to be involved.

55. Ibid., Mar. 3, 1920.

56. *Zhongshan Xianzhi*, 22: 82.

57. Zhang Yinhuan, 1: 31.

58. Despite their opposition to Chinese exclusion laws, according to Arnold Shankman, "in general blacks of the late nineteenth and early twentieth centuries found the 'mooneyed Celestials' to be 'absurd, unwholesome, and unacceptable [for] . . . Americanization.' " Shankman, p. 9. For another discussion of the same issue, see Hellwig, pp. 25–44.

59. *The Chinese-Western Daily*, Oct. 1, 1919. Editorial.

60. Ibid., Oct. 21, 1920. The alien land act was enacted in 1913 and amended in the 1920s.

61. Ibid., June 13, 1919. American News section.

62. Ibid., Jan. 24, 1920. City News section.

63. *Young China*, Mar. 4, 1942. Important News section.

64. *Chinese Times*, Mar. 3, 1942.

65. Ibid., May 1, 1942. Historically used to characterize Japanese pirates operating in Chinese coastal waters, the pejorative term "Wo" also connotes hostility.

66. *Chinese World*, Feb. 20, 1942.

67. *The Chinese-Western Daily*, May 12, 1919. City News section.

68. *Chinese World*, Mar. 10, 1942.

69. Ibid., July 8 and 9, 1943.

70. Ibid., Sept. 2, 1901. Advertisement section.

71. Ibid., Sept. 4, 1908.

72. Ibid., May 19, 1914. Editorial.

73. Ibid., Sept. 7, 1908. Editorial.

74. Ibid.

75. Ibid., Oct. 30, 1908. Editorial.

76. Ibid., Oct. 31, 1908. American News section.

77. *Young China*, July 12, 1916. Editorial.

78. Zhonghua Huiguan, letter to the minister. *The Chinese-Western Daily*, Dec. 17, 1917.

79. *The Chinese-Western Daily*, Nov. 30, 1918. Editorial.

80. Ibid., Oct. 18, 1918.

81. Ibid., Oct. 8, 1918.

82. Ibid., Sept. 28, 1918.

83. *The Chinese-Western Daily*, July 22, 1920. Editorial.

84. During the Civil War some Chinese joined the Union army. One, named Hong Neok Woo, who had come to America on the *Susquehana* of Commodore Perry's expedition, enlisted as a private in Company 1, 50th Regiment Infantry of Pennsylvania Volunteer Emergency Militia. (Worner, pp. 52–55.) Another Chinese named Chen, who had come to Boston in 1847 at the age of eleven, also joined the Union army during the Civil War. (*The Chinese-Western Daily*, Nov. 5, 1920. City News section.)

85. *The Chinese-Western Daily*, July 25, 1914. City News section.

86. The Beijing government was then headed by Yuan Shikai, a former high-ranking Qing official, who had replaced Sun Yat-sen in early 1912 as president of the new Republic in a political compromise. As the Beijing government was becoming more and more unpopular, Sun and his followers tried to regroup in the south. But Chinese San Franciscans' dislike for the Beijing government represented more than pro-Sun political partisanship. In fact, the popularity of Sun, once the symbol of the 1911 revolution, significantly declined in Chinese San Francisco.

87. *San Francisco Chronicle*, Aug. 21, 1915, p. 10.

88. *The Chinese-Western Daily*, Feb. 22, 1915. City News section.

89. Letter to the commissioner written on Apr. 10, 1915. *Young China*, Mar. 13, 1915. City News section.

90. *The Chinese-Western Daily*, July 9, 1914. Editorial.

91. Ibid., Feb. 13, 1915.

92. Ibid., Jan. 4, 1921.

93. Such perceptions were clearly expressed in an editorial in *Young China*, May 24, 1924.

94. *Young China*, Jan. 26, 1916. Editorial.

95. Ibid., Mar. 24, 1917.

96. *The Chinese-Western Daily*, Oct. 19, 1914.

97. According to estimates in Chinese newspapers, the number of Chinese who voted in elections probably increased from about two hundred in the early 1910s to about four to five hundred in the late 1930s. (*The Chinese-Western Daily*, May 11, 1911; *Young China*, Sept. 28, 1911; *The Chinese-Western Daily*, Mar. 3, 1937, Editorial.) On Mar. 3, 1937, *The Chinese-Western Daily* mentioned that of about two thousand eligible Chinese voters in San Francisco, usually less than five hundred came out to vote. Overall, Chinese voters remained a quite modest political force, and it is safe to say that the actual number of Chinese votes cast during any given election throughout this period never exceeded a thousand.

98. *The Chinese-Western Daily*, Mar. 3, 1937. Editorial.

99. We must note that not all of them were native born. Chinese-born immigrants whose fathers were American citizen fathers were citizens themselves, also. A significant number of them, including many American-born children who had been sent back to China for education, had not been educated in America.

100. *The Chinese-Western Daily*, Oct. 25, 1907. Editorial.

101. Ibid., Sept. 7, 1908.

102. *Young China*, Mar. 24, 1917. Editorial.

103. Although it soon grew to include people in many other cities, during this period the alliance was dominated by Chinese San Franciscans.

104. These numbers come from *Proceedings of the Tenth Convention of the Chinese American Citizens Alliance*, a report of the San Francisco Lodge, Sept. 6, 1925. (The documents included in the proceedings are in Chinese.) At this time the Los Angeles lodge, the second largest one, had a membership of seven hundred. Others were even smaller. The membership of the Chicago lodge, for instance, was less than three hundred. It must be noted that the non-U.S.-born American citizens had the same rights as did others in the organization, with the following exceptions: they could not be elected officials of the alliance, nor could they act as the local chapter's head or as its English or Chinese secretary.

105. The quotation is a translation from a text printed in *The Chinese-Western Daily*, Aug. 12, 1921. City News section.

106. Fessler, p. 191.

107. Section 1 of Article 7 of the 1927 Constitution of the Chinese American Citizens Alliance (San Francisco, 1928).

108. Preamble to the Constitution of the Chinese American Citizens Alliance. The spirit of mutual aid was written into all the constitutions of this fraternity, including that of the Native Sons of the Golden State.

109. Section 2 of Article 7 of the Constitution of the Native Sons of the

Golden State, cited from Liu Pei Chi, *Meiguo Huaqiao Shi*, p. 240. Liu's book includes the entire text of the constitution, pp. 236–41.

110. "Xiuzheng Xukuan Guitiao" (Amended bylaws of the life insurance funds) in *Proceedings of the Tenth Convention of the Chinese American Citizens Alliance*, a report of the San Francisco Lodge, Sept. 6, 1925, pp. 37, 38, 41. The amendment was adopted at the tenth convention of the alliance.

111. *The Chinese-Western Daily*, Apr. 1, 1900. American News section.

112. Ibid., Sept. 4, 1908. Similar incidents continued to occur later on, however. See for example a news report in the *Chinese Nationalist Daily*, Aug. 26, 1929. American News section.

113. Ibid., Aug. 26, 1929.

114. *Young China*, Aug. 8, 1925. City News section; report of the executive board at the tenth convention of the alliance, Sept. 15, 1925, p. 24.

115. W. Kong, p. 520. Kong was one of the first Chinese Americans to use the notion of "Chinese Americans." As further evidence of his Chinese American consciousness, he referred to white Americans as "other Americans."

116. The community constantly reminded the native-born that they, like others, were also the subjects of discrimination. See *Young China*, Apr. 1, 1916; Dec. 9, 11, 12, 1919; *The Chinese-Western Daily*, Oct. 25, 1907. Editorial.

117. The preface to its constitution, cited from Liu Pei Chi, *Meiguo Huaqiao Shi*, p. 236.

118. Article five of the constitution, which was included in a public announcement. *Young China*, Feb. 18, 1916. Advertisement section.

119. *Proceedings of the Tenth Convention of the Chinese American Citizens Alliance*, a report of the San Francisco Lodge, Sept. 6, 1925, p. 53.

120. *Young China*, Mar. 24, 1917. Editorial.

121. Chinese American Citizens Alliance, letter to the Zhonghua Huiguan. *Young China*, Jan. 18, 1916. American News section.

122. Ibid.

123. Powers, p. 129.

124. "Guarding the Gates Against Undesirables," p. 400.

125. Powers, p. 124.

126. *New York Times*, Jan. 26, 1924, 15: 8.

127. Wise was paraphrased in the *New York Times*, Jan. 7, 1924, 3: 3. The quota system was based on the nation's demographic character of 1890. For a discussion of the development of U.S. immigration laws, see Hutchinson. For their effects on Asians, see McKenzie. Two Ph.D. dissertations on the 1924 act have also been written: "Exclusion by Prejudice: Anti-Japanese Discrimination in California and

the Immigration Act of 1924," by Herbert Patrick LePore, and "Legislating 'Normalcy': The Immigration Act of 1924," by Peter Heywood Wang.

128. Stidger.

129. For Japanese reaction to the law, see Makela.

130. See for example *Chinese World*, May 27 and June 1, 1924, and *Young China*, May 31, 1924.

131. *The Chinese-Western Daily*, May 23, 1924. Editorial.

132. In early 1930 Congress passed a law allowing the wives of Chinese American citizens to come to the United States.

133. *Proceedings of the Tenth Convention of the Chinese American Citizens Alliance*, a report of the San Francisco Lodge, Sept. 6, 1925, p. 39.

134. Ibid., p. 52.

135. Treadway, p. 920.

136. *The Chinese-Western Daily*, Apr. 8, 1924. Important News section.

137. John McNab, letter to Dr. Howard Markel, June 9, 1927, in Wong Yu Fong, p. 30.

138. Dr. H. S. Cumming, letter to Wong Yun Fong, Dec. 5, 1927, ibid., p. 70.

139. *Chinese World*, Nov. 17, 1927.

140. Dr. H. S. Cumming, Letter to Wong Yun Fong, Nov. 18, 1927, in Wong Yu Fong, p. 62.

141. John McNab did acknowledge the effort made by another Chinese, Wong Yun Fong, who, as the secretary of the Zhonghua Huiguan, coordinated and assisted the activities of others. But Wong was not in as good a position as Lam was to become a hero.

142. *The Chinese-Western Daily*, Dec. 5, 1927. Contrary to Li's assertion, Lam did claim credit for himself.

CHAPTER 9: PERSISTENCE OF TRANS-PACIFIC TIES

1. Huang Dingchong, "Jierzhongde Zuguo" (The motherland in hunger), in Yishe Teken (Journal of the Yi Society), Zhonghua School (Apr. 26, 1943): 32.

2. Diary entry for Apr. 3, 1939. Wah-chung Leung's papers, which include a diary and various long and short memoirs. These are all written in Chinese, except for a few special terms.

3. Huang Dingchong, "Jierzhongde Zuguo" (The motherland in hunger) : 31–32.

4. Diary entry for May 24, 1939. Wah-chung Leung's papers.

5. Scholars have long recognized the collective nature of individuals' memories.

Maurice Halbwachs, one of the first modern theorists of memory, asserted over seventy years ago, that "everyone has a capacity for memory that is unlike that of anyone else. . . . But individual memory is nevertheless a part or an aspect of group memory." See Halbwachs, p. 52.

6. Hu Zhaozhong, p. 87.

7. As I have noted previously, Chinese America suffered from an extremely unbalanced ratio of men to women. In 1890, according to Fessler, the ratio was "a crazy 2,688 to 100." During the period being discussed in this chapter the imbalance lessened. But the improvement was very gradual. The ratio was still around 7 to 1 in 1920 and about 3 to 1 in 1940. See Fessler, p. 188.

8. *Chinese Nationalist Daily*, Dec. 4, 1930. American News section.

9. Chinese medicine had long been under attack by the white medical profession. In 1941, when a Chinese medical doctor, Kuang Pei, was fighting a legal battle for the legitimacy of herbal medicine, a Chinese group in Oakland published a 304-page book that included testimonies in support of Chinese herbal medicine. An advertisement for this book in the *Chinese Times* and other Chinese newspapers stated that "[people in] Western medicine have tried very hard to abolish Chinese medicine. First, they argued that [Chinese medical experts] practised without a license. . . . Second, [they] charge in court that Chinese medicine was ineffective and accused that the sale of [Chinese] medicine was a fraud." (*Chinese Times*, May 7, 1941. Advertisement section.)

10. The three examples are from a far larger sampling of *The Chinese-Western Daily*. The prevalence of such medical advertisements is also found in other Chinese newspapers during this period. In fact, many advertisers promoted their businesses in more than one newspaper.

11. Medical advertisements in the three issues of *The Chinese-Western Daily*:

Date	total commercial ads	medical ads	sexuality-related ads
Feb. 15, 1916	87	29 (33%)	22 (25%)
Dec. 8, 1925	69	29 (42%)	23 (33%)
Jan. 5, 1940	61	22 (36%)	15 (25%)

12. J. Yung, *Unbound Feet*, p. 72. Yung uses the census figures to suggest that the number of Chinese prostitutes had decreased. She acknowledges that Chinese prostitution continued through the 1920s. The Chinese-language newspaper advertisements indicate that it lasted much longer.

13. *The Chinese-Western Daily*, Dec. 30, 1917.

14. Ibid., May 8, 1920.

15. Ibid., Dec. 8, 1925.

16. *Chinese World*, May 21, 1941.

17. *Chinese Times*, Mar. 8, 1942.

18. *The Chinese-Western Daily*, Dec. 10, 1917.

19. Ibid., Feb. 15, 1916; Dec. 10, 1917.

20. Ibid., Dec. 8, 1925. Advertisement section.

21. Wah-chung Leung's papers. The exact date of this statement is not given. He also wrote regretfully of his extensive gambling activities, another curse of the bachelor life.

22. Wah-chung Leung's memo of Nov. 29, 1939.

23. Xie Zhujun, *Shifei ji* or *Huiyi yan* (On right or wrong, or words upon returning to [home] community) (Canton, 1936): 36. If the folklore in the Chinese community is any indication, we must note that single men in their 30s were still regarded as ideal matches. One folk song went: "men in their 30s are a flower; and women in their 30s are tea grounds." See Hu Zhaozhong, p. 213.

24. *The Chinese-Western Daily*, Mar. 24, 1914. Advertisement section.

25. According to official records, from 1908 to 1930 nearly ninety thousand Chinese were recorded as having departed from the United States. An overwhelming majority of those who returned were men.

26. *The Chinese-Western Daily*, May 11, 1926; Feb. 10, 1935. City News section.

27. Ibid., Apr. 24, 1914.

28. Announcement of the Consulate. Ibid., Feb. 28, 1931.

29. *The Chinese-Western Daily*, Oct. 5, 1921. Advertisement section.

30. *Xukuanbu shouzhi baogaolu* (Financial report of life insurance department), filed at the tenth convention of the Chinese American Citizens Alliance in 1925, pp. 12–15.

31. The original receipt of the departure fee, issued by the alliance.

32. Brochure printed by *Chinese World*.

33. Wah-chung Leung's diary entry for the Qingming festival, 1943.

34. *The Chinese-Western Daily*, Apr. 25, 1930. City News section.

35. George Leung, "The Chinese Theatre," in E. K. Moy. No page number was given.

36. Riddle, p. 140. The theater was no longer the only main institution of public entertainment but faced increasing competition, especially from the movie industry.

37. My discussion here is based on program flyers from the Mandarin Theatre, all from the 1920s. They are located in the Asian American Studies Library, University of California, Berkeley.

38. George Leung, "The Chinese Theatre," in E. K. Moy.

39. *Young China*, Aug. 15, 1918. Editorial.

40. Lin had a long-standing involvement with education in Chinese San Francisco. At the time he was the principal of the Gangzhou School.

41. *The Chinese-Western Daily*, Mar. 2, 1927. Editorial.

42. Yi Ying Ma, p. 53. The data were collected from sample groups of Chinese students in school during the spring of 1944.

43. In July 1915 the Zhonghua Huiguan approved the appointment of a new principal and two new teachers. Ding Dianliang, the principal, was a graduate of a normal school. The two teachers were Huang Zhaoqiang, who was a graduate of the Canton High School, and Cen Haisheng, who was also a normal school graduate. It became official by the late 1920s that the school's board members had to be appointed by the Zhonghua Huiguan. And one of the qualifications for teachers was that they have a diploma from a normal or high school in China.

44. Public announcement concerning a fund-raising drive for the school, in *The Chinese-Western Daily*, Jan. 5, 1940. City News section. Later an independent Chinese school was established at the high school level.

45. *Young China*, Aug. 21, 1919. City News section.

46. *Ershiernianlaide Nanqiao* (Twenty-two years of the Nanqiao School), printed by the school in 1943.

47. Thereafter, its enrollment remained at about two hundred. The early 1930s was a booming time for all Chinese schools. Later they were unable to maintain the same level of enrollment, largely because the war in China prevented people from coming to the United States. The enrollment of upper-division students, in particular, fell from its earlier peak levels.

48. *The Chinese-Western Daily*, July 27, 1937. Editorial.

49. The teaching of Chinese was widespread in the community. Organizations catering to the younger generation in the community, such as the Chinese YMCA and the Chinese American Citizens Alliance, offered Chinese classes. At its eighteenth convention in 1941, the Chinese American Citizens Alliance stressed the importance of teaching the Chinese language to its members. According to Wu Junsheng and others, many parents hired private Chinese-language tutors for their children.

50. *The Chinese-Western Daily*, July 27, 1937. Editorial.

51. The use of these books was not confined to the Xiehe School. Advertisements for similar textbooks appeared in the Chinese newspapers. These textbooks tell us a great deal about China as well as about the American schools that used them. The emphasis on natural sciences and world geography, for instance, reflects the changes taking place in twentieth-century Chinese society.

52. "Qinshu" (relatives), in *Xinguowen* (New Chinese language) (Shanghai: Shegwu Yinshuguan, 1911, 1913), 8: 12.

53. *The Chinese-Western Daily*, Jan. 17, 1939. Advertisement section.

54. Twenty others were from families that had a long-standing friendship with the family of the deceased. *Young China*, Oct. 22, 1943. Advertisement section.

55. *Guowen jiaokeshu* (Chinese-language textbook) (Shanghai: Shegwu Yinshuguan, 1902, 1907), 1: 32–33.

56. *Fuxing shuohua fanben* (Conversation textbook) (Changsha, Hunan Province: Shegwu Yinshuguan, 1934), 7: 34.

57. "Aiguo" (Patriotism), in *Xinguowen* (New Chinese language), 8: 11.

58. *Xinzhuan lishi jiaokeshu* (New Chinese History Textbook) (Shanghai: Shegwu Yinshuguan, 1924, 1926), 2: 23–24.

59. *The Chinese-Western Daily*, June 28, 1920. City News section.

60. Ibid., Nov. 11, 1921.

61. Bylaws of the Nanqiao School. Printed by the school in 1943.

62. Yi Ying Ma, pp. 30 and 48. Influenced by the assimilation ideology that prevailed in the academy at the time, Ma concluded that Chinese schools were "no longer necessary" and were "detrimental to the best interest of Chinese-American children." Ma herself had been educated in China before coming to the United States for graduate school. She once taught Chinese in an evening Chinese school in Chinese San Francisco.

63. *The Chinese-Western Daily*, July 27, 1937. Editorial.

64. One Chinese San Franciscan who participated in welcoming him remembers that the general once called Chinese Americans "bamboo shoes," meaning that they were empty inside their body. Interview, Nov. 7, 1995. As he noted in his autobiography, while visiting the Chinese community in Marysville Cai did comment critically, in reference to the numerous temples, that the Chinese there were "so superstitious." See Cai Tingkai, 2: 442. The autobiography was first completed in 1939.

65. *The Chinese-Western Daily*, Mar. 8, 1915; Sept. 11, 1915. City News section.

66. Ibid., Feb. 24, 1915, Advertisement Section, and Feb. 24, 1915, American News section; *Young China*, Oct. 12, 1915.

67. *The Chinese-Western Daily*, Mar. 12, 1915. City News section.

68. *Young China*, July 1, 1919. City News section.

69. *The Chinese-Western Daily*, Oct. 22, 1932. Advertisement section.

70. A flyer titled "Jinggao Laodongmingzhong," (An address submitted respectfully to all working people), distributed by the San Francisco Anarchist League in January 1932.

71. *Young China*, Mar. 21, 1918. Editorial.

72. Ibid., Nov. 23, 1934. Editorial.

73. Ibid., Jan. 17, 1939. Advertisement section.

74. Ibid., June 25, 1942. Editorial.

75. Ibid., July 31, 1928. City News section.

76. Telegram to the Chinese government. Ibid., July 18, 1937.

77. Ibid., Aug. 22, 1937.

78. Its full name in Chinese was Lumeihuaqiao tongyiyijuan jiuguozonghui (the General fund-raising association of the Chinese in America to save China). Its name in English was the China War Relief Association of America.

79. *The Chinese-Western Daily*, Dec. 11, 1937.

80. Ibid., Mar. 20, 1938. American News section.

81. Ibid., Aug. 2, 1939. City News section.

82. Ibid., Dec. 17, 1939. Editorial.

83. See Him Mark Lai, *Cong huaqiao dao huaren*, p. 300. According to a conservative estimate, Lai states, Chinese America as a whole donated about 24 million American dollars during the war.

84. *The Chinese-Western Daily*, Aug. 10, 1936. City News section.

85. Ibid., Apr. 21, 1938.

86. Huang Zhenwu, pp. 363–64.

87. Wah-chung Leung's diary entries for the Qingming festival and Mar. 1, 1943.

88. *Chinese Times*, Mar. 14, 1942. Editorial.

89. Japanese forces began their campaign in South China early in 1938 and took Canton in October.

90. *The Chinese-Western Daily*, July 18, 1937.

91. Ibid., Aug. 10, 1937. Announcement.

92. Ibid., Feb. 12, May 16, 1941. City News section.

CHAPTER 10: THE ROAD TO 1943

1. *New York Times*, Aug. 8, 1905, 6: 2.

2. *The Chinese-Western Daily*, Aug. 27, 1918. Editorial.

3. *Proceedings of the Alliance's Tenth Convention in Chicago*, 1925. p. 55. The documents included in the proceedings are in Chinese.

4. Townsend, p. 54. For Arthur H. Smith's view about the Chinese, see his *Chinese Characteristics*, which is largely devoted to discussing the Chinese people's "grave defects" (p. 14). One of these "defects" was their lack of trust and sincerity, which Smith discusses in two long chapters.

5. *Young China*, Nov. 11, 1941.

6. Riggs, p. 35.

7. "How to Tell Japs from the Chinese," *Life* (Dec. 1941): 81.

8. "How to Tell Your Friends from the Japs," *Time* (Dec. 22, 1941): 33.

9. "How to Tell Japs from Chinese," *Science Digest* 11 (Feb. 1942): 22.

10. *The Chinese-Western Daily*, June 10, 1938. City News section.

11. Ibid., June 18, 1938.

12. *San Francisco Chronicle*, Feb. 10, 1940, p. 1.

13. The Chinese, Low Fat Yuen, was the magistrate, and the two other judges, municipal judge Peter Mullins and superior judge Thomas M. Foley, were his assistants.

14. *San Francisco Chronicle*, Feb. 10, 1940, p. 4.

15. Ibid., Feb. 11, 1940. p. 1; *The Chinese-Western Daily*, Feb. 25, 1940. City News section.

16. *Chinese World*, Feb. 5, 1940.

17. *Young China*, Feb. 10, 1940. Special issue for the Bowl of Rice movement. Chinese in other cities also combined the Bowl of Rice pageants with traditional Chinese holidays. In 1941 Chinese in Los Angeles held the Bowl of Rice pageant during the Mid-Autumn Festival (Aug. 7–8).

18. *Chinese Times*, Feb. 9, 1940.

19. For example, women played a leading role in receiving him during his stay in Marysville. See Cai Tingkai, 2: 442.

20. See J. Yung, *Unbound Feet*, p. 55.

21. Man Yun, "Zhankai Huaqiaofunu Yundong" (Develop Chinese American women's movement), *Chinese Times*, Mar. 8, 1942.

22. Bowl of Rice pageant program flyer.

23. During the 1930s Chinese Americans in New York City, for example, believed that " 'to save China' and 'to save ourselves' were inseparable," as Renqiu Yu notes in his *To Save China, To Save Ourselves*, p. 82.

24. "The Significance of the Second Bowl of Rice Party," *Chinese Times*, Feb. 9, 1940.

25. Delkin, p. 28.

26. Its Chinese translation was published in the *Chinese Times*, Oct. 12, 1941. City News section.

27. *San Francisco Chronicle*, Apr. 27, 1941, p. 8.

28. *Young China*, Jan. 13, 1943. Editorial.

29. *Chinese World*, Dec. 19, 1941.

30. *The Chinese-Western Daily*, Dec. 27, 1941. City News section.

31. Ibid., Nov. 27, 1942. American News section.

32. *Young China*, May 15, 1943. Advertisement section.

33. According to the advertisement of a Chinese employment agency in 1941, for example, the monthly wage for a domestic servant was about $75, and for various restaurant workers it was between $55 and $90. See *Chinese Times*, June 6, 1941.

34. *Young China*, Nov. 18, 1943. Advertisement section.

35. *Chinese Times*, Jan. 1, 1943. Editorial. On October 9, 1942, the American government announced its decision to renounce its extraterritorial privileges in China. On Jan. 11, 1943, it signed a new treaty with China.

36. In November 1942 she had come to the United States for treatment of an injury she had suffered while visiting Chinese troops.

37. *San Francisco Chronicle*, Mar. 26, 1943, p. 11.

38. J. S. Gurley, "Madame Chiang in America," in *Current History* 4 (Apr. 1943): 138.

39. Program of "A Night for China."

40. *San Francisco Chronicle*, Mar. 26, 1943, p. 11.

41. Ibid., Mar. 26, 1943, p. 1.

42. Boothe, p. 23.

43. *New York Times Magazine*, Sept. 14, 1941, p. 8.

44. *Life*, Mar. 8, 1943, p. 11.

45. *New York Times*, Mar. 8, 1943.

46. See for example *New York Times*, Aug. 29, 1934, p. 12, and Aug. 30, 1934, p. 21. In like fashion, the *San Francisco Chronicle* indicated that he spoke through an interpreter. See *San Francisco Chronicle*, Nov. 5, 1934, p. 13.

47. *Literary Digest* 118 (Sept. 12, 1934): 12.

48. In fact, at the time that they were ignoring Cai's arrival, the San Francisco newspapers devoted extraordinary energy to covering the arrival of Sir Charles Kingsford-Smith, a native of Australia who flew from Honolulu. He set an aviation record in 1931 when he flew from Australia to England, landing on November 4. In Smith the mainstream media and society had clearly found a figure and an event that they could relate to.

49. *Young China*, Mar. 27, 1943.

50. *Chinese Times*, Mar. 26, 1943.

51. The translated quote is from the *San Francisco Chronicle*, Mar. 29, 1943, p. 1.

52. Ibid., p. 8.

53. *Chinese Times*, Mar. 28, 1943. Editorial.

54. *Jiangfuren youmei jiniance*, p. 46.

55. *Young China*, Mar. 27, 1943.

56. Ibid., Mar. 25, 1943. Editorial.

57. "Shuobing" (On disease), *The Chinese-Western Daily*, May 3, 1943. Advertisement section.

58. The presents also included gold medals. Some of the money was in Chinese currency. The dollar figure is calculated on the basis of the numbers provided in *Jiangfuren youmei jiniance*, p. 80. Chinese Americans elsewhere donated a great deal of money as well. While Mme. Jiang was in Chicago the Chinese in the city and the surrounding areas raised $85,640. Ibid., p. 64.

59. *The Chinese-Western Daily*, May 3, 1943, Mar. 25, 1943. Editorial.

60. C. Fong et al., pp. 3 and 213.

61. Ling-chi Wang, "Politics of the Repeal of the Chinese Exclusion Laws," C. Fong et al., p. 80.

62. "America, Asia and the Future," *Collier's* 112 (Oct. 1943): 82.

63. *Chinese Nationalist Daily*, Jan. 12, 1941. Editorial.

64. Transcripts of Japanese broadcast propaganda were made available during the congressional hearing on the repeal of Chinese exclusion. One such transcript included the following statement: "The Chungking authorities must certainly know that Chinese are rigidly prohibited from emigrating to the United States and that this ban on Chinese immigration was established in the latter portion of the last century after a campaign of venomous vilification of the character of the Chinese people." See U.S. Congress, House. Committee on Immigration and Naturalization. p. 82.

65. Dower, p. 167.

66. After the 1882 Chinese exclusion act went into effect, the American government made numerous efforts to restrict Asian immigration into the country. The 1908 Gentlemen's Agreement terminated Japanese immigration. Besides restricting general immigration, the 1917 immigration act set up the Asiatic Barred Zone, banning immigration from the Far East. The 1924 immigration act, known as the Oriental Exclusion Act, banned Asian immigration almost entirely. The immigration of the Filipinos, the only Asian group not included in the 1924 act, was restricted by the 1934 Tydings-McDuffie Act. In addition, through its decisions, the Supreme Court repeatedly denied Asian immigrants eligibility for citizenship on the basis of the 1790 naturalization act, which stipulated that only free white men were eligible for naturalization (African American men became eligible after the Civil War).

67. Cited from LaFeber et al., p. 193.

68. Daniels, *Concentration Camps*, xvi. Japanese elsewhere in the United States, especially in Hawaii, also faced discrimination before and during World War II. See Okihiro, *Cane Fires*.

69. Lowe, p. 23.

70. *The China Daily News*, Oct. 23, 1943.

71. Riggs, p. 53.

72. "Are We Are Afraid to Do Justice?" p. 687.

73. Villard, p. 633.

74. Spinks, p. 92. J. J. Singh, president of the India League of America, made the same point in a letter to the editors of *The Nation* 158 (May 1944): 607.

75. Howard, p. 151.

76. "Are We Are Afraid to Do Justice?" p. 687.

77. Lasker, p. 699.

78. Walsh, p. 671.

79. Criticism of the repeal act itself also escalated over time. In a 1945 letter to *Asia and the Americas*, Fong Man-hee and Cheng Tze-nan questioned its wisdom and legality. "Is race," they asked, "the determining factor of international law and legislation? Is this revision of anti-Chinese legislation a new discrimination in itself?" See *Asia and the Americas* 45 (Feb. 1945): 45.

80. Anup Singh, "A Quota for India Too," *Asia and the Americas* 44 (Apr. 1944): 157.

81. W. Kong, p. 520.

82. Her earlier, sterner criticism of the Western world's "superiority complex" in an article she had written in China never surfaced during her American tour, which was a public relations campaign. That article appeared in the *New York Times Magazine* (Apr. 1942): 5 and 36. A translation of the text also circulated in Chinese San Francisco. Having been educated in America, she was certainly aware of America's anti-Chinese discriminatory policies. The fact that she did not mention Chinese exclusion during her tour does not suggest that she had forgotten it. Within a week after the passage of the repeal bill, she sent Congress a thank-you telegram. For Chinese nationalists like herself, the U.S. government's exclusion policies not only represented racism against Chinese Americans but also brought humiliation upon the Chinese nation. She expressed her nationalistic sentiments in her *China Shall Rise Again* by emphasizing the importance of "passionate patriotism" (p. 17).

83. Ling-chi Wang, "Politics of the Repeal of the Chinese Exclusion Laws," in Fong et al., p. 67.

84. *The Chinese-Western Daily*, June 1, 1943. Editorial.

85. *The China Daily News*, Mar. 5, 1943. Editorial.

86. Ibid., Mar. 2, 1943.

87. The letter was made public later. The citation is from the *New York Times*, Mar. 3, 1943, 12: 2.

88. Deng Wentao, "Yingfu zhongzuqishi zhiwojian," (My view on how to deal with discrimination), *Chinese Times*, Nov. 7, 1943.

89. Lin Ruochong, "Tanqishi," (On discrimination), ibid., Nov. 29, 1943.

90. *The Chinese-Western Daily*, June 1, 1943. Editorial.

91. *Young China*, Oct. 23, 1943. Editorial.

92. *The China Daily News*, Oct. 23, 1943.

93. *Young China*, Oct. 15, 1943. Editorial.

CONCLUSION

1. Siu, pp. 2, 3, and 294. This work was first completed as a Ph.D. dissertation in 1953 at the Department of Sociology in the University of Chicago.

2. Ibid., p. 294.

3. Barth, p. 1.

4. Daniels, *Asian America*, p. 16. Numerous immigration scholars have discussed the high return rate of non-Asian immigrants who came to the New World during the late nineteenth and early twentieth centuries. See Archdeacon, p. 139, and Bodnar, pp. 53–54. The few groups that did not have a high return ratio, such as the Eastern European Jews, represented "the exception to the rule," as Alan M. Kraut has argued in his *The Huddled Masses*, pp. 17–18. In addition, Sucheng Chan has pointed out that "sojourner" is a problematic analytical concept. She has written: "the term sojourner is not useful analytically because . . . it is extremely difficult to determine, in retrospect, the motivations of a group of people who left few records of their personal lives." S. Chan, "Public Policy," p. 9.

5. Lydon, pp. 487–88.

6. Ibid., p. 488.

7. Coolidge, p. 441.

8. We must note that a similar debate is being carried on among scholars of Chinese Canada. Scholars such as Anthony B. Chan argue that Chinese immigrants went to Canada with the intention to settle but were forced to become "sojourners."

As Yuen-fong Woon's rebuttal shows, the argument offered by Chan and others that the immigrants intended to settle permanently is historically weak. See A. B. Chan, "The Myth of the Chinese Sojourner," pp. 33–42, and A. B. Chan, "Orientalism and Image Making," pp. 37–46. Also see Yuen-fong Woon, pp. 673–90.

9. *The Oriental*, Feb. 15, 1855.

10. We must note that the word "qiao" has been incorrectly translated as "sojourner" according to present-day usage of the word. It is a mistranslation that

has contributed to the "sojourner" thesis that I criticize here. The word "qiao" first appeared in the official *Suishi* (History of the Sui Dynasty [581–618]) to describe the people who emigrated to settle south of the Yangtze River during the late third and early fourth centuries—it was one of the largest population movements in Chinese history. See *Suishi*, 24: 4, which was first compiled early during the Tang Dynasty (618–907) and was reprinted by the Han Fen Lou Publishing House. Further, among all the Chinese and Japanese scholars who have studied the term "huaqiao," there is no consensus regarding when it first occurred. Nor has there been a consensus in Chinese society about the exact scope of "huaqiao," because of the complicated Chinese diaspora. For a discussion of the genesis of the term, see Gungwu Wang, pp. 122–24.

11. In 1907 it declared that honorific titles would be given to such investors.

12. *Daqing fagui daquan*, book 22, 2: 995–99.

13. Wang Yanwei, 1: 49.

14. *Chinese Nationalist Daily*, Dec. 19, 1928. Editorial.

15. Ibid., Dec. 19 and 20, 1928. Editorial.

16. *Chinese Times*, Nov. 1, 1941. Current Affairs section.

17. Ibid.

18. As I have indicated, the number of Chinese American citizens had already exceeded that of noncitizens by 1940. The number of males per 100 females declined from 295 in 1940 to 110 in 1970.

19. Omi and Winant, p. 97.

20. For further discussions of the significance and limitations of the 1965 act, see Reimers, *Still the Golden Door*, pp. 61–91, and Abrams and Abrams, pp. 3–29.

Selected Bibliography

PRIMARY SOURCES

Archival collections

Ah Quin. Diaries and other personal and family documents. San Diego Historical Society.

California Historical Society collections (political leaflets, legal documents, and various other items).

Genealogy of the Lu Family, first compiled in 1834 in Xiangshan (later renamed Zhongshan) County, Guangdong; recompiled in the United States by the descendants of Lu (spelled "Look" at the time) Bintai, who was given the name "Look Eli" when he came to the United States in 1860. Asian American Studies Library of the University of California at Berkeley (AASL).

Ng Poon Chew, Papers. AASL.

The Chinese American Citizens Alliance. Various constitutions and other documents. AASL.

Chinese-school textbook collection. AASL.

Collection of program flyers issued by the Mandarin Theatre. AASL.

Dr. Thomas Quin Kong. Private collection (Ah Quin's 1892 diary, a genealogy, photographs, and various artifacts).

Wah-chung Leung. Diaries, a memoir, and other documents.

National Archives. Manuscript schedules of the 1850 population census for select Northern California counties.

National Archives. Manuscript schedules of the 1860 population census for San Francisco.

National Archives. Manuscript schedules of the 1870 population census for San Francisco.

National Archives. Manuscript schedules of the 1880 population census for San Francisco.

Restaurant menus of Chinese restaurants in the 1930s and early 1940s.

Cynthia Soo. Private collection (correspondence, photographs, a genealogy, and other documents).

Periodicals (The titles, frequency of publication, and location of some of the periodicals listed here vary. For those that remained in business after 1943, I list only their starting date.)

Daily Alta California. San Francisco, 1850–91.

The American Review of Reviews, monthly. New York, 1907–28.

Asia: Journal of the American Asiatic Association. New York, 1917–42.

Atlantic Monthly. Boston, 1858–1932.

The California China Mail and Flying Dragon or *Fei Lung*, primarily in English. San Francisco, 1867.

The Californian Illustrated Magazine. San Francisco, 1891–94.

The China Mail. Hong Kong, 1845–67.

Chinese American Weekly or *Meihua Zhoubao.* New York, 1942–.

Chinese Free Press or *Datong Ribao.* (Datong daily; the word "datong" refers to a Chinese political utopia where harmony, equality, and justice prevail.) San Francisco, 1903–27.

Chinese Nationalist Daily or *Minqi Ribao.* New York, 1915–.

Chinese Repository, monthly. Canton, 1832–51.

Chinese Times or *Jinshan Shibao* (Gold Mountain Times), daily. San Francisco, 1924–.

The Chinese-Western Daily or *Chung Sai Yat Po* (spelled "Zhongxi Ribao" in Mandarin, meaning "Chinese and Western daily").San Francisco, 1900–.

Chinese World or *Shijie Ribao* (World Daily). San Francisco, 1909–69.

Christian Century, weekly. Chicago, 1902–.

The Cosmopolitan, monthly. Rochester, New York, 1886–1925.

The Golden Hills' News or *Jingshan Rixinlu*, bilingual weekly, San Francisco, 1854–[55?].

Harper's Weekly, weekly. New York, 1857–.

Kung Sing (Laborers' voice), monthly. San Francisco, 1924–[?].

Lippincott's Magazine, monthly. Philadelphia, 1881–85.

New York Times, 1851–.

North American Review, quarterly. Boston, 1821–.

The Oriental or *Dongya xinlu* (meaning "news of the eastern frontiers of the ocean"), bilingual weekly. San Francisco, 1855–57.

Oriental or *Tang-Fan gongbao* (meaning "news concerning the Chinese and fan people"), weekly. San Francisco, 1875–[?].

Overland, monthly. San Francisco, 1887–1935.

San Diego Union. San Diego, 1897–.

San Francisco Call.

Scribner's Monthly Magazine, monthly. New York, 1881–1925.

Young China or *Shaonian Zhongguo chenbao* (Young China Morning Paper), daily. San Francisco, 1911–.

Other Primary Sources

A Ying. *Fanmeihuagongjinyue wenji* (Collection of the literature in protest against American anti-Chinese exclusion). Beijing: Zhonghua Shuju, 1960.

Abeel, David. *Journal of a Residence in China and the Neighboring Countries from 1830–1833*. New York: Leavitt, Lord, & Co., 1834.

American Baptist Home Mission Society. "Fifteenth Annual Report." New York, 1882.

American Board of Commissioners for Foreign Missions. *Historical Sketch of the American Board of Commissions for Foreign Missions*. Boston, 1895.

Andrews, S. "The Gods of Wo Lee." *Atlantic Monthly* 25 (Apr. 1870): 469–79.

———. "Wo Lee and his Kinsfolk." *Atlantic Monthly* 25 (Feb. 1870): 223–33.

Anti-Chinese Union of San Francisco. *Constitution and By-laws of the Anti-Chinese Union of San Francisco*. San Francisco: M. Weiss, Printer, 1876.

"Are We Are Afraid to Do Justice?" *Christian Century* 60 (June 1943): 687–88.

Asbury, Herbert. *The Barbary Coast, An Informal History of the San Francisco Underworld*. New York: Alfred A. Knopf, 1933.

Ayers, James J. *Chinese Exclusion*. Speech delivered in the Committee of the Constitutional Convention, Dec. 9, 1878. Los Angeles: Evening Express Newspaper and Printing Co., 1878.

Baird, Robert. *The Christian Retrospect and Register: A Summary of the Science, Moral and Religious Progress of the First Half of the XIXth Century*. New York: M. W. Dodd, 1851.

Baldwin, Esther E. *Must the Chinese Go? An Examination of the Chinese Question*. Boston: Rand, Avery, 1886; reprint of third edition, San Francisco: R and E Research Associates, 1970.

Bamford, Mary E. *Angel Island: The Ellis Island of the West*. Chicago: Women's American Baptist Home Mission Society, 1917.

———. *A Story of San Francisco's Chinatown*. Chicago: D. C. Cook, 1899.

Bari, Valeska, comp. *The Course of Empire: First Hand Accounts of California in the Days of the Gold Rush of '49*. New York: Coward-McCann, 1931.

Barrows, Charles Dana. *The Expulsion of the Chinese. What Is a Reasonable Policy for the Times. A Sermon*. San Francisco: S. Carson, 1886.

Barry, John D. *The City of Domes*. San Francisco: J. J. Newbegin, 1915.

Becker, Samuel E. W. *Humor of a Congressional Investigation Committee: A Review of the Joint Special Committee to Investigate Chinese Immigration*. Washington, D.C.: Government Printing Office, 1877.

Bee, Fred. A. "Opening Argument of F. A. Bee Before the Joint Committee of the Two Houses of Congress on Chinese Immigration." San Francisco, 1876.

———. *The Other Side of the Chinese Question*. San Francisco: Woodward and Co., 1886.

Bode, William Walter. *Lights and Shadows of Chinatown*. San Francisco: Press of H. S. Crocker, 1896.

Boone, William J., M. D. *Address in Behalf of the China Mission*. New York: W. Osborn, 1837.

Boothe, Clare. "Madame Chiang Kai-Shek: Why the Wife of China's Generalissimo Is Considered One of the World's Great Women." *Scholastic* 41 (Sept. 28–Oct. 3, 1942): 23–24.

Brace, Charles L. *The New West; Or California in 1867–1868*. New York: G. P. Putnam and Son, 1869.

Brooks, Benjamin S. *Appendix to the Opening Statement and Brief of B. S. Brooks, on the Chinese Question, Referred to the Joint Committee of the Senate and House of Representatives, Consisting of Documentary Evidence and Statistics Bearing on the Question Involved*. San Francisco: Women's Co-operative Printing Union, 1877.

———. *Brief of the Legislation and Adjudication Touching the Chinese Question Referred to the Joint Commission of Both Houses of Congress*. San Francisco: Women's Co-operative Printing Union, 1877.

———. "Opening Statement of B. S. Brooks, Before the Joint Committee of the Two Houses of Congress, on Chinese Immigration." San Francisco, 1876.

———. *The Chinese in California: To the Committee on Foreign Relations of the United States Senate*. N.p., [1876?].

Brown, D. Mackenzi, ed. *China Trade Days in California: Selected Letters from the Thompson Papers, 1832–1863*. Berkeley: University of California Press, 1947.

Browne, J. Ross. *Report of the Debates in the Convention of California on the*

Formation of the State Constitution in September and October 1849. Washington, D.C.: John T. Towers, 1850.

Buel, J. W. *Metropolitan Life Unveiled; Or the Mysteries and Miseries of America's Cities.* St. Louis, Mo.: Anchor, 1882.

Cai Tingkai. *Cai Tingkai zizhuan* (Autobiography of Cai Tingkai). 3 vols. Taipei: Longwen chubanshe, 1989.

California State Legislature. "Report of Joint Select Committee Relative to the Chinese Population of the State of California." *Appendix to the Journals of the Senate and Assembly*, v. 3. Sacramento, Calif.: State Printing Office, 1862.

California State Legislature, Assembly. *Majority and Minority Reports of the Committee on the Mines and Mining Interests.* 1853 session in the assembly, Doc. 28; Sacramento, Calif.: State Printing Office.

California State Legislature, Senate, Special Committee on Chinese Immigration. *Chinese Immigrants: The Social, Moral and Political Effect.* Sacramento, Calif.: State Printing Office, 1878.

———. *Chinese Immigration: The Social, Moral, and Political Effect of Chinese Immigration.* Sacramento, Calif.: State Printing Office, 1876; reprint, San Francisco: R and E Research Associates, 1970.

California Supreme Court. See *Chin Kem You v Ah Joan, Transcript on Appeal.* San Francisco, 1885.

Capp, Charles S. *The Church and Chinese Immigration: A Consideration of the Question: "What Ought to Be the Attitude of the Church and Christian People Toward the Efforts Made to Prevent the Coming of Chinese to This Country.* San Francisco, 1890.

Carey, Joseph. *By the Golden Gate, or, San Francisco, the Queen City of the Pacific Coast: With Scenes and Incidents Characteristic of Its Life.* Albany, N.Y.: The Albany Diocesan Press, 1902.

Chen Hansheng. *Huagong chuguo shiliao huibian* (Compilation of historical documents concerning Chinese laborers overseas). 7 vols. Beijing: Zhonghua Shuju, 1985.

Chen Lanbin. *Shimei jilue* (Brief records of a diplomatic mission to the United States). In *Xiaofanghuzhai yudichungchao* (Collected texts on geography from the Xiaofanghu study), book 44.

Chiang, May-ling Soong (Madame Chiang Kai-shek). *China Shall Rise Again.* New York: Harper, 1941.

Chinatown Declared a Nuisance! San Francisco: n.p., 1880.

Chinese Chamber of Commerce of San Francisco (The Six Chinese Companies). *San Francisco Chinatown on Parade in Picture and Story.* Ed. H. K. Wong. San Francisco, 1961.

Chinese Consolidated Benevolent Association (The Six Chinese Companies). *To His Excellency Grant, President of the United States.* N.p., 1876.

———. *Memorial of the Six Chinese Companies: An Address to the Senate and House of Representatives of the United States. Testimony of California's Leading Citizens Before the Joint Special Congressional Committee.* San Francisco: Alta, 1877; reprint, San Francisco: R and E Research Associates, 1970.

Chinese Equal Rights League, New York. *Appeal of the Chinese Equal Rights League to the People of the United States for Equality of Manhood.* New York: The League, 1892.

Chinese Hospital of San Francisco. Oakland: Carruth & Carruth, Printers, 1899.

Clark, Helen F. *The Lady of the Lily Feet and Other Stories of Chinatown.* Philadelphia: Griffith and Rowland, 1900.

Coleman, William T. *The Chinese Question Considered by a Calm and Dispassionate Merchant; A Forcible Argument Against Further Mongolian Immigration.* San Francisco, [1882?].

Condit, Ira M. *The Chinaman as We See Him, and Fifty Years of Work for Him.* Chicago: Fleming H. Revell, 1900.

———. *The Force of Missions in a New China.* 2nd. ed. Oakland, Calif., [1903?].

Conwell, Russell Herman. *Why and How: Why the Chinese Emigrate, and the Means They Adopt for the Purpose of Reaching America.* Boston: Lee and Shepard, 1871.

Cui Guoyin. *Chushi meirimiguo riji* (Journal of Chinese minister to the United States, Spain, and Peru). 2 vols. 1894, reprint, Taipei: Wenhai.

Culin, Stewart. "China in America: A Study in the Social Life of the Chinese in the Eastern Cities of the United States." Originally presented at the 36th meeting of the American Association for the Advancement of Science, New York, 1887. Philadelphia: n.p., 1887.

———. *Chinese Drug Stores in America.* Originally published in the *Journal of Pharmacy* (Dec. 1887); reprinted as a pamphlet, Philadelphia, 1887.

———. "Chinese Secret Societies in the United States." *Journal of American Folklore* 3 (Jan.–Mar. 1890): 39–43.

———. "Divination and Fortune-Telling among the Chinese in America." *The Overland Monthly* 25, no. 146 (Feb. 1895): 165–72.

———. *The Gambling Games of the Chinese in America. Fan T'an: The Game of Repeatedly Spreading out. And Pak Kop Piu or the Game of White Pigeon Ticket.* Philadelphia: The University of Pennsylvania Press, 1891.

———. *The I Hing or "Patriotic Uprising." Chinese Secret Societies. Customs of the Chinese in America.* Baltimore, 1890, reprint, San Francisco: R and E Research Associates, 1970.

———. "Popular Literature of the Chinese Laborers in the United States." *Oriental Studies: A Selection of Papers Read Before the Oriental Club of Philadelphia, 1888–1894*. Boston: Ginn, 1894, pp. 52–62.

———. *The Practice of Medicine by the Chinese in America*. Philadelphia: n.p., 1887; reprinted from the Medical and Surgical Reporter.

Daoguangchao chouban yiwu shimo (A complete record of the management of the barbarian affairs of the Qing Dynasty: The reign of the Emperor Daoguang). Beijing, 1929–30.

Daqing fagui daquan (Complete statutes of the Great Qing [Dynasty]). Reprint, Taipei, 1972.

Davis, Horace. "Chinese Immigration." Speech delivered in the House of Representatives, Washington, D.C., June 8, 1878.

Davis, Sir John Francis. *China, During the War and Since Peace*. 2 vols. London: Longman, Brown, Green, and Longmans, 1852.

Day, Horace B. *The Opium Habit*. New York: Harper, 1868.

Del Mar, Alexander. *Why Should the Chinese Go? A Pertinent Inquiry from a Mandarin High in Authority*. San Francisco: Bruce's Book and Job Printing House, 1878.

Delkin, James Ladd. *Flavor of San Francisco: A Guide to "The City."* Stanford, Calif.: Stanford University Press, 1943.

Densmore, G. B. *The Chinese in California: Description of Chinese Life in San Francisco, Their Habits, Morals and Manners*. San Francisco: Oettit and Ross, 1880.

Ding Weiliang (W. A. P. Martin). "Meiguo Jinshan" (American Gold Mountain). In Ding Weiliang, comp. *Zhongxi jianwenlu xuanbian* (Selected accounts of things seen and heard in the West and China), 1877; reprint, Taipei: Wenhai.

Disturnell's Strangers' Guide to San Francisco and Vicinity. San Francisco: W. C. Disturnell, 1883.

Dobie, Charles Caldwell. *San Francisco's Chinatown*. New York: D. Appleton, 1936.

Downing, C. Toogood. *The Fan-Qui in China in 1836–7*. 3 vols. London: H. Colburn, 1838.

Doxey, William. *Doxey's Guide to San Francisco and the Pleasure Resorts of California*. San Francisco: W. Doxey, 1897.

Edholm, M. G. C. "A Stain on the Flag." *The Californian* 1 (1892): 159–70.

The Elite Directory for San Francisco and Oakland: A Residence Address, Visiting, Club, Theatre and Shopping Guide, Containing the Names of Over Six Thousand Society People. San Francisco: Argonaut, 1879.

Enping Xianzhi (The gazetteer of Enping County). 1934; reprint, Cheng-wen, n.d.

Fan Duanang. *Yuezhong jianwen* (Things seen and heard in Guangdong), [1730?]; reprint, Fugang: Guangdong gaodengjiaoyu chubanshe, 1988.

Farquhar, Francis P., ed. *Up and Down California in 1860–1864: The Journal of William Brewer.* London: H. Milford, 1930; reprint, Berkeley: University of California Press, 1966.

Farwell, Willard B. *The Chinese at Home and Abroad, Together with the Report of the Special Committee of the Board of Supervisors of San Francisco on the Condition of the Chinese Quarter of that City.* San Francisco: A. L. Bancroft, 1885.

Fitch, George H. "In a Chinese Theater." *The Century Magazine* 24, no. 1 (1882), pp. 189–92.

Frost, Jennett B. *California's Greatest Curse.* San Francisco: J. Winterburn, 1879.

General Harrison's Record on the Chinese Question. N.p., 1882.

Genthe, Arnold. *Old Chinatown: A Book of Pictures.* Text by W. Irwin. New York: M. Kennerley, 1913.

George, Henry. "Chinese Immigration." In John Lalor, ed., *Encyclopedia of Political Science, Political Economy and the Political History of the United States.* Chicago: Rand, McNally, 1883, pp. 409–14.

Gibson, Otis. *"Chinaman or White Man, Which?" Reply to Father Buchard.* San Francisco: Alta, 1873.

——. *The Chinese in America.* Cincinnati, Ohio: Hitchcock and Walden, 1877.

——. *[To] Hon. Horace Davis, M. C. Sir: While I Do Not Share in the Woful Prophecies of Impending Ruin to Our Country on Account of Chinese Immigration . . . .* San Francisco, 1880.

Gompers, Samuel, and Herman Gutstadt. *Meat vs. Rice: American Manhood Against Asian Cooliesm*, published by American Federation of Labor and printed as U.S. S. Doc. 137, 1902; reprinted with introduction and appendices, San Francisco: Asiatic Exclusion League, 1908.

Gong, Eng Ying. *Tong War!: The First Complete History of the Tongs in America, Details of the Tong Wars and Their Causes, Lives of Famous Hatchetmen and Gunmen, and Inside Information as to the Workings of the Tongs, Their Aims . . . .* New York: N. L. Brown, 1930.

Green, Mrs. E. M. "The Chinese Theater." *The Overland Monthly* 41, no. 2 (1902): 118–25.

Grimm, Henry. *"The Chinese Must Go": A Farce in Four Acts.* San Francisco: A. L. Bancroft, 1879.

Guangdong tongzhi (The general gazetteer of Guangdong). First published in 1818; revised in 1822; recompiled in 1864; reprint, Shangwu yinshuguan, 1934.

Guangdong wenshi ziliao (Historical documents concerning Guangdong). Comp. Research Commission on Historical Documents of the Political Consultative Conference of Guangdong Province. Canton: Guangdong renmin chubanshe, 1963–92.

"Guarding the Gates Against Undesirables." *Current Opinion* 16 (Apr. 1924): 400–401.

Hardy, Iza Duffus. *Between Two Oceans: or, Sketches of American Travel*. London: Hurst and Blackett, 1884.

Hart, Jerome A. "The New Chinatown in San Francisco." *The Bohemian Magazine* 16, no. 5 (May 1909): 593–605.

Healy, Patrick Joseph. *Reasons for Non-Exclusion with Comments on the Exclusion Convention*. San Francisco: the author, 1902.

The Heathen Chinee Songster: A Choice Collection of the Latest Copyright Songs, Minstrel Melodies, and Popular Ballads of the Day. New York: Beadle, 1871.

Helms, Ludvig Verner. *Pioneering in the Far East*. London: W. H. Allen, 1882; reprint, London: Dawsons, 1969.

Helper, Hinton R. *The Land of Gold. Reality Versus Fiction*. Baltimore, Md.: H. Taylor, 1855.

Hernisz, Stanislas, comp. *A Guide to Conversation in the English and Chinese Language for the Use of American and Chinese in California and Elsewhere*. Boston: J. P. Jewett, 1854.

Hertslet, Godfrey E. P. *Hertslet's China Treaties: Treaties &c., Between Great Britain and China; China and Foreign Powers; and Orders in Council, Rules, Regulations, Acts of Parliament, Decrees, &c., Affecting British Interests in China*. 2 vols. London: Harrison, 1908.

Himmelwright, Abraham Lincoln A. *The San Francisco Earthquake and Fire: A Brief History and Disaster*. New York: Roebling Construction, 1906.

Ho Yow. "Chinese Exclusion, A Benefit or A Harm." *North American Review* 173 (Sept. 1901): 314–30.

Holcombe, Chester. *The Real Chinaman*. New York: Dod, Mead, 1895.

———. "Chinese Exclusion and the Boycott." *Outlook* 81 (Dec. 30, 1905): 1066–72.

Holt, Hamilton, ed. *The Life Stories of Undistinguished Americans As Told by Themselves*. New York: J. Pott, 1906; reprint, New York: Routledge, 1990.

Howard, Harry Paxton. "Justice to Our Allies." *Commonweal* 36 (Jan. 1942): 151–53.

Hu Qiuyuan, and Wang Ping, eds. *Jindai zhongguo dui xifang ji lieqiang renshi zhiliaohuibian* (Compilation of sources concerning modern China's understanding of the West and the powers). 2 vols. Taipei: Zhongyang Yanjiuyuan jindaishi yanjiusuo, 1972.

Hu Zhaozhong, comp. *Meizhou guangdonghuaqiao liuchuangeyao huibian* (Anthology of folk songs circulating among the Cantonese in America). Hong Kong: Qiuguzhai, 1970.

Huang Juezi. "A Request to Repair the Leaking Hole to Strengthen the

Foundation of the Country." In Yang Jialuo, ed., *Yiapian zhanzheng wenxian Huibian* (Historical documents concerning the Opium War). Taipei, 1973.

Huang Sande. *Hongmeng Geming Shi* (A history of the revolution of the Hongmeng). 1936.

Hubbard, Frederick Heman. *The Opium Habit and Alcoholism.* New York: A. S. Barnes, 1881; reprint, New York, 1981.

Huggins, Dorothy H., comp. *Continuation of the Annals of San Francisco.* San Francisco: California Historical Society, 1939.

Hunter, William C. *The "Fan Kwae" at Canton Before Treaty Years, 1825–1844.* London: K. Paul, Trench, 1882.

International Opium Commission. *Report of the International Opium Commission.* 2 vols. Shanghai, North-China Daily News & Herald, 1909.

Jenness, Charles Kelley. *The Charities of San Francisco: A Directory of the Benevolent and Correctional Agencies.* San Francisco: Book Room Print, 1894.

Jiangfuren youmei jiniance (Anthology commemorating Mme. Jiang's American tour). Comp. Meizhou guomin ribao (Chinese nationalist daily of America). San Francisco, [1943?].

Joint Special Commission to Investigate Chinese Immigration. *Report of the Royal Commission on Chinese Immigration* (Ottawa: Printed by the order of the Commission, 1885).

Jones, David D. *The Surnames of the Chinese in America Spelled According to the David Jones System of Spelling Chinese Names; with Notes on Various Subjects of Interest to the Chinese and Those Who Do Business with Them.* San Francisco: The Chinese Name Spelling Co., 1904.

Kane, Harry H., M.D. *Opium-Smoking in America and China: A Study of Its Prevalence, and Effects, Immediate and Remote, on the Individual and Nation.* New York: G. P. Putnam's Sons, 1881. Reprint, New York: Arno, 1976.

Kimball, Charles P. *The San Francisco City Directory.* San Francisco: Journal of Commerce Press, 1850.

Kong, Walter. "How We Grill the Chinese," *Asia* 42 (spring 1942): 520–23.

Kuang, Bingshun (B. S. Fong). *Meizhou huaqiaogaikuang ji kangzhan yilai aiguo yundong baogaoshu* (A report of the conditions of the Chinese in America and the Patriotic Movement since the beginning of the War of Resistance). San Francisco: n.p., 1941.

La Fevre, Benjamin. *Biographies of S. Grover Cleveland, and Thomas A. Hendricks, with a Description of the Leading Issues and the Proceedings of the National Convention Together with a History of the Political Parties of the United States: Comparisons of Platforms on All Important Questions, and Political Tables for Ready Reference,* New York: Baird & Dillon, 1884.

Langley, Henry G., comp. *The San Francisco Directory*. San Francisco: Henry G. Langley, 1870s and 1880s.

Lasker, Bruno. "End Exclusion Now." *New Republic* 108 (May 1943): 698–99.

Layres, Augustus. *Both Sides of the Chinese Question, or Critical Analysis of the Evidence for and Against Chinese Immigration as Elicited Before the Congressional Commission*. San Francisco: A. F. Woodbridge, 1877.

Legge, James. *Christianity in China: Nestroianism, Modern Catholicism, Protestantism*. Boston, 1888.

Liang Chaojie. *Meiyou shici cungao chuji* (Poetry written during the American journey). San Francisco: Chinese World, 1931.

Liang Qichao. *Xindalu youji* (My journey to the new continent), 1904; reprinted in Shen Yunlong, *Jindai Zhongguo shiliao congkan* (Historical documents concerning modern China). Taipei: Wenhai, 1967, 10: 377–490.

Liang Tingnan and Fang Tungshu, eds. *Yuehaiguan zhi* (The discourse on the Canton maritime customs). 30 vols., 1838; reprint, Taipei: Cheng-wen, 1968.

Lin Zexu. *Lin zehsu ji: Riji* (Complete Works of Lin Zexu: Diaries), edited by the History Department of Sun Yat-sen University. Beijing: Zhonghua shuju, 1962.

———. *Sizhou zhi* (Gazetteer of the four continents). 1839.

Lin Zhen. *Xihau jiyou cao* (Account of a journey to the West Sea), 1849. Reprinted in 1985, together with a few other documents, Changsha, China: Hunan renmin chubanshe, 1985.

Linthicum, Richard. *Complete Story of the San Francisco Horror*. San Francisco: Herbert D. Russell, 1906.

Liu Guoxin. "Prostitute in Canton Since the Late Qing Dynasty." *Guangdong wenshi ziliao* (Historical documents concerning Guangdong). Comp. Research Commission on Historical Documents of the Political Consultative Conference of Guangdong Province. Canton, 1963, 10: 197–211.

Lloyd, Benjamin E. *Lights and Shades in San Francisco*. San Francisco: A. L. Bancroft, 1876.

Lo Hsiang-lin, comp. *Yuedongzhifeng* (meaning "Folk songs in East Guangdong"; the author's own English translation is *Folksongs of Hakka, Kuangtung*). Taipei: The Orient Cultural Service, 1947.

Loomis, A. W. "Chinese 'Funeral Baked Meats.' " *The Overland Monthly* 3, no. 1 (July 1869): 21–29.

———. "Chinese in California, Their Sign-Boards." *The Overland Monthly* 1, no. 2 (Aug. 1868): 152–56.

———. "Occult Science in the Chinese Quarter." *The Overland Monthly* 3, no. 2 (Aug. 1869): 160–69.

———. "Holiday in the Chinese Quarter." *The Overland Monthly* 2 (Feb. 1869): 144–53.

———. "Medical Art in the Chinese Quarter." *The Overland Monthly* 2, no. 6 (1869): 496–506.

———. "Chinese Women in California." *Overland* 2, no. 4 (1869): 344–51.

———. "The Oldest East in the New West." *The Overland Monthly* 1, no. 4 (Oct. 1868): 360–69.

———. "Our Heathen Temples." *The Overland Monthly* 1, no. 5 (Nov. 1868): 345–61.

Lowenstein, M. J., comp. *Official Guide to the Louisiana Purchase Exposition*. St. Louis, Mo.: The Official Guide Company, 1904.

Lu Chuanpu jiaxun (Family precepts of Lu Chuanpu). San Francisco: Chong Jan, 1933.

Ma, Yi Ying. "Effects of Attendance at Chinese Language Schools upon San Francisco Children." Ph.D. diss., University of California, 1945.

Martin, W. A. P. *The Awakening of China*. New York: Doubleday, Page, 1907.

———. "The Awakening of China." *World's Work* 11 (June 1906): 7124–28.

Masters, Frederick J. "Can a Chinaman Become a Christian?" *The Californian Illustrated Magazine* 2, no. 5 (Oct. 1892): 622–32.

———. "Opium and Its Votaries." *The Californian Illustrated Magazine* 2 (1892): 631–45.

———. "Pagan Temples in San Francisco." *The Californian Illustrated Magazine* 6 (1892): 727–41.

McDowell, Henry Burden. "The Chinese Theater." *The Century Illustrated Monthly Magazine* 29, no. 1 (Nov. 1884): 27–44.

———. "A New Light on the Chinese." *Harper's New Monthly Magazine* 86 (Dec. 1892): 3–17.

McLeod, Alexander. *Pigtails and Gold Dust: A Panorama of Chinese Life in Early California*. Caldwell, Idaho: Caxton, 1947.

Medical Missionary Society and the Ophthalmic Hospital at Canton. *Address with Minutes of the Medical Missionary Society in China*. Canton, 1838.

———. *Minutes of the Annual Meeting of the Medical Missionary Society in China; and the Fifteenth Report of its Ophthalmic Hospital at Canton, for the years 1848–1849*. Canton, 1850.

Methodist Missionary Society. *China and the Chinese: A Compend of Missionary Information from Various Source*. Toronto: Methodist Missionary Society, 1892.

Mitchell, John H. "Chinese Immigration. Absolute Exclusion the Only Effective Remedy." Speech delivered in the U.S. Senate, Washington, D.C., Jan. 12, 1888.

A. W. Morgan & Co.'s San Francisco City Directory. San Francisco: F. A. Bonnard, Sept. 1852.

Morgan, John Tyler. *The Chinese Question; Arguments Against Exclusion Answered and Arguments in Favor of Exclusion Presented.* Portland, Ore.: Multnomah, 1901.

Moy, Earnest K. *The Pacific Coast Tour of Mei Lan-Fang.* San Francisco: The Pacific Chinese Dramatic Club, n.d.

Murray, Hugh. *An Encyclopaedia of Geography.* London: Longman, Rees, Orme, Brown, Green, & Longman, 1834.

Nanhai Xianzhi (The gazetteer of Nanhai County), 1836; revised, 1872; reprint, Taipei: Cheng-wen, n.d.

————, 1910; reprint, Taipei: Cheng-wen, n.d.

Ng Poon Chew. *The Treatment of the Exempt Classes of Chinese in the United States: A Statement from the Chinese in America.* San Francisco: the author, 1908.

Nordhoff, Charles. *California, for Health, Pleasure and Residence: A Book for Travellers and Settlers.* New York: Harper, 1872.

Norr, William. *Stories of Chinatown, Sketches from Life in the Chinese Colony of Mott, Pell and Doyers Streets.* New York: the author, 1892.

The Pacific Telephone and Telegraph Company. San Francisco and Oakland Chinese Telephone Directory. 1935; 1942.

Panyu Xianzhi (The gazetteer of Panyu County), 1871; reprint, Taipei: Cheng-wen, n.d.

Parker's San Francisco Directory. San Francisco: James M. Parker, 1852.

Phelan, James D. "Why the Chinese Should be Excluded." *North American Review* 173 (Nov. 1901): 663–76.

Pond, William Chauncey. *Gospel Pioneering: Reminiscences of Early Congregationalism in California, 1833–1920.* Oberlin, Ohio: The News Printing Company, 1921.

Poole, F. "The Law and the Gospel in 'Chinatown.'" In *A Record of Applied Christianity.* Philadelphia, Pa.: The Christian League of Philadelphia, 1898.

Powers, H. H. "Grave Consequences." *Atlantic Monthly* 134 (June 1924): 124–33.

Presbyterian Home Mission. "Mission to the Chinese in California." Annual report. 1854–91.

Qu Dajun. *Guangdong xinyu* (New things about Guangdong), [1700?]; reprint, Hong Kong: Zhonghua Shuju, 1974.

Quincy, Josiah, ed. *The Journals of Major Samuel Shaw: The First American Consul at Canton.* Boston: W. Crosby and H. P. Nicholas, 1847.

Rae, William F. *Westward by Rail: Journey to San Francisco and Back and a Visit to the Mormons.* London: Longmans, Green, 1870.

Rasmussen, Louis J., ed. *San Francisco Ship Passenger Lists.* 4 vols. Colma, Calif.: San Francisco Historic Record & Genealogy Bulletin, 1965.

Roberts, William Kemuel. *The Mongolian Problem in America: A Discussion of the Possibilities of the Yellow Peril: With Notes upon American Diplomacy in Its Relation to the Boycott*. San Francisco: Organized Labor Print, 1906.

Sala, George A. *America Revisited: From the Bay of New York to the Gulf of Mexico, and From Lake Michigan to the Pacific*. 2 vols. London: Vizetelly, 1882.

San Francisco Municipal Reports, 1860–1910, published by the order of the Board of Supervisors.

Sargent, Aaron A. "Immigration of Chinese." Speech delivered in the U.S. Senate, March 7, 1878. Washington, D.C.: Government Printing Office, 1876.

Seward, George F. *Chinese Immigration: Its Social and Economic Aspects*. New York: Arno, 1881.

Shearer, Frederick E., ed. *The Pacific Tourist*. New York: Adams and Bishop, 1879.

Shepherd, Charles R. *The Ways of Ah Sin*. New York: Fleming H. Revell, 1923.

Shunde Xianzhi (The gazetteer of Shunde County), 1853; reprint, Taipei: Chengwen, 1967.

———. Beijing: Zhonghua Shuju, 1996.

Smith, Arthur H. *Chinese Characteristics*. New York: Fleming H. Revell, 1894.

A Social Manual for San Francisco and Oakland. San Francisco: The City Publishing Company, 1884.

Soule, Frank, John H. Gihon, and James Nisbet. *Annals of San Francisco*. New York: D. Appleton, 1855; reprint, Palo Alto: Lewis Osborne, 1966.

Speer, William. *Answer to Objections to Chinese Testimony, and Appeal for Their Protection by Our Laws*. San Francisco: The Chinese Mission House. 1857.

———. *China and California: Their Relations, Past and Present*. San Francisco: Marvin and Hitchcock, 1853.

———. *An Humble Plea, Addressed to the Legislature of California in Behalf of the Immigrants from the Empire of China to This State*. San Francisco: Steret, 1856.

———. *The Oldest and the Newest Empire: China and the United States*. Chicago: Jones, Junkin, 1870.

Spinks, Charles Nelson. "Repeal Chinese Exclusion." *Asia* 42 (Feb. 1942): 92–94.

Starr, M. B. *The Coming Struggle, or, What the People on the Pacific Coast: Think of the Coolie Invasion*. San Francisco: Bacon, 1873.

Stoddard, Charles Warren. *A Bit of Old China*. San Francisco: A. M. Robertson, 1912.

Stout, Arthur B. *Chinese Immigration and the Psychological Causes of the Decay of a Nation*. San Francisco, Agnew and Deffebach, 1862.

Taylor, Benjamin F. *Between the Gates*. 6th ed., Chicago: S. C. Griggs, 1879.

Taylor, Philip A. M. *The Distant Magnet: European Emigration to the U.S.A.* London: Eyre and Spottiswoode, 1971.

Taylor, William. *Seven Years' Street Preaching in San Francisco, California*. New York: Carton & Porter, 1856.

Tisdale, William. "Chinese Physicians in California." *Lippincott's Magazine* 63 (March 1899): 411–16.

Todd, Frank Morton. *The Chamber of Commerce Handbook for San Francisco, Historical and Descriptive: A Guide for Visitors.* San Francisco: San Francisco Chamber of Commerce, 1914.

——. *The Story of the Exposition.* 5 vols. New York: G. P. Putnam's Sons, 1921.

Towner, Charles. "*The Heathen Chinee," Songs & Chorus.* Lyrics by Bret Harte. Chicago: Root and Cady, 1870.

Townsend, Ralph. *Ways That Are Dark: The Truth About China.* 3rd ed., New York: G. P. Putnam, 1934.

U.S. Bureau of the Census. *Abstract of the Twelfth Census of the United States, 1910.* Washington, D.C.: Government Printing Office, 1904.

——. *Historical Statistics of the United States: Colonial Times to 1957.* Prepared by the Bureau of the Census with the cooperation of the Social Science Research Council. Washington, D.C.: Government Printing Office, 1960.

——. *Chinese and Japanese in the U.S.* Washington, D.C.: Government Printing Office, 1914.

——. *Statistical Abstract of the United States.* Washington, D.C.: U.S. Government Printing Office, 1981.

U.S. Census Office. *Census Reports.* Vol. 1. *Twentieth Census of the United States Taken in the Year 1900: Population,* part I. Washington, D.C., Government Printing Office, 1901.

——. *Census Report of the Social Statistics of Cities.* Washington, D.C.: Government Printing Office, 1887.

——. *A Compendium of the Ninth Census.* Washington, D.C.: Government Printing Office, 1872.

——. *A Compendium of the Tenth Census,* part I. Washington, D.C.: Government Printing Office, 1883.

——. *A Compendium of the Tenth Census,* part II. Washington, D.C.: Government Printing Office, 1888.

——. *Ninth census.* Vol. 1. *The Statistics of the Population of the United States, Embracing the Tables of Race, Nationality, Sex, Selected Ages and Occupations.* Washington, D.C.: Government Printing Office, 1872.

——. *Population of the United States in 1860: Compiled from the Original Returns of the Eighth Census.* Washington, D.C.: Government Printing Office, 1864.

——. *Seventh Census of the United States, 1850: An Appendix, Embracing Notes upon the Tables of Each of the States, Etc.* Washington, D.C.: Government Printing Office, 1853.

——. *Tenth Census of the United States: Statistics of the Population of the United*

State by States, Counties, and Minor Civil Divisions. Washington, D.C.: Government Printing Office, 1881.

U.S. Congress. House. Committee on Immigration and Naturalization. *Repeal of the Chinese Exclusion Acts.* Hearings, 78th Cong., 1st sess. Washington, D.C.: Government Printing Office, 1943.

————. *Facts Concerning the Enforcement of the Chinese-Exclusion Laws.* Compilation from the records of the Bureau of Immigration, 59th Cong., 1st sess., House doc. no. 847. Washington, D.C.: Government Printing Office, 1906.

————. Select Committee on Depression of Labor and Business. *Causes of General Depression in Labor and Business.* Washington, D.C.: Government Printing Office, 1879.

U. S. Congress, Joint Select Committee on Immigration and Naturalization. *Chinese Immigration,* 51st Cong., 2nd. sess., March 2, 1891. Washington, D.C.: Government Printing Office, 1891.

U.S. Congress, Joint Special Committee to Investigate Chinese Immigration. *Report of the Joint Special Committee to Investigate Chinese Immigration,* 44th Cong., 2nd sess., report no. 689. Washington, D.C.: Government Printing Office, 1877.

U.S. Congress. Senate. Committee on Immigration. *Chinese Exclusion: Testimony Taken before the Committee on Immigration, United States Senate, on Senate Bill 2960 and Certain Other Bills before the Committee Providing for the Exclusion of Chinese Laborers.* Washington, D.C.: Government Printing Office, 1902.

————. Committee on Immigration. *Immigration of Chinese into the United States: A Pamphlet Containing a Collection of Excerpts and Arguments in Opposition to the Passage of a Law to Prohibit the Immigration of Chinese into the United States.* Washington, D.C.: Government Printing Office, 1902.

U.S. Immigration Commission. *Dictionary of Races of Peoples.* Washington, D.C.: Government Printing Office, 1911.

U.S. Industrial Commission on Immigration. *Reports of the Industrial Commission on Immigration.* Vol. 15. Washington, D.C.: Government Printing Office, 1901.

U.S. Laws. *Treaty, and Regulations Relating to the Exclusion of Chinese.* Washington, D.C.: Government Printing Office, 1903.

U.S. Library of Congress. Division of Bibliography. *Select List of References on Chinese Immigration,* comp. under the direction of A. P. C. Griffin. Washington, D.C.: Government Printing Office, 1904.

U.S. Supreme Court. *Immigration of Chinese Laborers. Its Injurious Effect. Legislation of Long Restricting It. The Validity of That Legislation Considered with Reference to the Treaty with China of 1880.* Washington, D.C.: Government Printing Office, 1884.

Views of San Francisco Before and After Earthquake. San Francisco: E. P. Chalton, 1906.

Villard, Oswald Garrison. "Justice for the Chinese." *Christian Century* 60 (May 1943): 633–34.

Walsh, Richard J. "Our Great Wall Against the Chinese." *New Republic* 107 (Nov. 1942): 671–72.

Wang Xiqi, comp. *Xiaofanghuzhai yudichungchao* (Collected texts on geography from the Xiaofanghu study). Shanghai: Zhuyitang, 1877–97.

Wang Yanwei, et al., comp. *Qingji waijiao shiliao* (Historical materials concerning foreign relations of the Qing Dynasty). 269 vols. Beijing: Gugongbowuyuan, 1931–33.

Warner, F. W. *Guide Book and Street Manual of San Francisco, California.* San Francisco: H. S. Crocker, 1882.

Wei Yuan, comp. *Haiguo tuzhi* (Illustrated treatise on the ocean kingdoms), 1844; reprint, Taipei: Cheng-wen, 1967.

Wells Fargo and Co.'s Express. *Directory of Principal Chinese Business Firms* (in San Francisco, Oakland, Los Angeles, Virginia City, Victoria, and Denver). San Francisco, 1882.

———. *Directory of Principal Chinese Business Firms* (in San Francisco, Sacramento, Marysville, Portland, Stockton, San Jose, and Virginia city of Nevada). San Francisco, 1878.

West, Henry J. *The Chinese Invasion; Revealing the Habits, Manners and Customs of the Chinese, Political, Social and Religious, on the Pacific Coast, Coming in Contact with the Free and Enlightened Citizens of America . . . .* San Francisco: Bacon, 1873.

Wheeler, Osgood Church. *The Chinese in America: A National Question.* Address delivered in Metropolitan Temple, San Francisco, Dec. 21, 1879, and in the State Capitol at Sacramento, Jan. 16, 1880. Oakland, Calif.: Times Publishing Co., 1880.

Williams, Frederick Wells. *Anson Burlingame: The First Chinese Mission to Foreign Powers.* New York: Scribner's, 1912.

———, ed. *The Life and Letters of Samuel Wells Williams,* New York: G. P. Putnam's Sons, 1889; reprint, Wilmington, Del.: Scholarly Resources, 1972.

Williams, Samuel Wells. *Chinese Immigration.* New York: Scribner's, 1879.

———. *The Middle Kingdom: A Survey of the Geography, Government, Literature, Social Life Arts, and History of the Chinese Empire and Its Inhabitants.* Rev. ed., 2 vols., 1895, New York: Charles Scribner's; reprint, New York 1966.

Wold, Ansel, comp. *Biographical Directory of the American Congress, 1774–1927.* H. Doc. 783. 69th Cong., 2nd sess., 1928.

Woltor, Robert. *A Short and Truthful History of the Taking of California and Oregon by the Chinese in the Year A. D. 1899*. San Francisco: A. L. Bancroft, 1882.

Wong, Mrs. Clemens. *Chinatown*. San Francisco: n.p., 1915.

Wong Yu Fong, comp. *Historical Review of Clonorchiasis*. San Francisco, 1927.

Workingmen's Party of California. *The Labor Agitators; or the Battle for Bread*. San Francisco: Geo. W. Greene, n.d.

Xiao Ninyu. "Yuedong shibolun" (On the foreign ships in East Guangdong). In Wei Yuan, comp. *Haiguo tuzhi* (Illustrated treatise on the ocean kingdoms). Taipai: Cheng-wen, 1967.

Xie Qinggao. *Haiwai fanyi lu* or *Hailu* (Record of the seas). Ed. and notes by Feng Chengjun, Taipei, 1962.

Xinning Xianzhi (The gazetteer of Xinning County), 1839; revised 1891; reprint, 1965.

Xu Jiyu. *Yinghuan zhilue* (Brief record of the ocean circuit), manuscript version, reprint, Taipei: Wenhai, 1974.

———. *Yinghuan zhilue* (Brief record of the ocean circuit), 1848. In Hu Qiuyuan and Wang Ping, eds., *Jindai zhongguo dui xifang ji lieqiang renshi zhiliaohuibian* (Compilation of sources concerning modern China's understanding of the West and the powers). 2 vols. Taipei: Zhongyang yanjiuyuan jindaishi Yanjiusuo, 1972.

Yuan, Tung-li. *A Guide to Doctoral Dissertations by Chinese Students, 1905–1960*. Washington, D.C.: published under the auspices of the Sino-American Cultural Society, Inc., 1961.

Yung, Wing. *My Life in China and America*. New York: H. Holt, 1909.

Zengcheng Xianzhi (The gazetteer of Zengcheng County), 1820; reprint, Taipei: Cheng-wen.

Zhang Deyi. *Hanghai shuqi* (Recounting the ocean-navigation wonders, or accounts of trips to Europe and America). Changsha, Hunan Province: Hunan renmin chubanshe, 1980.

Zhang Guiyong, et al., eds. *Zhongmei guanxi shiliao* (Historical sources concerning Sino-American relations: The reigns of the Emperors Jiaqing, Daoguang and Xianfeng). Taipei: Zhongyang yanjiuyuan jindaishi yanjiusuo, 1968.

Zhang Yinhuan. *Sanzhou riji* (Journal of the journey to three continents). 8 vols. Beijing, 1896.

Zhi Gang. *Chushi taixi ju* (Accounts of my first visit to the West). Reprint, Changsha, Hunan Province: Hunan renmin chubanshe, 1980.

Zhongshan Xianzhi (The gazetteer of Zhongshan [previously Xiangshan] County), 1873; reprint, n.p., 1961.

Zhu Shijia. *Meiguo huagong shiliao* (Documents concerning the United States' persecution of Chinese laborers). Beijing: Zhonghua Shuju, 1959.

Zhu Shoupeng, ed. *Guangxuchao donghualu* (Records of the Donghua in the reign of the Emperor Guangxu), 1909; reprint, Beijing, 1958 and 1984.

SECONDARY SOURCES

Abrams, Elliot, and Franklin S. Abrams. "Immigration Policy—Who Gets in and Why." *Public Interest* 38 (winter 1975): 3–29.

Anderson, Margo J. *The American Census: A Social History.* New Haven: Yale University Press, 1988.

Archdeacon, Thomas. *Becoming American: An Ethnic History.* New York: Free Press, 1983.

Arkush, R. David, and Leo O. Lee, eds. and trans. *Land Without Ghosts: Chinese Impressions of America from the Mid-Nineteenth Century to the Present.* Berkeley: University of California Press, 1989.

Armstrong, W. M. "Godkin and Chinese Labor: a Paradox in Nineteenth Century Liberalism." *American Journal of Economics and Sociology* 12 (1962): 91–102.

Bailyn, Bernard. *Voyagers to the West.* New York: Knopf, 1986.

Barlow, Janelle M. "The Images of the Chinese, Japanese, and Koreans in American Secondary School Textbooks, 1900–1970." Ph.D. diss., University of California, Berkeley, 1972.

Barnett, Suzanne Wilson. "Practical Evangelism: Protestant Missions and the Introduction of Western Civilization into China, 1820–1850." Ph.D. diss., Harvard University, 1973.

———. "Protestant Expansion and Chinese Views of the West." *Modern Asian Studies* 6 (1970): 1–20.

Barnett, Suzanne Wilson, and John King Fairbank, eds. *Christianity in China: Early Protestant Missionary Writings.* Cambridge: Committee on American-East Asian Relations of the Department of History in Collaboration with the Council on East Asian Studies/Harvard University, 1985.

Barnhart, Jacqueline Baker. *The Fair But Frail: Prostitution in San Francisco, 1849–1900.* Reno: University of Nevada Press, 1986.

Barry, Theodore Augustus, and B. A. Patter. *San Francisco, California, 1850.* Oakland: Biobooks, 1947.

Barth, Gunther. *Bitter Strength: A History of the Chinese in the United States, 1850–1870.* Cambridge: Harvard University Press, 1964.

BeDunnah, Gary P. *A History of the Chinese in Nevada: 1855–1904.* San Francisco: R and E Research Associates, 1973.

Bell, Daniel. "Ethnicity and Social Change." In Nathan Glazer and Patrick Moynihan, eds., *Ethnicity: Theory and Experience.* Cambridge: Harvard University Press, 1975, pp. 141–174.

Benderson, Eric Stuart. "Communist China's Treatment of the Overseas Chinese: The Dilemma of Manipulation or Protection." M.A. thesis, Columbia University, 1969.

Benedict, Burton. *The Anthropology of World's Fairs: San Francisco's Panama Pacific International Exposition of 1915*. Berkeley, Calif.: Lowie Museum of Anthropology, 1983.

Bernard, William S., ed. *American Immigration Policy—A Reappraisal*. New York: Harper, 1950.

Bodnar, John. *The Transplanted: A History of Immigrants in Urban America*. Bloomington: Indiana University Press, 1985.

Book, Susan W. *The Chinese in Butte County, California, 1860–1920*. San Francisco: R and E Research Associates, 1976.

Boorstin, Daniel J. *The Americans: The Democratic Experience*. New York: Random House, 1965.

Breslin, Thomas A. *China, American Catholicism, and the Missionary*. University Park: Pennsylvania State University Press, 1980.

Brettel, Carol B. *Men Who Migrate, Women Who Wait: Population and History in a Portuguese Parish*. Princeton: Princeton University Press, 1986.

Britton, Roswell S. *The Chinese Periodical Press, 1800–1912*. Taipei: Cheng-wen, 1966.

Brownstone, David M. *The Chinese-American Heritage*. New York: Facts on File, 1988.

Buell, Paul D., and Christopher Muench. "Chinese Medical Recipes from Frontier Seattle." *The Annals of the Chinese Historical Society of the Pacific Northwest* (1984): 100–105.

Buhle, Paul. "Anarchism and American Labor." *International Labor and Working Class History* 23 (spring 1983).

Burchell, R. A. *The San Francisco Irish, 1848–1880*. Manchester: University Press, 1979.

Caldwell, Dan. "The Negroization of the Chinese Stereotype in California." *Southern California Quarterly* 53 (1971): 123–31.

Cather, Helen V. *The History of San Francisco Chinatown*. San Francisco: R and E Research Associates, 1974.

Chan, Anthony B. "The Myth of the Chinese Sojourner." In K. Victor Ujimoto and Gordon Hirabayashi, eds. *Visible Minorities and Multiculturalism: Asians in Canada*. Toronto: Butterworths, 1980, pp. 33–42.

——. "Orientalism and Image Making: The Sojourner in Canadian History." *Journal of Ethnic Studies* 9 (1981): 37–46.

Chan, Kim M. "Mandarins in America: The Early Chinese Ministers to the United States, 1878–1907." Ph.D. diss., University of Hawaii, 1981.

Chan, Loren B. "The Chinese in Nevada: A Historical Survey." *Nevada Historical Society Quarterly* 25 (1982): 266–314.

Chan, Marlorie K. M., and Douglas W. Lee. "Chinatown Chinese: A Linguistic and Historical Re-evaluation." *Amerasia* 8 (1981): 111–31.

Chan, Sucheng. *Asian Americans: An Interpretive History.* Boston: Twayne, 1991.

———. "European and Asian Immigration into the United States in Comparative Perspective, 1820s to 1920s." in Virginia Yans-McLaughlin, ed., *Immigration Reconsidered: History, Sociology, and Politics.* New York: Oxford University Press, 1990, pp. 37–75.

———. "The Exclusion of Chinese Women, 1870–1943." In Sucheng Chan, ed., *Entry Denied.* Philadelphia, Pa.: Temple University Press, 1991.

———. "Public Policy, U.S.–China Relations, and the Chinese American Experience: An Interpretive Essay." In Edwin G. Clausen and Jack Bermingham, eds., *Pluralism, Racism, and the Search for Equality.* Boston: G. K. Hall, 1981, pp. 5–38.

———. "Selected Bibliography on the Chinese in the United States, 1850–1920." *Immigrant History Newsletter* 16 (1984): 7–15.

———. *This Bittersweet Soil: The Chinese on California Agriculture, 1860–1910.* Berkeley: The University of California Press, 1986.

———. "Using California Archives for Research in Chinese American History." In Douglas W. Lee, ed., *Annals of the Chinese Historical Society of the Pacific Northwest.* Seattle, Wash.: Chinese Historical Society of the Pacific Northwest, 1983, pp. 49–55.

———, ed. *Entry Denied: Exclusion and the Chinese Community in America, 1882–1943.* Philadelphia, Pa.: Temple University Press, 1991.

Chang, F. Yung. "A Study of the Movement to Segregate Chinese Pupils in the San Francisco Public Schools Up to 1885." Ph.D. diss., Stanford University, 1936.

Chang, Hao. *Liang Ch'i-ch'ao [Liang Qi-chao] and Intellectual Transition in China, 1890–1907.* Cambridge: Harvard University Press, 1971.

Chang, Hsin-pao. *Commissioner Lin and the Opium War.* New York: W. W. Norton, 1970.

Chang, Pao-min. *Continuity and Change: A Profile of Chinese Americans.* New York: Vantage, 1983.

Chapin, Howard M. "The Chinese Yunk Ke Ying at Providence." *Rhode Island Historical Society* (Providence) 27 (January 1934): 5–12.

Char, Tin-yuke. *The Bamboo Path: Life and Writings of a Chinese in Hawaii.* Honolulu: Hawaii Chinese History Center, 1977.

Char, Tin-yuke, comp. *The Sandalwood Mountains: Readings and Stories of the Early Chinese in Hawaii.* Honolulu: The University of Hawaii Press, 1975.

Chen, Helen. "Chinese Immigration into the United States: An Analysis of Changes in Immigration Policies." Ph.D. diss., University of Illinois at Champaign–Urbana, 1980.

Chen, Jack. *The Chinese of America*. San Francisco: Harper and Row, 1980.

Chen Kuangmin. *Meizhouhuaqiao tongjian* (The Chinese in the Americas). New York: Overseas Chinese Culture Publishing, 1950.

Chen, Ta. *Chinese Migration With Special Reference to Labor Conditions*. Washington, D.C., Government Printing Office, 1923.

——. *Emigrant Communities In South China: A Study of Overseas Migration and Its Influence on Standards of Living and Social Change*. New York: Institute of Pacific Relations, 1940.

Chen, Yong. "The Internal Origins of Chinese Emigration to California Reconsidered." *The Western Historical Quarterly* 28: 4 (winter 1997): 521–46.

Cheng, David Te-chao. *Acculturation of the Chinese in the United States: A Philadelphia Study*. Ph.D. diss., University of Pennsylvania; published in Fuochow, China: The Fukien Christian University Press, 1948.

Cheng, Lucie. "Free, Indentured, Enslaved: Chinese Prostitutes in 19th Century America." In Lucie Cheng and Edna Bonacich, eds., *Labor Immigration under Capitalism: Asian Workers in the United States before World War II*. Berkeley: The University of California Press, 1984, pp. 402–34.

Cheng, Lucie, and Liu Yuzun, with Zheng Dehua. "Chinese Emigration, the Sunning Railway and the Development of Toisan." *Amerasia* 9, no. 1 (spring 1982): 59–74.

Chetin, Helen. *Angel Island Prisoners, 1922*. Berkeley, Calif.: New Seed Press, 1982.

Chih, Ginger. *Immigration of Chinese Women to the U.S.A. 1900–1940*. M.A. thesis, Sarah Lawrence College, 1977.

Chin, Art. *Golden Tassels: A History of the Chinese in Washington, 1857–1977*. Seattle, Wash.: Chin, 1977.

Chin, Frank, et al., eds. *Aiiieeeee! An Anthology of Asian-American Writers*. Washington, D.C.: Howard University Press, 1974.

Chinese Historical Society of America. *The Life, Influence and the Role of the Chinese in the United States, 1776–1960*. San Francisco: The Society, 1976.

Chinn, Thomas W. *Bridging the Pacific: San Francisco Chinatown and Its People*. San Francisco: Chinese Historical Society of America, 1989.

Chinn, Thomas W., H. Mark Lai, and Philip P. Choy, eds. *A History of the Chinese in California: A Syllabus*. San Francisco: Chinese Historical Society of America, 1969.

Chiu, Ping. *Chinese Labor in California, 1850–1880: An Economic Study*. Madison: The State Historical Society of Wisconsin, 1963.

Chow, Willard T. *The Reemergence of an Inner City: The Pivot of Chinese Settlement in the East Bay Area of the San Francisco Bay Area*, San Francisco: R and E Research Associates, 1977.

Chu, Doris C. J. *Chinese in Massachusetts: Their Experiences and Contributions.* Boston: Chinese Culture Institute, 1987.

Chu, Li-min. "The Image of China and the Chinese in the Overland Monthly, 1868–1875, 1883–1935." San Francisco: R and E Research Associates, 1974.

Cohen, Lucy M. *Chinese in the Post–Civil War South.* Baton Rouge, Louisiana State University Press, 1984.

Colman, Elizabeth. *Chinatown, USA.* New York: Asia Press in association with the John Day Company, 1946.

Commons, John R. *Races and Immigrants in America.* New York: Macmillan, 1907.

Coolidge, Mary Roberts. *Chinese Immigration.* New York: Henry Holt, 1909.

Coppel, Charles A. *Indonesian Chinese in Crisis.* New York: Oxford University Press, 1983.

Courtney, William J. *San Francisco's Anti-Chinese Ordinances.* San Francisco: R and E Research Associates, 1974.

Cowan, Robert Ernest, and Boutwell Dunlap. *Bibliography of the Chinese Question in the United States.* San Francisco: A. M. Robertson, 1909.

Crouch, Archie R., et al. *Christianity in China: A Scholar's Guide to Resources in the Libraries and Archives of the United States.* Armonk, N. Y.: M. E. Sharpe, 1989.

Daley, William. *The Chinese-Americans.* New York: Chelsea House, 1987.

Daniels, Roger. "American Historians and East Asian Immigrants." *Pacific Historical Review* 43 (1974): 448–72.

———. *Asian America: Chinese and Japanese in the United States Since 1850.* Seattle: The University of Washington Press, 1988.

———. "Changes in Immigration Law and Nativism Since 1924." *American Historical Review* 76 (1986): 159–80.

———. "Chinese and Japanese in North America: The Canadian and American Experiences Compared." *The Canadian Review of American Studies* 17 (1986): 173–86.

———. *Concentration Camps: North America.* Malabaz, Fla.: Krieger, 1989.

———, ed. *Anti-Chinese Violence in North America.* New York: Arno Press, 1978.

Davis, Fred. *Yearning for Yesterday: A Sociology of Nostalgia.* New York: Free Press, 1979.

Davison, Mary. "The Babies in Chinatown." *Cosmopolitan* 28, no. 6 (Oct. 1900): 605–12.

Di Leonardo, Micaela. *The Varieties of Ethnic Experience: Kinship, Class, and Gender among California Italian-Americans*. Ithaca, N. Y.: Cornell University Press, 1984.

Dicker, Laverne Mau. *The Chinese in San Francisco: A Pictorial History*. New York: Dover Publications, 1979.

Dikötter, Frank. *The Discourse of Race in Modern China*. London: Hurst, 1992.

Dillon, Richard H. *The Hatchetmen: The Story of the Tong Wars in San Francisco's Chinatown, 1962*. New York: Ballantine Books, 1972.

Ding You. "The 1905 Anti-American Movement in Guangdong." *Jindaishi ziliao* (Documents concerning modern history). Institute of History, the Chinese Academy of Sciences, 1958, issue no. 5, pp. 8–55.

Ding Zemin. *Meiguo paihuashi* (A history of Chinese exclusion in the United States). Beijing: Zhonghua shuju, 1952.

Divine, Robert A. *American Immigration Policy 1924–1952*. New Haven, N.J.: Yale University Press, 1957.

Dong, Lorraine. "The Forbidden City Legacy and Its Chinese American Women." In *Chinese America: History and Perspectives, 1992*. San Francisco: Chinese Historical Society of America, pp. 125–48.

Dong, Lorraine, and Marlon K. Hom. "Chinatown Chinese: The San Francisco Dialect." *Amerasia Journal* 7 (1980): 1–30.

Douglas, Mary. "Deciphering a Meal." In Clifford Geertz, ed., *Myth, Symbol, and Culture*. New York: Norton, 1971, pp. 61–81.

Dower, John W. *War Without Mercy: Race and Power in the Pacific War*. New York: Pantheon, 1986.

Downs, Jacques M. "American Merchants and the China Opium Trade, 1800–1840." *Business Review* 42 (1969): 418–42.

Dowdell, Dorothy, and Joseph Dodwell. *The Chinese Helped Build America*. New York: J. Messner, 1972.

Drake, Fred W. *China Charts the World: Hsu Chi-yu [Xu Ji-yu] and His Geography of 1848*. Cambridge: Harvard University Press, 1975.

———. "A Nineteenth-Century View of the United States of America from Hsu Chi-yu's [Xu Ji-yu] *Ying-huan Chih-lueh*." In East Asia Regional Studies Program, ed., *Papers on China*. Cambridge: Harvard University Press, 1964, no. 19.

Duara, Prasenjit. "De-constructing the Chinese Nation." *The Australian Journal of Chinese Affairs*, no. 30 (July 1993): 1–26.

DuFault, David V. "The Chinese in the Mining Camps of California: 1818–1870." *Historical Society of Southern California Quarterly* 41 (1959): 155–70.

Eberhard, Wolfram. "Economic Activities of a Chinese Temple in California." *Journal of the American Oriental Society* 82 (1962): 362–71.

Edson, Christopher Howard. *The Chinese in Eastern Oregon, 1860–1890.* San Francisco: R and E Research Associates, 1974.

Elsensohn, M. Alfred. *Idaho Chinese Lore.* Cottonwood: Idaho Corp. of Benedictine Sisters, 1970.

Evans, William S. Jr. "Food and Fantasy: Material Culture of the Chinese in California and the West, circa 1850–1900." In Robert L. Schuyler, ed., *Archaeological Perspectives on Ethnicity in America: Afro-American and Asian American Culture History.* Farmingdale, N.Y.: Baywood, 1980, pp. 89–96.

Fairbank, John King, ed. *The Missionary Enterprise in China and America.* Cambridge: Harvard University Press, 1974.

———. *Trade and Diplomacy on the China Coast: The Opening of the Treaty Ports, 1842–1854.* 2 vols. Cambridge: Harvard University Press, 1953.

———. *The United States and China,* 1958; reprint, Cambridge: Harvard University Press, 1983.

Fan, Tin-chiu. *Chinese Residents in Chicago.* Saratoga, Calif.: R and E Research Associates, 1974.

Farrar, Nancy. *The Chinese in El Paso.* El Paso: Texas Western Press, 1971.

Faure, David. *The Rural Economy of Pre-Liberation China: Trade Expansion and Peasant Livelihood in Jiangsu and Guangdong, 1870 to 1937.* New York: Oxford University Press, 1989.

Fay, Peter Ward. *The Opium War, 1840–1842: Barbarians in the Celestial Empire in the Early Part of the Nineteenth Century and the War by Which They Forced Her Gates Ajar.* Chapel Hill: The University of North Carolina Press, 1975.

Fell, Marie Leonore. *The Foundation of Nativism in American Textbooks, 1783–1860.* Washington, D.C.: Catholic University of America Press, 1941.

Feng Ziyou. *Huaqiao geming zushi shihua* (A history of overseas Chinese revolutionary organizations). Taipei: Zhengzhong Shuju, 1958.

Fenn, William Purviance. *Ah Sin and His Brethren in American Literature.* Beijing, 1933. Ph.D. diss., College of Chinese Studies (Peking) cooperating with California College in China, 1933.

Fessler, Loren W., ed. *Chinese in America: Stereotyped Past, Changing Present.* New York: Vantage, 1983.

Field, Margaret. "The Chinese Boycott of 1905." In East Asia Regional Studies Program, ed., *Papers on China.* Cambridge: Harvard University Press, 1964, no. 11.

Fields, Barbara J. "Ideology and Race in American History." In J. Morgan Kousser and James M. McPherson, eds., *Region, Race, and Reconstruction.* New York: Oxford University Press, 1982, pp. 143–77.

Fishman, A. Joshua, Vladimir C. Nahirny, John Hofman, and Robert G. Hayden.

Language Loyalty in the United States: The Maintenance and Perpetuation of Non-English Mother Tongues by American Ethnic and Religious Groups. The Hague: Mouton, 1966.

Fitzgerald, Stephen. *China and Overseas Chinese; a Study of Peking's Changing Policy, 1949–1970*. Cambridge: Cambridge University Press, 1972.

Fones-Wolf, Ken, and Elliott Shore. "The German Press and Working-Class Politics in Gilded-Age Philadelphia." In Elliott Shore, Ken Fones-Wolf, and James P. Danky, eds., *The German-American Radical Press: The Shaping of a Left Political Culture, 1850–1940*. Urbana: University of Illinois Press, 1992.

Fong, Collen, Robert A. Fung, Marlon K. Hom, and Vitus C. W. Leung. *The Repeal and Its Legacy: Proceedings of the Conference on the 50th Anniversary of the Repeal of the Exclusion Acts*. Brisbane, Calif.: Fong Brothers, 1994.

Fong, Lawrence M. "Sojourners and Settlers: The Chinese Experience in Arizona." *Journal of Arizona History* 21 (1980): 227–56.

Fritz, Christian G. "Due Process, Treaty Rights, and Chinese Exclusion, 1882–1891." in Sucheng Chan, ed., *Entry Denied: Exclusion and the Chinese Community in America, 1882–1943*. Philadelphia: Temple University Press, 1991, pp. 25–56.

Gall, Susan B., and Timothy L. Gall, eds. *Statistical Record of Asian Americans*. Detroit, Ill.: Gale Research, 1993.

Gans, Herbert J. *The Urban Villagers: Group and Class in the Life of Italian-Americans*. New York: Free Press, 1962.

Gardner, John B. "The Image of the Chinese in the United States, 1885–1915." Ph.D. diss., University of Pennsylvania, 1961.

Ge Gongzheng. *Zhongguo baoxueshi* (A history of newspapers in China). Shanghai: Shangwu Yinshuguan, 1926.

Geertz, Clifford. *The Interpretation of Cultures*. New York: Basic Books, 1973.

Gillenkirk, Jeff. *Bitter Melon: Stories from the Last Rural Chinese Town in America*. Seattle: The University of Washington Press, 1987.

Glazer, Nathan, and Patrick Moynihan. *Beyond the Melting Pot: The Negroes, Puerto Ricans, Jews, Italians, and Irish of New York City*. Cambridge: MIT Press, 1963.

Glick, Clarence Elmer. *Sojourners and Settlers, Chinese Migrants in Hawaii*. Honolulu: The University of Hawaii Press, 1980.

Goldberg, George. *East Meets West; the Story of the Chinese and Japanese in California*. New York: Harcourt Brace Jovanovich, 1970.

Goldstein, Jonathan. *Philadelphia and the China Trade, 1682–1846: Commercial, Cultural, and Attitudinal Effects*. University Park: Pennsylvania State University Press, 1978.

Gordon, Milton M. *Assimilation in American Life: The Role of Race, Religion, and National Origins*. New York: Oxford University Press, 1964.

Griego, Andrew. "Mayor of Chinatown: The Life of Ah Quin." M.A. thesis, San Diego State University, 1979.

Griswold, Wesley S. *A Work of Giants: Building the First Transcontinental Railroad*. New York: McGraw-Hill, 1962.

Gulick, Edward V. *Peter Parker and the Opening of China*. Cambridge: Harvard University Press, 1973.

Guo Tingyi. *Jindai zhongguo de bianju* (The changes in modern China). Taipei: Lianqing chuban shiye gongsi, 1987.

Gutman, Herbert G. *Work, Culture and Society in Industrializing America: Essays in American Working-Class and Social History*. New York: Knopf, 1966.

Halbwachs, Maurice. *On Collective Memory*. Edited, translated, and with an introduction by Lewis A. Coser. Chicago: The University of Chicago Press, 1992.

Hall, Stuart. "Cultural Identity and Diaspora." In Jonathan Rutherford, ed., *Identity, Community, Culture, Difference*. London: Lawrence & Wishart, 1990, pp. 222–37.

Handlin, Oscar, ed. *Immigration as a Factor in American History*. Englewood Cliffs, N.J.: Prentice-Hall, 1959.

———, ed. *The Uprooted: The Epic Story of the Great Migrations That Made the American People*. Boston: Little, Brown, 1951; reprint, New York: Grosset and Dunlap, 1957.

———, ed. *Race and Nationality in American Life*. Boston: Little, Brown, 1957.

Hansen, Gladys C. *The Chinese in California; A Brief Bibliographic History*. Portland, Ore.: R. Abel, 1970.

Hansen, Gladys C., and Emmet Condon. *Denial of Disaster*. San Francisco: Cameron, 1989.

Hansen, Marcus Lee. *The Immigrant in American History*. Cambridge: Harvard University Press, 1940.

———. "The Third Generation in America." *Commentary* 14 (1952): 492–500.

Hareven, Tamara K. *Family Time and Industrial Time: The Relationship Between the Family and Work in a New England Industrial Community*. New York: Cambridge University Press, 1982.

Hastings, Lansford W. *The Emigrants' Guide to Oregon and California* (Cincinnati: G. Conclin, 1845), p. 133.

Hawgood, John A. *The Tragedy of German America*. New York: Putman, 1940.

He Zuo, comp. "The 1905 Patriotic Movement Against the United States." *Jindaishi ziliao* (Documents concerning modern history), no. 1 (1956).

Heizer, Robert F., et al. *The Other Californians*. Berkeley: The University of California Press, 1971.

Helmer, John. *Drugs and Minority Oppression*. New York: Seabury, 1975.

Hellwig, David J. "Black Reactions to Chinese Immigration and Anti-Chinese Movement, 1850–1910." *Amerasia Journal* 6 (1979): 25–44.

Higham, John. "Current Trends in the Study of Ethnicity in the United States." *Journal of American Ethnic History* 2 (fall 1982): 5–15.

———. *Send These To Me: Immigrants in Urban America*. Baltimore, Md.: The Johns Hopkins University Press, 1984.

———. *Strangers in the Land, Patterns of American Nativism 1860–1925*. New Brunswick, N.J.: Rutgers University Press, 1955; reprint, New York: Atheneum, 1972.

Hobsbawn, Eric, and Terence Ranger, eds. *The Invention of Tradition*. New York: Cambridge University Press, 1983.

Hoexter, Corinne K. *From Canton to California: The Epic of Chinese Immigration*. New York: Four Winds Press, 1976.

Hofstadter, Richard. *Social Darwinism in American Thought*. Boston: Beacon, 1944.

Hoy, William. *The Chinese Six Companies*. San Francisco: The Chinese Consolidated Benevolent Association (Chinese Six Companies), 1942.

———. *The Story of Kong Chow Temple*. N.p., n.d.

Huang Zhenwu. *Huaqiao yu zhongguo geming* (Overseas Chinese and the Chinese revolution). Taipei: Guofang Yanjiuyuan, 1963.

Hune, Shirley. "Politics of Chinese Exclusion: Legislative Executive Conflict, 1876–1882." *Amerasia Journal* 9 (1982): 5–27.

Hune, Shirley, Hyung-chan Kim, Stephen S. Fugita, and Amy Ling, eds. *Asian Americans: Comparative and Global Perspectives*. Pullman: Washington State University Press, 1991.

Hunt, Michael H. *Ideology and U.S. Foreign Policy*. New Haven, N.J.: Yale University Press, 1987.

———. *The Making of a Special Relationship: the United States and China to 1914*. New York: Columbia University Press, 1983.

Hutchinson, Edward Prince. *Legislative History of American Immigration Policy, 1798–1965*. Philadelphia: University of Pennsylvania Press, 1981.

Hyde, Stuart W. "The Chinese Stereotype in American Melodrama." *California Historical Society Quarterly* 34 (1955): 357–67.

Ichioka, Yuji. *The Issei: The World of First Generation Japanese Immigrants*. New York: Free Press, 1988.

———. "Japanese Associations and the Japanese Government: A Special Relationship, 1909–1926." *Pacific Historical Review*, 46 (1977): 409–38.

Isaacs, Harold R. *Images of Asia: American Views of China and India*. New York: Capricorn, 1962.

Janisch, Hudson N. "The Chinese, the Courts, and the Constitution: A Study of the Legal Issues Raised by Chinese Immigration to the United States, 1850–1902." J.D. diss., University of Chicago, 1971.

Jiang Zuyuan. *Guangdong jianshi* (A concise history of Guangdong Province). Canton: Guangdong renmin chubanshe, 1987.

Johnsen, Leigh Dana. "Equal Rights and the 'Heathen Chinese': Black Activism in San Francisco, 1865–1875." *Western Historical Quarterly* 11 (1980): 57–68.

Johnson, Arthur M., and Barry E. Supple. *Boston Capitalists and Western Railroads: A Study in the Nineteenth-Century Railroad Investment Process*. Cambridge: Harvard University Press, 1967.

Jones, Claire. *The Chinese in America*. Minneapolis, Minn.: Lerner, 1972.

Jue, Willard G. "Chin Gee-hee, Chinese Pioneer Entrepreneur in Seattle and Toishan." *The Annals of the Chinese Historical Society of the Pacific Northwest* (1983), pp. 31–38.

Kalisch, Philip A. "The Black Death in Chinatown: Plague and Politics in San Francisco, 1900–1904." *Arizona and the West* 14 (1972): 113–36.

Kedrus, Gail H. "The Lee Family Association of New York: A History of Its Early Years, 1899–1927." M.A. thesis, Columbia University, 1981.

Keim, Margaret Laton. "The Chinese as Portrayed in the Works of Bret Harte: A Study of Race Relations." *Sociology and Social Research* 25, no. 5 (May–June 1941): 441–50.

Ken, Sally. "The Chinese Community of Augusta, Georgia, from 1873 to 1971." *Richmond County History* 4 (1972): 51–60.

Kettner, James H. *The Development of American Citizenship, 1608–1870*. Chapel Hill: The University of North Carolina Press, 1978.

Kim, Elaine H. *Asian American Literature: An Introduction to the Writings and Their Social Context*. Philadelphia, Pa.: Temple University Press, 1982.

Kim, Hyung-chan. *A Legal History of Asian Americans, 1790–1990*. Westport, Conn.: Greenwood Press, 1994.

———,ed. *Asian Americans and the Supreme Court: A Documentary History*. New York: Greenwood Press, 1992.

Kraut, Alan M. *The Huddled Masses: The Immigrant in American Society*. Wheeling, Ill.: Harlan Davidson, 1982.

Krebs, Sylvia. "John Chinaman and Reconstruction Alabama: The Debate and the Experience." *Southern Studies* 21 (1982): 369–83.

Kung, Shien-Woo. *Chinese in American Life: Some Aspects of Their History, Status, Problems and Contributions*. Seattle: The University of Washington Press, 1962.

Kwong, Peter. *Chinatown, New York, Labor and Politics, 1930–1950*. New York: Monthly Review Press, 1979.

———. *The New Chinatown*. New York: Hill and Wang, 1987.

LaFeber, Walter, Richard Polenburg, and Nancy Woloch. *The American Century*. New York: Alfred A. Knopf, 1986.

Lai Bojiang and Huang Jinming. *Yuejushi* (A history of Cantonese opera). Beijing: Zhongjuo xiju chubanshe, 1988.

Lai, Him Mark. "The Chinese-American Press." In Sally M. Miller, ed., *The Ethnic Press in the United States*. New York: Greenwood, 1987, pp. 27–43.

———. *Cong huaqiao dao huaren* (From Overseas Chinese to Chinese Americans). Hong Kong: Sanlian shudian, 1992.

———. *A History Reclaimed: an Annotated Bibliography of Chinese Language Materials on the Chinese of America*. Los Angeles: Resource Development and Publications, Asian American Studies Center, UCLA, 1986.

Lai, Him Mark, Genny Lim, and Judy Yung, eds. *Island: Poetry and History of Chinese Immigrants on Angel Island, 1910–1940*. San Francisco: Hoc Doi [History of Chinese detained on island], 1980.

Lai, Him Mark, and Wei-chi Poon. "Notes on Chinese American Historical Research in the United States." *Amerasia Journal* 12 (1985–86): 101–11.

Lee, Bill Lann. "Yung Wing and the Americanization of China." *Amerasia Journal* 1 (1971): 25–32.

Lee, James. "Migration and Expansion in Chinese History." In William H. McNeill and Ruth S. Adams, eds. *Human Migration: Patterns and Policies*. Bloomington: Indiana University Press, 1978, pp. 20–47.

Lee, Rose Hum. *The Chinese in the United States of America*. Hong Kong: Hong Kong University Press, 1960.

———. "The Decline of Chinatowns in the United States." *American Journal of Sociology* 54 (1948–49): 422–32.

———. *The Growth and Decline of Chinese Communities in the Rocky Mountain Region*. New York: Arno Press, 1978.

Leonard, Jane Kate. *Wei Yuan and China's Rediscovery of the Maritime World*. Cambridge: Council on East Asian Studies, Harvard University Press, 1984.

LePore, Herbert Patrick. "Exclusion by Prejudice: Anti-Japanese Discrimination in California and the Immigration Act of 1924." Ph.D. diss., Brigham Young University, 1973.

Lesser, Jeff H. "Always 'Outsiders': Asians, Naturalization and the Supreme Court." *Amerasia Journal* 12 (1985–86): 83–100.

Leung, Peter C. Y. *One Day, One Dollar: Locke, California, and the Chinese Farming Experience in the Sacramento Delta*. El Cerrito, Calif.: Chinese/Chinese American History Project, 1984.

Levenson, Joseph Richard. *Liang Ch'i-Ch'ao [Liang Qi-chao] and the Mind of Modern China*. Cambridge: Harvard University Press, 1959.

———. *Modern China and Its Confucian Past: The Problem of Intellectual Continuity*. Garden City, N.Y.: Doubleday, 1964.

Li Changfu. *Zhongguo zhiminshi* (A history of Chinese [overseas] colonization). Shanghai: Shangwu yinshuguan, 1937.

Li Dingyi. *Zhongmei zaoqi waiqiaoshi* (A history of early Sino-American relations). Taipei: Chuanjiwenxue chubanshe, 1978.

Li Huiying. *Huaqiaozhengce yu haiwai minzuzhuyi (1912–1949)* ([China's] policy concerning overseas Chinese and overseas Chinese nationalism, 1912–49). Taipei: Guoshiguan, 1997.

Li, Po-ju, comp. *Chinamen in Arizona Heritage: An Annotated Bibliography*. Tokyo: Tai-shan Sinological Researches Institute, 1986.

Li, Tien-Lu. *Congressional Policy of Chinese Immigration*. South Nashville, Tenn.: The Publishing House of the Methodist Episcopal Church, 1916.

Liang Jiabin, "Biography of Liang Qinggui." In *Guangdong wenxian* ([Historical] documents concerning Guangdong), 7, no. 1 (1977).

———. *Guangdong shisanhang kao* (A study of the thirteen hang [co-hong] in Guangdong), Shanghai: Guoli Bianyiguan, 1937.

Lim, Genny, ed. *The Chinese American Experience: Papers from the Second National Conference on Chinese American Studies*. San Francisco: Chinese Historical Society of America, 1984.

Lin Chongyong. *Lin Zexu zhuan* (A biography of Lin Zexu). Yangmingshan, Taiwan: Zhonghua Dadian Bianyinhui, 1967.

Lin, Yu-tang. *Chinatown Family: A Novel*. New York: J. Day, 1948.

Liu, Ling. *The Chinese in the Americas; A Guide to Their Life and Progress*. Los Angeles: East-West Culture, 1949.

Liu Pei Chi. *Meiguo huaqiao shi* (A history of the Chinese in the United States). Taipei: Liming wenhua shiye gongsi, 1976.

———. *Meiguo huaqiao yishi* (An informal history of the Chinese in America). Taipei: Liming wenhua shiye gongsi, 1981.

———. *Meiguo huaqiao jiaoyu* (Overseas Chinese education in the United States). Taipei, 1959.

Lo Hsiang-lin. *Liang Cheng de chushimeiguo* (Liang Cheng: Chinese minister in Washington). Hong Kong: Zhongguo wenhua yanjiushuo, 1977.

Lo, Karl, and Him Mark Lai. *Chinese Newspapers Published in North America, 1854–1975*. Washington, D.C.: Center for Chinese Research Materials and Association of Research Libraries, 1977.

Loewen, James W. *The Mississippi Chinese: Between Black and White*. Cambridge: Harvard University Press, 1971; reprint, Prospect Heights, Ill.: Waveland, 1988.

Loo, Chalsa M. *Chinatown: Most Time, Hard Time*. New York: Praeger, 1991.

Lou, Raymond. "The Chinese American Community of Los Angeles, 1870–1900: A Case Study of Resistance, Organization, and Participation." Ph.D. diss., University of California, Irvine, 1982.

Louie, Emma Woo. "A New Perspective on Surnames Among Chinese Americans." *Amerasia Journal* 12 (1985–86): 1–22.

Low, Victor. *The Unimpressible Race: A Century of Educational Struggle by the Chinese in San Francisco*. San Francisco: East/West, 1982.

Lowe, Lisa. *Immigrant Acts*. Durham, N.C.: Duke University Press, 1996.

Lum, William Wong, comp. *Asians in America: A Bibliography of Master's Theses and Doctoral Dissertations*. Davis: Asian American Studies Division, Department of Applied Behavioral Research, University of California, 1970.

Luo, Zhiping. *Qingmo mingchu maiguo zaihua de qiyetouzhi (1818–1937)* (American investments in China during the Late Qing and early Republic period, 1818–1937). Taipei: Guoshiguan, 1996.

Lydon, Sandy. *Chinese Gold: The Chinese in the Monterey Bay Region*. Capitola, Calif.: Capitola, 1985.

Lyman, Stanford M. *Chinese Americans*. New York: Random House, 1974.

Lyon, James K. *Bertolt Brecht in America*. Princeton: Princeton University Press, 1980.

Ma, L. Eve Armentrout (Eve Armentrout-Ma). "The Big Business Ventures of Chinese in North America, 1850–1890: An Outline." In Genny Lim, ed., *The Chinese American Experience*. San Francisco: Chinese Historical Society of America and the Chinese Culture Foundation, 1984.

———. "Chinese Traditional Religion in North America and Hawaii." *Chinese America: History and Perspectives* San Francisco; Chinese Historical Society of America and the Chinese Culture Foundation, 1988, pp. 131–47.

———. *Revolutionaries, Monarchists, and Chinatowns: Chinese Politics in the Americas and the 1911 Revolution*. Honolulu: University of Hawaii Press, 1990.

———. "Urban Chinese at the Sinitic Frontier: Social Organizations in United States' Chinatowns, 1849–1898." *Modern Asian Studies* 17 (1983): 107–35.

MacNair, Harley Farnsworth. *The Chinese Abroad, Their Position and Protection: A Study in International Law and Relations*. Shanghai: The Commercial Press, 1924.

MacPhail, Elizabeth C. "San Diego's Chinese Mission." *Journal of San Diego History* 23 (1977): 9–21.

———. "Shady Ladies in the Stingaree District: When the Red Lights Went Out in San Diego." *Journal of San Diego History* 20 (1974): 1–28.

Makela, Lee Arne. "Japanese Attitudes Towards the United States Immigration Act of 1924." Ph.D. diss., Stanford University, 1972.

Mann, Arthur. *The One and the Many: Reflections on the American Identity.* Chicago: The University of Chicago Press, 1979.

Mark, Diane Mei Lin, and Ginger Chih. *A Place Called Chinese America.* Dubuque, Iowa: Kendall Hunt, 1982.

Mark, Gregory Yee. "Racial, Economic and Political Factors in the Development of America's First Drug Laws." *Issues in Criminology* 10 (1975): 49–72.

Marks, Robert B. "Rice Prices, Food Supply, and Market Structure in Eighteenth-Century South China." *Late Imperial China* 12, no. 2 (Dec. 1991): 64–116.

———. *Tigers, Rice, Silk, and Silt, Environment and Economy in Late Imperial South China.* New York: Cambridge University Press, 1997.

Massey, Douglas. "Social Class and Ethnic Segregation: A Reconsideration of Methods and Conclusion." *American Sociological Review* 46 (1981): 641–50.

May, Ernest R., and John King Fairbank, eds. *America's China Trade in Historical Perspective: The Chinese and American Performance.* Cambridge: Harvard University Press, 1986.

McClain, Charles J. *In Search of Equality: The Chinese Struggle Against Discrimination in Nineteenth-Century America.* Berkeley: University of California Press, 1994.

McClain, Charles J., and Laurene Wu McClain. "The Chinese Contribution to the Development of American Law." In Sucheng Chan, ed., *Entry Denied: Exclusion and the Chinese Community in America, 1882–1943.* Philadelphia, Pa.: Temple University Press, 1991, pp. 3–24.

McClellan, Robert. *The Heathen Chinee: A Study of American Attitudes Toward China, 1890–1905.* Columbus: Ohio State University Press, 1971.

McCunn, Ruthanne Lum. *Chinese American Portraits: Personal Histories.* San Francisco: Chronicle Books, 1988.

McCutchen, James M. *China and America; a Bibliography of Interactions, Foreign and Domestic.* Honolulu: The University of Hawaii Press, 1972.

McEvoy, Arthur F. "In Places Men Reject: Chinese Fishermen at San Diego, 1870–1905." *Journal of San Diego History* 23 (1977): 12–24.

McKee, Delber L. *Chinese Exclusion Versus the Open Door Policy, 1900–1906: Clashes over China Policy in the Roosevelt Era.* Detroit, Ill.: Wayne State University Press, 1977.

———. "The Chinese Must Go! Commissioner General Powderly and Chinese Immigration, 1897–1902." *Pennsylvania History* 44 (1977): 37–51.

———. "The Chinese Boycott of 1905–1906 Reconsidered: The Role of Chinese Americans." *Pacific Historical Review* 55 (May 1986): 165–91.

McKenzie, Roderick Duncan. *Oriental Exclusion: The Effect of American Immigration Laws, Regulations, and Judicial Decisions Upon the Chinese and*

Japanese on the American Pacific Coast. Chicago: The University of Chicago Press, 1928.

Mei, June. "Socioeconomic Developments Among the Chinese in San Francisco, 1848–1906." In Lucie Cheng and Edna Bonacich, eds., *Labor Immigration under Capitalism: Asian Workers in the United States before World War II.* Berkeley: The University of California Press, 1984, pp. 370–401.

——. "Socioeconomic Origins of Emigration: Guangdong to California, 1850 to 1882." in Lucie Cheng and Edna Bonacich, eds., *Labor Immigration under Capitalism: Asian Workers in the United States before World War II.* Berkeley: The University of California Press, 1984, pp. 219–45.

Miller, R. M., ed. *The Kaleidoscopic Lens: How Hollywood Views Ethnic Groups.* Englewood Cliffs, N.J., 1980.

Miller, Stuart C. *The Unwelcome Immigrant: The American Image of the Chinese, 1785–1882.* Berkeley: The University of California Press, 1969.

Minke, Pauline. *Chinese in the Mother Lode, 1850–1870.* San Francisco: R and E Research Associates, 1974.

Minnick, Sylvia Sun. *Samfow: The San Joaquin Chinese Legacy.* Fresno, Calif.: Panorama West, 1988.

Morison, Samuel Eliot. *The Maritime History of Massachusetts, 1783–1860.* Boston: Houghton Mifflin, 1941.

Morse, Hosea Ballou. *The Chronicles of the East India Company Trading to China, 1635–1834.* 5 vols. New York: Oxford University Press, 1926–29; reprint, Taipei: Cheng-wen, 1966.

Moy, James S. *Marginal Sights: Staging the Chinese in America.* Iowa City: University of Iowa Press, 1993.

Musto, David F. *The American Disease: Origins of Narcotic Control.* New York: Oxford University Press, 1987.

Nee, Victor, and Brett de Bary Nee. *Longtime California: A Documentary Study of an American Chinatown.* New York: Pantheon, 1973; reprint, Stanford, Calif.: Stanford University Press, 1986.

Nelli, Humbert S. *From Immigrants to Ethnics: The Italian Americans.* New York: Oxford University Press, 1983.

Netten, Neil. "The Origins of Ethnic Radicalism in Northern Minnesota, 1900–1920." *International Migration Review* 4, no. 2 (spring 1970): 44–56.

Ng-Quinn, Michael. "National Identity in Premodern China: Formation and Role Enactment." In Lowell Ditter and Samuel S. Kim, eds. *China's Quest for National Identity.* Ithaca: Cornell University Press, 1993, pp. 32–61.

Nora, Pierre. "Between Memory and History: Les Lieux de Memoire," *Representation* 26 (spring 1989): 7–25.

Novak, Michael. *The Rise of the Unmeltable Ethnics: Politics and Culture in the Seventies*. New York: Macmillan, 1972.

Okihiro, Gary Y. *Cane Fires: The Anti-Japanese Movement In Hawaii, 1865–1845*. Philadelphia, Pa.: Temple University Press, 1991.

Okihiro, Gary Y., et al., eds. *Reflections on Shattered Windows*. Pullman: Washington State University Press, 1988.

Omi, Michael, and Howard Winant. *Racial Formation in the United States from the 1960s to the 1990s*. New York: Routledge, 1994.

Ong, Paul. "Chinese Labor in Early San Francisco: Racial Segmentation and Industrial Expansion." *Amerasia Journal* 8 (1981): 69–92.

Ong, Paul M., Edna Bonacich, and Lucie Cheng. *The New Asian Immigration in Los Angeles and Global Restructuring*. Philadelphia, Pa.: Temple University Press, 1994.

———. *Margins and Mainstreams: Asians in American History and Culture*. Seattle: University of Washington Press, 1994.

Ophthalmolic Hospital at Canton. *The Fourteenth Report of the Ophthalmolic Hospital*. In *Chinese Repository*, v. 17. March 1848.

———. *The Fourteenth Report of the Opthamolic Hospital*. Canton, 1845.

Ourada, Patricia. "The Chinese in Colorado." *Colorado Magazine* 29 (1952): 273–84.

Palmer, Albert Wentworth. *Orientals in American Life*. New York: Friendship Press, 1934.

Park, Robert. *Race and Culture*. Glencoe, Ill.: Free Press, 1950.

Pascoe, Peggy. "Gender Systems in Conflict: The Marriages of Mission-Educated Chinese American Women, 1874–1939." In Ellen Carol DuBois and Vicki L. Ruiz, eds., *Unequal Sisters: A Multicultural Reader in U. S. Women's History*. New York: Routledge, 1990, pp. 123–40.

Paul, Rodman W. "The Origin of the Chinese Issue in California." *The Mississippi Valley Historical Review* 25 (1938): 181–96.

Paulsen, George E. "The Abrogation of the Gresham-Yang Treaty." *Pacific Review* 40, no. 4 (Nov. 1971): 457–77.

———. "The Gresham-Yang Treaty." *Pacific Historical Review* 37 (1968): 281–97.

Peffer, George Antony. "Forbidden Families: Emigration Experiences of Chinese Women under the Page Law, 1875–1882." *Journal of American Ethnic History* 6 (1986): 28–46.

———. "From under the Sojourner's Shadow: A Historiographical Study of Chinese Female Immigration to America, 1852–1882." *Journal of American Ethnic History* 2 (spring 1992): 41–67.

Persons, Stow. *Ethnic Studies at Chicago, 1905–1945*. Urbana: The University of Illinois Press, 1987.

Phillips, Jackson C. *Protestant America and the Pagan World: The First Half Century of the American Board of Commissioners for Foreign Missions, 1810–1860.* Cambridge: East Asian Research Center, Harvard University, 1969.

Pitt, Leonard. "The Beginnings of Nativism in California." *Pacific Historical Review* 30 (1960): 23–38.

Pomerantz, Linda. "The Chinese Bourgeoisie and the Anti-Chinese Movement in the United States, 1850–1905." *Amerasia Journal* 11 (1984): 1–34.

Pozzetta, George E., ed. *Themes in Immigration History.* New York: Garland, 1991.

Pusey, James R. *China and Charles Darwin.* Cambridge: Council on East Asian Studies, Harvard University, 1983.

Quinn, Arthur. *The Rivals: William Gwin, David Broderick, and the Birth of California.* New York, 1994.

Ralph, Julian. "The Chinese Leak." *Harper's New Monthly Magazine* (Mar. 1891): 515–25.

Reimers, David M. *Still the Golden Door: The Third World Comes to America.* New York: Columbia University Press, 1985, 1992.

———. "An Unintended Reform: The 1965 Immigration Act and the Third World Immigration to the United States." *Journal of American Ethnic History* 3 (fall 1983): 9–28.

Remer, Charles F. *A Study of Chinese Boycotts: With Special Reference to Their Economic Effectiveness,* 1933; reprint, Taipei: Cheng-wen, 1966.

Rhoades, Edward J. M. "The Chinese in Texas." *Southwest Historical Quarterly* 81 (1977): 1–36.

Riddle, Ronald. *Flying Dragons, Flowing Streams: Music in the Life of San Francisco's Chinese.* Westport, Conn.: Greenwood Press, 1983.

Riggs, Fred W. *Pressures on Congress: A Study of the Repeal of Chinese Exclusion.* New York: King's Crown Press, Columbia University, 1950.

Rodecape, Lois. "Celestial Drama in the Golden Hills: The Chinese Theater in California, 1849–1869." *California Historical Quarterly* 23 (June 1944): 97–116.

Ronan, Charles E., and Bonnie B. C. Oheds. *East Meets West: The Jesuits in China, 1582–1773.* Chicago: Loyola University Press, 1988.

Rouse, Roger. "Question of Identity: Personhood and Collectivity in Transnational Migration to the United States." *Critique of Anthropology* 15, no. 4: 351–80.

Rowbotham, Arnold H. *Missionary and Mandarin: The Jesuits at the Court of China.* Berkeley: University of California Press, 1942; reprint, New York: Russell & Russell, 1966.

Rudolph, Frederick. "Chinamen in Yankeedom: Anti-Unionism in Massachusetts in 1870." *American Historical Review* 53 (1947): 1–29.

Rydell, Robert W. *All the World's a Fair: Visions of Empire at American International Expositions*. Chicago: University of Chicago Press, 1984.

Said, Edward W. *Oriententalism*. New York: Vintage, 1978.

Saloutos, Theodore. *The Greeks in the United States*. Cambridge: Harvard University Press, 1964.

Salter, Christopher L. *San Francisco's Chinatown: How Chinese a Town*. San Francisco: R and E Research Associates, 1978.

Salyer, Lucy E. "Laws Harsh as 'Tigers': Enforcement of the Chinese Exclusion Laws, 1891–1924." In Sucheng Chan, ed. *Entry Denied: Exclusion and the Chinese Community in America, 1882–1943*. Philadelphia, Pa.: Temple University Press, 1991, pp. 57–93.

Sanchez, George J. *Becoming Mexican American: Ethnicity, Culture, and Identity in Chicano Los Angeles, 1900–1945*. New York: Oxford University Press, 1993.

Sandmeyer, Elmer C. *The Anti-Chinese Movement in California*. Urbana: The University of Illinois Press, 1939.

Sarna, Jonathan D. "From Immigrants to Ethnics: Toward a New Theory of Ethnicization." *Ethnicity* 5 (1978): 370–78.

Saxton, Alexander. "The Army of Canton in the High Sierra." *Pacific Historical Review* 35 (1966): 141–52.

——. *The Indispensable Enemy: Labor and the Anti-Chinese Movement in California*. Berkeley: The University of California Press, 1971.

Schaff, Philip. "Progress of Christianity in the United States of America." *The Princeton Review* (Sept. 1879): 209–52.

Schillar, Nina Glick, Linda Basch, and Christina Blanc-Szanton, eds. *Towards a Transnational Perspective on Migration: Race, Class, Ethnicity, and Nationalism Reconsidered*. New York: New York Academy of Sciences, 1992.

Schuman, Howard, and Jacqueline Scott. "Generations and Collective Memories." *American Sociological Review* 54 (June 1989): 359–81.

Seager, Robert II. "Some Denominational Reactions to the Chinese Immigration to California, 1856–1892." *Pacific Historical Review* 28 (1959): 49–66.

Semmel, Bernard. *Imperialism and Social Reform*. Cambridge: Harvard University Press, 1960.

Shankman, Arnold. "Black on Yellow: Afro-Americans View Chinese-Americans, 1850–1935." *Phylon* 39, no. 1 (spring 1978): 1–17.

Shen Yiyao. *Haiwai paihua bainianshi* (A century of Chinese exclusion overseas). Hong Kong: Wanyou tushu gongsi, 1970.

Shumsky, Neil Larry. *The Evolution of Political Protest and the Workingmen's Party of California*. Columbus: Ohio State University Press, 1991.

Shumsky, Neil Larry, and Larry M. Springer, "San Francisco's Zone of Prostitution, 1880–1934." *Journal of Historical Geography* 7, no. 1 (1981): 71–89.

Siu, Paul C. P. *The Chinese Laundryman: A Study of Social Isolation*. New York: New York University Press, 1987.

Skinner, G. William. "Chinese Peasants and the Closed Community: An Open and Shut Case." *Comparative Studies in Society and History* 13, no. 3 (1971): 270–81.

Smith, Henry Nash. *Virgin Land: The American West as Symbol and Myth*. Cambridge: Harvard University Press, 1970.

Spence, Jonathan. *The Memory Palace of Matteo Ricci*. New York: Viking Penguin, 1984.

Spitzer, Alan. "The Historical Problem of Generations." *American Historical Review* 78 (1973): 1353–85.

Spoehr, Luther W. "Sambo and the Heathen Chinee: Californians' Racial Stereotypes in the Late 1870's." *Pacific Historical Review* 42 (1973): 185–203.

Steinberg, Stephen. *The Ethnic Myth: Race, Ethnicity, and Class in America*. New York: Atheneum, 1981.

Steiner, Stan. *Fusang: The Chinese Who Built America*. New York: Harper and Row, 1979.

Stelle, Charles C. "American Trade in Opium to China Prior to 1820." *Pacific Historical Review* 9 (1940): 425–44.

———. "American Trade in Opium to China, 1821–1839." *Pacific Historical Review* 10 (1941): 57–74.

Stevens, George B., and W. Fisher Markwich. *The Life, Letters, and Journals of the Rev. and Hon. Peter Parker, M.D.*, 1896; reprint, Wilmington, Del.: Scholarly Resources, Inc., 1972.

Stevens, Larry. *Chinese Americans: A Brief History*. Stockton, Calif.: Hammer, 1970.

Stidger, Oliver P. *High Lights on Chinese Exclusion and Expulsion. The Immigration Law of 1924 As It Affects Persons of Chinese Descent in the United States, Their Business Interests, Their Rights and Their Privileges*. San Francisco: Chinese Chamber of Commerce of San Francisco, 1924.

Stockard, Janice E. *Daughters of the Canton Delta: Marriage Patterns and Economic Strategies in South China, 1860–1930*. Stanford, Calif.: Stanford University Press, 1989.

Storti, Craig. *Incident at Bitter Creek: The Story of the Rock Springs Chinese Massacre*. Ames: Iowa State University Press, 1991.

Sujuki, Bob H. "Education and the Socialization of Asian Americans: A Revisionist Analysis of the 'Model Minority' Thesis." *Amerasia Journal* 4 (1977): 23–51.

Sulentic, Joe. *Deadwood Gulch: the Last Chinatown*. Deadwood, S. Dak.: Deadwood Gulch Art Gallery, 1975.

Sun, Shirley. *Three Generations of Chinese—East and West*. Oakland, Calif.: Oakland Museum, 1973.

Sun Zhongshan quanji (Complete works of Sun Yat-sen). 11 vols. Beijing: Zhunghua Shuju, 1981.

Sung, Betty Lee. *An Album of Chinese Americans*. New York: F. Watts, 1977.

———. *Mountain of Gold: The Story of the Chinese in America*. New York: Macmillan, 1967.

———. *The Story of the Chinese in America*. New York: Collier Books, 1975.

Swisher, Earl. *China's Management of the American Barbarians: A Study of Sino-American Relations, 1841–1861, with Documents*. New Haven, N.J.: Far Eastern Publications, Yale University, 1953.

Tachihana, Judy M. "Outwitting the Whites: One Image of the Chinese in California Fiction and Poetry, 1849–1924." *Southern California Quarterly* 61 (1979): 379–89.

Takaki, Ronald T. *Iron Cages: Race and Culture in Nineteenth-Century America*. New York: Oxford University Press, 1979.

———. *Strangers from a Different Shore: A History of Asian Americans*. New York: Penguin, 1989.

Teng, Ssu-yu, and John King Fairbank. *China's Response to the West*, 8th printing of the 1963 edition. New York: Atheneum, 1970.

Thelen, David, ed. *Memory and American History*. Bloomington and Indianapolis, Ind.: The Organization of American Historians, 1990.

Thernstrom, Stephan, et al., eds. *Harvard Encyclopedia of American Ethnic Groups*. Cambridge: Belknap Press of Harvard University, 1980.

Tom, Kim Fong. *The Participation of the Chinese in the Community Life of Los Angeles*. San Francisco: R and E Research Associates, 1974.

Tong, Ben R. "The Ghetto of the Mind: Notes on the Historical Psychology of Chinese America." *Amerasia Journal* 1 (1971): 1–31.

Tong, Benson. *The Unsubmissive Women: Chinese Prostitutes in Nineteenth-Century San Francisco*. Norman: University of Oklahoma Press, 1994.

Topley, Marjorie. "Marriage Resistance in Rural Kwangtung [Guangdong]." in Margery Wolf and Roxane Witke, eds., *Women in Chinese Society*. Stanford, Calif.: Stanford University Press, 1975, pp. 67–88.

Trauner, Joan B. "The Chinese as Medical Scapegoats in San Francisco, 1870–1905." *California History* 57 (spring 1978): 70–87.

Treadway, Walter Lewis. "Keeping the Alien Out of America." *The Current History Magazine* (Sept. 1924): 913–20.

Tsai, Shih-shan H. "Reaction to Exclusion: The Boycott of 1905 and Chinese National Awakening." *The Historian* 39 (1976): 95–110.

———. *China and the Overseas Chinese in the United States, 1868–1911.* Fayetteville: The University of Arkansas Press, 1983.

———. *The Chinese Experience in America.* Bloomington: Indiana University Press, 1986.

———. "The Chinese in Arkansas." *Amerasia Journal* 8 (1981): 1–18.

Tung, William L. *The Chinese in America, 1820–1973: A Chronology and Fact Book.* Bobbs Ferry, N. Y.: Oceana, 1974.

Uchida, Naosaku. *The Overseas Chinese: A Bibliographical Essay Based on the Resources of the Hoover Institution.* Stanford, Calif.: Hoover Institute on War, Revolution, and Peace, Stanford University, 1959.

Varg, Paul A. *Missionaries, Chinese, and Diplomats: The American Protestant Missionary Movement in China, 1890–1952.* Princeton, N.J.: Princeton University Press, 1958.

Vecoli, Rudolph J. "European Americans: From Immigrants to Ethnics." *International Migration Review* 6 (1972): 403–34.

———. "Contadini in Chicago: A Critique of the Uprooted." *Journal of American History* 51 (1964): 404–17.

von Brandt, M. *Chinese Pigtails and What Hangs Thereby.* New York: Tucker, 1900.

Wakeman, Frederic Jr. *Strangers at the Gate: Social Disorder in South China, 1839–1861.* Berkeley: The University of California Press, 1966.

Walker, Clarence E. *Deromanticizing Black History: Critical Essays and Reappraisals.* Knoxville: The University of Tennessee Press, 1991.

Wang, Gungwu. "A Note on the Origins of Hua-ch'iao [huaqiao]." in Gungwu Wang, *Community and Nation, Essays on Southeast Asia and the Chinese.* Singapore: Published for the Asian Studies Association of Australia by Heinemann Educational Books (Asia), 1981, pp. 122–24.

Wang, Peter Heywood. "Legislating 'Normalcy': The Immigration Act of 1924." Ph.D. diss., University of California, Riverside, 1971.

Weiss, Melford S. *Valley City: A Chinese Community in America.* Cambridge: Shenkman, 1974.

Wells, Mariann Kaye. *Chinese Temples in California.* San Francisco: R and E Research Associates, 1971.

Wen Guangyi. "The Meaning of 'Huaqiao' and 'Huaren', and the Periodization of the History of Overseas Chinese." In *Huaqiao, Huaren lishi luncon* (Forum of the history of Chinese sojourning overseas and ethnic Chinese) 1 (1985): 1–5.

Wilson, Carol Green. *Chinatown Quest: One Hundred Years of Donaldina Cameron House.* San Francisco: California Historical Society, 1974.

Wittke, Carl. *The German Language Press in America.* Lexington: University of Kentucky Press, 1957.

Wolf, Margery, and Roxane Witke, eds. *Women in Chinese Society*. Stanford: Stanford University Press, 1975.

Wong, Bernard P. *Chinatown, Economic Adaptation and Ethnic Identity of the Chinese*. Fort Worth, Tex.: Holt, Rinehart and Winston, 1982. 1981, pp. 122–24.

Wong, James I. *A Selected Bibliography on the Asians in America*. Palo Alto, Calif.: R and E Research Associates, 1981.

Wong, K. Scott. "Liang Qichao and the Chinese of America: A Re-evaluation of His 'Selected Memoir of Travels in the New World.' " *Journal of American Ethnic History* 11, no. 4 (summer 1992): 3–24.

Wong, K. Scott, and Sucheng Chan, eds. *Claiming America: Constructing Chinese American Identities*. Philadelphia, Pa.: Temple University Press, 1998.

Woo, Wesley Stephen. "Chinese Protestants in the San Francisco Bay Area."

Woon, Yuen-Fong. "The Voluntary Sojourner Among the Overseas Chinese: Myth or Reality." *Pacific Affairs* 56, no. 4 (winter 1983–84): 673–90.

Worner, William Frederic. "A Chinese Soldier in the Civil War." *Historical Papers and Addresses of the Lancaster County Historical Society* 25 (1921): 52–55.

———. *Protestant Work Among the Chinese in the San Francisco Bay Area, 1850–1920*. Ann Arbor, Mich.: University of Microfilms International, 1984.

Wright, Doris Marion. "The Making of Cosmopolitan California." *California Historical Society Quarterly* 19 (1940): 323–43.

Wu, Cheng-tsu, ed. *"Chink!" A Documentary History of Anti-Chinese Prejudice in America*. New York: World, 1972.

Wu, Ching-chao. "Chinatowns: A Study of Symbiosis and Assimilation." Ph.D. diss., University of Chicago, 1928.

Wu Shangyin, *Meiguohuaqiao bainianjishi* (A chronology of a century of Chinese Americans). Hong Kong: the author, 1954.

Wu, William F. *The Yellow Perils: Chinese Americans in American Fiction, 1850–1940*. Hamden, Conn.: Archon Books, 1982.

Wu Xinci. "The Qing Government's Policy Toward Overseas Chinese, 1644–1795." In *Huaqiao, huaren lishi luncon* (Forum of the history of Chinese sojourning overseas and ethnic Chinese) 1 (1985): 19–36.

Wunder, John R. "Chinese in Trouble: Criminal Law and Race in the Trans-Mississippi West Frontier." *The Western Historical Quarterly* 17 (1986): 25–41.

Wynne, Robert Edward. *Reaction to the Chinese in the Pacific Northwest and British Columbia, 1850–1910*. New York: Arno, 1978.

Yen, Tzu-kuei. "Chinese Workers and the First Transcontinental Railroad of the United States of America." Ph.D. diss., St. John's University, 1977.

Yu, Connie Young. "Rediscovered Voices: Chinese Immigrants and Angel Island." *Amerasia Journal* 4 (1977): 123–39.

Yu, Renqiu. "Chinese American Contributions to the Educational Development of Toisan, 1910–1940." *Amerasia Journal* 10 (1983): 47–72.

———. *To Save China, to Save Ourselves: The Chinese Hand Laundry Alliance of New York*. Philadelphia, Pa.: Temple University Press, 1992.

Yuan, D. Y. "Voluntary Segregation: A Study of New York's Chinatown." *Phylon* 27 (1963): 155–68.

Yuan, Tung-li. *A Guide to Doctoral Dissertations by Chinese Students, 1905–1960*. Washington, D.C.: The Sino-American Cultural Society, 1961.

Yuk Ow, Him Mark Lai, and P. Choy, eds. *Yumei Sanyi Zonghuiguan jianshi* (A brief history of the Three-District Association in America). San Francisco, 1975.

Yung, Judy. *Chinese Women of America: A Pictorial History*. Seattle: The University of Washington Press, 1986.

———. "The Social Awakening of Chinese American Women as Reported in Chung Sai Yat Po, 1900–1911." In Ellen Carol DuBois and Vicki L. Ruiz, eds., *Unequal Sisters: A Multicultural Reader in U. S. Women's History*. New York: Routledge, 1990, pp. 195–207.

———. *Unbound Feet: A Social History of Chinese Women in San Francisco*. Berkeley: University of California Press, 1995.

Zhang Cunwu. *Guangxu Sanshiyinian zhongmei gongyue fengcao* (The tidal wave against the labor treaty between the United States and China in the thirty-first year of the Guangxu emperor). Taipei: Zhongyang yanjiuyuan xiandaishi yanjiusuo, 1961.

Zheng Hesheng. *Jinshi zhongxishiri duizhaobiao* (Modern Chinese and Western historical dates in contrast). Shanghai: Shangwu Yinshuguan, 1936.

Zhongguo xiquzhi guangdong juan (The history of theater in China: Guangdong). 4 vols. Compilation Committee, comp. Canton, 1987.

Zhu Qianzhi. *Fusangguo kaozheng* (A study of Fusang Country). Shanghai: Shangwu yinshuguan, 1940.

Zo, Kil Young. *Chinese Emigration into the United States, 1850–1880*. New York: Arno, 1978.

Index

Library of Congress Cataloging-in-Publication Data

Chen, Yong
   Chinese San Francisco, 1850–1943 : a trans-Pacific community / Yong
      Chen.
         p.   cm.—(Asian America)
      Includes bibliographical references and index.
   ISBN 0-8047-3605-7 (cl. alk. paper) : ISBN 0-8047-4550-1 (pbk. alk. paper)
      1. Chinese Americans—California—San Francisco—History.
   2. San Francisco (Calif.)—History.   I. Title.   II. Series.

   F869.S39 C515 2000
   979.4'61004951073—dc21   99-055529

This book is printed on acid-free, archival-quality paper.
Original printing 2000
Last figure below indicates year of this printing:
08 07 06 05 04 03 02

Typeset by BookMatters in 11/14 Adobe Garamond
Designed by Janet Wood